THE COLD WAR WILDERNESS
OF MIRRORS

THE COLD WAR WILDERNESS OF MIRRORS

Counterintelligence and the U.S. and Soviet Military
Liaison Missions 1947–1990

ADEN C. MAGEE

CASEMATE
Philadelphia & Oxford

Published in the United States of America and Great Britain in 2021 by
CASEMATE PUBLISHERS
1950 Lawrence Road, Havertown, PA 19083, USA
and
The Old Music Hall, 106–108 Cowley Road, Oxford OX4 1JE, UK

Hardback Edition: ISBN 978-1-61200-993-3
Digital Edition: ISBN 978-1-61200-994-0

A CIP record for this book is available from the British Library

Printed and bound in the United States of America by Sheridan

Typeset by Lapiz Digital Services.

For a complete list of Casemate titles, please contact:

CASEMATE PUBLISHERS (US)
Telephone (610) 853-9131
Fax (610) 853-9146
Email: casemate@casematepublishers.com
www.casematepublishers.com

CASEMATE PUBLISHERS (UK)
Telephone (01865) 241249
Email: casemate-uk@casematepublishers.co.uk
www.casematepublishers.co.uk

The views expressed in this publication are those of the author and do not necessarily reflect the official policy or position of the Department of Defense or the U.S. government.

Front cover image: A communist border guard mans the Berlin Wall, keeping a lookout for persons attempting to escape from East Berlin. (U.S. National Archives)

Contents

Past is Prologue

"The myriad of stratagems, deceptions, artifices and all other devices of disinformation which the Soviet bloc and its coordinated intelligence services use to confuse and split the West have confronted our policy makers with an ever-fluid landscape where fact and illusion merge—a kind of *wilderness of mirrors* where honest statesmen are finding it increasingly difficult to separate the facts of Soviet actions from the illusion of Soviet rhetoric."

JAMES JESUS ANGLETON, CHIEF OF CIA COUNTERINTELLIGENCE, 1954–74

In December 1988, the newly assigned commander of the Department of Defense's (DoD's) elite Counterintelligence Special Operations element in Europe met with the Chief of Counterintelligence for the U.S. Army Europe (USAREUR) at the USAREUR headquarters in Heidelberg, West Germany. The operational commander was a U.S. Army captain and counterintelligence special agent with highly specialized training and experience. The USAREUR Chief of Counterintelligence was a seasoned colonel who did not fit the standard role of an intellectually introverted counterintelligence officer. The two men were cut from the same cloth. The captain was hand-picked to establish an unprecedented counterintelligence capability in Europe and to lead sensitive operations against the main enemy. The colonel was brought in specifically to attack the hard problems that had perpetuated for decades.

The colonel had received his marching orders from the senior intelligence general in Europe, and now the captain was getting his. On that day, the two leaders agreed to endeavor to solve one of the greatest mysteries in the history of counterintelligence—the enigma that was the Soviet Military Liaison Mission.

Ultimately, they did not succeed because the Cold War clock ran out on them; but sometimes, the journey can be as interesting as the destination.

The history, evolution, and norms of operations that developed among the MLMs, and the events that occurred leading to this intended decisive point to address the Soviet Military Liaison Mission, is an epic and mostly untold story in and of itself. The story of the intense but short period that followed has never been told.

Introduction

Spying is commonly referred to as the world's second-oldest profession. Spying is generally associated with intelligence collection which is the acquisition of information that a competing nation holds as secret, and the disclosure of which is counter to that nation's best interests. Counterintelligence is information gathered and activities conducted to identify, deceive, exploit, disrupt, or protect against intelligence collection. In basic terms, intelligence collection is offense and counterintelligence is defense, but to borrow from another adage, sometimes the best defense is a good offense. The primary battles and methods of "warfare" during the Cold War were intelligence collection and counterintelligence.

As will be detailed, the two Cold War superpowers approached warfare in this arena and on foreign soils differently. The key players on the Soviet side were the Committee of State Security, the Komitet Gosudarstvennoi Bezopasnosti (KGB), and the Russian military intelligence service, the Glavnoye Razvedyvatel'noye Upravlenie (GRU). On the U.S. side the key players were the Central Intelligence Agency (CIA) and the DoD intelligence and counterintelligence elements. Although these may appear to be similar constructs for combat in the domains of intelligence and counterintelligence, as will be detailed throughout the pages, they differed significantly. These differences had substantial implications for how this story played out.

From the historic perspective, there are many stories in the world of espionage and intrigue, intelligence and counterintelligence, and spy and counterspy, that will never be told. If not for the following pages, there would be more undocumented missions and operations to be lost in the sands of time. This book provides a small time capsule of Cold War history that would have been lost in the shadows of the decades after the close of the Cold War, if not told here.

A good story benefits from an interesting dynamic among a protagonist and antagonist, and this one certainly has that, in the form of the U.S. and Soviet Military Liaison Missions (MLMs), which were established after the conclusion of World War II, and remained microcosms of the epic standoff for the following four-plus decades of the Cold War. The U.S. and Soviet MLMs collected intelligence against their main enemy for the entirety of the Cold War, and the sides were in a continuous process of attempting to counter collection activities of the MLMs.

This was a cat-and-mouse dynamic that was in play for each hour of each day of the Cold War, with very few exceptions.

The MLMs were persistent fixtures in postwar Germany and played a prominent role during the entire Cold War era. However, these artifacts have been almost completely overlooked by authoritative works in Cold War history. The very few works that do memorialize the MLMs are largely anecdotal and presented almost exclusively from the standpoint of the Allied MLMs. This lack of research and notoriety is due largely to the fact that the MLMs and the countries they represented vigilantly discouraged publicity about their existence because their anonymity served to avoid questions regarding their purpose. Only occasionally did news about the MLMs escape into the public domain during their existence. U.S. and Soviet authorities consistently sheltered the missions' activities from unnecessary publicity, which may have otherwise left them more exposed to downturns in superpower relations. In addition, since the MLMs were largely regarded as sore reminders of German occupation and postwar reparations, the Germans who hosted these missions had little motivation to preserve their legacies.

Formerly classified annual U.S. MLM (USMLM) Unit History reports from 1964 through 1988 have been declassified and provide a strong record of unit activities, but these reports did not capture all of the events as they applied to USMLM. The Moscow Institute for Military History has rejected requests for information regarding Soviet MLM, Frankfurt (SMLM-F). Such a disclosure would require approval from the Russian chief of the general staff. Former members of the Soviet missions do not want to be cited and are not available for interviews. Details that likely reside in the secretive military history archives have not been approved for release, and likely never will. And even if the archives were opened or the Soviet cold warriors spoke, it would still be impossible to separate fact from rhetoric. In contrast, many of the details regarding SMLM-F and the U.S. activities to monitor SMLM-F have been released exclusively to the author through the U.S. Freedom of Information Act. First-hand information from the very few shadow warriors who actually operated against SMLM-F have provided very credible details regarding that enigmatic element.

In parallel with the MLM dynamic playing out in the sectors of German occupation, there was a strategic landscape of which the MLMs were a microcosm. The intelligence, counterintelligence, and disinformation battle between the two superpowers was playing out—as history has demonstrated—in a manner that should have been expected in a strategic struggle between a free, open, and democratic system that was under continuous covert and clandestine attack from a closed, centrally controlled, and ruthless apparatus. This book provides a substantial historical backdrop to demonstrate how the MLM intelligence collection and counterintelligence dynamic evolved, leading to the climactic final years of the Cold War.

Although there were many trials and tribulations along the way, the MLMs continued to operate in a relatively steady manner from 1947 through the 1970s. Then in the 1980s (the decade of the spy), a number of factors converged to illuminate concerns that the Soviet MLM may have been operating in the shadows, and perhaps even hiding in plain sight. During this entire period as well, there was a strategic chess game of espionage and intrigue that could have been a macrocosm for what may have been developing among the MLM players.

There are a few publications that discuss the history of the MLMs, but they focus almost exclusively on the Allied missions that operated in East Germany and the challenges they faced, to include East German and Soviet counterintelligence efforts. However, this is the first and only publication to address, in detail, the Soviet MLMs and the counterintelligence efforts focused against one in particular. And while this book focuses on the dynamics that drove and led to a counterintelligence capability that reached its zenith just as the threat decided to quit, it provides a very interesting perspective regarding Cold War counterintelligence and the mindset that drove an almost compulsive mission focus. Therefore, there is much history that must be referenced and juxtaposed as it related to the U.S./Soviet dynamic ranging from the strategic level to the manner in which the grand game of chess played out with the pawns, rooks, and knights on the ground.

This book is organized into three parts that logically and thought-provokingly build a historical analysis of the MLMs and examine their operations within the context of the larger national counterintelligence and intelligence strategies/frameworks of the opposing superpowers. Part I provides an unprecedented history of the MLMs, offering both a broad understanding of the historic evolution of the U.S. and Soviet MLMs, how their actions were related, and how they differed. This level of detail is necessary to provide perspective as it applies to the deeper issues surrounding the SMLM-F enigma and the U.S. counterintelligence effort to unlock the mystery.

Part II focuses on the MLMs as microcosms of the larger strategic framework, and provides the lesser- and never-known details on the episodes that shaped the evolution of the MLMs. Based on volumes of previously classified documents, and first-hand accounts of the cold warriors who either operated in the MLMs or operated against the MLMs, this work is replete with information that has never before been published, and much of which dispels information previously accepted as facts.

In addition to the never-before-documented histories and insights regarding the competing MLMs, Part III brings the epic Cold War case study to a conclusion with the untold story of the highly sensitive and elite counterintelligence element established to counter perhaps the most sophisticated and enigmatic of Soviet threats.

From the counterintelligence and intelligence professional perspective, this book is an absolute must-read. In addition to being a unique story, within a story, within another story, the book applies some of the most important and relevant counterintelligence and intelligence principles to the lesser-known, and many never-known, episodes recounted in the pages. Although now decades removed, the Cold War provided a wealth of lessons that are enduring. This book helps to complete the record by documenting many that would otherwise escape history by fading from human memory. The lessons learned when the bar was the highest are the ones that should be retained, and the Cold War Soviet adversary set the absolute highest counterintelligence, intelligence, and disinformation bar ever.

PART I

MILITARY LIAISON MISSION
HISTORY AND EVOLUTION

CHAPTER I

The History of the Military Liaison Missions

The Formative Years

In November 1944, several months before the conclusion of the war in Germany, the U.S., Britain, and Soviet Union signed the Agreement on Control Machinery in Germany, which detailed how the Allies would administer Germany after its unconditional surrender. Article 2 of the agreement specified that "Each Commander-in-Chief (CINC) in his zone of occupation will have attached to him military, naval and air representatives of the other two CINCs for liaison duties." After its liberation, France was viewed as a fourth Allied power.

The first gathering of the Allied powers' leadership in the wake of Germany's defeat occurred in July 1945 at Potsdam, Germany. The Western leaders agreed that the best protection against a revival of German aggression was to enable the nation to rebuild and restore the German people to a prominent place in the political and economic systems in Europe. The Potsdam Declaration, which was executed as a communiqué and was therefore not a peace treaty according to international law, declared that Germany should be viewed as a single political and economic unit, but would be temporarily divided into zones to be administered by an army of occupation. The four powers divided "Germany as a whole" into four occupation zones for administrative purposes, creating what became collectively known as Allied-occupied Germany. The Allies agreed to a joint occupation, with each country taking charge of a zone and a sector of Berlin. The Soviet leadership vocally supported the talk of democracy and self-determination, but in parallel, the Soviets were employing their vast security and espionage apparatus to actively spread Communism throughout war-torn Europe.

Following the partition of Germany, cooperation between the Soviet Union and what then became known as the "Allied" powers (U.S., Britain, France) soon faded. The Allies partnered in the occupation by merging their three zones of West Germany and West Berlin, while the Soviet Union managed the affairs of its zones in eastern Germany and Berlin. In contrast to the spirit of the Potsdam Declaration, the Soviets rapidly reconstituted the Communist Party in the eastern sector of Germany, which took its orders from Moscow, and placed its members in

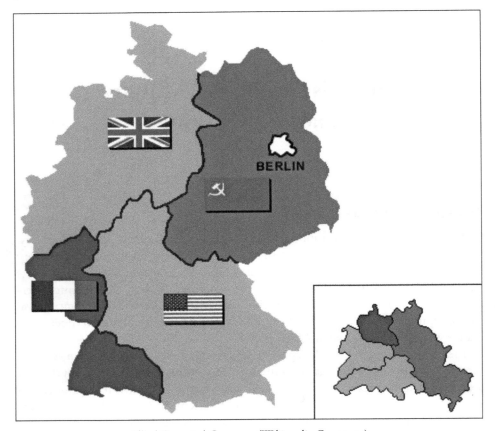

Allied Occupied Germany. (Wikimedia Commons)

every key position of political and administrative authority. This dynamic was the beginning of the East/West divide.

The rapid decline in political cooperation and the high degree of uncertainty regarding the Allies' and Soviets' intentions in central Europe prompted the occupying military forces to establish reliable channels of communications between the sides to manage the increased risks between the Soviets and the Western alliance. The powers agreed that it was in their best interests to recognize Article 2 of the Agreement on Control Machinery in Germany and establish liaison mechanisms. As a result, the U.S. and Soviet MLMs were established to maintain interzonal "liaison"—or communication—between the CINCs of the U.S. European Command and the Group of Soviet Forces in Germany (GSFG). After several exchanges of views during 1946, the American and Soviet sides reached an accord—the Agreement on Military Liaison Missions Accredited to the Soviet and

United States Commanders in Chief of the Zones of Occupation in Germany—which was signed on 5 April 1947 by Lieutenant General Clarence Huebner, Deputy CINC, U.S. European Command (USEUCOM), and Colonel-General Mikhail Malinin, Deputy CINC, GSFG. This agreement establishing the U.S. and Soviet MLMs became commonly referred to as the Huebner–Malinin Agreement. Per the agreement, the U.S. established the U.S. Military Liaison Mission (USMLM) in Potsdam, near the GSFG headquarters, and the Soviets established the Soviet Military Liaison Mission, Frankfurt (SMLM-F), in Frankfurt where the USEUCOM headquarters was located at the time. Over time, the abbreviation SMLM was coined "smell 'em," USMLM was "U smell 'em," and SMLM-F was "smell 'em F."

The GSFG concluded similar accords with the British and French military commanders, establishing the other two Allied MLMs in Potsdam and a Soviet MLM near the French headquarters in Baden-Baden, and the third Soviet MLM near the British headquarters in Bunde. The Soviet MLM in the British sector was named the Soviet Exchange Mission (SOXMIS) and the Soviet mission in the French sector was named the Mission Militaire Sovietique (MMS). The British MLM in the Soviet zone was named the British Exchange Mission (BRIXMIS), and the French mission was named the French MLM (FMLM). Although authorized under Article 2 of the Agreement on Control Machinery in Germany, the Allies did not have a need to establish MLMs in each other's zones.

The staffing of the MLMs was based on specific agreements. The U.S. and Soviets agreed to 14 personnel per side. The British and Soviets agreed to missions of 37 personnel per side, and the French and Soviets agreed to missions of 18 personnel. The relatively small size of the U.S. MLM and its Soviet counterpart was primarily the result of vocal opposition from U.S. counterintelligence agencies to the prospect of Soviet operatives roaming freely in the U.S. sector of Germany.

In addition to the staff size, the only other difference between the U.S. agreement with the Soviets and that of the French and British was the provision which included a clause excluding "political representatives." This exclusion was unique to the U.S./Soviet agreement and reflected that U.S. military leadership did not want to be influenced by the State Department, which at the time was taking a very hardline approach to diplomacy with the Soviets. By ensuring that the agreement applied only to military matters, any requirements for U.S. Senate ratification were successfully avoided. The U.S. Constitution requires that all treaties be ratified by the U.S. Senate, but since the Huebner–Malinin Agreement was enacted under the provisions of the previously ratified Agreement on Control Machinery in Germany, it was viewed as having the standing of a legally binding international treaty/agreement.

There were 17 specific provisions ("regulations") in the Huebner–Malinin Agreement which established a relatively flexible framework for the MLMs. The agreement specified that the mission would be accredited to the respective U.S. and Soviet CINCs, with their primary tasks being to maintain liaison between both CINCs and their staffs. It will never be known what the actual crafters of the agreement intended, but there was one pivotal provision of the agreement that enabled the MLMs to operate as they did for the following 43 years. This open-ended provision specified that "each member of the missions would be given identical travel facilities to include identical permanent passes in Russian and English languages permitting complete freedom of travel wherever and whenever it will be desired over territory and roads in both zones, except places of disposition of military units, without escort or supervision."

From the point of the Huebner–Malinin Agreement through the duration of the Cold War, military members of the competing alliances were stationed within each other's sectors, with significant freedom of movement. The MLMs exercised a quasi-diplomatic status that was assumed by the two field commanders in that they negotiated directly on issues of concern between the two headquarters, first as occupiers of the two zones of occupation and subsequently as guarantors of the two Germanys. Almost immediately, however, the emphasis was narrowly focused on relations between the occupying armies, with broader diplomatic issues being handled in traditional diplomatic channels. As a result, what should have been a coordinated effort by the victorious Allies to first control and then revive a unified Germany, turned into an East/West contest of wills over what the geopolitical map of Europe would become in the postwar years.

The original intent and need for the MLMs based on the Agreement on Control Machinery in Germany was to foster communication and cooperation. The MLMs were initially intended to be established for purely liaison purposes—to provide a face-to-face communications channel between the U.S., British, and French leadership and their GSFG counterparts. However, the wording in the Huebner–Malinin Agreement (and British and French agreements) citing "except places of disposition of military units" demonstrated an adversarial and non-transparent relationship from the beginning. Due to the nearly immediate mistrust and lack of understanding regarding the other's military intentions, liaison and cooperation rapidly became a much lower priority than the compelling need to anticipate each other's military intentions. The inadequacy of intelligence on both sides engendered a mutual paranoia about the risk of surprise attack which increased the probabilities of war as a result of misunderstanding. The scenario most feared by Cold War policymakers was the outbreak of a major superpower conflict in Germany, and tensions regarding this central issue remained consistently high through the ensuing 43 years of the standoff. From the outset, the U.S. and the Soviets realized that the MLMs provided unparalleled access, and the most direct and accurate information regarding combat force dispositions in the opposing zones.

By the fall of 1947, the focal point of the East/West conflict was Germany, with particular interest on the struggle for control of Berlin. With the closing of Czechoslovakia by the Communist coup in February 1948, the "Iron Curtain" was dropping into place, and the Soviet and Allied MLMs were focused less on liaison and nation-building, and more on East/West competition. The complete breakdown of East/West cooperation and joint administration in Germany was marked by the imposition of the Berlin Blockade—the Soviet attempt to limit the ability of the Allies to travel to their sectors of Berlin, from June 1948 to May 1949. To demonstrate unity in the face of Soviet belligerence, the Allies merged their three Western zones to form the Federal Republic of Germany (FRG) in May 1949. The Soviets followed suit in October 1949 with the establishment of the German Democratic Republic (GDR). By this time, the East/West divide was formalized. The FRG was commonly referred to as West Germany and the GDR as East Germany.

In 1949, the Allied occupying powers turned over sovereignty to West Germany for the area comprising the three sectors of the Allied forces. Later that year, the West German government signed its constitution, referred to as the "Basic Law." The law was explicit in the West German intent to ultimately reunify the separated parts of Germany—which was a reference to East Germany—under "Germany as a whole." The law expressed that West Germany was constitutionally bound to pursue reunification with peoples living outside the territory under the control of West Germany. To achieve the objective of the Basic Law, the West German leadership understood that although the occupying forces were a wartime punishment and a national humiliation, their maintaining some semblance of a postwar reconstruction effort was the best possible path to the reunification of Germany. This meant that as long as the occupying forces remained in the Germanys, the international community, or at least the North Atlantic Treaty Organization (NATO), would view the two Germanys as "Germany as a whole" with the objective that they would one day be reunified. Although many of the articles agreed to in the Agreement on Control Machinery in Germany were no longer in practice among the Allies and Soviets by 1949, the West Germans believed that as long as the Article 2 provision for MLMs remained in practice, the spirit of the agreement would remain intact and that reunification would remain the ultimate objective of all concerned.

Whereas the Allies allowed West Germany to develop based on open and democratic principles, East Germany developed a government and security system that was among the most controlling and repressive ever. In February 1950, the East Germans established the Ministerium für Staatssicherheit (MfS)—the State Security Service commonly known as the Stasi. The Stasi was one of, if not the most, effective and oppressive intelligence and secret police agencies ever.

Shortly after the U.S. and Soviet MLMs were established, GSFG consolidated its headquarters (HQ) in Wunsdorf, East Germany, which was 30 miles from Potsdam. In 1952, USEUCOM transferred all of its responsibilities to U.S. Army Europe (USAREUR) in Heidelberg, over 50 miles from Frankfurt. So, by 1952, neither of the MLMs was collocated with the HQ they were accredited to and intended to be direct liaison channels to.

After East Germany was recognized as a sovereign country in 1955, both the West and East German governments recognized that there was only a fragile legal standing for the MLMs under international law, and both regularly repeated this contention. Although the two Germanys played a vital role for their respective occupiers, the absence of a peace treaty ending World War II limited their sovereignty in respect to the occupying forces. East Germany was most adamant that with the cessation of major parts of the Potsdam Declaration, and the formation of two German states, that the basis for the existence of the Allied missions on their territories had been voided. The West Germans generally held the same position, but were more tolerant of the MLMs for pragmatic purposes; in addition to their Basic Law reunification aspirations, West Germany, as a member of NATO, recognized that the MLMs did, at a practical level, serve a purpose in preventing its country from once again becoming the largest battleground in the history of the world, or worse yet, a nuclear wasteland.

Alternatively, as West and East Germany steadily grew more ideologically divergent, the East Germans realized that if reunification were to eventually occur on their terms, it would only happen with the strong support of the Soviets. Therefore, while the reunification of Germany was viewed by the Allies and their West German host as an ultimate objective, the Soviets and East Germans were content with the widening schism, and continually took actions to increase the divide. The only issue, however, that the Soviets and their most loyal Soviet Bloc partner did not see eye to eye on was the MLMs. East Germany's political leaders, and by extension its police forces, denied the legitimacy of the Allied MLMs, so the GSFG forces stationed throughout the country continually had to work with the East Germans to ensure compliance with the Huebner–Malinin Agreement. Against their strongest desires, East Germany acquiesced to its Communist Bloc master by allowing the missions to operate.

Despite the fact that the missions were obviously viewed as a penalty for wartime wrongs and antagonized their respective German allies, the U.S. and Soviets denied attempts by the East and West German governments to force the MLMs to deal directly with the local German authorities. As a testament to the enduring value of the MLMs to the postwar powers, the MLMs were always given priority over relations with their German proxies. Although the MLMs continued to operate in accordance with the agreements signed when they were still allies, the Soviet Union and the Western Allies had significantly divergent objectives for the former German territories.

The Evolution of Military Liaison Mission Cooperative Norms

The Huebner–Malinin Agreement included a provision stating the agreement could be changed or amplified by mutual consent to cover new subjects if the sides agreed it was necessary. The agreement was never modified from its original form, but there were a number of governing protocols that were mutually agreed to and followed although not officially documented. One protocol that was not delineated in the accord but agreed to by both sides was that MLM personnel would wear uniforms anytime outside the MLM compound. Another was that MLM vehicles would have distinctive license plates to make them readily distinguishable. Although these rules served a counterintelligence purpose, they also served to ensure that the hosting German governments and their citizens recognized and respected the MLMs' special status. Also, by mutual agreement, the U.S. and Soviet Union accredited ten vehicle passes in each other's sector of operation.

With the exception of a few agreed-upon but undocumented side accords, the MLMs established some ground rules, largely through trial and error, that were accepted by both sides within the broad guidelines of the Huebner–Malinin Agreement. Within the first five years of MLM operations, the sides established standards of operations—"cooperative norms"—that were practiced throughout the duration of the MLMs' existence. Corresponding "competitive norms" among the MLMs and their respective hosts evolved along differing trajectories based on how the cooperative norms were complied with and enforced.

The cooperative norms which developed over time were characterized by the MLMs' operational practices. These were mutually agreed-upon practices and were considered norms because both sides practiced these without objection, when remaining within certain boundaries. The gray areas residing within the relatively vague provisions of the Huebner–Malinin Agreement facilitated the establishment of cooperative and competitive norms which basically represented the "rules of the game." Within the context of the Huebner–Malinin Agreement, which was

SMLM-F license plate. (Author)

open to some interpretation, the U.S. and Soviet MLMs effectively established cooperative norms that enabled the MLMs to endure the entirety of the Cold War. The liaison function among the MLMs developed into a standard process, but it was the additional norms that put the day-to-day competition into motion. Both sides played by "unwritten rules of the game."

A treaty is a formal written agreement entered into by actors in international law, usually sovereign states and international organizations, that is binding under international law. The Huebner–Malinin Agreement had the standing as a treaty between the U.S. and Soviet Union, and was therefore binding under international law. When two countries enter into a treaty, all actions taken under the provisions of the treaty are legitimized if they are allowed to continue without becoming cause to break the treaty. Therefore, all of the "unwritten rules of the game" become legitimized through precedent and repetition, if allowed to continue under the provisions of the treaty.

The key provision of the Huebner–Malinin Agreement which established the rules of the game was Regulation 10, which stated:

> Each member of the mission will be given identical travel facilities to include identical permanent passes in Russian and English languages permitting complete freedom of travel wherever and whenever it will be desired over the territory and roads in both zones, except places of disposition of military units, without escort or supervision.

The agreement did not specify how "freedom of movement" could be exercised or how the exception to "places of disposition of military units" would be enforced. These two open-ended clauses led to the most fascinating manifestation of the evolution of the MLMs, resulting in the two additional cooperative norms of touring and travel restrictions. These, in addition to the stated purpose of liaison, developed into the primary cooperative norms.

Liaison

As their title reflects, the MLMs were originally established to specifically perform "liaison duties." Officer positions were listed as "Liaison Officers" in official documents, and non-commissioned officers (NCOs) were listed as "Liaison NCOs." One provision of the Huebner–Malinin Agreement clearly specified the primary purpose of the MLMs, which was that "the task of the mission will be to maintain liaison between both Commanders-in-Chief and their staffs." However, there were no specific protocols for how the "diplomatic" side of the MLMs was to be conducted, so it simply developed.

As the U.S. and Soviet MLMs settled in as recognized entities, they each implemented similar structures to formalize their liaison functions. USAREUR employed the Allied Contact Section (ACS) in Frankfurt as the day-to-day interface with SMLM-F for logistics and administrative support, and routine communications between USAREUR and the mission. The GSFG employed the Soviet External Relations Bureau (SERB) to perform this same function between its headquarters and USMLM. Since neither MLM was collocated with the HQ they were accredited to and intended to be direct liaison channels to, the ACS and SERB were essentially the only entities the MLMs "liaised" with, with the exception of the rare visits to the hosting HQ.

Although their activities remained mostly in the shadows for those many years, MLM liaison was recognized as the most consistent means of direct communication among the superpowers during the Cold War. In retrospect, many geopolitical Cold War scholars who believed that there was limited communication between the U.S. and Soviet forces were unaware that this little-known direct and interpersonal channel of communication existed.

The MLMs resolved disputes by a code of military honor. Their meetings were generally marked by a friendly cooperative spirit, and both sides endeavored to resolve arising disputes as quickly and quietly as possible. USMLM officers were transferred from the mission if it became apparent that their conduct was excessively provocative and objectionable to the GSFG command, and the Russians responded in a similar manner. This norm of cooperation also fostered a mutual interest in preserving the MLMs. Particular care was generally taken during periods of international crisis to respect the MLMs' privileges under the Huebner–Malinin Agreement and maintain cordial liaison relations.

Although the expansion of the MLM's intelligence role downgraded the liaison function to secondary status, the liaison function also supported the intelligence mission by contributing to the overall picture of their counterpart's outlook and intentions. Mission members and hosts leveraged periodic contact with their counterparts to develop biographical sketches of each officer and to elicit their views on current events and the East/West relationship. In addition to official engagements, each side hosted social events to foster improved relations between the MLMs and their hosts.

The Huebner–Malinin Agreement exclusion of diplomatic personnel made the MLM liaison function unique. The West German government never interfered with the SMLMs as agreed to, and the U.S. Embassy in West Germany did not involve itself with MLM business. Although USMLM did not communicate directly with the East German government, it was the only U.S. presence/representation in East Germany prior to 1974.

Intelligence Collection (Tours)

Although the MLMs were ostensibly established to provide a direct channel of communications between the two militaries, the staffing structure and freedom of movement provision of the Huebner–Malinin Agreement made clear that the missions were also always intended to perform an "observer" function.

Within the vague, but pivotal Regulation 10 of the agreement, the MLMs found the latitude to set the big game into perpetual motion. The ambiguously worded provision which permitted "complete freedom of movement … except places of disposition of military units, without escort or supervision," established the very grayest of gray areas. This gray area essentially resulted in a 43-year game of cat and mouse that played out every day in East Germany and the U.S. sector of West Germany.

Intelligence collection was the cooperative norm that defined the East/West sparring match that endured among the MLMs and their hosts. The MLMs exercised quasi-diplomatic privileges and immunities as well as the right to unencumbered travel by vehicle or on foot in the zone where accredited, except in the otherwise undefined places of disposition of military forces. As the rules of game rapidly evolved, the mutually accepted form of intelligence collection was reconnaissance missions referred to as "tours." MLM officers and enlisted personnel traveling in this manner were known as tour teams. With the exception of official documents

USMLM tour vehicle. MLM touring became the most enduring cooperative norm. (USMLM Association)

that identified officer and NCO positions as liaison positions, they were commonly referred to as tour officers and NCOs. Touring was immediately recognized as the central cooperative norm which endured as the primary mission of the MLMs. This began an intelligence-collection and counterintelligence dynamic that continued at a steady pace until the very end of the Cold War.

During the first five years of the MLMs, USMLM maintained a relatively low touring profile due to Soviet overt surveillance and other forms of harassment. In contrast during this period, SMLM-F took a very aggressive approach to the "freedom of movement" rights by vigorously tracking U.S. military activity and demonstrating a blatant disregard for West German laws. In fact, SMLM-F provocations led USAREUR to consider discontinuing the missions in 1952, but the notion was dismissed due to the value of USMLM intelligence. After a series of tit-for-tat provocations in 1953 and into 1954, relations stabilized and touring patterns normalized.

After East Germany was granted sovereignty in 1954, their internal security agency (Stasi) and local police departments assumed the coordinated responsibility for monitoring USMLM tour activities, which was a violation of the Huebner–Malinin Agreement. Alternatively, the U.S. never authorized the West Germans to monitor SMLM-F, and the U.S. exercised a relatively hands-off approach to SMLM-F. As was the case for the large portion of the MLMs' existence, the U.S. refrained from provocative actions against SMLM-F in an effort avoid any reprisals from the Soviets and East Germans against USMLM that would negatively impact the intelligence-collection mission. However, East German monitoring of and reaction to USMLM remained consistently aggressive and rarely appeared to change in response to events in West Germany. When USMLM complained about aggressive East German activities such as overt surveillance, the Soviets regularly stated that they had no control over the East Germans; however, there were many cases over the years wherein East German behavior did change after complaints to the Soviets, demonstrating that they did have influence over the East Germans. In some cases, the Soviets likely directed the East Germans to moderate their harassment of USMLM just to demonstrate to USAREUR that they could do so.

A nuance that complicated liaison and impacted the disruption of USMLM collection was that under the Soviet system, the KGB was responsible for all aspects of state counterintelligence—foreign and domestic. Therefore, although USMLM was accredited to the GSFG, the KGB was responsible for the counterintelligence monitoring of SMLM-F. By 1954, the Stasi had become the KGB's proxy intelligence organization given the responsibility to repress USMLM collection. As such, when USMLM complained to the GSFG SERB regarding Stasi activity such as the unauthorized surveillance or harassment of tour vehicles, the complaint would need to be channeled, if they chose to do so, through the KGB for resolution. Alternatively, complaints regarding East German forces could be resolved directly between the GSFG and the East German military, again, if SERB chose to raise the issue at all.

Restricted Areas

A technical interpretation of the "except places of disposition of military units" clause implied that the MLMs agreed that they would refrain from traveling in any areas where military activity was taking place. However, as tours (and intelligence collection) became the primary effort of the MLMs, it became apparent that a norm was established that would not be self-regulating. The need to formalize a process to restrict movement quickly emerged, and the sides established a travel restriction regime which became a cooperative norm for the duration.

The clause under Regulation 10 which restricted freedom of travel alluded to a restriction, but there was no provision to distinguish freedom of travel areas from those which fell under the disposition of military forces exemption. As such, this broad clause in the agreement was eventually addressed through the establishment of officially designated restricted travel areas.

In 1951, the Soviets implemented the first effort to enforce the exception to the freedom of travel by designating areas as restricted areas. The restricted areas concept rapidly evolved to constitute counterintelligence efforts undertaken bilaterally as a measure to control intelligence activities in the U.S. and Soviet occupational zones. These restrictions became institutionally recognized as Permanent Restricted Areas (PRAs) and Temporary Restricted Areas (TRAs). This process of designating restricted areas was formalized in 1952 through the exchange of maps with PRAs and TRAs clearly delineated by shaded areas.

PRAs were designed to protect major installations, airfields, missile sites, training areas, and in the case of the Soviets in East Germany initially, all border areas. PRAs remained in effect unless removed or altered by the U.S. or Soviets in a newly issued PRA map. TRAs were areas that were temporarily restricted for periods ranging from three to 30 days, primarily to restrict touring activities during sensitive military training exercises. Updated TRA maps were issued several times a year.

Although not specified by the agreement, the exchange of restricted area maps became the norm by which the sides drew their red lines. While there had been no formal changes to the Huebner–Malinin Agreement in regard to restricted areas, the standards established by exchanging PRA and TRA maps established this as a practice, that legal scholars would contend, eventually became binding as a recognized point of agreement under international law.

Violations of PRAs and TRAs were taken seriously by the MLMs and were rare occurrences. USMLM did not violate PRAs or TRAs as a matter of policy. PRAs or TRAs were not penetrated without expressed approval of Headquarters USAREUR, or in the very rare occasions when Chief USMLM (CUSMLM) approved immediate exploitation to fill high-priority gaps in intelligence holdings. In the rare cases wherein a USMLM tour vehicle entered a PRA or TRA by accident, this was immediately reported by the erring tour officer to the CUSMLM and then to USAREUR leadership in case of a Soviet protest. Although SMLM-F initially demonstrated little regard for restricted areas, this behavior was adjusted by the early 1950s due to the need to enforce the restrictions on USMLM through reciprocity. At that point, the Soviets were also careful not to violate PRAs or TRAs.

It was mutually understood that highways passing through restricted areas and roads bordering on restricted areas were authorized for MLM travel unless explicitly marked as restricted. This nuance, however, was not widely understood (or at least acknowledged) by East German and Soviet forces, resulting in many claims of restricted area violations when USMLM tours were observed traveling in such non-restricted areas. Although the East German security forces regularly reported USMLM tours violating PRAs and TRAs, in virtually all cases, the USMLM tours were traveling on highways through the restricted area or on roads bordering the restricted areas, as authorized. On many other occasions, accusations of USMLM PRA/TRA violations were determined to be the result of map-reading errors by sighting/reporting elements or the use of outdated PRA/TRA maps by Soviet or East German forces. All told, the East German and Soviet statistics on USMLM PRA/TRA violations were believed to have been greatly exaggerated over the years, but this did not negate the fact that USMLM did perform their touring mission very aggressively.

The Evolution of Competitive Norms

The "cooperative norms" to institutionalize touring as the practice to exploit the freedom of movement and to place boundaries on these freedoms through restricted areas appropriately evolved due to the broad nature of the Huebner–Malinin Agreement. Within these cooperative norms, a subset of "competitive norms" evolved to address the privileges and restrictions vaguely imposed in the agreement. The competitive practices that evolved through a process of trial and error developed largely based on tour activities, and as efforts to deter intelligence collection in sensitive areas. The competitive norms consisted primarily of efforts by the hosting forces to monitor and restrict MLM tours, or in reaction to objectionable MLM actions while on tour. The large majority of competitive norms were borne out of the dynamic among USMLM and the Soviets and East Germans in the Soviet zone, and were rarely practiced among the players in the U.S. zone.

MLM Restriction Signs

The unilaterally imposed competitive norm that caused the most contention and controversy among USMLM and its Soviet hosts was the employment of MLM

Restriction Signs (MRSs). Although the MLMs agreed to areas recognized under the Huebner–Malinin Agreement as "places of disposition of military units" by exchanging maps with designated PRAs and TRAs, the Soviets and East Germans regularly placed MRSs in efforts to further restrict MLM presence in many more locations.

MRSs were posted by Soviet and East German forces to block access to installations and training locations that were not located within PRAs or TRAs. In most cases, these were expansive training or storage areas that were not secured or marked by fences or other physical barriers. The U.S. (and Allies) did not recognize the legitimacy of MRSs because they were not officially declared and mutually accepted through a formal process. Although the Allies' official position was that the areas marked by MRSs were not legitimate, USMLM recognized that there was an increased risk of Soviet or East German security measures in these areas, and there is evidence to suggest from many recurring incidents that Soviet and East German military forces considered the MRS-marked areas as authoritative as the PRAs and TRAs, and enforced them as such.

The majority of incidents involving alleged USMLM restricted area violations occurred in areas only marked by MRSs. The fact that USMLM personnel were

MLM Restriction Signs that were posted over large portions of the Soviet sector (East Germany). (USMLM Association)

declared persona non grata after violating a PRA, but never for violating an area marked by an MRS, demonstrated that the Soviets also recognized that the MRSs had no standing under the Huebner–Malinin Agreement and the mutually recognized norms.

Incidents

Issues that arose while the USMLM or SMLM-F were conducting tour activities that required discussion and remediation between the MLM and their host were characterized as "incidents." Any event could rise to the level of an incident, but the more common occurrences were claims of restricted area violations, complaints of surveillance, vehicle accidents (to include intentional rammings), the forceful detention of tour vehicles or personnel, shooting incidents, or other forms of harassment/deterrence. Incidents of actual PRA/TRA violations were very rare for both SMLM-F and USMLM. Incidents not only applied to actions taken by hosting security forces against touring MLMs; MLM tour activities deemed to be dangerous or otherwise objectionable were also protested as incidents.

There were two officially recognized categories of incidents: minor incidents and serious incidents. A minor incident was defined as an occurrence for which a resolution could be accomplished at the Chief of MLM and Chief of SERB (CSERB) or Chief of ACS (CACS) level, or which required no additional action. A serious incident was defined as a relatively grave occurrence for which resolution required action at a higher level than that of the Chief of MLM and CSERB or CACS. Actions taken for serious incidents frequently included an exchange of letters at the USAREUR/GSFG Chief of Staff or higher level.

In the context of the MLMs, a serious incident usually involved the intended or actual use of physical force against a tour team. Both sides authorized the detention of MLM tour vehicles, but the Soviets and East Germans employed the measure more frequently and aggressively. All other activities qualifying as incidents were strictly prohibited by USAREUR rules of engagement in regard to SMLM-F, and were therefore exclusively conducted by Soviet or East German elements targeting USMLM tours. Incidents were a common, unavoidable part of USMLM operations. The most frequent incidents other than detentions were vehicle rammings and shootings. Many incidents involving USMLM were commonly the result of security forces and other military elements acting in reaction to USMLM presence in what was, or what was perceived to be, a restricted area. Occurrences of surveillance were reported as incidents by USMLM when the surveillance reached the level of being dangerous harassment.

By the time of East Germany's initial grant of sovereignty in 1954, the East Germans had clearly assumed responsibility for the monitoring and surveillance of USMLM, although a blatant contradiction to the Huebner–Malinin Agreement provision of "without escort or supervision." In general, the Soviet and East German militaries were very aggressive in efforts to obstruct USMLM movement and intelligence collection. Although other factors contributed to the USMLM operational approach, the aggressive and often dangerous countermeasures employed by Soviet and East German forces directly led to a more aggressive intelligence-collection approach by the U.S. (and Allies). In contrast to the Soviet and East German approach to USMLM, the U.S. never authorized or requested direct West German support or interference as it applied to SMLM-F and the enforcement of the Huebner–Malinin Agreement. In addition, U.S. forces rarely attempted to directly interfere with a SMLM-F tour except in the very rare occasions when they were discovered blatantly violating a restricted area. These dynamics, which were relatively unique to each MLM and their U.S. or Soviet host, largely resulted in diametrical incident environments among the two MLMs.

Surveillance

Covert surveillance is conducted in a manner to observe the surveillance target without the target detecting that it is under surveillance. Conversely, overt surveillance is conducted in a manner that places maintaining contact (observation) with the target as a higher priority than ensuring that the surveillance activity goes undetected. In fact, overt surveillance is often conducted with the expressed purpose of ensuring that the target is very aware that it is under surveillance. In some cases, this serves as a form of intimidation, or as a show of force as may be the case when a foreign diplomat is overtly followed during periods of increased political tensions between countries. In the case of the MLMs, overt surveillance would also serve the purpose of making it known that the tour vehicle was under scrutiny and to discourage any nefarious activity.

The employment of surveillance on an MLM vehicle or member was a violation of Regulation 10 of the Huebner–Malinin Agreement specifying that the MLMs should be "permitted complete freedom of travel ... *without escort or supervision.*" This provision implied that surveillance as a form of supervision, and particularly overt surveillance which was also a deterrent to freedom of travel, would be in violation of the agreement.

During the first five years of the MLMs, overt surveillance was regularly conducted by both the U.S. and the Soviets. The Soviets initially employed very aggressive overt surveillance coverage of USMLM vehicles which resulted in a very high detention rate and influenced the mission's less aggressive initial approach to intelligence collection. During the initial years, Soviet agents conducted covert surveillance of USMLM in an apparent effort to determine whether USMLM was conducting clandestine or other activities in violation of the Huebner–Malinin Agreement.

The initial overt surveillance of SMLM-F was conducted by U.S. Army military police highway patrol detachments. The employment of overt surveillance by both sides began a tit-for-tat cycle which demonstrated that surveillance, although technically prohibited by the agreement, represented one of the methods the opposing generals could use to punch and counterpunch. When USAREUR retaliated against overt surveillance of USMLM by ordering overt surveillance of SMLM-F, the activities targeting USMLM would immediately and invariably be paused. When reinitiated, USAREUR would retaliate and achieve the same positive response.

In 1952, the U.S. and Soviets agreed to cease surveillance of MLM personnel and vehicles. As a result, USAREUR ceased all surveillance of Soviet vehicles and personnel, and the Soviets terminated the overt surveillance of USMLM vehicles by Soviet and East German security agencies. With one exception, the U.S. did not conduct overt surveillance operations against SMLM-F for the remaining duration of the MLMs. Conversely, the Soviets did not adhere to the non-surveillance agreement of 1952, but rather, acquired a fleet of high-performance, American-made vehicles and attempted to continue covert surveillance against USMLM. The transition to covert surveillance was readily detected and largely ineffective because the American-made vehicles were not common in the Soviet zone, and the surveillance vehicles readily stood out.

The fundamental difference between surveillance targeting USMLM and surveillance targeting SMLM-F was the differences among the occupying forces' relationship with their German partners. The U.S. played the role of a true occupying force with a special relationship with the Soviet occupiers, and never asked the West German government to conduct surveillance; nor did the West German government take a great interest in exercising sovereignty as it applied to SMLM-F, with the exception of two pivotal but brief periods in the evolution of West Germany. Alternatively, the East Germans assumed the mission to autonomously surveil and otherwise harass USMLM. The Soviets did, however, exercise a degree of influence when they wanted the East Germans to increase intensity, or to decrease or pause surveillance operations when USAREUR raised significant protests.

Throughout the MLM era, the U.S. conducted surveillance far less frequently and almost always in a covert manner, whereas the Soviet/East German approach to surveillance was largely persistent, overt, and aggressive. The East German surveillance of USMLM was highly indicative of the Stasi obsession with disrupting USMLM intelligence-collection activities and detecting the conduct of clandestine intelligence activities.

Detentions

A "detention" was defined as an incident wherein a tour's freedom of movement was physically restricted. As the term implies, a detention was a form of capture wherein the tour vehicle was stopped, and the tour personnel were taken into custody. Detentions were normally executed by two or more vehicles operating in coordination to physically box in and immobilize a tour vehicle. With restricted areas being the mouse-bait, the tactic of the detention became the cat's preferred method of enforcement. Detentions were a method employed to entrap and penalize restricted-area violations, to counter aggressive intelligence-collection activities, or as a form of reciprocity for a detention occurring against a counterpart MLM. Detentions first became the method employed early and often by the Soviets and East German military and security forces to enforce restricted areas, and very quickly became a mutually recognized measure. Although detentions became the primary enforcement and punishment mechanism for restricted-area violations, there were never any written protocols for detentions; they just evolved and became competitive norms of the game. And although most detentions occurred outside of restricted areas, the intent was to forcibly stop a tour vehicle while violating a restricted area as red-handed proof of a Huebner–Malinin Agreement violation.

Detentions and related Soviet and East German attempts to disrupt USMLM tour teams were the antagonistic behavior that would become the overall characterization of U.S./Soviet MLM dynamic in postwar Germany. Detentions of SMLM-F tours were not unheard of, but they were exponentially less common than detentions against USMLM. The relatively rare detentions of SMLM-F were the result of opportune and proactive military units. The majority of USMLM detentions occurred based on the coordinated surveillance by Stasi and regional police forces, in coordination with military forces. Detentions were regularly effected by road blockades, being forced off the road, the mechanical breakdown of a tour vehicle, or by being detained while on foot in the vicinity of an installation or other sensitive intelligence target. Detentions became so commonplace to USMLM tours that tour officers jokingly referred to a detention as a "clobber."

Detentions on both sides of the divide were always addressed afterward at the Chief of MLM and CSERB/CACS level. In the most egregious cases, formal complaints were exchanged between USAREUR and GSFG. As a common element of the detention process, the detaining MLM host reserved the authority to retain the detained personnel's accreditation documents before being released to their MLM, which essentially restricted those personnel to their mission compound until the documents were returned. As a typical act of reciprocity, if a SMLM-F tour was detained and their personnel's accreditation documents were kept for three days, the GSFG would rapidly orchestrate a detention of a USMLM tour and keep the detained personnel's accreditation documentation for four or more days.

Both the USAREUR and GSFG forces had widely trained and practiced MLM detention response protocols. USAREUR issued a SMLM sighting/detention instructions card that was carried by every soldier. The Soviets had differing detention and detention resolution procedures from those employed by USAREUR, but their procedures were uniformly understood and generally complied with by all Soviet and East German forces. Once a detention was effected, a well-rehearsed and choreographed form of political theater would then ensue. However, the procedures practiced by the Soviets and the U.S. differed significantly.

Other Incidents

Although SMLM-F did have isolated traffic incidents which were discussed as incidents, the majority of incidents other than surveillance and detentions were essentially associated with USMLM actions and East German and Soviet countermeasures. USMLM vehicles had tires slashed and windows smashed by shovels and rifle butts, and tour personnel were even dragged from vehicles, bound, and interrogated. It was not uncommon for USMLM equipment to be confiscated during detentions, which was sometimes returned and sometimes not. Vehicle rammings were an extreme form of detention, and evidence exists to demonstrate that this tactic was intended to have more lasting effects than simply to detain a vehicle. There was never an incident of U.S. or West German forces firing gunshots in the vicinity of SMLM-F, but as will be detailed, aimed shots at, and warning shots in the vicinity of, USMLM were relatively common occurrences. Only twice did the occurrence of dangerous shooting or vehicle-ramming incidents rise to the level of a protest that threatened the viability of the Huebner–Malinin Agreement and the MLMs. The fact that these types of incidents continued to occur throughout the existence of the MLMs established and sustained precedents that demonstrated they were tacitly accepted as competitive norms. Like no other gesture, accepting these risks as norms demonstrated the level of risk the U.S. would accept to allow the USMLM intelligence-collection mission to continue.

A Period of Relative Calm

The dynamics among the Allied and Soviet MLMs transformed quickly and settled into a long period of relatively steady-state activities after tacit norms and other unwritten rules became mutual practice. Although the period of 1954 to 1979 was a period of relative calm in relation to the initial and concluding periods of the MLMs, it was still a daily game of move and countermove that continued around the clock. As will be detailed in subsequent chapters, this 25-year period was rife with activities that established the MLM battlefields as the most emblematic of the Cold War. It was also during this period that the game of Soviet manipulation and deception played out on a global scale, while elements of which were perhaps obscured by the very visible and contentious dynamic that was a perpetual theater among the MLMs.

Quasi-diplomatic Status

One of the more interesting manifestations of the MLMs was the de facto diplomatic immunity status that was never declared but always assumed. The privilege of "complete freedom of travel" did not directly equate to diplomatic immunity. The only provision of the Huebner–Malinin Agreement that explicitly referenced diplomatic immunity was one which granted couriers "the same immunity which is extended to diplomatic couriers."

One of the two primary principles of diplomatic immunity is extraterritoriality, which is the state of being exempted from the jurisdiction of local law. Extraterritoriality is largely recognized as embassies, homes, offices, and vehicles being considered to be situated on the soil of the home country. However, the Huebner–Malinin Agreement only specified extraterritoriality as a privilege granted for the "buildings of each mission," meaning that MLM vehicles or personnel did not technically enjoy this element of immunity when not on their respective compounds.

The second primary principle of diplomatic immunity—inviolability—means that diplomats are untouchable. Only on rare occasions did U.S. forces not recognize inviolability by detaining SMLM-F vehicles. Even during detentions, U.S. forces never violated the principle of extraterritoriality by entering or taking the contents from a SMLM-F vehicle, demonstrating that the U.S. recognized this diplomatic immunity principle although not officially granted. The West German government always treated SMLM-F as though they were granted absolute diplomatic immunity.

Although there were no provisions which specified full rights of diplomatic immunity to MLM personnel, with few exceptions these privileges were assumed and recognized by all. In fact, the status of the MLMs was historically unique in that the MLMs maintained a status of superiority over their host countries, ignored the sovereignty of these governments' conventions, and freely traveled throughout the countries in a belligerent manner that was well beyond that of any other officials enjoying diplomatic status in any other country in the world.

The Soviets and East Germans recognized and respected the extraterritoriality of the USMLM compound, but the vehicles and tour personnel were not always given such consideration, particularly when it was perceived that they were violating a restricted area or operating in the area of sensitive military activity. Generally, however, the Soviets and East Germans did treat USMLM as though they were extended the privileges of extraterritoriality and inviolability at all other times in which they did not perceive a direct security threat.

Although not always practiced by the East Germans and Soviets, the MLMs quasi-diplomatic status enabled them to travel throughout the Germanys with much more freedom than diplomats in any other country were granted. Generally, foreign diplomats in any country must submit a travel request with a travel plan before traveling outside a prescribed radius from their embassy or consulate. The MLMs had no such restrictions unless traveling outside of the Allied or Soviet sectors. In addition, the privilege of inviolability for individuals with diplomatic status is generally waived when such an individual is detected in the act of committing a crime, but this did not apply to the MLMs.

USMLM had to recognize the East German authorities because they represented a daily hazard, but never from the perspective of any judicial consequences. The East Germans' and Soviets' actions suggested that they only failed to recognize the principle of inviolability for USMLM personnel when it was perceived that USMLM tours were violating the provisions of the Huebner–Malinin Agreement or associated cooperative norms. And while they did not always recognize inviolability, the reconciliation of all incidents involving USMLM ultimately concluded with the Soviets granting them the privilege of diplomatic immunity. In fact, USMLM personnel were protected by this immunity after incidents in which East German citizens would have been arrested and jailed for perpetrating the same acts.

When East German elements detained USMLM tours, they expeditiously turned them over to Soviet authorities, demonstrating that they would always defer to the Soviets to resolve any East German claims against USMLM. One incident in 1968 that demonstrated the manner in which USMLM members were treated as though they were granted diplomatic immunity, involved an East German allegation that a USMLM tour vehicle caused serious injury to a motorcycle driver. The tour vehicle was detained by the Stasi and turned over to the local Soviet Kommandant, who was the district military police commander. The East Germans alleged that the USMLM vehicle was in a restricted area, made an illegal U-turn on the highway, caused a following motorcycle to lose control which seriously injured the operator, and fled the scene of the accident without rendering assistance to the injured individual. The USMLM tour personnel denied all charges stating that the U-turn was a legal maneuver and that they did not witness an accident. The tour was eventually released and allowed to return to the USMLM compound, but in a very rare occurrence, the CSERB immediately notified CUSMLM that the USMLM tour officer was declared persona non grata. Whether or not the USMLM tour personnel legitimately believed that they were not at fault, the expulsion of the USMLM tour officer demonstrated that the East Germans protested the incident to the Soviets in the strongest terms, compelling the CSERB to take action. This also demonstrated that although the East Germans had taken a USMLM tour into custody for allegedly causing serious injury to one of their citizens, they immediately turned the tour personnel over to Soviet officials, as they always did, and relied on the Soviets to act in their interest. This was a classic case of diplomatic immunity wherein the USMLM member was simply expelled whereas an East German citizen committing the same alleged crime would have been arrested to face a court trial.

As another example, in 1972, two USMLM enlisted drivers were observed removing flags that were on public display in Leipzig, East Germany. Local police were called to the scene and attempted to detain (pull over) the USMLM vehicle departing the scene of the crime, but the USMLM vehicle successfully evaded the attempt. The Soviets presented a protest claiming that the USMLM members were guilty of "hooliganism" and traffic violations, to include reckless endangerment when fleeing the scene of a crime. Following a quick USMLM investigation, the two personnel were removed from the mission and the stolen flags returned to the East Germans through the SERB. Obviously, being allowed to simply be removed and have no further action taken, after having not responded to police when fleeing the scene of a crime, demonstrated that USMLM personnel were treated as though having diplomatic immunity status.

Since West German authorities were completely hands off in regard to the MLMs, SMLM-F never appeared to acknowledge that the West Germans even existed. SMLM-F regularly violated West German traffic laws, usually to bypass annoying traffic jams, but were never detained by West German police for such actions. SMLM-F enjoyed absolute inviolability and immunity as it applied to U.S. military forces and West German authorities, with the exception of the occasional detention or detention attempt.

A prime example of SMLM-F immunity was an event that was reported to USAREUR by West German authorities in 1978. The West Germans reported that a SMLM-F vehicle stopped in the middle of a highway for no apparent reason, causing four vehicles to collide while avoiding the SMLM-F vehicle. The SMLM-F vehicle departed the scene of the accident despite being requested by the West German police to remain. USAREUR launched a protest through ACS and USMLM, to which the Soviets uniformly replied that a stopped West German vehicle caused the SMLM-F vehicle to stop, which was not consistent with any of the statements taken at the scene of the accident. Although any West German citizen would have been charged with causing multiple accidents and fleeing the scene, the incident was dropped after the Soviets' unsubstantiated retort. The West Germans knew they had no recourse given the SMLMs' "special" status.

Even in official, senior-level discussions as late as 1986, the U.S. and Soviets agreed that the MLMs did not fall under any West or East German jurisdiction.

One More Push for Sovereignty

Until the final decade of the Cold War period, the only event that significantly challenged the legitimacy of the MLM institutions was not one of contention among the superpowers, rather, one that compelled them to unify in the face of their increasingly defiant hosts. The Treaty Concerning the Basis of Relations

Between the Federal Republic of Germany and the German Democratic Republic, which was signed on 21 December 1972 and went into effect in June 1973, was the first official recognition by West Germany and East Germany of each other's sovereignty. This treaty paved the way for the two German states to be recognized by the international community and led to both being admitted into the United Nations on 18 September 1973.

Viewing this as the point at which the possibility of German reunification was least likely, the West Germans became increasingly vocal in questioning the legitimacy of the MLMs on sovereign German territories. This period also marked one of the most dangerous in USMLM history as the East Germans undertook a coordinated campaign of harassment and challenges to USMLM's freedom of movement that continued until after a life-threatening shooting incident in October 1973. In the face of the challenges, the U.S. and Soviets once again placed the priority of the MLMs over the demands of their German partners, and stood united in maintaining the legitimacy of the Huebner–Malinin Agreement.

One Final Period of Relative Calm

After the period of challenges to the MLMs' status as occupying-force symbols, the dynamic among the MLMs and their respective hosts normalized again in deference to the traditional occupying powers. This then resumed the period of relative status quo which remained in practice until the fourth decade of the Cold War. In this context, status quo meant aggressive intelligence collection by USMLM (and Allied MLMs) with aggressive Soviet and East German countermeasures to include surveillance, detentions, and isolated shooting incidents, and a much less contentious dynamic among the Soviet MLMs and their Allied hosts.

This period of relative calm persisted until the Soviet invasion of Afghanistan in 1979, which proved to be the most adversarial period between the superpowers, and which had cascading impacts on the MLMs and the nature of operations conducted among them.

Into the Final Decade

The situation in Afghanistan and other international dynamics made 1979 and the early 1980s the most politically and operationally contentious period in U.S./Soviet relations. In anticipation of the Soviet invasion of Afghanistan in 1979, the U.S. began providing covert support to the opposition Mujahedeen. Although the U.S. and Soviets had been fighting proxy wars around the globe for the previous three decades, this was the first time the U.S. was taking actions that directly threatened Soviet military forces. In reaction to the December 1979 invasion, the U.S. enacted economic sanctions and trade embargoes against the Soviet Union, led a boycott of the 1980 Moscow Olympics, and stepped up its aid to the Afghan insurgents.

In March 1983, perhaps marking the lowest point in U.S./Soviet relations, U.S. President Ronald Reagan referred to the Soviet Union as the "Evil Empire." Soviet General Secretary Mikhail Gorbachev characterized the world situation in the first half of the 1980s as the most explosive, difficult, and unfavorable of the postwar decades. This was the first time in MLM history that there was a direct correlation between international relations and MLM activities. There was a notable increase in dangerous harassment activities directed toward the Allied MLMs, so it is not surprising that the only two Allied MLM deaths would occur during this period. The U.S. policy toward SMLM-F did not overtly change during this period, but there was a different mindset developing regarding the SMLM-F threat.

The French Harbinger

In 1979, when relations between the U.S. and the Soviet Union began to rapidly deteriorate, the Soviets, East German military, and Stasi implemented tactics to facilitate detentions by ambush. The early 1980s were marked by a dangerous campaign of harassment and physical threats involving vehicle rammings and shootings on the part of the Soviets and the East Germans. The first incident occurred in 1979 wherein an East German military vehicle rammed a USMLM tour vehicle, forcing it off the road and rolling it twice. Rammings and other violent detention methods continued to target USMLM until the last such event in January 1984. It is likely that these tactics were discontinued after the tragic event occurring two months later.

On 22 March 1984, an FMLM vehicle was struck by an East German military vehicle, instantly killing the passenger-side FMLM tour officer named Philippe Mariotti. Since the East German government did not entertain official contacts with the FMLM, it would have been problematic for the French to make Mariotti's death a political issue—which of course might have brought into question the validity of the MLMs continuing to operate in sovereign German territories. This incident was the most serious in a recurrence of provocations that demonstrated the fragile nature of the MLMs' quasi-diplomatic status. However, even this most egregious violation of the intent of the Huebner–Malinin Agreement was not addressed as an issue that would challenge the validity of the MLMs. Mariotti's death was the first of the two examples of what extreme risks the Allied MLMs would tolerate to avoid bringing into question the propriety of MLM intelligence collection in third-country territories.

The Mariotti incident did apparently prompt GSFG to issue guidance regarding the harsh treatment of MLM tours, and there was a noticeable decline in these aggressive actions immediately following the incident. But this lull was short-lived, and the East Germans were not the only risk.

The Last Casualty of the Cold War

Just over a year after Mariotti's death, a USMLM tour officer was shot and killed while attempting to photograph Soviet military assets at a Soviet military facility in East Germany. On 24 March 1985, army Major Arthur Nicholson and his driver, Staff Sergeant Jessie Schatz, conducted standard tour activity by following a convoy of Soviet tanks returning from a training range and then stopped to examine a tank shed that they happened upon. According to Schatz, an undetected Soviet soldier fired a shot from his AK-47 which barely missed his head, and then fired two shots at Nicholson who was running away from the sentry and toward the tour vehicle. Nicholson suffered a fatal wound and died shortly after lying on the ground, bleeding without medical aid.

As could be expected, the U.S.'s position on the event was based on Sergeant Schatz's account and the Soviets' position was based on the sentry's account, both of which affixed fault on the other. Regardless, it was a senseless killing and only the second death in the nearly 40-year history of the MLMs. The Soviets, however, refused to apologize for the event (until years later), and even the USAREUR investigations, the most thorough of which was completed in 1987, concluded that the killing was an isolated incident involving the poor judgement of a lone sentry.

Although the Nicholson incident was the one in the history of the MLMs which brought the most notoriety to the previously little-known World War II occupation-force relics, it was far from recognized as a relation-altering international incident. The shooting occurred during the first months of Mikhail Gorbachev's presidency in which the U.S. saw great promise for reform. President Reagan's only comment on the event condemned the killing, but basically indicated that it would be back to business as usual.

Throughout the entire Cold War, the Nicholson shooting was the only time that an American in uniform was killed by a Soviet in uniform. Consistent with the out-of-the-public-eye nature of the MLMs and many related Cold War activities, Major Nicholson was posthumously promoted to lieutenant colonel and is memorialized as the "last casualty of the Cold War." However, since casualty actually means killed or injured, Nicholson was not technically the last casualty, as there were other incidents resulting in injury after his killing. Therefore, he would have been more accurately termed the last killed in action (KIA) casualty of the Cold War.

During the nearly 13-month period following Nicholson's death, the U.S. insisted on a series of talks to address the issue of MLM safety, and the Soviets dogmatically played along. Despite the U.S.'s honorable intentions, it was clear from the beginning and immediately acknowledged that the Soviets would not acquiesce to the two fundamental demands of an official apology and compensation for Nicholson's family. In the end, despite all of the finger-pointing between USAREUR and the

GSFG regarding which side was at fault, neither side ever questioned the legitimacy of the MLMs.

During the "Nicholson negotiations," the U.S. was careful to coordinate the negotiation objectives with its Allied partners; and, while the French had already demonstrated their position the year before in the death of Mariotti, the British were adamant that the U.S. should not risk any bargaining position that might result in restrictions to Allied collection operations. In the end, the talks (negotiations) to elicit Soviet concessions and to affix mutually agreed-upon responsibility for Nicholson's death were diluted by the U.S.'s underlying position, which was to avoid a rush to alter the mutually accepted norms or to establish any clear and well-defined procedures that might bring color to the gray areas wherein the MLMs had lived and operated since 1947.

An Inflection Point

The Nicholson negotiations were initially viewed by USAREUR as a success in that they resulted in increased access for intelligence collection in East Germany; but upon further review by counterintelligence professionals, and as will be detailed, the Soviets' negotiating position and the results of the talks were one of the many related dynamics that shaped USAREUR's concerns regarding the nature of SMLM-F intelligence activities.

As the MLMs entered their fifth decade in 1987, the U.S. counterintelligence effort was posturing to enter a new era to address questions regarding the true nature of the SMLM-F intelligence-related activities in West Germany. In late 1988, Army Counterintelligence established a highly specialized counterintelligence unit to unravel the SMLM-F mystery in a dedicated and sophisticated manner.

On 9 November 1989, a few sections of the Berlin Wall were opened, resulting in thousands of East Germans crossing freely into West Berlin and West Germany for the first time in nearly 30 years. At the Malta Summit on 3 December 1989, Soviet President Mikhail Gorbachev and U.S. President George H. W. Bush mutually declared the end of the Cold War. On 1 October 1990, two days before German reunification, the MLMs were disestablished.

Insights on History

The fact that the MLMs continued to operate for more than four decades with little more standing than what amounted to a gentlemen's agreement after the Agreement on Control Machinery in German essentially disintegrated, is a little-known footnote in Cold War history. Because the agreements governing the MLMs were made during the occupation period and between the victorious powers, the original accords remained intact, giving the MLMs quasi-diplomatic status until they ceased operations in 1990. Throughout the Cold War, the MLMs exercised extraterritoriality rights that were considered the reserved rights of the occupying powers. It was in this vestigial legal gray zone that the American, British, French, and Soviet MLMs operated, accredited only to each other, and communicating directly with each other over the heads of all other actors, especially their East and West German hosts.

Both sides tacitly agreed to exploit the flexibility of the Huebner–Malinin Agreement to create what in effect became a system of mutual inspection. A cooperative regime was fostered and (for the most part) carefully respected by both in order to avoid undesired provocations. By an unspoken agreement, both U.S. and Soviet authorities sheltered the MLMs' activities from publicity, which may otherwise have left the mechanism more exposed to downturns in superpower relations. Constant and direct communications between the MLMs diffused tensions and ultimately ensured that the beneficial, transparency-building intelligence collection continued over the years. This allowed the interactive intelligence-liaison relationship to perpetuate the development of competitive norms between the two players.

Given the cat-and-mouse games involving surveillance, detentions, and even more serious incidents such as vehicle rammings and shootings, it is remarkable and improbable that the MLM framework was able to persist as a visible microcosm of the Cold War given the multitude of political gyrations among the superpowers throughout contentious periods, which included the Korean War; the East German uprising of 1953; the Russian invasion of Hungary in 1956; the U-2 shoot-down incident in 1960; construction of the Berlin Wall beginning in 1961; the Cuban revolution, the Bay of Pigs invasion, and the Missile Crisis of 1962; the Russian invasion of Czechoslovakia in 1968; the Vietnam War; and, the many other proxy wars between the U.S. and Soviet Union during the Cold War era. Despite these and other geopolitical challenges, the MLMs generally remained immune from any impacts of strategic U.S./Soviet relations during the first three decades of the Cold War.

The fact that the U.S. and Soviets allowed to set in motion a dynamic wherein the MLMs operated as intelligence-collection platforms with tacit recognition and acceptance on all sides is likely the reason the MLMs persisted long after the need for a direct liaison relationship resident in each other's sector had passed. The MLMs endured in spite of all detractors because they provided what experts regarded as the best on-site intelligence that could be gathered on Europe's heavily armed central fronts. Further insulating the MLMs was a culture which developed and was perpetuated by U.S. and Soviet personnel who would serve two or more times at an MLM during their careers, and even some who served at an MLM and ACS or SERB. In fact, the practice of referring to intelligence-collection missions as tours was a term of culture that was an early and obvious effort to disassociate the MLMs from their primary intelligence functions.

The cooperative and competitive norms established through trial and error among the MLMs evolved into the spoken and unspoken rules of the game. The competitive norms which became common practices/occurrences were established largely as a response to the touring patterns of the respective MLMs. But despite all the measures implemented and executed specifically to deter and prevent intelligence collection, the viability/legitimacy of tours and their underlying intelligence-collection objectives was never questioned as an acceptable practice.

Although the MLMs and their respective hosts operated as though they generally played by the same written and unwritten rules, the dynamic among USMLM and the GSFG and East German security forces differed significantly from that of SMLM-F and USAREUR and the West German government. The primary difference was that the rules were more aggressively enforced in the Soviet sector, and the Soviets did allow the East Germans to exercise a high degree of sovereignty in countering USMLM. A much higher frequency of detentions in East Germany was a direct result of the dynamic among aggressive Stasi surveillance process, which compelled USMLM to collect more aggressively, which in turn stimulated a more aggressive response from the East Germans or Soviets.

The PRA and TRA (and MRS in the case of the Soviets) restrictions were part of the overall effort to systematize a counterintelligence response to touring. However, with restricted areas containing the most sensitive military activities, it was intuitive to all involved that there was relatively little activity of intelligence interest that was not taking place in a restricted area. Therefore, although intended as a counterintelligence measure, restricted areas focused intelligence attention and became the mouse-bait in the cat-and-mouse game that played out every day for decades.

When the Soviets released their most restrictive PRA map in 1984, PRAs covered 39 percent of East Germany, and USAREUR estimated that MRSs covered an additional 40 percent of the area. And again, Soviet forces, and the East Germans in particular, enforced MRS areas with the same sense of urgency as PRAs/TRAs. The issue of restricted areas was one area in which USAREUR never reached a level of equity or quid pro quo with the Soviets until the final four years of the MLMs. This was based on a long-standing but unsuccessful effort to convince the Soviets to concede reciprocity and decrease the percentage of restricted areas in East Germany. USAREUR consistently restricted travel in an average of 19–22 percent of the area of West Germany in an effort to convince the Soviets to extend parity. In fact, USAREUR needed to be creative in developing restricted areas in the effort to raise the percentage of coverage and gain a semblance of parity with the high percentage of restricted areas in the Soviet sector. One method USAREUR arbitrarily employed to increase the percentage of restricted areas was to restrict travel in the large urban areas in the U.S. sector, to include the SMLM-F base location of Frankfurt.

Although there are many additional examples, the two Allied fatalities occurring within nearly a year of each other in 1984 and 1985 best reflected the contrasting risk environments among that in which SMLM-F operated and that in which the Allied MLMs operated. Whereas the U.S. had very rigid and widely trained restrictions regarding the use of force against SMLM-F touring activities, which resulted in no major dangerous incidents or injuries to SMLM-F personnel over the years, USMLM regularly encountered risks posed by Soviet and East German elements.

As recorded history would tell it, the period between the conclusion of the Nicholson negotiations and the end of the MLMs was the most uneventful of the era—but this was not necessarily the case.

CHAPTER 2

The Evolution of the Military Liaison Mission Game

The development of the norms practiced by the MLMs was a rapid evolutionary process. Cooperative norms were established within the provisions of the agreement, and competitive norms were established as commonly conducted, and therefore acceptable, practices within the bounds of the cooperative norms. Although the basic rules as set forth in the Huebner–Malinin Agreement were intended to provide both of the signatories equal freedoms to operate, the U.S. and Soviets chose divergent approaches, both in the manners in which they operated their MLM and in the manner in which they hosted their counterpart MLM. Despite the common framework governing the MLMs, there were many differences in the manner which each side chose to develop and exercise their applicable cooperative and competitive norms—the rules by which each side chose to play.

Applicable to international law, the Huebner–Malinin Agreement stood as an official agreement between two nation-states. As such, it established the legal bounds under which both parties agreed to operate within the agreement. Any activities conducted under the auspices of the agreement were considered as being governed and authorized by the agreement. Actions by either side could be protested, negotiated, and reconciled, but only actions that raised to the level of "breaking" the agreement and being cause for dissolution could be considered beyond acceptable norms. Therefore, all of the cooperative and competitive norms that were allowed to continue over the years, even when uniformly protested but under the level of calling them a "deal-breaker," established legal precedents as acceptable actions under international law among the two nation-states.

Coupled with the detailed history of the MLMs, an examination of the manner which the MLMs evolved provides a window into one of the more unique microcosms of the Cold War. Both MLMs and their hosting counterparts developed standards of action which were reinforced by accompanying narratives during liaison engagements and other interactions. These narratives—some very subtle and some not so—served to establish the record of what each side agreed was acceptable as legal precedents under international law.

Intelligence Collection and Counterintelligence

Before a deep dive into the evolution of the MLMs, it is instructional to understand how the East and West configured for combat and operated in the intelligence arena. The Western intelligence and counterintelligence agencies generally operated in the same manner, as did the Soviets and their Soviet Bloc republics' agencies. However, there were distinguishable differences among the Soviet Bloc human intelligence (HUMINT) and counterintelligence processes and those of the U.S.

The intelligence-collection means that was most emblematic of Cold War spy/counterspy intrigue was HUMINT. HUMINT is a category of intelligence derived from information collected and provided by human sources. A HUMINT source is a person who wittingly or unwittingly conveys by any means information of potential intelligence value. Generally, HUMINT is distinguished as overt or clandestine. The Allied MLMs quickly evolved as overt HUMINT collectors, meaning that they did not employ any extraordinary operational tradecraft to conceal the identity of operators or methodologies employed. Military exchanges and liaison engagements facilitated overt HUMINT collection as well. In contrast to overt HUMINT, clandestine HUMINT is the acquisition of protected intelligence information in a manner designed to protect the source, and conceal the operation, identity of operators and sources, and actual methodologies employed. Clandestine HUMINT is most commonly associated with the recruitment and control of spies to commit espionage. Although it is known that USMLM only operated overtly and did not conduct clandestine HUMINT activities, this was never confirmed (or denied) to be the case for SMLM-F.

Counterintelligence is the discipline that focuses on countering all adversarial intelligence threats, with the most potentially severe threat being clandestine HUMINT.

Soviet HUMINT and Counterintelligence

Soviet HUMINT

The KGB was the last in a succession of post-Russian Revolution and Cold War Soviet internal security agencies dating back to 1917, and was the main security agency from 1954 until the dissolution of the Soviet Union in 1991. Democratic countries like the U.S. tend to decentralize intelligence and security functions in many different agencies, among other reasons, to prevent any one agency from becoming too powerful. In contrast, the Soviets consolidated virtually all intelligence, counterintelligence, and security functions under the KGB to ensure that this all-powerful and centrally controlled behemoth remained singularly loyal to the Communist Party. The KGB protected against threats from within Russia and maintained an extensive international network to conduct intelligence collection and other active measures.

The KGB conducted clandestine HUMINT operations from residencies operating in official foreign elements such as embassies and consulates, and also ran operations out of the range of Russian foreign commercial entities and non-aligned cover organizations. The 15 constituent Soviet Socialist Republics comprising the Soviet Union each had their own governments closely resembling the central government of the USSR, with intelligence and security services that duplicated the KGB's structural organization and were subordinated to the main KGB. The Soviets' most effective and closely aligned junior service was the East German Stasi.

The only exception to the KGB's control of all intelligence and security functions was the GRU. The GRU was the foreign military intelligence agency of the General Staff of the Soviet Armed Forces of Russia. The GRU was subordinate to the Russian military command and reported directly to the minister of defense and the chief of the general staff. In addition to controlling the military intelligence service, the GRU controlled the majority of the Russian special forces (Spetsnaz). The GRU was the Soviet military's agency responsible for collecting intelligence regarding the intent and capability of any nation to wage war, which of course meant the U.S. and NATO were the primary intelligence-collection targets. The GRU conducted HUMINT operations across the spectrum of overt/tactical to clandestine/strategic. The GRU managed an extensive international clandestine HUMINT operation, which was the primary source of information regarding U.S. and NATO plans and capabilities to counter Soviet Bloc military actions. Like the KGB, the GRU operated residencies out of all official foreign diplomatic entities and other organizations which enabled their foreign presence in target countries.

The KGB and GRU operated independently and aggressively to achieve their global intelligence-collection objectives. Throughout the Cold War, the two organizations did display some attributes of competing organizations, but for the most part, appeared to coexist in a collegial manner. They both operated independent residencies out of official foreign presences, commercial entities, and other available cover organizations. They both also ran networks of "illegals" in every target country. GRU clandestine activities were not subordinated to the KGB, but the KGB did report directly to the Central Committee of the Communist Party, so it wielded a little more power in that regard. Although known instances were rare, when the GRU recruited an asset that the KGB assessed would better serve its requirements, the KGB would be able to effect the transfer.

Soviet Counterintelligence

While the GRU was the lone exception to the KGB's primacy over intelligence collection, there were no such exceptions in regard to counterintelligence responsibilities. The KGB was singularly responsible for counterintelligence and rigorously monitored all aspects of Soviet government and society with an iron fist. The KGB even had counterintelligence jurisdiction over the GRU, and regularly recruited sources inside their ranks without GRU knowledge. The KGB's counterintelligence authority over the GRU was a primary source of friction between the two organizations. The discovery of spies within the ranks of the Red Army, and in particular the GRU, were crown jewels for the KGB.

U.S. HUMINT and Counterintelligence

U.S. HUMINT

The U.S. National Security Act of 1947 established the CIA, which grew out of the World War II-era Office of Strategic Services and other smaller postwar intelligence organizations. The CIA served as the primary U.S. civilian intelligence-gathering organization in the government. Later, the Defense Intelligence Agency (DIA) became the main military intelligence body. As the CIA and DIA evolved, their HQ elements became very focused on providing intelligence support to the National Security Council and other policymaking bodies, while practicing a very decentralized approach to operations in the field. The army approach was similar in that it provided a regional support element for counterintelligence and HUMINT to each of the geographic theaters of operations, to include USAREUR.

As the central coordinator, the CIA had jurisdiction for all foreign intelligence activities. As such, any U.S. government agency conducting HUMINT operations targeting another country was required to coordinate with, and gain approval from, the CIA. U.S. HUMINT operated under a relatively rigidly managed echelon structure. The CIA conducted strategic (clandestine) HUMINT operations and the DoD conducted tactical (overt) HUMINT operations. The CIA ran its intelligence collection operations out of "stations" in U.S. embassies and consulates. The CIA operated essentially all clandestine HUMINT programs throughout the Cold War, and even resisted efforts by the DoD to build such programs.

Unlike the DoD's Soviet intelligence counterpart (the GRU), DoD HUMINT was largely restricted to conducting tactical, battlefield HUMINT functions such as ground reconnaissance, interrogations, and debriefings. In addition to USMLM, the DoD's primary source of tactical HUMINT in central Europe was the U.S. Army Joint Interrogation Centers (JICs) in West Germany. Although termed "interrogation," the large majority of HUMINT was developed through "debriefings" of cooperative/non-hostile sources consisting primarily of migrants, refugees, asylum seekers, and defectors fleeing East Bloc countries. The DoD's primary focus on HUMINT was preparation for tactical-level battlefield interrogation and debriefing operations. The JICs provided relevant intelligence on Soviet Bloc military forces and established the processes and expertise that would be employed for the interrogation and debriefing capability in the event of conflict.

U.S. Counterintelligence

In contrast to the Soviets, U.S. agencies that collected or utilized classified information to perform their missions operated their own counterintelligence service/capability to protect their organization from foreign intelligence-collection threats. Each of the DoD services had a relatively robust counterintelligence service. In addition to having its own counterintelligence capability to protect its internal organization from foreign threats, the CIA had jurisdiction over all counterintelligence activities conducted outside the U.S., meaning that the DoD services and all other organizations with a counterintelligence service operating outside the U.S. were required to coordinate counterintelligence activities reaching a certain investigative/operational threshold with the CIA. This coordination threshold was generally limited to priority counterespionage investigations and operations targeting foreign intelligence services such as the KGB and GRU. The CIA had the authority to assume control of any DoD-initiated investigation or operation, but rarely did so.

What's the Difference?

The primary difference between the U.S. and Soviet HUMINT programs was that the U.S. drew a rigid distinction between tactical/overt HUMINT and strategic/clandestine HUMINT. Whereas the KGB and GRU conducted HUMINT operations across the spectrum without constraints, the U.S. CIA retained the authority to manage clandestine HUMINT while establishing tactical HUMINT as the purview of the DoD.

The primary different between U.S. and Soviet counterintelligence was that the U.S. executed in a very decentralized manner whereas the Soviet KGB managed all counterintelligence in a very well-resourced and centrally controlled manner. The KGB trained and managed all counterintelligence personnel and agencies to operate employing uniformly (ruthless) procedures. In contrast, among the FBI, CIA, and DoD alone, there were six distinct counterintelligence programs that trained and operated in a decentralized manner under very loosely managed coordination practices. It was very apparent from the beginning of the Cold War, in 1945, that the Soviets had a centrally orchestrated, deliberate, and comprehensive grand strategy. The U.S. developed its first-ever unifying national counterintelligence strategy 60 years later, in 2005.

Tours and Intelligence Collection: How the Players Played the Game

The respective MLMs developed their methods of operations within the parameters of the established norms. After touring was established as a cooperative norm, the MLMs established their operational procedures based on their approaches to touring.

Many of these procedures were influenced by the manner in which the hosting forces reacted to MLM tour activities. Although the Huebner–Malinin Agreement was intended to provide the two parties the same capabilities and accesses, the U.S. and Soviet MLMs actually operated in a very dissimilar manner. Since the very small sampling of literature available on the MLMs is written from the standpoint of the USMLM, these previously undocumented juxtapositions between the two missions' operating models are enlightening. The manners in which USMLM and SMLM-F operated are provided in a "compare and contrast" format to highlight these differences.

Uniforms

One protocol that was not delineated in the accord but agreed to by both sides was that MLM personnel would wear uniforms anytime outside the MLM compound. Although these rules served a counterintelligence purpose, they also served to ensure that the hosting German governments and their citizens recognized and respected the MLMs' special status. The agreement to wear uniforms was also ostensibly intended to make MLM personnel more overt and reduce the risk of incidents due to misidentification.

USMLM Uniforms

USMLM personnel wore military dress uniforms when attending official functions. When on tour, however, USMLM tour personnel wore camouflaged fatigues and combat boots. The obvious reason for this choice of uniform was to remain hidden and discreet when on tour. The USMLM choice of tour uniform was unique among the Allied missions, with the British citing that they preferred to wear uniforms that, when confronted by Soviet or East German security forces, made clear that they were British military and not unidentifiable aggressors. The USMLM wearing of camouflaged uniforms became a talking point for the Soviets in the aftermath of the Nicholson shooting.

SMLM-F Uniforms

Tour teams occasionally wore utility uniforms with a camouflaged pattern, but they rarely exited their vehicle, and when they did, always remained in the vicinity of the vehicle where they could be most readily identified as SMLM-F based on the vehicle license plate. Most of the time when on tour, SMLM-F personnel wore basic uniforms with badges and insignia. On the rare occasions they did exit the vehicle while on tour, SMLM-F members regularly wore their military headgear to highlight the Soviet hat crest as an overt symbol of their unique uniform. By wearing their headgear, this made them very distinguishable as SMLM-F personnel in the event they were confronted by U.S. forces. When not on tour but outside the compound, however, the Soviets regularly wore uniforms without decorations or insignia and without headgear, which allowed them to blend in well with businessmen among the urban populous. This method of dress made SMLM-F personnel much less distinguishable when traveling among citizens in West German towns. Overcoats worn during the colder months made them even less distinguishable as uniformed personnel. In addition to choosing to dress in a manner that tended to blend more with the local populous when outside the compound but not on tour, SMLM-F personnel regularly departed the compound by vehicle and foot wearing civilian clothing. USAREUR was aware of occasions of SMLM-F personnel departing the compound in civilian clothes but chose not to make an issue of this non-tour-related violation of the norms, primarily because the USMLM wearing of camouflaged fatigues was not consistent with the intent of the uniform norm, and USAREUR did not want to open that debate. This nuance characterized the sensitive balance that USAREUR had to maintain in that any issue that arose as it applied to SMLM-F could be used as ammunition and backfire on USMLM.

Base of Operations

There were significant differences in how the USMLM and SMLM-F played the game. The primary basis for the vast differences among the two is directly attributable to differences among the bases of operations. Various factors gave USMLM significant advantages, which the U.S. readily exploited. The Soviets uncharacteristically allowed the significant disproportionality to continue while they regularly commented on how keenly aware they were of the disparity.

USMLM Base of Operations

GSFG provided USMLM with a lakeside villa in Potsdam on a 4.5-acre compound, which was referred to as the "Potsdam House." Over time, the practical inconveniences of living inside East Germany with the American sector of West Berlin and all of its facilities and security just across the Glienicke Bridge prompted a shift in operations. In 1947, USMLM began the process of establishing its primary base of operations in West Berlin. While the Potsdam House continued to be used for representational purposes and as a forward perch to launch and recover reconnaissance missions (tours), by 1953, all other activities were transferred and conducted from a large compound built for the Nazi General Staff in the Dahlem residential district of West Berlin. The expansive compound consisted of a large four-floor brick structure containing approximately 33 rooms and 8,674 square feet of floor space. This large building was able to accommodate all USMLM administrative, communications, and mission planning needs, as well as housing a vehicle maintenance shop.

SMLM-F Base of Operations

In comparison to USMLM which operated with a robust support facility less than 15 miles from the Potsdam House, the SMLM-F compound was located nearly

COBETCKAЯ BOEHHAЯ MИCCИЯ CBЯЗИ
ПРИ ГЛАВНОКОМАНДУЮЩЕМ
АМЕРИКАНСКОЙ АРМИЕЙ В ЕВРОПЕ
SOVIET MILITARY LIAISON MISSION
TO COMMANDER IN CHIEF
US ARMY EUROPE
SOWJETISCHE MILITÄRMISSION
AKKREDITIERT BEIM OBERBEFEHLSHABER
DER US ARMEE EUROPA

EXTRATERRITORIAL

NO ENTRY WITHOUT PERMISSION OF THE CHIEF
SOVIET MILITARY LIAISON MISSION

EINTRITT VERBOTEN OHNE ERLAUBNIS DES CHEFS
DER SOWJETISCHEN MILITÄRMISSION

SMLM-F compound in Frankfurt, West Germany.

220 miles from the inner German border station at Herleshausen, and nearly 350 miles from the GSFG HQ.

SMLM-F did leverage the inequity of the dual USMLM bases of operations to compel USAREUR to construct a new compound facility in 1959. The compound, which SMLM-F occupied until the mission was disestablished in 1990, was located on prime downtown Frankfurt real estate and was therefore relatively small in comparison to the USMLM facility. In addition, since the facility only housed a maximum of 14 military personnel and only a few accompanying families, there was not a great demand for an expansive site.

The SMLM-F compound consisted of three buildings. One was a duplex residence for the chief and deputy chief of mission consisting of two apartments with four bedrooms each and adjacent carports for two vehicles. The second building was a six-apartment family housing complex with three three-bedroom apartments and three two-bedroom apartments. The third building had the offices to manage the SMLM-F operational and administrative activities, with the second floor having a series of bedrooms with bathrooms in between for bachelor SMLM-F personnel and visitors. The facility was fenced with a guardhouse at the compound entrance.

Staffing

The USMLM West Berlin base of operations was the singular component that made all other comparisons between the USMLM operating model and the SMLM-F operating model so diametric. This disproportionality began with the staffing structures of the two MLMs. The U.S. predisposition to begin the MLMs with a relatively small staff of 14 and then assess the need to grow after operations began was fortuitous, as the U.S. unilaterally instituted a staff augmentation process while the Soviets sustained their limited manning.

USMLM Staffing

The USMLM staff structure fluctuated slightly throughout the years, but it consistently remained a very robust organization, particularly in relation to SMLM-F. The 14 accredited members were supported by up to an additional 56 members consisting of rotating tour officers and drivers, administrative and support staff, and a robust intelligence analysis and production staff.

USMLM was a 70-person organization when at its most robust during the 1980s. The army staffed the majority of USMLM, providing 11 officers, 29 enlisted, six civilians, and four locally hired (U.S. citizen) augmentees, for a total of 50 personnel. The air force staffed the air division with five officers and 14 enlisted personnel for a total of 19 personnel. Until 1986, there was a restricted area along the East German coast which restricted the observation of naval activities, so the naval element was manned with one Marine Corps officer who served as a ground team tour officer. The six tour officers and tour NCOs that were accredited at any given time were considered elements of the larger ground division and air division operations that were managed out of the West Berlin facility.

The only two personnel who were permanently accredited were the CUSMLM and the NCO in charge (NCOIC). The CUSMLM was an army colonel. The other 12 personnel accreditations were fluidly changed among personnel on a rotational basis. The standard allocation of manning for the 12 rotational positions was four ground reconnaissance teams with one tour officer and one tour NCO each, and two air reconnaissance teams with one tour officer and one tour NCO each. The highest-ranking tour officer with time in grade was normally designated as the Deputy CUSMLM (DCUSMLM), and the air force usually provided a senior lieutenant colonel to fill that position. All photo lab technicians were provided by the air force.

SMLM-F Staffing

SMLM-F was staffed with a general major (1-star general) mission commander, three support personnel, five tour officers, and five enlisted tour drivers. The senior tour officer also performed as the DCSMLM-F and was normally an army colonel. SMLM-F was normally a three-year assignment, and the tour officers and NCOs assigned to SMLM-F were not augmented or substituted on a recurring basis as was the case with USMLM.

SMLM-F was the smallest of the Soviet MLMs with 14 personnel, but it was the only Soviet MLM that was consistently staffed at its fully authorized strength. Although the French and British agreed with the Soviets to maintain MLMs of 18 and 31 personnel respectively, the Soviet MLM in the French sector was normally understaffed at less than 14 personnel and the Soviet MLM in the British sector rarely reached a strength of 20 personnel.

Vehicles

Although not a provision of the Huebner–Malinin Agreement, the U.S. and Soviets agreed to accredit up to 10 vehicles per mission, but this is where the similarities between the two missions ended in regard to vehicles. Each MLM was issued 10 sets of mutually agreed to, uniquely identifying, license plates. The plates issued to SMLM-F were numbered 1–10 and those issued to USMLM were numbered 20–29. Any vehicle with a set of the license plates was considered accredited.

USMLM Vehicles

Although only 10 vehicles at any one time would be officially accredited for use, USMLM maintained a fleet of (on average) 25 vehicles. The additional vehicles were held in reserve at the West Berlin mission headquarters to ensure that replacements were immediately available in the event of mechanical breakdown or damage to an accredited tour vehicle. The West Berlin support staff included a transportation division, and mechanics were on the premises of the West Berlin mission headquarters to ensure that no intelligence tours were impacted due to vehicle maintenance problems. Tour vehicles were replaced approximately every 25,000–30,000 miles to keep breakdowns at a minimum during operations.

USMLM toured in standard four-wheel-drive vehicles that were modified with a special suspension to allow for more road clearance and a stiffer ride over unimproved roads. Vehicles were reinforced with special plating under the chassis to protect the engine and transmission from tree stumps and rocks. Vehicles were modified with an additional 35-gallon fuel tank, rollbar, heavy-duty shock absorbers, enhanced electrical system, winch, and other alterations that enabled extended cross-country operations and made the vehicles safer, more rugged, and better able to withstand the constant off-road beatings. Vehicles were modified with toggle switches to manipulate vehicle lights to facilitate stealth and antisurveillance. Among the modifications was a switch to disable all vehicle lights to enable the vehicle to completely black out when eluding surveillance or approaching a target area at night. Other vehicle modifications included a switch to disable one brake light and one headlight to project the signature of a motorcycle at night. Infrared lights were installed in the vehicles to enable the tour vehicle to go "lights out" driving by shutting down all

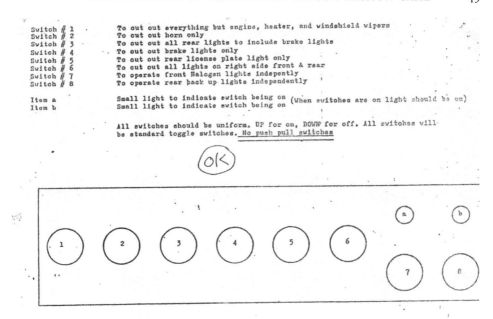

Switch # 1	To cut out everything but engine, heater, and windshield wipers
Switch # 2	To cut out horn only
Switch # 3	To cut out all rear lights to include brake lights
Switch # 4	To cut out brake lights only
Switch # 5	To cut out rear license plate light only
Switch # 6	To cut out all lights on right side front & rear
Switch # 7	To operate front Halogen lights indepently
Switch # 8	To operate rear back up lights independently
Item a	Small light to indicate switch being on (When switches are on light should be on)
Item b	Small light to indicate switch being on

All switches should be uniform. UP for on, DOWN for off. All switches will be standard toggle switches. No push pull switches

OK

Instructions for the use of specially configured vehicle light and other controls to facilitate stealth and antisurveillance.

of the standard vehicle lights, donning night-vision goggles, and turning on the infrared lights for stealth driving at night. The vehicles also had a switch which allowed the driver to cut off the horn (to prevent the possibility of blowing it by mistake). Vehicles were painted olive drab for camouflage to enable them to blend in and be less detectable when stationary in forested locations.

In addition to the installed equipment, USMLM tour vehicles carried equipment for maintaining mobility in all conditions to include mud, snow, ice, sand, swamps, and fields. This equipment included an axe, a shovel, and a toolbox. Probably the most commonly used equipment was a heavy-duty winch and 50 feet of steel cable to pull the vehicle free when stuck in mud, water beds, snow, or other difficult terrain. Also, to support these efforts, each vehicle carried two four-foot "cheater boards" to place under the rear wheels to gain traction when stuck or to place across narrow ditches. And finally, two nylon tow straps, a steel tow cable, and a tow chain were carried to enable a tour vehicle to tow another vehicle that had become disabled back to the compound.

USMLM vehicles were modified for the specific type of operations conducted, but there were no technical collection capabilities such as communications intercept equipment installed in the vehicles or carried on tour, as was widely suspected by East German authorities. Whether or not the USAREUR Deputy Chief of Staff for

USMLM on tour. (USMLM Association)

Intelligence (DCSINT) or other U.S. intelligence agencies might have considered employing USMLM vehicles as technical collection platforms, the regularity at which USMLM vehicles were detained and equipment confiscated by East German or Soviet elements would have precluded any serious consideration of such efforts. Vehicles were equipped with VHF radios to report to base stations in Berlin and Potsdam without actually driving to their locations. The 50-mile range of the radios did not facilitate communications from all over East Germany, but was sufficient to allow a tour to report significant indicators without having to cross into West Berlin or rely on East German commercial communications.

USMLM installed curtains in their vehicles that could be pulled down over the back seat and rear windows to conceal equipment and activities inside the vehicle. CSERB initially asserted that the curtains were in violation of GSFG vehicle policy and demanded that they be removed, but USMLM countered that their vehicles had the rights of extraterritoriality and were not bound by Soviet rules. Tours also carried large camouflage sheets and nets to cover the vehicle when parked and positioned as an observation post or in a hide site.

There were claims by USMLM that their vehicles had the rights of extraterritoriality, but the specific wording of the Huebner–Malinin Agreement did not extend such privileges. The Soviet and East German practices generally demonstrated that USMLM enjoyed the privilege of extraterritoriality except when perceived to be

USMLM vehicles needed special equipment to keep them mobile in a range of circumstances, to include when the driver underestimated the depth of standing water. (USMLM Association)

located in the vicinity of sensitive military activity, in which cases, USMLM vehicles were often searched and equipment confiscated.

SMLM-F Vehicles

In contrast to the U.S. approach to maintain the maximum number of vehicles authorized with a robust reserve available for rapid replacements, SMLM-F commonly maintained seven or eight of their authorized 10 vehicles at their Frankfurt compound.

None of the SMLM-F vehicles were modified to facilitate extended or off-road touring as was the case with USMLM vehicles, nor were there any indications that they manipulated vehicle lights for stealth or antisurveillance purposes. SMLM-F tour vehicles traveled on improved roads and it was the very rare exception that a tour vehicle was sighted off-road or on unimproved roads.

Although SMLM-F did not conduct activities that would indicate that their tour vehicles were employed as technical intelligence collection platforms, there are no recorded incidents involving U.S. or West German security elements detaining a SMLM-F vehicle and inspecting the interior or confiscating equipment. There was no credible information to suggest that SMLM-F vehicles were platforms for any other type of collection other than overt HUMINT collection when on tour. In an apparent response to the USMLM refusal to remove vehicle curtains, SMLM-F

SMLM-F on tour. (Author)

installed curtains in their vehicles that could be pulled down over the back seat and rear windows. SMLM-F personnel were regularly sighted in highway rest areas and other locations apparently manipulating equipment located in the trunk of a tour vehicle. This activity was only observed in areas where the only likely targets of intelligence interest were military movements, so this was assessed to be, at worst, the use of communications receivers to monitor tactical military unit communications, which would not have been a sophisticated or concerning intelligence-collection capability.

Tour Patterns

The tour patterns of the Soviet and U.S. MLMs were as would be expected given the examination of the respective bases of operations and vehicle specifications. USMLM fully exploited the Huebner–Malinin Agreement and the Soviets both accepted and did not attempt to compete against the inequitable practices USMLM employed to maximize intelligence collection. SMLM-F, on the other hand, were handicapped by factors that compounded the degree of inequity in their operational processes relative to USMLM. Although it was not envisioned that intelligence collection would become the primary function of the MLMs when the Huebner–Malinin Agreement was enacted, the SMLM-F operating process was much more consistent with the original intent of the agreement, whereas the USMLM approach stressed all limits of the governing protocols.

The intelligence target environment differed significantly in the U.S. and Soviet MLM sectors, which certainly influenced the U.S.'s and Soviets' differing tour patterns. The target environment in East Germany consisted of 20 Soviet divisions and an air army, six East German divisions, and more than 3,000 military installations dispersed in an area of 41,828 square miles. In an area slightly smaller than the Soviet sector of East Germany, the U.S. sector had four U.S. divisions at the height of occupation and no NATO forces of significant intelligence interest to the Soviets. In addition, the U.S. had a policy of not abusing occupation powers by not infringing unnecessarily on the West German territory, and therefore only conducted very small unit training around U.S. Army garrison locations. With the exception of one large annual exercise, the majority of U.S. training for major maneuvers was conducted at one of the three primary training ranges, two of which were in the U.S. sector at Grafenwoehr and Hohenfels, West Germany. In contrast, GSFG and East German units were dispersed throughout the country and regarded East Germany as one large military maneuver area.

USMLM Tour Patterns

On average, USMLM conducted 506 tours per year for a combined mileage of 260,000. USMLM conducted tours ranging in duration from one to four days. A one-day tour typically lasted 10–12 hours and covered an average distance of 400 miles. A two-day tour involved two 10–12-hour days and covered an average distance of 650 to 800 miles. Three- and four-day tours also consisted of work days of 10–12 hours over distances of 900–1,200 and 1,150–1,600 miles respectively. Up to four teams per day would go out during the periods of high-interest Soviet/ Warsaw Pact military maneuvers. The standard operating model for the most effective coverage of a region was multiple-, one-, and two-day tours working simultaneously. To facilitate two-, three-, and four-day tours, teams frequently returned to the Potsdam House for resupply. Additional tours were regularly dispatched to replace a fatigued team, focus attention on a particular area or target of interest, or widen coverage. The pace of USMLM touring steadily increased through the years, logging an average of over 537 tours and roughly 900 tour days per year during their final 10 recorded years.

The most standard USMLM tour was a two-day tour. A week prior to any tour, the tour officer would receive a schedule identifying the general touring area, the name of the driver, and the duration of the tour. Two days prior to the execution of the tour, the tour officer would receive a list of collection requirements from the

Operations Section and begin preparation for the actual tour. The tour officer would develop the initial tour route based on hours of daylight, the distance and condition of routes between targets, and additional factors such as MRSs and priority targets which might require more time of coverage. The officer would then review target folders for each of the planned targets containing detailed information based on observations of the target by previous Allied MLM collection missions, to include photographs. The typical tour would range from five to 15 targets.

TRAs were normally imposed to cover significant training activities and became the key focus of USMLM when in effect. As with PRAs, TRAs were not violated without high-level approval. TRAs were usually linked with established PRAs to deny mission travel over a greater size of an area. TRAs were higher risk areas because of heightened East German and Soviet vigilance to counter USMLM collection activities when a given TRA was in effect. TRAs did, however, signal to USMLM where their greatest collection opportunities were located. The primary collection methodology in these cases was to observe the periphery of a TRA along primary routes of military traffic into and out of the TRA to observe for equipment and other military activity of intelligence interest.

Tour equipment was consistent with the overt collection mission and included binoculars, cameras with a wide array of lenses, video cameras, tape recorders, night-vision goggles, compasses, maps, and rations. No collection gear or "spy"

USMLM ready to collect intelligence from a vehicle observation post on tour. (USMLM Association)

paraphernalia was ever carried. They did not conduct meets with agents, service dead drops, or conduct any other clandestine activity associated with espionage operations (with one isolated exception in 1956).

Tour officers would commonly depart the tour vehicle and maneuver on foot to establish a better vantage point for observation. This tactic enabled the vehicle to remain hidden while the tour officer moved in closer to a collection target. When the officer was out of the vehicle, the driver would remain in the vehicle with the doors locked and observe for any risks. The tour driver did not use a radio to communicate with the dismounted tour officer due to the risk of intercept and detection. Therefore, the driver would honk the horn to alert the tour officer when he needed to return to the vehicle so the team could depart the area, normally when Soviet or East German forces were entering the area.

Whereas PRAs and TRAs were established to protect areas of major military activities, the installations which housed equipment and units were normally inside or near urban areas where the troops and their families resided, and therefore many were not inside restricted areas. One collection mission termed "installation coverage" demonstrated how brazen USMLM collection operations were in comparison to SMLM-F. Installation coverage was conducted on a periodic basis according to a master matrix to reconfirm the activities associated with GSFG and East German installations. These missions were referred to as "over the wall" operations, because they required that pictures be taken of the equipment inside the installation to confirm the type of units and activities associated with the installations. As the reference implies, in cases where there was no natural vantage point from which to observe the interior of an installation, the tour vehicle would be driven up to the installation fence/barrier and the tour officer would climb to the top of the vehicle and put the camera on automatic for a matter of seconds before the security force reacted. These missions required precision planning, patience, and luck. The keys to a successful mission were identifying the best window to approach the installation and for the driver to judge when the tour officer needed to get back in the vehicle to enable egress without detention. These missions were relatively successful, resulting in less than 5 percent of USMLM detentions, but detentions and the many other "over the wall" missions that were detected without detentions demonstrated that the Soviets and East Germans were aware of these activities which could be characterized as "denied-area collection operations."

Allied cooperation was a significant aspect of USMLM tour activities and served to multiply the overwhelming intelligence-collection capacity advantage that the Allies exercised in comparison to the Soviets. The Agreement on Control Machinery in Germany was originally devised under an assumption that the four Allied powers would cooperatively work to rebuild a unified Germany. After the three MLM agreements were signed and the schism among the three remaining Allies and the Soviet Union developed, the establishment of the MLMs was to the Allies' strong advantage in regard to intelligence collection. This essentially gave the Allies a three-to-one ratio in intelligence-coverage capability.

The combined effort of the British, French and U.S. MLMs was an outstanding example of Allied cooperation and coordination. To avoid duplication of effort and maximize Allied collection efforts against targets in East Germany, the country was divided into three primary tour areas and a fourth "local" area which was defined within a 19-mile (30-kilometer) radius around Berlin. During a large portion of the Allied MLM era, each MLM was responsible for one primary tour area on a rotating basis for a two-week period. During the later years, the Allied MLMs exercised a dual-responsibility relationship with two MLMs operating in the same area. The MLMs would further combine their efforts on occasions when a high-priority target or sustained activity warranted the concentrated efforts of all three MLMs. The Allies regularly conducted tri-mission operations to maximize intelligence collection on high-priority military activity. A common example of a high-priority, coordinated effort was to observe all the rail routes into and out of a specific PRA or TRA when it was suspected that a new weapon system or piece of equipment would be deployed to the area. According to BRIXMIS officers, when the MLMs were assigned sectors of responsibility, USMLM was the only MLM ever known to infringe on another MLM's sector to "snipe" priority intelligence targets.

Teams of all three Allied MLMs returning from operational tours would stop at the Potsdam House immediately upon their return to East Berlin. They would prepare a "highlight" with significant observations of current intelligence value. These reports were sent to each Allied mission and the interested U.S. intelligence elements. Detailed reports were produced the day following the tour and disseminated widely. Coordination among the three Allied missions made it possible for each of the Allies to receive reports from an average of six reconnaissance teams in the Soviet zone at any given time.

To ensure complete and efficient coverage of targets in East Germany, tri-mission ground and air operations meetings were held at least once a week. At these meetings, mutual requirements were agreed to and integrated plans finalized. A quarterly chiefs of mission meeting served to focus attention on important policy matters affecting all three missions and to discuss other issues of mutual interest.

SMLM-F Tour Patterns

In contrast to USMLM which would perform as many two-, three-, or four-day tours as they would one-day tours, SMLM-F tours were essentially all one-day tours, and rarely extended beyond nine hours or into the hours of darkness. SMLM-F tours settled into a relatively standard practice over the years with tours normally departing the mission by 8:00 AM and returning to the mission by 5:00 PM. SMLM-F rarely toured during hours of darkness or on weekends, presumably due to the relative decrease in U.S. military activities at those times.

SMLM-F rarely had more than one vehicle out of the compound at any given time on a tour, and when more than one vehicle left the compound, the vehicles normally departed for non-tour purposes such as to travel to East Germany, the other SMLMs, the Bonn embassy, or for leisure purposes such as to shop at the American post exchange (PX). The purpose and locations of many of the SMLM-F short-duration, non-tour compound departures were unknown.

Frankfurt was located far to the west in the U.S. sector, and therefore, was not as well situated given SMLM-F's primary collection targets. Most SMLM-F tours involved travel to the major training areas at Grafenwoehr or Hohenfels, or the area of primary military interest which was the "Fulda Gap" area of inner German border where it was known that any major Soviet Bloc military offensive would pass through. Grafenwoehr is 190 miles from Frankfurt with a travel time of nearly three hours and 15 minutes, and Hohenfels is 183 miles from Frankfurt with a travel time of just under three hours. Therefore, a basic tour to these areas consisted of travel to the location, perhaps one to two hours conducting reconnaissance around the training area to determine which U.S. units were undergoing training and what type of training might be under way, and then return travel to Frankfurt. Stops to observe convoys on the highway or to eat would further cut into the time spent collecting on military activity in the target area, as they would invariably plan to return to their Frankfurt compound by 5:00 PM.

Although SMLM-F tours would regularly target areas other than Grafenwoehr and Hohenfels, the touring patterns associated with tours to these locations was among the idiosyncrasies that confounded logic. The two training areas were less than one hour (45 miles) of vehicle travel apart. However, SMLM-F very rarely collected against both areas during a single tour; rather, they would target one or the other. The fact that they would not collect against both sites when there was activity of interest ongoing at both locations, after having traveled over three hours to reach the general area, was simply not an efficient use of the overall travel time expended. The only logical explanation for this tour pattern was that they placed limiting tours to nine hours and returning to the Frankfurt compound by 5:00 PM above extended intelligence-collection efforts. Another argument could be made that they simply did not really need to collect intelligence and were simply going through the motions so as not to not appear completely disinterested.

SMLM-F tours did not appear to be as deliberately planned or target-specific focused as USMLM tours were known to be. The SMLM-F tour approach appeared to be one of travel to a location of likely military activities and scout for targets of opportunity to observe. SMLM-F tour personnel always observed military activities from inside the tour vehicle. The only times they departed the vehicle was to stretch their legs, picnic at a rest-stop table, open the trunk for supplies or to check equipment, or to urinate.

Although there were no incidents to reinforce the notion, SMLM-F tours reflected the Soviet mentality that a sentry had a responsibility to protect his post through whatever means necessary. Whether it was a lack of drive to collect intelligence or an overabundance of caution, SMLM-F tours did not allow themselves to be placed in a position that might draw hostile fire. The strong propensity to remain in the vehicle except at times when no U.S. military forces were in the area would suggest that no intelligence target was worth the risk of being perceived as an aggressor or exposing oneself to potential gunfire.

SMLM-F carried cameras but were rarely observed taking photographs. The only other equipment that SMLM-F were known to carry were binoculars. They occasionally appeared to be speaking into a tape recorder, but this was never confirmed. Consistent with the understanding that SMLM-F vehicles very rarely, if ever, traveled off-road, they were never observed carrying any special equipment that would facilitate off-road travel.

West German highways were notorious for their *Staus*, or traffic jams. SMLM-F tour vehicles regularly encountered traffic jams, particularly when returning from a tour during mid- to late-afternoon hours. When a SMLM-F vehicle encountered such a standstill, the driver would regularly turn on the four-way emergency flashers and travel down the breakdown lane for miles while bypassing the traffic jam. This common maneuver demonstrated the impunity of SMLM-F from West German police interventions. This would also serve as an effective surveillance detection or antisurveillance maneuver if that were the intent.

The Soviet MLMs had interzonal travel restrictions which constrained cooperative collection missions such as those which the Allied MLMs were able to perform given that the Allies all collected in the same Soviet sector. There were no instances that suggested that the Soviet MLMs performed precoordinated tour activities.

Intelligence Support Activities

Intelligence is a requirements-driven process. USMLM did not conduct their tour activities for the sake of doing so. The relatively high tempo of USMLM (and Allied MLM) tours and collection activities was driven by the high demand for the intelligence on GSFG and East German equipment and order of battle from USAREUR and national intelligence agencies. The disparity among the intelligence-collection (touring) capabilities among the Soviet and Allied MLMs was apparent. And while this level of disparity was largely due to factors such as the USMLM West Berlin base of operations for which there was no effort on the part of the Soviets to replicate, the Soviets' intelligence-collection approach never appeared to be one that could be characterized as "driven." The only rationale for the disparity among the two is that there was not a similar level of demand, or requirements, from GSFG or Moscow for the type of intelligence that USMLM very aggressively collected on a daily basis with the support of a robust analysis, production, and dissemination process.

USMLM Intelligence Support Activities

USMLM was placed under the USAREUR DCSINT—specifically the HUMINT Operations Division. USMLM had many visitors per year, and the visiting agencies demonstrated that intelligence collection was essentially the only USMLM activity of external interest. Through the mid-1950s, USMLM reporting was disseminated under the codename VOUCHER, meaning that it was considered a sensitive intelligence-collection source at the time. The VOUCHER designation was lifted by 1960, suggesting that the determination had been made by that point that USMLM would not be involved in clandestine collection or other sensitive intelligence support activities. This also meant that all USMLM reporting could be widely disseminated to all USAREUR commands and intelligence elements.

The USMLM intelligence program was another significant aspect of the USMLM mission that benefited from its proximity to the West Berlin facility. From the outset, the U.S. intended to leverage the proximity of the U.S. sector of Berlin to the Potsdam House to facilitate intelligence operations. A memorandum from HQ USEUCOM dated 29 April 1947 issued instructions to CUSMLM that there be designated a "rear echelon" facility in Berlin "for the purpose of preparing and processing documents of a confidential nature." USMLM leveraged the West Berlin facility to provide support to its comprehensive intelligence process.

By the 1960s, USMLM had become a fine-tuned intelligence collection, analysis, and production operation. The Berlin HQ provided essential services which could not have been adequately maintained at the Potsdam House. Many of the additional 56 personnel located in the West Berlin facility provided intelligence analysis and other types of intelligence support. In fact, over 90 percent of the functions performed at the West Berlin USMLM facility were in direct support of USMLM touring (intelligence collection) in the Soviet zone of Germany. A key component of the intelligence analysis and production function was the elaborate photographic laboratory that processed an average of 15,000 to 20,000 rolls of film per year and reproduced over 500,000 prints for dissemination.

USMLM intelligence information report (IIR) statistics demonstrated why the unit was recognized as the most productive intelligence-collection element in the DoD, and perhaps within the entire U.S. intelligence community. The highest production year on record was the first year USMLM began reporting IIR statistics, which was 1975 with 1,497 IIRs. Production remained relatively high from 1976–8 with 1,337, 1,438, and 1,259 IIRs produced respectively. Production was reduced to 970 IIRs in 1979 due to the more restrictive environment imposed after stressed relations due to the events leading up to and after the Soviet intervention in Afghanistan. Numbers were again up in 1980 (1,216 IIRs) and 1981 (1,269 IIRs). Production declined steadily beginning in 1982 and again further in the aftermath of the Nicholson incident, but IIR production remained high in relation to other collection elements with an average of over 900 IIRs per year.

By 1964, USMLM tours began actively collecting trash and other items left behind at vacated training sites for intelligence exploitation. By 1974, this trash-collection activity developed into a formal program named Project SANDDUNE, and by 1976, this secret exploitation of Soviet garbage dumps accounted for 40 percent of all USMLM ground intelligence reports. By 1979, this effort accounted for over 50 percent of reporting and a dedicated SANDDUNE section was established with augmentation from national-level U.S. intelligence agencies. Information gained from these sources during the 1980s was a valuable and always entirely reliable source for Western intelligence services. The term "dumpster diving" has long been in the counterintelligence lexicon as an effective method of intelligence collection against targets that practice poor operations security (OPSEC) by throwing sensitive information in the trash. Project SANDDUNE was the epitome of dumpster diving.

During the late 1970s and into the early 1980s, satellite imagery provided near-real-time imagery of large Soviet Bloc military formations, which rendered USMLM observations much less critical than they had been over the previous three decades. Until this point, USMLM collection was focused on indications of hostility and observations regarding military training and new equipment. After the detection of large military formations became the focus of satellite imagery, USMLM expanded

USMLM tour officer collecting "trash" at a vacated GSFG training site. (USMLM Association)

its collection and analysis focus to a wider range of interests which included nuclear weapons, troop morale, equipment production, technical data, health and ethnic issues, and literacy.

Although USMLM was regularly cited by Soviet and East German officials for committing acts of espionage, USMLM did not engage in any type of clandestine activity associated with espionage in the true sense of the word (with one isolated exception in 1956, and the exceptions of occasional support to the National Security Agency, or NSA). On rare occasions, USMLM tours did support NSA activities by dropping specially configured "rocks" or "sticks" at designated locations, and employed special handheld devices in an attempt to collect against the Soviet laser capability.

SMLM-F Intelligence Analysis

Although SMLM-F represented the GSFG, they reported directly to the GRU. The GRU staffed the Intelligence Directorate providing direct military support to GSFG and the Operational Group which managed sensitive operations such as clandestine intelligence collection. General SMLM-F tour activities and collection requirements would come from and be reported to the Intelligence Directorate. Any SMLM-F clandestine collection or support to other clandestine or covert operations would have been managed by the Operational Group. Operational Group requirements would take priority over Intelligence Directorate requirements.

Much less is known about SMLM-F intelligence analysis and production support provided by the GRU. However, SMLM-F tours were clearly not as focused, aggressive, and extensive in comparison to USMLM, strongly indicating that there was a similarly less-robust intelligence support effort for the standard tour-type activities. There were no reports to indicate that SMLM-F tours focused on recently vacated training areas to collect trash or other items left behind in a manner similar to Project SANDDUNE.

As with most diplomatic missions worldwide, the "communications room" was the most highly secured location of the mission. One provision of the Huebner–Malinin Agreement specified that "each mission will have its own radio station for communication with its own headquarters." The communications room in the SMLM-F facility was never seen by Western eyes. Whenever the ACS, support staff, or any other non-Soviet persons were in the facility housing the communications room, a SMLM-F member was posted with a weapon at the door to the room. Occasionally, the Soviets would request accreditation for technical personnel to travel to Frankfurt to upgrade the communications room. Signals intelligence (SIGINT) confirmed that the mission transmitted encrypted communications daily. These transmissions were normally sent in the middle of the night, so it was logically assumed that the tour officers would pass off their day's tour collection notes which would be typed up and transmitted by night-shift personnel. There was never any indication of a dynamic exchange of information that would suggest rear-echelon intelligence analysis support to SMLM-F that would be comparable to that employed by USMLM.

Whereas SMLM-F tours were rarely observed photographing military activity, the SMLM-F compound was modest in size relative to the USMLM facilities and could not have possibly housed a photo development and reproduction capability of nearly the magnitude of the USMLM operation. Even if they had maintained a modestly sized photo lab, this could not have been hidden from ACS or maintenance personnel, confirming the lack of even a marginally operational photo lab.

Non-tour Travel Activity

The non-tour travel activity of the MLMs was very different due to their divergent living environments. East Berlin was a depressed and semi-hostile environment, whereas West Berlin offered all the best in entertainment and shopping to the USMLM members and their families. SMLM-F personnel did not have such a similar choice to make, but Frankfurt and other urban areas in the U.S. sector were in stark contrast to the urban landscapes of Russia and Eastern Europe. The Soviets freely leveraged the opportunity to travel among the free and open Western culture.

USMLM Non-tour Travel

USMLM personnel and their families resided in West Berlin, which is where they spent all their local, off-duty time. Since USMLM personnel and vehicles were always a Stasi target when traveling in East Germany, there was no such thing as leisure in the East, and USMLM personnel and families were therefore restricted from spending their leisure time in East Berlin. The only non-tour travel USMLM personnel conducted in East Germany was to visit the Allied MLMs, attend official functions, travel to meetings at SERB, or travel to meetings at the GSFG headquarters.

SMLM-F Non-tour Travel

Since the U.S. sector of West Germany was technically SMLM-F's "neighborhood," most of the non-tour and non-official travel was travel in and around the Frankfurt area. The guard force at the SMLM-F compound immediately notified the designated USAREUR office when a SMLM-F vehicle departed the compound, citing vehicle number and the vehicle occupants. Unless a vehicle departed early in the morning on a weekday it was known to be leisure travel and not a tour. When a SMLM-F vehicle was not on tour on the highway or near military activity, there were much fewer, and in many cases no, sighting reports. Since U.S. Counterintelligence only conducted limited surveillance of SMLM-F when touring, SMLM-F non-tour travel was never physically monitored. Every year there were days in the tens to hundreds that the Soviets departed the compound for four hours or less in what was assessed to be non-tour/non-official travel, for which U.S. Counterintelligence had no idea what the destination or purpose of the travel had been, due to a lack of sighting reports.

One provision in the Huebner–Malinin Agreement specified that "The respective missions or individual members of the missions may purchase items of Soviet or United States origin which must be paid for in currently specified by the headquarters controlling zone where purchase is made." This stipulation was interpreted to mean that the MLMs were allowed to shop at the post exchanges of their hosts. While this was of no benefit to USMLM, this was a considerable privilege for SMLM-F members, of which they took full advantage. Western clothing, movies, and entertainment technologies were the favored items of purchase. There was no specified limit for purchases, and the Soviets clearly made purchases for themselves, families, friends, and likely for personal gain. In 1986, ACS prohibited a SMLM-F member from shopping at the post exchange due to his suspected "speculation" with purchases of audiovisual equipment, meaning he was accused of exploiting the privilege for personal gain.

The Counter-USMLM Process

USMLM collection was the most recognizable and persistent Allied risk to Soviet and East German military security. In addition to PRA and TRA restrictions, MRSs which read "ATTENTION! Passage of Members of Foreign Military Liaison Mission PROHIBITED!" in English, French, Russian, and German languages were mass produced and posted over as much as 40 percent of the countryside. Since USMLM was perceived as the primary intelligence-collection and security threat, purpose-built GSFG and East German security measures were established to counter the effectiveness of USMLM tours. Characteristically, Soviet and East German installations were well barricaded with guard towers appropriately situated to enable all-around security monitoring on a 24-hour basis. Soviet and East German units training in the field employed security measures that were specifically practiced to counter USMLM collection. For example, manned security posts were positioned along all routes leading into exercise areas, forcing USMLM vehicles to bypass them by traveling off-road or driving through them. Given that the East Germans viewed USMLM as the persistent threat that was known to be conducting multiple collection missions every day, they established a robust process to counter this recognized national security risk.

The Soviet and East German approach to countering the USMLM collection threat was best characterized as brute force. USMLM tours could be equated to aggressive ground reconnaissance missions, which certainly further exacerbated the aggressive counter-reconnaissance tactics employed. This dynamic often led to physical acts such as rammings, detentions, and deterrence by gunfire.

The cycle of reportable incidents involving Stasi surveillance and USMLM antisurveillance, and aggressive collection techniques that often resulted in detentions, rammings, gunshots, and other forms of physical attack, was largely the USMLM dynamic within the dynamic. Although such incidents invariably resulted in strong protests from USAREUR, with the exception of two relatively short periods, these incidents were discussed but were never cause to allow a dispute to disrupt the pace of operations. Although activities and incidents such as surveillance and vehicle detentions and rammings were certainly not within the spirit of the Huebner–Malinin Agreement, and in most circumstances were outright violations, the fact that they continued to occur supported the contention that they were accepted as norms. Therefore, from a legal precedent standpoint, it could be validly argued that the U.S. allowed such dangerous and eventually life-ending incidents to become tacitly recognized norms, by allowing them to continue without a protest that would seriously threaten the sustainment of the Huebner–Malinin Agreement.

The risk of physical harm was largely one-sided, but this was not always the case. On occasion, reportable incidents were the result of aggressive USMLM collection methods which led to attempts to avoid surveillance or detentions, and resulted in injuries to Soviet or East German security forces.

The East German and Soviet USMLM Monitoring Process

In 1961, a Stasi defector reported that the Stasi had a department dedicated to operations against USMLM that conducted operations independent of the GSFG and without prior coordination or approval. This report is very consistent with all other intelligence developed on the topic of East German monitoring of USMLM. It was immediately apparent after East Germany was extended full diplomatic recognition by the Soviets in 1954 that East German intelligence and security elements were either delegated or assumed USMLM monitoring responsibilities, with the Stasi as the lead agency. The East Germans centrally managed the USMLM monitoring process out of their central surveillance headquarters, MfS Department "K" in Potsdam. The CSFG also had a reporting system headed by its security organization at Zossen/Wunsdorf.

The Stasi approach and ability to monitor and disrupt USMLM touring was immersive. East Germany was a surveillance state like no other in history. Its surveillance focus was on its internal population for those who were not loyal to the Communist Party. As the effectiveness of their internal security surveillance state procedures improved, so did their ability to monitor USMLM tours. At the height of Stasi dominance shortly before the collapse of Communism in 1989, estimates suggested there were a staggering 97,000 people employed by the Stasi with an additional nearly 200,000 informers living among the populace, resulting in an unprecedented ratio of one Stasi officer for every 63 individuals. With the additional paid and unpaid informers included in these figures, the ratio could have been as high as one in five. All along the thousands of miles of East German highways, Stasi agents posed as gas-station attendants, waiters, and tourists, all of which reported on their fellow East Germans, as well as any sighting of USMLM.

The centralized USMLM monitoring process employed an extensive spot-reporting system to trigger and vector surveillance operations. This process also included periodic announcements over standard East German radio broadcasts directing citizens to immediately report any sighting of USMLM to the People's Police (Volkspolizei/VOPO). Given that East Germany was a surveillance state, the amount of real-time reporting on USMLM locations was extensive. Although the Stasi conducted all activities from an extreme perspective of proactive paranoia, their ultimate agenda was to develop overwhelming evidence that the U.S. was inappropriately exploiting the Huebner–Malinin Agreement to convince the Soviets to discontinue the accord.

Surveillance

During the first five years of the MLMs, the Soviets aggressively conducted overt surveillance of USMLM tours. In 1952, the U.S. and Soviets agreed to cease surveillance of MLM personnel and vehicles. As a result, USAREUR ceased all surveillance of Soviet vehicles and personnel, and the Soviets terminated the overt surveillance of USMLM vehicles by Soviet and East German security agencies. However, this change prompted the Soviets to attempt the covert surveillance of USMLM with civilian vehicles, which continued with little success for a few years.

After 1954, surveillance by Soviet or East German military personnel was rarely encountered. The Stasi was clearly responsible for surveillance of USMLM, but the Soviets were still able to compel the Stasi to cease such activities on demand. When USMLM did complain to the Soviets regarding East German surveillance, it appeared that the East Germans responded by curtailing surveillance for at least a discernable period of time. Over the years, however, East German surveillance was a consistent irritant and risk to USMLM touring operations.

To obstruct USMLM intelligence collection, the East German authorities relied largely on active surveillance. Surveillance was a method by which the East German officials asserted the sovereign rights of East Germany to regulate the actions of USMLM, to document the intelligence role of USMLM, and to disrupt the effectiveness of USMLM reconnaissance teams. The anti-USMLM surveillance process matured into practices that remained relatively standard throughout the extended game of cat and mouse. Surveillance in the Soviet zone of Germany was an immersive and nationally coordinated process, normally conducted by the Stasi and VOPO. This centrally controlled process involved the coordination of the Stasi at regional levels and the VOPO agencies at the various local levels to attempt to provide blanket coverage across the countryside.

The Stasi conducted surveillance to monitor USMLM collection activities and to coordinate the detention of USMLM teams on charges such as speeding, reckless driving, taking illegal photos, or violating restricted areas. The primary objective was to document evidence of intelligence activities in violation of the Huebner–Malinin Agreement, and to have discredited individuals declared persona non grata. The ultimate objective was to detain USMLM teams where charges of "espionage" would have some validity when presented to the Soviet authorities.

The tours' entry point into East Germany was the Glienicke Bridge, which crossed the Havel River and marked the boundary between West Berlin and Potsdam. Also nicknamed "Freedom Bridge," the Glienicke Bridge was the site where Gary Powers was exchanged for Colonel Rudolf Abel in 1962, and the location of many other quiet exchanges of spies and recovered remains of soldiers between the Soviets and Allies over the years. No regular traffic was allowed on the bridge which was barricaded by a guard station manned by Soviet soldiers. Therefore, this was the first chokepoint where Stasi surveillance would be alerted to an upcoming USMLM tour. USMLM tour vehicles were stopped at the guard station where the guards reviewed the accreditation documents, placed a phone call, and then raised the barrier and allowed them to pass. USMLM tours occasionally picked up on Stasi surveillance immediately after crossing the bridge, but this was not always the case because Stasi agents understood that tours invariably traveled to the Potsdam House before departing into the countryside, where the real surveillance would be initiated.

When a USMLM tour vehicle departed the Potsdam compound, a Stasi surveillance vehicle would normally be waiting to initiate surveillance. There was a guard station at the entrance to the Potsdam compound manned by VOPO or East German military guards who notified Stasi and VOPO when USMLM vehicles entered and departed the compound. USMLM tour personnel would very commonly detect surveillance shortly after departing the compound to begin the tour.

While USMLM tours were known to be out on missions, the vast network of East German informants provided sighting reports to the central control office. The location and direction of travel was rapidly disseminated to the agencies having jurisdiction to vector surveillance assets and establish surveillance observation of the tour vehicles. Surveillance teams were relatively effective at handing off the surveillance of USMLM tours as they traveled between jurisdictions, demonstrating a high degree of coordination and capability.

Surveillance activities were primarily coordinated among the Stasi and the VOPO through the central coordination center using two-way radio communications to execute surveillance operations and pass USMLM vehicles from one jurisdiction to another. Overt surveillance was largely the function of uniformed VOPOs using relatively low-performance cars of East German manufacture. The Stasi surveillance teams were also equipped with low-performance sedans but did employ a few relatively high-performance sedans.

Covert surveillance elements were the most dangerous because their mission was to covertly locate a tour engaged in intelligence-collection activities, photograph this activity, and create a situation whereby the tour could be boxed in and detained. Stasi agents generally attempted to surveil covertly, resorting to overt, aggressive tactics when it became obvious that they had been detected, or when they had good prospects of detaining USMLM tours in the act of collecting intelligence.

Stasi and VOPO clearly led the coordinated surveillance effort, but USMLM tours were forced to navigate a wide range of surveillance elements that were very effectively organized, possessed a full range of communications support, and were augmented by numerous individuals and organizations hostile to their presence. These included the East German national police apparatus to include the Grenzpolizei (Border Police), Bereitschaftspolizei (Alert Police), and Transportpolizei (Railway Police). This vast network was augmented by political officials, foresters, collective enterprise managers, and "do-gooder" citizens. This USMLM tracking apparatus was also augmented by personnel referred to as "narks." These narks were on-call individuals who would assist in locating USMLM vehicles suspected of being in their local area. The locals not only increased the force deployed against the USMLM tours, but also provided their own intimate knowledge of the local area roads and trails. A tour vehicle sighted by any of the category of personnel was reported to Department K, and USMLM sightings reported to the CSFG security headquarters were also immediately passed to Department K.

Taking advantage of high-speed, radio-equipped cars, the Stasi was able to assign at least two cars to overtly surveil USMLM tour vehicles, while constantly shifting other high-speed cars to critical points along the various routes open to the USMLM team. By using blocking tactics, the Stasi would attempt to influence the route taken by a USMLM tour so that the tour team would be detained at a time and place of their choosing. The Stasi made excellent use of PRAs to not only deny access to targets of interest, but to effectively channel routes of travel, thus greatly aiding their surveillance elements in the orchestration of detentions. The Stasi would often attempt to pass USMLM vehicles to set up roadblocks. The aggressive and dangerous tactics demonstrated that Stasi agents were prepared to act with apparent disregard for life and property.

One prevalent method of surveillance that developed over the years was to employ high-performance vehicles as the leaders of the so called "rat pack." This tactic involved the employment of "packs" of low-performance vehicles at various locations within and around a sensitive area, particularly during the imposition of a TRA. The East Germans would employ as many as 30 vehicles to saturate an area when operating as a rat pack. The rat pack would attempt to close in on and contain a USMLM vehicle in an area to enable Stasi high-performance vehicles with radio communications to move in for a detention attempt when it was anticipated that USMLM was attempting to observe sensitive military activities.

Although the specific details remain unknown, the communications process employed to coordinate and maintain surveillance of USMLM and other Allied MLMs, mostly during a period of antiquated communications capabilities, must have been comprehensive based on MLM observations alone. The East German whole-of-sector approach to MLM surveillance could only have been executed through an integrated communications system employing fixed-site cable telephone communications and mobile radios with a robust base station and repeater network. The fact that the East Germans dedicated the amount of resources they did in the form of personnel, vehicles, and communications infrastructure, against the up-to-12 MLM tours at any given time, epitomized how effective they were as a surveillance state.

The Stasi maintained detailed information on individual tour officers and were aware of techniques used by tour officers and the likely intelligence targets that a given officer might be inclined to pursue. The Stasi and local VOPO maintained a list (or working knowledge) of observation posts and hide sites commonly used by USMLM tours when in a particular area, and would check these known locations when it was suspected that a tour vehicle was in the area. Stasi and VOPO personnel commonly dismounted from vehicles and maneuvered on foot to observe sites, coordinate detention attempts, or check the site for evidence of occupation such as tire tracks.

USMLM Antisurveillance

The surveillance countermeasures available for use by USMLM were limited, particularly against overt surveillance efforts. After years of operating, the USMLM methods of operation and areas of interest were well known to the East Germans. Among the limited tactics used to counter surveillance were to avoid populated areas, continually stay on the move, and move primarily during the hours of darkness.

The immersive nature of East German security elements made extended USMLM travel on improved roads ineffective as ingress routes to intelligence-collection targets. In most cases, however, surveillance of USMLM was more of an irritant than an impediment to operations. Essentially all USMLM vehicle modifications enabled antisurveillance. Since the USMLM vehicles were ruggedized and equipped for off-road travel, whereas Stasi and VOPO surveillance vehicles were not, USMLM vehicles would regularly maneuver off-road to counter and evade surveillance. USMLM used preplanned, off-road escape routes to elude surveillance vehicles that were not well suited for off-road pursuit. Although most vehicle modifications serving an antisurveillance purpose were obvious, even the increased fuel capacity served this purpose, as every time a USMLM vehicle stopped to refuel at an East German gas station, the VOPO and Stasi would be notified and enabled to reestablish surveillance.

For USMLM tours, losing the surveillance at the time of their choosing was normally a perfunctory task. When the tour officer determined that they needed to lose surveillance in order to move to the target area undetected, the tour vehicle would accelerate, often on a stretch of highway. When this was conducted at night, the driver would observe to the rear to determine when the following vehicle was in a blind spot where they could not see the lights of the following Stasi vehicle, and then flip the toggle switch to disable the tour vehicle's rear and brake lights. USMLM tour officers had a number of favored off-road hide sites where they would turn into when well ahead of a lost Stasi surveillance vehicle. After turning unobserved into a hide site, the vehicle would be turned off and the tour members would observe the Stasi vehicle speeding down the road past their location. The tour vehicle would normally stay in the hide site until after dark, if not already. The tour vehicle would then move to the target area under the cover of darkness, often in "lights out" mode with infrared lights on and wearing night-vision goggles. The team would then sleep until the early morning military activity was expected to begin.

Detentions

Since USMLM detentions were relatively common, the post-detention adjudication process was much more decentralized and efficient than the process practiced by USAREUR/ACS. Each GSFG region had a designated Kommandant, a local military police commander, who was the only individual USMLM tour officers were authorized to speak with during the detention process. In fact, the Soviets demanded that USMLM only speak with a properly accredited, pass-carrying Kommandant, because he alone could speak with the authority of the Chief of Staff, GSFG. East German authorities detaining USMLM personnel quickly turned them over to the Soviets, who then immediately dismissed the East German authorities. Again, this was the MLM game that the occupying powers played above the heads of their respective German hosts. In some cases, when the circumstances of a detention did not involve another incident such as damage to a vehicle or personal injury, the USMLM vehicle would be escorted to the Kommandant's facility. In other cases, the Kommandant would travel to the site of a detention to conduct an investigation. All Kommandants were uniformly familiar with the provisions of the Huebner–Malinin Agreement and USMLM detention resolution procedures.

In cases when a USMLM vehicle was detained in an area that was not blatantly in the area of military activities, Soviet and East German forces would commonly orchestrate the appearance of such. This was done by moving an MRS into the area where pictures could be taken with the sign near the detained vehicle, or by calling in military units so that incriminating pictures could be taken with the USMLM vehicle near military equipment.

When the Kommandant arrived on the scene, he would collect the USMLM personnel's accreditation documents and conduct an investigation by questioning the detaining party and the tour officer. The Kommandant would then produce an incident report, known as an "*Akt*," which is the Russian term for a legal document or indictment. When the Kommandant completed the Akt and presented it to the tour officer, the tour officer, as a matter of policy, would refuse to sign the document. This was a proforma response to both refuse any admission of guilt and to avoid the possibility of signing a document that could be altered afterward. After the tour officer and Kommandant discussed the Akt, the Kommandant would then contact SERB for disposition instructions for the USMLM tour. In most cases, after the prescribed warnings and lectures about mission travel freedom, as authorized by the Huebner–Malinin Agreement, the USMLM tour would be authorized to depart, with a warning not to push the agreement provisions too far.

Since the Soviet detention resolution process was decentralized (and more regularly practiced), it would generally take much less time than the USAREUR process. For this reason, SERB would regularly instruct the Kommandant to needlessly hold the USMLM tour for a period of time after the issue had been resolved. This was directed by SERB as a reciprocity measure to penalize USMLM for the amount of time the most recent, previous SMLM-F detention had taken to resolve. In most cases, the circumstances of the detention were resolved at the local level and the USMLM tour would be released on their own cognizance and could even continue to tour and collect intelligence if it so opted. But for this very reason, the Soviets would commonly hold the detained USMLM tour until nightfall to deny them the opportunity to continue collection when observation was good and more military activity of collection interest was taking place.

If the detention involved a potential PRA or TRA violation, or some other serious incident potentially instigated by the USMLM tour, the Kommandant may have been instructed by SERB to retain the tour personnel's accreditation documents. In cases of perceived egregious USMLM malfeasance, the tour would be escorted back to the Potsdam House by a SERB-arranged security detail. In such cases, the documents would be transferred to SERB who would determine how long the documents would be held before being returned. In a few rare cases, USMLM personnel would be declared persona non grata and not have their documents returned.

Ability to Orchestrate Detentions

Whereas the U.S. rarely demonstrated the ability to orchestrate a detention on demand in response to a detention of USMLM or another act against USMLM warranting reciprocity, the Soviets and East Germans were well practiced at orchestrating detentions. This was particularly impactful when the Soviets needed to demonstrate a level of effectiveness in orchestrating on-demand detentions in response to actions in the U.S. sector. One example of this proclivity occurred shortly after a SMLM-F tour was detained in West Germany with the tour members having their accreditations withheld for 10 days. The day following the return of the SMLM-F accreditation documents, the Soviets displayed their talent and inclination to exert retribution, retaliation, and reciprocity by detaining a

USMLM tour vehicle in a non-restricted area after the tour vehicle had experienced minor engine problems. During the course of the detention, several Soviet tactical columns moved through the area enabling the Soviets to take pictures and charge the tour with observing military activity. After the standard accusations, denials, and negotiations, the USMLM personnel were released to return to West Berlin without their Soviet accreditation documents. Predictably, the USMLM accreditations were returned after 10 days.

A candid conversation between CUSMLM and CSERB disclosed how well practiced the Soviets and East Germans were in orchestrating detentions during a February 1979 protest of the ramming and detention of a USMLM tour. The CSERB responded to the protest by asserting that the tour officer had violated PRAs six times in 1978 and the detention was a measure to discourage further such actions. Unofficially, however, CSERB admitted to CUSMLM that an eight-hour detention had been orchestrated in direct retaliation for the seven-hour detention of a SMLM-F tour two weeks prior. Obviously, this messaging was intended to be reported to USAREUR to remind the leadership that the detention of a SMLM-F tour would prompt an in-kind response.

In 1983, CSERB confided to CUSMLM that Soviet forces had guidance to "capture a tour like a fish in a net." Later that same year, CSERB responded to the detention of a USMLM vehicle by stating that the vehicle had been regularly detected during the previous three days in an area of sensitive military activity, and that the detention was conducted to "bring this activity to a halt." Again, later in the year, CSERB responded to the protest of the ramming of a USMLM vehicle by admitting that the Soviet units did have contingency plans for detaining mission tours, but deliberate rammings were not a part of such plans.

Many detention attempts and many detention-related vehicle collisions occurred when a USMLM vehicle was "running a column." When a tour vehicle passed a military convoy/column either head on or from behind, experienced column commanders regularly demonstrated the ability to orchestrate a detention (or at least vehicle ramming). Whether the USMLM vehicle was running the column as a calculated collection opportunity or because circumstances left no other option, the vehicle was usually more vulnerable to detention, particularly if there was not sufficient space for the vehicle to immediately maneuver off-road.

Although relatively rare, USMLM personnel were treated harshly during detentions. USMLM equipment was also commonly confiscated during detentions. Although these incidents were always protested in the strongest terms, they were never raised to the level of questioning the validity of the Huebner–Malinin Agreement. As was the trend during the lifespan of the MLMs, the U.S. was willing to endure high risks to enable collection missions to continue at pace. By allowing these events to repeat themselves time and time again, these abuses of tour personnel and equipment were technically accepted norms.

Often getting dangerously close to their collection targets, USMLM was the best first-hand source of information on the latest Soviet equipment.

In July 1971, a USMLM tour was detained inside a PRA at a Soviet airfield. The USMLM tour officer and driver were forcibly pulled from the vehicle by 12 soldiers, thrown to the ground, and had their hands tied. All of the equipment was seized by the Soviets and the tour members were interrogated for several hours. When CUSMLM met with CSERB two weeks later to request the return of the confiscated equipment, he was informed the tour officer and driver involved in this PRA violation would not have their accreditation documents returned and that they had been declared persona non grata. The Soviets eventually returned some of the equipment confiscated during the incident. USMLM did not protest the rough treatment of the USMLM members who were unquestionably apprehended red-handed violating a PRA. CSERB was also very slow to issue accreditation documentation for the replacements for the disaccredited tour personnel after they arrived.

Incidents of harsh treatment of USMLM personnel continued as evidenced by a 1982 detention in which a USMLM tour was attacked by a group of Soviet soldiers. The vehicle sunroof was smashed and the tour personnel were forcefully pulled from the vehicle. While the USMLM members lay on the ground with their hands tied, the Soviets ransacked the vehicle and confiscated all the equipment in the vehicle. The incident resulted in a USAREUR general officer protest, but while the formality of back and forth among the leadership ensued, USMLM continued to operate as business as usual. Coincidentally, the USMLM tour driver involved in this incident was one Staff Sergeant Schatz.

Detention by Ramming

The coordination of East German surveillance and efforts to detain USMLM vehicles was common. Throughout the years, the rammings of USMLM vehicles by East German and Soviet military vehicles appeared to be the result of spontaneous efforts by military units detecting USMLM intelligence-collection activities. One more dangerous twist to this dynamic was the tactic of ramming USMLM vehicles with East German military vehicles to disable the tour vehicle and effect a detention. There were many instances wherein the ramming of a tour vehicle was clearly a coordinated effort, and this practice matured and was deliberately employed when needed.

One of the most aggressive and dangerous periods involving serious incidents to include vehicle rammings targeting USMLM occurred in 1973 during the period immediately prior to and after the signing of the Treaty Concerning the Basis of Relations Between the Federal Republic of Germany and the German Democratic Republic, in which the East and West German governments recognized each other as sovereign states for the first time. This treaty led to the two German states being recognized by the international community and being admitted into the United Nations. During this period, East German military and security forces endeavored to test their newly perceived sovereignty by conducting unprecedentedly aggressive and dangerous surveillance coverage, vehicle rammings, and detention efforts. USMLM conducted monthly protests of the increasingly aggressive and dangerous East German activities. In a periodic meeting between CUSMLM and CSERB in June, CSERB unceremoniously announced the Soviet rejection of all USMLM protests concerning harassment and surveillance, and a Soviet affirmation that the East Germans would be allowed to continue unlimited surveillance and harassment of USMLM. On 10 July, USMLM provided SERB with a counterprotest to this Soviet position which was never officially responded to—meaning that the issue of the propriety of aggressive measures, to include vehicle rammings, was not mutually resolved. By not elevating the issue until gaining a positive resolution that ensured the safety of USMLM personnel, the U.S. allowed the violent and potentially life-threatening practice to stand as an acceptable norm.

In 1979, when relations between the U.S. and the Soviet Union began to rapidly deteriorate, the Soviets, East German military, and Stasi implemented tactics to facilitate detentions by ambush. The first incident occurred in 1979 wherein an East German military vehicle rammed a USMLM tour vehicle, forcing it off the road and rolling it twice, requiring that the tour officer be hospitalized prior to a four-week recovery. In June 1980, there was a Soviet ramming attempt that caused a USMLM tour vehicle to crash into trees, causing the tour officer to sustain a broken collarbone and dislocated shoulder. Later that same month, an intentional ramming resulted in a tour driver sustaining broken ribs. This month alone demonstrated the hostile environment that USMLM allowed to persist by placing the intelligence-collection mission above challenging the viability of the Huebner–Malinin Agreement, if such actions were allowed to continue.

Rammings and other violent detention methods continued to target USMLM until the last such event in January 1984. It is likely that these tactics were discontinued after the tragic event occurring two months later—the March 1984 death of the FMLM officer, Philippe Mariotti, who was the victim of a violent East German military truck ramming. The Mariotti incident apparently prompted GSFG to issue guidance regarding the harsh treatment of MLM tours, and there was a noticeable decline in these aggressive actions immediately following the incident. It was discovered many years later that the MLMs had been the targets of a deliberate campaign of violence directed at their tours. It was not until many years after the incident and the end of the Cold War that documents were discovered disclosing that Mariotti's death was actually a homicide—a deliberate act planned and executed by the Stasi. Stasi documentation described the operation, in which the vehicles of Allied missions "are to be hindered in their reconnaissance" and "are to be offensively disturbed." In the case of Mariotti, heavy military trucks were positioned around a set of barracks, Mariotti's movements were carefully tracked, and then the deadly operation was executed as retaliation for Mariotti's purported record of aggressive tour activities.

Shooting Incidents as a Deterrent to Intelligence Collection

During the history of shooting incidents involving USMLM tours, the Soviets regularly reinforced their policy position that sentries standing guard had a responsibility to follow their orders to protect their post. Even during the periods of relative calm, there were incidents that demonstrated the Soviets' official stance on shooting incidents, which remained consistent through the history of the MLMs, to include in the case of the Nicholson shooting. During the entire existence of the MLMs, to include the aftermath of the Nicholson shooting, the Soviets remained resolute in their position that sentries on guard had standing orders to protect their posts by whatever means necessary.

The first incident in which a Soviet soldier fired a weapon at a USMLM vehicle occurred in 1951. Soviet soldiers regularly fired their weapons when sighting USMLM vehicles, and the history of shooting incidents confirmed that this was a consistently dangerous threat. Of the 35 shooting incidents prior to and including the Nicholson shooting, 12 hit vehicles or personnel with one or multiple rounds, 14 involved one or multiple rounds that were clearly aimed rounds with the intent to hit vehicles or personnel, and only nine were clearly warning shots. Evidently, when the Soviets or East Germans chose to fire on USMLM, nearly 75 percent were aimed shots with the intent to hit the tour vehicle, or worse.

In March 1957, USAREUR convened a Soviet Relations Advisory Committee (SRAC) meeting to decide how the command should respond to eight incidents occurring during the January 1955 to March 1957 period in which Soviet military personnel discharged firearms while detaining USMLM tours. The Soviet position on all of the shooting incidents was that these were standard Soviet security measures instigated by aggressive USMLM touring activities and efforts to aggressively avoid detention. Rather than resulting in a more rigid protest to the Soviets, as was originally envisioned, the committee determined that the only way to prevent future such shooting incidents was to direct USMLM not to undertake actions that might instigate such a Soviet response. The committee's determination resulted in instructions being issued for USMLM members to cease running to avoid apprehension. The rationale for this position was that it would "preclude Soviet firing with any pretext of justification," and that the "Soviet security measures do not appear to be other than we would expect of an alert interior guard system." The SRAC determination concluded that "to protest would not appear warranted even though our own actions might not be to fire under similar circumstances." This guidance, however, did not have a lasting impact on USMLM tour behavior. As the history of USMLM actions and incidents demonstrated, USMLM tours and the responses to Soviet and East German detention efforts were to run to avoid apprehension, which was counter to this directive. Ironically, the conclusion that prompted the USAREUR leadership to direct USMLM to exercise restraint in 1957 was the exact same rationale the Soviets professed as justification for the Nicholson shooting in 1985.

One of the more aggressive and dangerous periods involving serious incidents to include shootings targeting USMLM also occurred in 1973 after West Germany and East Germany recognized each other as sovereign states for the first time. The period of heightened East German assertiveness included a six-month period (May–October) which comprised five shooting incidents targeting USMLM tours. USMLM conducted monthly protests of the increasingly aggressive and dangerous East German activities and a more formal protest to the first shooting event in May 1973. As with the simultaneous vehicle-ramming protests during this timeframe, the Soviets never provided a response of substance—meaning that the issue of the propriety of aggressive measures, to include gunfire, was never mutually resolved.

On 28 October 1973, East German guards fired approximately 20 rounds at a USMLM tour vehicle at an East German installation near Leipzig as it departed the area at high speed. One round penetrated the driver's door and passed through the toe of the driver's boot, making this the most serious shooting incident involving a USMLM tour until the killing of Major Nicholson. The most serious shooting incident involving an Allied MLM prior to the Nicholson shooting occurred in 1959, when a Soviet traffic regulator fired on an FMLM vehicle, hitting the French tour officer in the hip and requiring that he be admitted to an East German hospital before returning to West Berlin.

The immediate aftermath of the 1973 Leipzig incident was very instructional in demonstrating the Soviet stance on shooting incidents that endured to the end of the MLM era—to include the post-Nicholson shooting deliberations. In response to this incident, General Michael Davison, CINC USAREUR, sent a protest letter to General Yevgeni Ivanovski, CINC GSFG, to protest the shooting. In response to the U.S. protest, the Soviet general was resolute in stating that the incident was instigated by USMLM's presence in an area of military activity, and that their failure to respond to the sentry's orders and attempt to flee the area caused the incident. The Soviet response once again stressed the position that a soldier on his post will act in strict compliance with regulations and will use his weapon against any transgressor who does not obey his orders. As with other incidents reaching this level of protest, after the requisite protest and retort, the event was considered addressed, and the MLMs moved forward. In fact, the USMLM history report from that year even downplayed the seriousness of the shooting incidents by stating that in the five shooting incidents that year, "only one tour car was actually hit."

Boot of USMLM tour driver with bullet hole from East German gunfire. (U.S. Government Public Record)

Following the October 1973 shooting incident there was an immediate and noticeable reduction in East German surveillance, harassments, and incidents, which demonstrated that the Soviets still exercised strong influence over East German authorities. The next shooting incident targeting a USMLM tour occurred nearly a year later, which was one of only two shooting incidents occurring over the next nearly five years. However, despite that apparently positive outcome from the debate, the issue of whether these tactics were proper and acceptable was never resolved. Therefore, the fact that these events continued to occur, albeit initially at a reduced level, would support a legal argument that they were tacitly legitimized based on a lack of determination on either side to definitively establish the propriety or impropriety of such actions under the context of the Huebner–Malinin Agreement.

In August 1978, CSERB met with CUSMLM to discuss an incident involving a USMLM tour that had allegedly removed the license plates from its vehicle in an attempt to penetrate a Soviet installation. According to the Soviets, the sentry fired a warning shot because the tour failed to obey a sentry's command to halt. Although USMLM denied the allegation of removing a license plate, CSERB discussed the potential consequences of such actions and firmly reminded CUSMLM that Soviet sentries were responsible for the protection of military installations and were under orders to fire aimed shots at intruders who refused to obey commands to halt. Again, these liaison engagements were intended to be documented exchanges to send high-level messaging to USAREUR leadership.

One event that strongly indicated that the risk of gunfire was a competitive norm in the Soviet sector was a CUSMLM protest of a February 1983 incident. CUSMLM asserted that a USMLM tour that was not even in a restricted area was fired upon by a Soviet officer. CSERB countered that the tour had approached a "most sensitive" field deployment and that the shot, fired by a facility guard and not a Soviet officer, was a warning shot and not directed at the tour vehicle. When CUSMLM disagreed, CSERB asserted that had the guard intended to fire on the tour there would have been holes in the tour vehicle. When pressed to provide specifics regarding what constituted a sensitive area, CSERB responded, "That's not important, you'll know when you're in one!"—implying that gunfire was the response USMLM should expect when in the vicinity of guarded locations. The discussion of that topic concluded with no further debate, which should have been interpreted as the Soviets informing CINC USAREUR that the risk of gunfire would persist, which it did, up to and beyond the killing of Major Nicholson.

USMLM Instigation

Very often, Soviet and East German forces would conduct inappropriate and unauthorized actions such as slashing vehicle tires, searching tour vehicles, confiscating equipment, and even abusing tour personnel. In some cases, such actions were in reaction to aggressive (and often dangerous) USMLM efforts to avoid detention.

It is clear from the overwhelming evidence that East German and Soviet security efforts to deter USMLM collection efforts prompted USMLM to adopt tactics that protected them from these adversarial efforts. USMLM was usually well justified in their complaints regarding aggressive surveillance, the reckless circumstances of the detention attempts, the abuse of USMLM personnel by GSFG or East German forces when detained, and incidents of life-threatening gunfire. However, understanding the East German and Soviet mindset of the time, there is rationale to the argument that USMLM activities stimulated or instigated many of these actions. In fact, virtually all such activities were the reaction to and the result of USMLM tour presence in areas perceived by the Soviets and East Germans as areas of sensitive military activity.

This dynamic established the vicious cycle of aggressive Stasi surveillance, which compelled USMLM to adapt more aggressive collection capabilities and methods, which often resulted in detention attempts, detentions, vehicle collisions, and gunfire targeting USMLM tours. Both sides committed significant resources in an effort to overwhelm the other's operational capability. USMLM tour activity could

USMLM drivers were known to use high-risk maneuvers to avoid Soviet and East German detention efforts. (USMLM Association)

be seen as antagonizing much of the Soviets' and the East Germans' aggressive and dangerous responses. In fact, most of the "liaison" among USMLM and the SERB revolved around which side instigated the dangerous situation that led to a given incident.

In virtually all cases of a USMLM complaint of dangerous Soviet or East German activities, the Soviets would counter the allegation by asserting that it was the undisciplined action on the part of the USMLM tour that created the dangerous situation. In many cases, the Soviets unilaterally protested unsafe actions by USMLM vehicles which threatened the safety of security personnel or civilians, usually when attempting to aggressively escape the possibility of detention.

The Soviet position was supported by the fact that USMLM had a much higher rate of accidents involving government forces and East German civilians than did their SMLM-F counterparts. In 1968, a USMLM officer was expelled by the Soviets for allegedly causing an accident that resulted in serious injury to an East German citizen. Among the many other examples was a 1982 incident in which a USMLM tour vehicle struck and seriously injured a Soviet officer while eluding a detention attempt in a restricted area. The Soviet account of the incident claimed that the USMLM vehicle "deliberately ran down a Soviet Army officer" and "inflicted grievous bodily harm." Five days following the incident, one of the two tour officers involved was turned away at Glienicke Bridge crossing point, and the SERB subsequently informed CUSMLM that the officer's presence in East Germany was no longer appropriate. Twelve days following the incident, a USMLM vehicle was violently rammed by a Soviet military vehicle.

USAREUR and USMLM regularly recognized that USMLM activities added fuel to the fire of some serious incidents. Similar to the 1957 USAREUR guidance that did not appear to affect USMLM behavior, by 1976, USMLM reported that they had adjusted their touring approach by replacing "escape and evade tactics which often led to exciting, but pointless high-speed chases and concerted efforts to detain tours," with a "more subdued, stealthful style of collection and a preparedness to accept detention, rather that escalate a situation." However, this approach was relatively short-lived, as the increasingly aggressive East German and Soviet tactics which evolved starting in 1979 compelled USMLM to resort to their more aggressive countersurveillance and counter-detention tactics.

Other Monitoring Activities

Telephone Monitoring

According to the Huebner–Malinin Agreement, "Each mission will be given facilities for telephone communication through the local telephone exchange at the headquarters." Even if there were a follow-on provision barring the monitoring of that telephone exchange, it would not have impacted the Stasi's "surveillance state" mentality. USMLM obviously operated under the assumption that the phone service provided to the Potsdam House under a provision of the Huebner Malinin Agreement was monitored by the Stasi. This was confirmed years after the MLMs ceased operations with the review of the Stasi files. In a report provided by the MfS Main Division VIII to the GSFG leadership two days after the killing of Major Nicholson, a summary of the actions they had taken included the "Surveillance of phone calls from the USMLM in Potsdam." USMLM regularly complained about the poor telephone reception at the compound which could also have been indicative of telephone communications intercept activity.

Agents Working on the USMLM Facility

As would be expected, the East German personnel working at the Potsdam facility, primarily as kitchen, custodial, maintenance, and guard force workers, were Stasi and/or Soviet informants who eavesdropped on conversations and read the private mail of USMLM members. A 1978 agreement protocol between the MfS and the KGB specifically stated that the KGB was allowed to recruit East German citizens for secret collaboration in order to use them for operating against members of the Military Liaison Missions from the U.S., Britain, and France accredited with the staff of the GSFG. Directly after the Nicholson shooting, the Stasi contacted their agents operating on the USMLM compound to collect the reactions of USMLM members. In addition to collecting biographical information on USMLM personnel, compound workers could have been trained as access agents to facilitate the recruitment of a USMLM member as an agent, but this does not appear to have been an objective. The belief that USMLM was the only intelligence element operating out of Berlin during the Cold War that was not penetrated by Soviet Bloc intelligence is a point of great pride for USMLM alumni. It is almost beyond question, however, that the reason that USMLM never detected or reported activity indicative of spy recruitment tradecraft was due to a calculated decision by the Soviets not to make the effort. So, it is likely more accurate to say that USMLM was the only intelligence element operating out of Berlin that the Soviets chose not to penetrate—for whatever reason. Although none of the specific exploits appear to have been documented, generations of USMLM personnel have referred to the flirtatious and generous "house girls" who had some innocuous purpose on the support staff and were always believed to have been emplaced by the KGB. There were never any reported indications of a "honey trap," but female support staff members regularly socialized at the Potsdam House bar, and were very friendly with USMLM members. Everything taking place involving the East German staff working in the USMLM compound would have been instigated by and reported to the Soviets and East Germans, so any flirtatious staff members would have been doing so at the behest of Eastern intelligence.

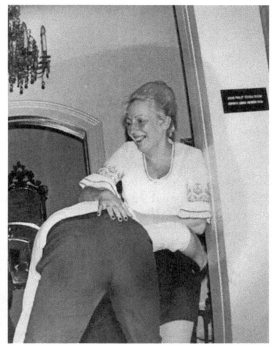

USMLM members were known to be friendly with the Soviet-provided East German workers. (USMLM Association)

Collection of USMLM Biographical Data

The collection of USMLM personnel biographical data by SERB and through other official contacts was the price of doing business in an MLM. SERB officers were GRU officers with English-language training and HUMINT-collection training to include information-elicitation techniques. However, the collection of biographical data on USMLM personnel was not limited to observations and elicitation made during USMLM/Soviet engagements.

The Stasi report provided to the Soviets the second day after the Nicholson shooting was particularly telling due to the information the Stasi claimed to have collected on Nicholson. The report disclosed that the East Germans were aware that Nicholson attended the U.S. Army Intelligence and Counterintelligence Officers' course seven years earlier and that he had attended the U.S. Russian Institute in Garmisch, West Germany. The report stated that Nicholson violated PRAs 15 times and MRSs 32 times during "intelligence gathering trips." The report further provided that Nicholson regularly violated traffic laws and on two occasions offered payments to East German citizens to avoid official reporting of collisions for which the USMLM tour vehicles were at fault. This level of detail on a standard tour officer indicated the level of monitoring and documentation that the Stasi invested in each tour officer. This also indicated that once officers were assigned to USMLM, the Stasi made the effort to investigate their backgrounds prior to the assignment.

USMLM personnel often returned for two or more additional assignments with USMLM. USMLM officers often served in other positions of interest to the KGB or Stasi such as military attaché positions. As a testament to the Stasi's obsession with USMLM, released Stasi documents disclosed that in at least one case, the Stasi continued to collect information on a USMLM officer whom they suspected of espionage after he departed USMLM and returned to the U.S. The Stasi documentation disclosed that after the officer's departure from USMLM, and while assigned to a position in the U.S., the Stasi intercepted letters and received a report from a codenamed informant who advised that the officer would be promoted and return to USMLM.

The Counter-SMLM-F Process

The monitoring of SMLM-F began as an ad hoc process of U.S. Army military police units tracking and reporting on SMLM-F travel throughout the U.S. sector. The Army Counterintelligence Corps (CIC) assumed responsibility for the SMLM-F "target" in the latter part of 1955, but was slow to establish a counterintelligence program to holistically address the SMLM-F threat. The CIC headquarters in Germany was an administrative headquarters with no authority to command and control operations, so there was no entity that maintained a strategic, big-picture perspective of operations across the West German zone of occupation. As such, the CIC operated in a completely decentralized, disconnected, and autonomous manner, with limited cross-regional coordination. This decentralized regional structure would constrain the CIC throughout the majority of the occupation of Germany.

Under the regional construct, the counterintelligence support elements were directly responsible to the army commanders in the region and were not uniformly focused on transregional threats such as SMLM-F. This approach differed significantly from the Soviet and East German methodology to manage its counterintelligence apparatus through a centrally orchestrated process. Throughout the majority of the Cold War era in West Germany, the regional counterintelligence structure persisted, with the region that encompassed the Frankfurt area having de facto responsibility for SMLM-F. The CIC Region III was the unit with this responsibility until 1962.

In 1962, the 165th Military Intelligence (MI) Battalion was activated and assumed responsibility for counterintelligence support to USAREUR units in the state of Hessen, and therefore Frankfurt, and therefore SMLM-F. This change of the unit in charge and alignment of regional support with the West German state system to improve coordination with West German agencies did not address the shortcoming in the area support construct as it applied to transregional threats such as SMLM-F. Army Counterintelligence continued to operate under the regional, area support structure, with counterintelligence elements taking direction from USAREUR army combat unit commanders, who tended to view the threat from their own very narrow perspectives. Since SMLM-F's primary intelligence-collection (military) interests were the major training facilities and other garrison locations well outside of the 165th MI Battalion area (and Region III before it), commanders had no practical reason to divert counterintelligence support from their own parochial priorities to the SMLM-F target. This, coupled with a lack of emphasis from the USAREUR level that was largely driven by a proclivity to not take action against SMLM-F that might impact USMLM operations, meant that SMLM-F went from slipping through the cracks to being largely ignored. In contrast to the immersive Stasi-led whole-of-country counterintelligence process targeting USMLM, SMLM-F was viewed primarily as an OPSEC threat and therefore a local, tactical counterintelligence concern. Also, in contrast to the East German and Soviet forces emplacement of active security measures to counter USMLM, U.S. forces in West Germany never perceived SMLM-F tours as a significant enough threat to take additional security measures solely to thwart their collection efforts.

During the mid-1960s, the 165th MI Battalion established a separate element—Detachment A, or Det A—as the element responsible for the surveillance of SMLM-F tours. Det A was well staffed relative to the other counterintelligence units, but only had the capability to surveil a maximum of three SMLM-F tours per week. Had SMLM-F toured at nearly the pace of USMLM, the Det A surveillance capability would have been readily overwhelmed and completely ineffective.

The relatively limited amount of resources dedicated to counterintelligence coverage of SMLM-F, in comparison to the Stasi effort targeting USMLM, reflected USAREUR priorities. Soviet Bloc intelligence services were aggressively operating throughout West Germany and the number of ongoing counterintelligence investigations was overwhelming. In addition, by the early 1970s, transnational and domestic terrorism had emerged as a major threat that further broadened the USAREUR counterintelligence mission. With these pressing threats, SMLM-F did not rate as a requirement to devote the resources that would have been necessary to actually study the SMLM-F problem in the detail necessary to gain results, if there really were any results to have been gained. The USAREUR tendency to discourage actions that might aggravate SMLM-F in a manner that might result in reprisals against USMLM was another factor that favored a more hands-off approach. To address a "hard target," which SMLM-F would have been if they were in fact involved in clandestine intelligence collection or other covert activities, would require substantial resources in both analytical and operational capabilities to be effective.

In 1977, the army established the U.S. Army Intelligence and Security Command (INSCOM), which finally began the process of bringing strategic counterintelligence under coordinated counterintelligence command-and-control structures. In West Germany, all counterintelligence elements were placed under the command and control of the 66th MI Group, and by the end of the decade, counterintelligence agents were no longer under the control of USAREUR and combat unit commanders, and were finally placed under the direction of professional counterintelligence leaders. In 1983, the 165th MI Battalion was deactivated, and all counterintelligence elements were placed under the command and control of the 527th MI Battalion.

The SMLM-F Monitoring Process

In accordance with the exception to freedom of movement in areas of disposition of military units noted in the Huebner–Malinin Agreement, USAREUR established PRAs around major garrison locations and training areas to designate the areas where SMLM-F was restricted from entering. Maps of the U.S. sector with shaded PRA locations were widely produced and distributed by USAREUR to SMLM-F and all U.S. military units. These maps could be found in virtually all DoD offices and common areas, and were carried by military personnel whenever on training maneuvers or when conducting other off-garrison travel. TRAs were established for periodic activities such as military training exercises and were detailed on TRA maps provided to SMLM-F and all USAREUR elements.

Beginning at least as early as 1960, USAREUR produced SMLM sighting/detention instructions cards for reporting sightings of SMLM-F vehicles and personnel. These cards provided the criteria under which SMLM-F vehicles could

THIS is what your sighting report should contain :

1. LICENSE NUMBER of SMLM vehicle

2. COLOR and MAKE of SMLM vehicle

3. TIME and DATE of sighting

4. LOCATION where SMLM vehicle was seen (give details like name of town, number of highway or autobahn, kilometer-stone marker or coordinates if possible, between which towns, on autobahn between which exits, etc)

5. DIRECTION OF TRAVEL of SMLM vehicle and if it was parked or moving

6. OCCUPANTS: Number, sex, type of clothing worn

7. SPECIAL OBSERVATIONS: Were occupants out of vehicle, using cameras, binoculars, maps, note books, etc? Was vehicle involved in running convoys, near military units or installations, near maneuver areas, etc?

AE Form 3231, 16 Apr 73
Previous edition is obsolete

THIS is what a license plate of a

SOVIET MILITARY LIAISON MISSION
(SMLM)
⬇ vehicle looks like

(The number being different in each case)

If you see a SMLM vehicle, notify

IMMEDIATELY

● TELEPHONE Mil 98 or
● TELEPHONE Mil 2311-6066 or
● TELEPHONE Civ 0611-151-6066

ACT QUICKLY! BE ACCURATE!

DETENTIONS
(Reference: USAREUR Reg 550-445)

1. IN THE FOLLOWING CIRCUMSTANCES SMLM SHOULD BE DETAINED:
   a. If in a permanent restricted area (PRA) or temporary restricted area (TRA) but NOT on autobahn in such areas.
   b. If SMLM shows interest in any military installations, exercises, etc.

2. A DETENTION MAY BE EFFECTED BY ANY MEMBER OF THE US FORCES. When making detention, no force should be used or lives endangered. If possible, SMLM vehicle should be boxed in by US vehicles to keep from leaving the scene. Once detention is affected, you

DO	DO NOT
3.a. Show military courtesy and ask the occupants for identification.	4.a. Interrogate or question SMLM personnel.
b. Make sure SMLM vehicle has no way to get away by suddenly driving through a ditch or similar action which must be expected.	b. Open doors of, or search, SMLM vehicle.
c. Secure the scene and direct traffic on highway to keep obstruction to a minimum, make double sure that MPs are coming to take over.	c. Tell the Russians why they are detained.
	d. Enter into arguments or allow Russians to intimidate you with threats which they might try.
	e. Release the SMLM vehicle unless instructed by USAREUR.

KNOW WHAT YOU ARE DOING! KNOW THE PRAs/TRAs NEAR YOUR BASE OR HOME!

USAREUR SMLM sighting/detention instructions card. (U.S. Government Public Record)

be detained and the instructions for actions on the scene of a detention. All U.S. military personnel were required to carry SMLM-F sighting/detention instructions cards, and stacks of these cards could be found in virtually any common area on a U.S. military installation for service members, family members, and other affiliates to carry. The SMLM sighting/detention instructions cards remained relatively consistent throughout the existence of the SMLMs. The phone numbers on the cards remained the same from 1964 to the end.

The reporting instructions on the cards directed that the reporter provide the SMLM tour vehicle license number, the date and time of the observation, the color and make of the vehicle, the location and direction of travel, and the number of, sex of, and type of clothing worn by the occupants. In addition to the basic identifying data, reporters were asked to provide any additional observations regarding military activity in the vicinity of the sighting and whether the personnel were out of the vehicle or using items such as cameras, binoculars, maps, or notebooks.

The USAREUR sighting/detention cards and the detailed PRA and TRAs maps were mass-produced by USAREUR and widely distributed throughout West Germany, which would suggest a rather robust SMLM-F monitoring program. In reality, however, USAREUR established the USAREUR SMLM Control Facility (USCF) as a fictitious front organization to distance the ACS and its interactions with SMLM-F from the DCSINT intelligence and counterintelligence functions, which did actually manage all USAREUR staff activities associated with SMLM-F and USMLM. The USCF was a façade USAREUR invented to have a name for the producer of items provided to SMLM-F such as PRA maps, license plates, and accreditation documents. USAREUR also used the USCF to project the façade of a robust organization that ostensibly produced and issued sighting/detention instructions cards and manned the sighting reporting line.

Since the inception and until the 1980s, the USCF was only the public face of due diligence. In reality, the USAREUR DCSINT branch "responsible" for SMLM-F was a very small (normally two-person) element that barely managed to produce maps and cards, man the sighting line, and produce detention reports in those rare cases. For example, during the 1970s, the USAREUR DCSINT Counterintelligence Analysis Branch receiving the sighting reports and ostensibly conducting trend/pattern analysis of SMLM-F activities was a two-person office, for which the SMLM-F responsibility was an additional duty. This office was consumed with issuing TRA maps in support of major USAREUR exercises and was unable to do little more in regard to SMLM-F, other than answer the sighting line and file the handwritten sighting reports in a bottomless cabinet of unanalyzed data.

Until the very final years, there was no analysis conducted to determine SMLM-F interests, patterns, and trends that might have provided insights regarding SMLM-F intelligence requirements and activities that may not have been within the parameters of their overt intelligence-collection charter. There was no dynamic operational interaction between the office receiving sightings of ongoing SMLM-F tours and the counterintelligence element that might have been conducting surveillance of SMLM-F, and therefore might benefit from this near-real-time locational data. This would have required a whole-of-sector approach similar to that employed by the East Germans, as opposed to a single surveillance element operating in isolation. This minimalist approach to monitoring SMLM-F activities remained the norm up to the final year of the Cold War, and even the lack of a dynamic interaction between the sighting desk and Det A surveillance operations persisted until 1985 when West Germany installed its first-generation (1G) mobile telephone network.

Counterintelligence Analysis: Trend and Pattern Analysis

Throughout the Cold War, the intelligence discipline was viewed in binary terms: as either collecting intelligence on threats, or preventing threats from collecting on U.S. interests. Whereas threat analysis was conducted with a multisource methodology (e.g., SIGINT, HUMINT, IMINT), and focused primarily on the threat of military intent and capabilities, counterintelligence was operationally executed in a very decentralized and compartmented manner with a focus on investigations and other counterintelligence operations. All-source analysis was viewed as everything other than counterintelligence, and counterintelligence was viewed as a completely independent discipline of intelligence. Counterintelligence agents were trained as investigators, and not as analysts. Throughout the Cold War, counterintelligence was viewed as multiple independent and compartmented investigations and operations, with no dedicated analytical elements piecing together the big-picture threat.

For the large majority of the existence of SMLM-F, the USAREUR DCSINT office with oversight for counterintelligence "operations" such as the surveillance of SMLM-F was the Counterintelligence Special Operations Division (SOD). Alternatively, the monitoring of SMLM-F touring activities through the sighting and reporting program was viewed as an OPSEC issue and managed out of the USAREUR Counterintelligence Support Division. Therefore, there was a process to monitor SMLM-F tour activities that was completely separated from the element with operational responsibility for the sensitive activities addressing the SMLM-F target.

In the early 1980s, counterintelligence analysis began to emerge as a necessary tool, due largely to the counterintelligence discipline having responsibility for countering the terrorism threat. In evaluating the counterintelligence analysis requirements in Europe, USAREUR recognized that there was a gap in the analysis of SMLM-F that had persisted for decades. When the 527th MI Battalion assumed responsibly for the strategic counterintelligence mission in West Germany in 1983, USAREUR tasked INSCOM to establish a dedicated counterintelligence analysis capability to study

SMLM-F. All were in agreement that this would be of value to both USAREUR as an analytical capability, and as an enabling capability for surveillance operations. USAREUR agreed to transfer the SMLM sighting reporting desk responsibility to Det A.

Det A developed information on SMLM-F tour activities through surveillance operations and other sources, but after assuming the sighting line and sighting analysis functions, the SMLM-F sighting and reporting program became the most consistent source of data for the analysis of SMLM-F activities. By 1983—for the first time in the 36-year existence of SMLM-F—the sighting line was manned with analysts who understood the SMLM-F target and could probe for details during sighting calls.

Counterintelligence Monitoring and Analysis

Needing a front organization to distance the Det A analysis effort from any overt association with SMLM-F, Det A assumed the mantle of the fictitious USCF. The illusive USCF would remain the alleged source of PRA maps and sighting cards, and the voice at the other end of the sighting line. The USCF became a key component of the analytical arm of Det A, but was still not openly associated with any counterintelligence activities. What was only known by a select few with the appropriate security clearance and an operational need-to-know, was that the USCF was established as the overt cover element of the larger counterintelligence effort targeting SMLM-F. The official USCF brand projected the appearance that the "facility" remained a USAREUR HQ element with the responsibility to monitor SMLM-F movement. The USCF was a widely publicized and acknowledged entity throughout USAREUR, but as a facility, it did not physically exist on any military installation or commercial facility in West Germany. The closest the average military member ever came to the entity known as USCF was the voice at the other end of the phone taking sighting report information and asking follow-up questions.

The USCF was responsible for monitoring SMLM-F activities when outside the Frankfurt compound. The SMLM-F compound gate guards immediately notified USCF when SMLM-F personnel departed or returned to the compound by foot or vehicle. Tracking the movements of SMLM-F was largely accomplished through reports provided to the USCF by on- and off-duty military personnel, cognizant military family members, and cooperating West German military and police elements. Current sightings of SMLM-F tour vehicles were obviously ideal, but due to the limitations involving U.S. forces reaching telephone communications, many of the reported sightings were made after the fact.

The Det A analysis cell analyzed SMLM-F tour activity to identify collection priorities, trends, and patterns. During the course of a SMLM-F tour, Det A analysts would receive sighting reports, assess the likely targets of collection, and notify the affected units that SMLM-F was either approaching or already in their area.

Although the USAREUR monitoring and reporting regime was not as immersive as the police state coverage in East Germany, sighting reports for any given tour were usually sufficient for Det A analysts to monitor and isolate SMLM-F travels to general areas and assess the likely intelligence interests based on U.S. military

USAREUR SMLM Control Facility logo provided a semblance of legitimacy to a non-existent organization. (Author)

SUBJECT: *SMLM Sighting Report !*

REFERENCE: USAREUR REG 550-445/USAFE REG 30-26

On 25 Nov 87, 1LT Eric Eastes,
an individual in your command reported the sighting of a vehicle of the Soviet Military Liaison Mission (SMLM).

The USAREUR SMLM CONTROL FACILITY (USCF) wishes to thank the sighter for his/her efforts. This reporting shows his/her awareness of the SMLM problem and reflects favorably on the unit security training program.

Every sighting report helps to better understand the activities of the SMLM. Please forward this card to the sighter with our expressed appreciation.

THANK YOU !

HQ AE FORM 122, JAN 85   HQ USAREUR AND SEVENTH ARMY

Sighting report note of appreciation. (Author)

activity in that area at the time. After each tour, Det A analysts prepared and provided USAREUR DCSINT a report detailing the SMLM-F collection activities and likely intelligence interests. To reinforce good behavior, USCF sent notes of appreciation to the commanders of units whose personnel called in a sighting report.

The Det A counterintelligence analysis effort was an integral component of the full-spectrum counterintelligence coverage approach for SMLM-F. Detailed analysis, to include target pattern and trend analysis, informed analysis-driven covert (discreet) surveillance operations targeting SMLM-F tours.

Surveillance

U.S. and West German forces were strictly prohibited from surveilling SMLM-F tour vehicles or obstructing their travel except under the circumstances authorized in sighting/detention cards. As a complete contrast to the Stasi surveillance and other harassment activities targeting USMLM, the West German security services never actively monitored or engaged SMLM-F tour vehicles or personnel. The U.S. did not extend any such authorities to the West Germans to monitor SMLM-F upon that nation's sovereignty, nor was West German assistance requested. The U.S. did not conduct overt surveillance of SMLM-F tours after the 1952 agreement, with the exception of an overt surveillance operation conducted by INSCOM counterintelligence agents under the direction of Det A immediately after the Nicholson shooting. The lack of German involvement and a U.S. policy to refrain from surveillance as agreed, led to a period in which the U.S. unilaterally refrained from surveillance operations despite very aggressive and overt surveillance against USMLM. In stark contrast to the surveillance approach in the Soviet sector, the U.S. counterintelligence elements with regional responsibility for the Frankfurt area sporadically conducted surveillance of SMLM-F in an ad hoc manner. In the mid-1960s, the 165th MI Battalion established Det A as a dedicated SMLM-F surveillance effort. Det A established a marginally effective capability to conduct surveillance of SMLM-F tour activities.

Det A only conducted surveillance of SMLM-F when on tour. Since Soviet tour personnel never departed their vehicle to conduct significant travel by foot while on tour, the surveillance operations were strictly vehicular surveillance operations. Vehicular surveillance operations are significantly less complex than combined vehicular and foot surveillance operations, such as those conducted against an espionage target in a large urban environment. In fact, Det A was restricted from surveilling SMLM-F anytime other than when they were known to be on tour in the vicinity of military activity, due to USAREUR sensitivities regarding violations of the Huebner–Malinin Agreement. In mid-1989, after concerns were raised and USAREUR's approach to SMLM-F had finally evolved, Det A developed the capability to conduct full-spectrum, combined vehicular and foot surveillance operations with the objective of observing SMLM-F non-tour activities when traveling in urban areas.

Throughout the SMLM-F/DoD counterintelligence standoff, the only surveillance conducted against SMLM-F were covert surveillance operations. In contrast to the overt and relatively aggressive Soviet and East German surveillance tactics, when the U.S. did conduct surveillance of SMLM-F, the intent was to do so covertly in an effort to observe SMLM-F activities without their knowledge that surveillance coverage was present. A primary purpose for this was USAREUR's respect for the "without escort or supervision" portion of the Huebner–Malinin Agreement provision allowing "complete freedom of travel wherever and whenever it will be desired over territory and roads in both zones, except places of disposition of military units, without escort or supervision." As such, USAREUR chose not to overtly demonstrate it was violating the agreement despite the obvious deterrent effects such actions had, as demonstrated daily by the aggressive East German surveillance efforts. As it related to the Huebner–Malinin Agreement concerns, another primary driver for this covert approach was USAREUR sensitivities to taking any actions that appeared provocative and might lead to negative reactions against USMLM collection efforts. In addition, the U.S. perspective was that SMLM-F were more likely to be observed and photographed violating a PRA or TRA if they did not suspect that they were under surveillance.

The only diversion from the covert surveillance approach and the only significant overt surveillance of SMLM-F since the 1952 moratorium occurred during the aftermath of the 24 March 1985 killing of Major Nicholson. Although the negotiations demanding Soviet concessions dragged on for over a year, SMLM-F tour operations resumed on 5 April 1985, just 12 days after Nicholson's death and six days after his funeral at Arlington National Cemetery. In response to the Nicholson murder, USAREUR directed the execution of Operation REMEMBRANCE '85 which began on 4 May 1985. This operation consisted of the overt surveillance of SMLM-F tour vehicles to place pressure on the Soviets during the initial period of negotiations. Det A was augmented by 22 additional counterintelligence agents which provided the capability to simultaneously track three SMLM-F vehicles. This was the only time that Det A was manned with the capability to conduct the surveillance of more than one SMLM-F tour at a time. However, after only one month of operations, on 4 June, augmentation was reduced to a level which only enabled the robust overt surveillance of one tour vehicle. The operation was officially ended on 27 July 1985. Ironically, the one-month period of maximum surge support was the only time that the U.S. employed the capability to surveil up to three SMLM-F tours simultaneously, whereas the Stasi employed a process to actively surveil (or at least attempt to surveil) USMLM tours at an average of two to three tours per day, every day for decades. Operation REMEMBRANCE was not cited as having any discernable influence regarding the Soviets' approach to the negotiations.

One version of the Intelligence and Security Command history page actually dedicated the majority of its section on the Soviet Cold War threat to the SMLM-F threat and the counterintelligence efforts to counter their intelligence-collection efforts. This page included the following:

> The seemingly endless Cold War between the United States and the Soviet Union went on unabated for nearly 45 years … Agents of both sides shared the same basic tools of the spy trade, including **cameras** and **specialized equipment**. The Military Liaison Mission was an agreed-upon means by which the Soviets and the Allies could monitor East and West Germany against a surprise mobilization by the other side. Counterintelligence personnel would follow the Soviet teams (facilitated by special **license plates** that identified a vehicle as belonging to an MLM) to ensure they did not stray into restricted areas and to determine their targets of interest.

This depiction largely characterizes how the MLMs were emblematic of the intelligence/counterintelligence dynamic on the front lines of the Cold War. This depiction also stands as a public acknowledgement that counterintelligence agents conducted surveillance of the SMLM-F vehicles when on collection missions. As history would have it, the legacy of counterintelligence agents actively following SMLM-F tours was largely based on the perception of the large-scale and aggressive overt surveillance in the aftermath of the Nicholson episode, and not the method of surveillance that was most prevalent throughout the period.

Although the process of covert surveillance was best characterized by Det A operations in the 1980s, the process was one that developed and matured throughout the years of the Cold War. Det A had a garage facility with a stable of 10 indigenous German vehicles which were specially configured for surveillance operations. The vehicles were leased so a vehicle could be readily exchanged for another type and color vehicle when it was assessed as having been "burned." Each vehicle was equipped with a radio system that included a coil concealed in the roof liner to pick up and broadcast communications so that the operator did not need to place a hand-transmitter to the face to talk, which could be detected by SMLM-F as an indication of surveillance. Communications capabilities were significantly upgraded after West Germany installed its 1G mobile telephone network and each surveillance vehicle was equipped with a mobile phone. Each vehicle was configured with a button on the dash console, that when depressed, disengaged the brake lights to enable a surveillance vehicle traveling in front of a SMLM-F vehicle to slow down without making it obvious to the following SMLM-F vehicle that it was doing so. The vehicles were high-performance BMW, Mercedes, and Passat sedans that were well suited for the German highways, which did not have speed limits. Det A personnel attended annual high-speed driving training provided by the German National Police Academy.

U.S. Army Counterintelligence agents received a clothing allowance to purchase civilian clothes consistent with their special agent duties. For the large majority of counterintelligence agents, clothing consisted of suits for men and business dress for women. The purpose for the more formal business dress was so that special agents were not acknowledged by their actual army rank, but viewed generically as agents ("suits" or "G-men"). Although standard counterintelligence agents wore civilian clothes, they were still generally required to maintain army-regulated grooming standards. Det A agents were among the very few in the army authorized to maintain "relaxed grooming standards," which primarily applied to men and meant they were authorized to have longer hair and facial hair. This relaxed grooming served two purposes: it allowed Det A agents to better blend with the West German populous when on surveillance operations, and it precluded agents from displaying attributes of U.S. Army personnel when potentially observed by SMLM-F tour members. Whereas the standard counterintelligence agents dressed to appear as an agent authority figure, the Det A dress was intended purely to blend with the West German populous, which had nuanced differences from the standard U.S. casual civilian dress and grooming at the time. Det A was an elite counterintelligence assignment and the rest of Army Counterintelligence enviously referred to the Det A swagger as "long hair and leather jacket."

The Anatomy of a Surveillance Operation

The typical SMLM-F tour surveillance operation employed six surveillance vehicles, referred to as callsigns. The standard manning for each callsign was a two-person team with a driver and passenger-side navigator. The navigator navigated by tracking the SMLM-F tour vehicle location and providing directions to the driver. The navigator was responsible for transmitting the location of the SMLM-F vehicle when their callsign was the one with control (having observation) of the SMLM-F vehicle. The navigator used a map book that did have maps, but Det A relied primarily on a unique method of surveillance tracking. Since the U.S. zone restricted SMLM-F travel to a finite area, and Army Counterintelligence had conducted surveillance of SMLM-F in that zone for decades, they developed "map books" that were actually not maps, but lists of every mile marker and every road interchange in the entire zone. This enabled the navigator to simply transmit an alpha-numeric location as the SMLM-F vehicle passed a location or changed direction at an interchange.

Surveillance operations usually began in a standard manner. Until 1986, PRAs in the greater Frankfurt area channelized SMLM-F travel along a route that would lead a tour vehicle to a traffic option that the vehicle would take to either of the two main highways (autobahns) that they would select depending on the intended tour destination (highways 3 and 5). A surveillance operator would be designated to deploy to a hide site overlooking the traffic option (trigger point) leading to the highways. The team would establish positions to pick up surveillance on the highway with a priority on traveling east if it were Highway 3, and south if it were Highway 5, since these were the directions of the primary USAREUR military activities. As with any SMLM-F vehicle departure, the SMLM-F facility contract guard force contacted the USCF when a tour vehicle departed the compound, who in turn immediately notified the Det A surveillance team regarding the vehicle (by number) and the tour officers they could expect to see emerging momentarily at the trigger point. In this case, the USCF was the overt tracking agency and a secure cutout between reporting sources and the surveillance team. When in position, or "on bumper," the callsigns would sit and wait until the trigger broadcasted the alert of "77-77," meaning that the SMLM-F vehicle had been sighted and that the initial direction of travel was forthcoming. Based on the tour vehicle's direction of travel out of the trigger point, the surveillance operator would inform the team which highway the tour vehicle would be entering. As the SMLM-F vehicle "broke the box," the callsigns that were positioned to initiate the surveillance along the SMLM-F direction of travel would execute the "pickup" and begin the surveillance follow. For those callsigns that had to position for the less likely directions of SMLM-F travel, recovering and rejoining the team was a minor challenge given the amount of time it would take the SMLM-F vehicle to reach its objective area and the fact that German highways had no speed limits at the time; all Det A surveillance operators were trained in high-speed driving and 120–140 miles per hour was a comfortable cruising speed in the high-performance vehicles.

Surveillance operations when traveling from Frankfurt to the tour's target area were generally basic highway follows. It would normally take the SMLM-F tour vehicle three or more hours to get to the day's objective collection area. The tour vehicle would conduct some basic and overt surveillance detection maneuvers and capitalize on ad hoc collection opportunities by pulling off the highway to photograph and record bumper numbers of military convoys encountered along the way. The actual surveillance operation would begin when the tour vehicle reached the vicinity of military activity, and exited the highway, making the target of the day's tour obvious. With the first sighting of the SMLM-F vehicle exiting the main highway, Det A analysts in the rear could immediately assess the tour's intelligence-collection interest and potentially impacted units with a high probability of confidence.

The surveillance team would know they were nearing the objective collection location when the SMLM-F tour team would become "switched on" and begin conducting a series of surveillance detection and then antisurveillance maneuvers … and so the game began.

One of the primary tenants of conducting covert surveillance is that the surveillance team will break contact with the target rather than risk compromise. In standard covert surveillance operations, this imperative is balanced by the assumption that if the standard espionage target is trained in surveillance countermeasures and is actively surveillance conscious, they will conduct the countermeasures in a manner that is not overtly noticeable by a potential surveillance effort—as even the display of the slightest operational tradecraft would be perceived as a sign that the target is preparing to conduct activity of interest ("switched on"), and prompt the team to intensify coverage. Det A's challenge was that SMLM-F did not share this need for discretion. Generally, the more overt and aggressive the surveillance countermeasures technique, the more effective it will be, and the SMLM-F drivers were trained and fearless.

Antisurveillance consists of actions taken to elude or evade possible, suspected, or identified surveillance. Since SMLM-F appeared to operate under the assumption that surveillance was always possible, they conducted antisurveillance as a standard practice prior to reaching their ultimate collection target area. As with surveillance detection, antisurveillance is based on an understanding of how a surveillance effort operates. The driving principle of most antisurveillance efforts is that a surveillance team will normally break contact with the target rather than accept a high risk of exposure. Antisurveillance strives to capitalize on this by placing the surveillance team in a position that forces it to either terminate the surveillance or risk compromise (detection). In reaction to SMLM-F surveillance countermeasures, the Det A surveillance team would regularly lose or have to break contact with the SMLM-F vehicle during the operation to avoid detection, and ensure compliance with USAREUR direction that surveillance operations remain covert.

When the surveillance team was forced to break contact and observation with a SMLM-F tour vehicle to avoid acting conspicuously in reaction to a standard SMLM-F antisurveillance measure, the team would contact the sighting line desk for support. For most of the timeframe, this required a tedious process of deploying a surveillance operator to find a public pay phone to call the sighting line and then to transmit this information to the team. This process was significantly improved in 1983 when analysts who understood SMLM-F intelligence interests and who had studied their trends and patterns would provide the best-informed assessment possible as to where SMLM-F was likely going and where the team would most likely to able to reestablish contact. Ideally, current SMLM-F sighting reports would be relayed to the surveillance team to more specifically close back in on and reestablish surveillance of the SMLM-F tour vehicle. This process was again significantly improved in 1985 when Det A vehicles were equipped with mobile phones capable of dynamically contacting USCF directly.

Even with the best equipment it was very difficult to take an identification-quality photograph from a moving callsign while catching an identifiable sign or landmark without detection. In addition, it was rarely feasible for a surveillance operator to discreetly take a photograph from a callsign within mutual observation range of a SMLM-F vehicle. Therefore, the callsign navigator was prepared to exit the vehicle on foot at a moment's notice. A specially configured backpack ("go-bag") with all

SMLM-F tour as observed by a Det A surveillance operator approaching through a wooded area. (Author)

the necessary equipment and provisions (camera, night-vision goggles, mobile radio, water, energy bars) was always carried on the backseat floor of the callsign. When necessary, the navigator would exit the callsign with the go-bag to maneuver in a concealed manner to an appropriate observation point. This normally occurred when a SMLM-F vehicle stopped at a location that did not allow for a callsign to securely stop and observe the SMLM-F vehicle, and it was assessed that the SMLM-F tour might conduct some activity of interest. In such cases, a foot operator would maneuver to a location where the SMLM-F activity could be observed, photographed, and reported on. Another common location for deploying an operator on foot was an area with a distinguishable sign or landmark where it was anticipated that the SMLM-F vehicle might pass by, which would facilitate a photograph of a SMLM-F vehicle with evidence of its presence in a restricted or sensitive area.

When SMLM-F completed the day's tour observation/collection activities, the surveillance reverted to a standard highway follow directly back to Frankfurt. When the tour vehicle exited the highway at the Frankfurt-Niederrad exit, the team would terminate the surveillance to avoid following on smaller roads and increasing the risk of detection, having a high degree of confidence that the tour vehicle would drive directly to the SMLM-F compound, as it invariably did. In a matter of a few minutes, USCF would notify the team of the tour vehicle's return to the compound, and the surveillance team would return to base.

When the surveillance team returned to the compound after a SMLM-F tour surveillance operation, they would conduct a debrief to recount the day's observations for Det A analysts. The analysts would incorporate the observations into the daily SMLM-F analysis report as though the observations were provided by sighting reports. In fact, for a standard, bland SMLM-F tour, the surveillance team would provide no insights in addition to what could have been derived from the day's sighting reports. Any other more sensitive information developed during the surveillance operation, or information that the reader might deduce was derived through physical surveillance, was provided to the appropriate consumers by a separate "sensitive sources and methods" distribution channel.

License Plates

One aspect of a surveillance operation in West Germany that highlighted the difficulties of a single-surveillance capability following a target traveling long distances across the countryside, was that of vehicle license plates impacting the ability of the surveillance team to remain discreet. A surveillance team's ability to blend in with its surroundings is key to the ability to remain discreet. Since the surveillance of SMLM-F was primarily a vehicle follow, this aspect of operating covertly was to ensure that Det A callsigns blended with the vehicles in their West German surroundings.

Unlike the U.S. wherein license plates are generally standardized based on the state the vehicle is registered to, German vehicles had license plates that were unique to the city or township to which the vehicle was registered. As such, license plates in Germany began with one, two, or three letters based on the city of origin, followed by random letters and numbers. License plates for the larger or more prominent cities started with one letter such as F for Frankfurt and M for Munich. Generally, the license plates from medium-sized cities with names that started with a letter already used by a larger city would begin with the first letter of the city and then a second letter (which may or may not be the second letter in the name) which indicated the city of origin. The license plates from smaller cities had three letters using the same lettering convention as the two-letter city plates. Matching license plates were displayed on the front and rear of a vehicle. A vehicle that did not bear a license plate from the city in which it is located, or one from a nearby city, was readily identified as foreign to the area. For example, a vehicle with a license plate beginning with a lone letter F would stand out and appear very out of place in the areas around the Grafenwoehr or Hohenfels training areas. This presented a unique security challenge for surveillance operations because a callsign beginning the day's operation with Frankfurt or other nearby license plates could end up anywhere in the sector, normally traveling a distance of 150–200 miles from Frankfurt. To address this challenge, Det A leveraged the USAREUR "occupying forces" status to exercise a support relationship and cover support process that was absolutely unique in the history of U.S. counterintelligence.

The West German government's Federal Office for the Protection of the Constitution (Bundesamt für Verfassungsschutz, or BfV) was Det A's primary partner for national counterintelligence support. Det A employed a local national (LN) investigator who maintained relations with the BfV for these type purposes. The BfV provided multiple sets of license plates for any city Det A requested. Det A had a large storage room at the garage complex that was filled with shelves of license plates that allowed Det A callsigns to blend in with local vehicles anywhere in the U.S. sector. Over 30 sets of plates with corresponding registration forms were acquired for each of the 10 Det A callsigns. When a Det A callsign was exchanged for another leased vehicle, over 30 new sets of license plates and registrations needed to be acquired for the new vehicle. Det A had a special "liaison" fund which ensured that the LN investigator was able to regale his BfV contacts with the finest cigars and liquor when asking for these time-consuming and sensitive "favors."

In preparation for surveillance operations, USCF analysts would attempt to predict where the tour might likely lead the surveillance team on a given day, based on military activities of potential SMLM-F interest and trend/pattern analysis from previous tours. Although this level of analysis did enable Det A members to prioritize the plates it selected for the day, they needed to be as prepared as possible for any contingency. Therefore, each callsign would depart the compound with at least 10 sets of license plates in a concealed trunk compartment.

License plates were referred to by the code term "socks." Socks changes were performed either to avoid continuing with a "pair of socks" that made it obvious that the callsign was not from the area so it could more readily blend with vehicles in the area, or to change the callsign's profile after it was potentially observed by the SMLM-F tour. During the course of a day's surveillance operation, it was common for a callsign to change socks three to five times. Each callsign was equipped with quick-change license-plate brackets that could release or secure plates to the bracket with a 180-degree turn of a screw using a small coin. Since a license plate (socks) change would take place during the course of an ongoing surveillance operation, time was of the essence. In addition, a socks change needed to take place in a location that could not be observed by third parties, or, in the worst-case scenario, by a SMLM-F vehicle actively conducting surveillance-detection maneuvers. One of the more common such locations were service roads (referred to as "illegals") that crossed under the main thoroughfare and were restricted to use only by official vehicles such as police vehicles.

When a callsign informed the team that it was "changing socks," it meant that the callsign was temporarily dropping out of the operation for a license-plate change. The navigator would then direct the driver to an appropriate socks-change location and decide which new plates to use. As the callsign was preparing to stop, the navigator would pull the registration for the current plates from the glove compartment. Once the callsign was stopped, the navigator would run to the rear of the callsign, pull the new set of plates from the trunk, and hand one of the plates to the driver. The driver would run to change the front plate while the navigator changed the rear plate. The driver would run and hand the replaced front plate to the navigator at the rear of the callsign, and then return to the callsign to be ready to drive. Simultaneously, the navigator would pair the replaced set of plates with its registration and return the plates to the secure compartment. The navigator would then run and enter the callsign, place the registration for the new plates in the glove compartment while the driver began to maneuver to the thoroughfare, and inform the team "socks change complete"—meaning that the callsign was maneuvering to re-enter the operation. From callsign stop to restart, the socks-change process should have taken no longer than 30 seconds.

USCF Credentials and Other Cover for Action

As with any covert surveillance, potential detection by the target is not the only risk of compromise to the operation. The observation of suspicious activities by a third party might cause that party to act in a manner that disrupts or completely compromises the operation. The primary threat in this regard was the ever-diligent West German police forces, whose unwitting and well-meaning actions often interfered with Det A operations. For example, being discovered by an Uzi-wielding German police officer while "changing socks" in an "illegal" with an open trunk containing an additional 10 sets of license plates made for a tense situation. For these and other such circumstances, each Det A member carried an English language and a German language picture credential. The English language credentials were signed by a general officer representing the CINC USAREUR and the German language credentials were signed by the German minister of the interior. Both credentials had the following language:

> THE INDIVIDUAL DESCRIBED HEREON IS A MEMBER OF THE ABOVE AGENCY AND ON AN OFFICIAL MISSION REPRESENTING THE COMMANDER-IN-CHIEF, US ARMY, EUROPE. ALL PERSONNEL ARE ENJOINED TO RENDER ASSISTANCE FOR THE ACCOMPLISHMENT OF THIS MISSION.

These credentials represented perhaps the longest-lasting and most assertive demand placed on the West Germans by an "occupying power." The credentials essentially gave Det A personnel the authority to operate throughout West Germany with impunity. There was never a case of any West German authority not immediately deferring when presented the credentials.

In situations wherein Det A agents needed a shallow "cover for action" to explain their presence to authorities or other curious third parties, but did not need to use their credentials which could attract unnecessary attention simply based on the levels of the signatories, they all carried business cards which identified them as a member of the "USAREUR Maneuver Topographical Survey Team." The cover organization's mission, which could be found in the USAREUR directory, was ostensibly to map evacuation routes for U.S. military dependents and other U.S. citizens in the event of war or other crises. The business cards displayed the organization heading, a post office box address, and a telephone number which would ring to a dedicated line at the USCF and be answered by an analyst acting as a front office member of the mythical Maneuver Topographical Survey Team. This "shallow cover" was particularly effective when Det A agents were on the roads developing map books, which was completely consistent with the cover mission.

SMLM-F Surveillance Countermeasures

The USMLM repertoire of antisurveillance methods was primarily limited to "brute force" tactics such as outrunning and traveling off-road to evade Stasi surveillance. The SMLM-F approach to surveillance countermeasures was much different, as their vehicles were not suited for off-road driving. In addition, Det A callsigns were among the very highest-performing vehicles on the road, and Det A surveillance operators could outrace virtually any car on the road.

Standard sophisticated hard targets conduct active surveillance countermeasures (active surveillance detection and antisurveillance) after having detected indications of surveillance through passive surveillance-detection measures. As an overt target, this was not the case with SMLM-F. When on tour, SMLM-F invariably conducted surveillance countermeasures along the highways and then most intensely when nearing the location of the tour's intended collection effort.

Active surveillance detection involves specific, usually preplanned maneuvers to isolate a surveillance asset and/or elicit a conspicuous and detectable reaction from a surveillance effort, if one is present. SMLM-F invariably employed surveillance detection as a standard security practice prior to conducting intelligence-collection activities. Effective surveillance detection methods are based on an understanding of how a surveillance effort operates. SMLM-F tour drivers actively endeavored to orchestrate unanticipated situations to force following surveillance vehicles to react in a manner which isolated them for detection. As a covert surveillance effort, Det A made operational security their highest priority, because if SMLM-F became aware of coverage, the surveillance effort was hindered, if not rendered completely ineffective. In addition, surveillance was technically a violation of the Huebner–Malinin Agreement provision of freedom of travel without escort or supervision, so a compromised surveillance could result in an official protest.

Some of the specific surveillance countermeasures consisted of time-proven maneuvers such as running red lights, rolling through rest stops without stopping, drastic decreases in speed after blind hills or curves, logical and illogical U-turns, and luring surveillance into intrusion points (e.g., dead-end streets, cul-de-sacs). Just one example of the very overt and hazardous, yet effective, antisurveillance maneuvers was for the SMLM-F vehicle to stop in a highway breakdown lane immediately after passing an exit ramp, and, after allowing any following surveillance vehicles to pass by, back up, and take the highway exit.

Detentions

The USAREUR SMLM sighting/detention instructions card authorized the detention of Soviet vehicles in PRAs and TRAs, but also specified that SMLM had unrestricted access to highways for travel through and bordering PRAs and TRAs. The detention instructions on the cards were interesting as they suggested that the USAREUR policy for tour detentions was as liberal, or more so, than the detention practices in the Soviet sector. The more liberal aspect of the instructions was that USAREUR units were authorized to detain SMLM vehicles anytime they were observed exhibiting "undue interest" in military activity, to include while traveling on highways. Whereas USMLM regularly complained about the Soviet practice of MRSs which they did not recognize as valid for warranting detentions, the USAREUR instructions basically authorized detentions anywhere in the sector if in the vicinity of military activity. However, despite being relatively open-ended, the instructions stipulated that the detention must be effected within the immediate vicinity of the installation or activity.

Although the card was originally intended to be followed as worded, in practice, the card was more propaganda than policy. Commanders and soldiers throughout USAREUR received annual training on SMLM-F detention procedures and were actually cautioned to only take such actions if they could ensure the absolute safety of tour personnel, and that detentions in PRAs or TRAs were actually the only ones that served a purpose. Throughout the years, personnel demonstrated the perception that by detaining a SMLM-F vehicle they were entering into a drawn-out process that detracted from the ongoing training activity, and that leadership viewed it as a distraction rather than an accomplishment that should be rewarded. After the card authorized detentions anywhere military activity occurred, the card then emphasized in bold lettering that no force should be used or lives endangered, which would tend to discourage such attempts. The detention instructions directed soldiers to show military courtesy, and to not open doors of, or search, SMLM-F vehicles nor interrogate SMLM-F personnel. When provided an instruction card that lists more things not to do than it does things to do, there is a tendency to err on the side of caution.

In the event of a detention, the detaining unit's chain of command would contact the USCF to report the detention, who would in turn report the details to ACS. The CACS or another ACS officer would then travel from the Frankfurt office to the location of the detention, which could take up to four or more hours. The responsible officer of the detaining unit would ensure the safety of the SMLM-F tour personnel until ACS arrived, often calling on military police units to support. There was never a recorded case of USAREUR forces searching a SMLM-F vehicle, confiscating equipment, or abusing personnel. After arriving at the detention location, SMLM-F personnel would surrender their accreditation documents to ACS and a discussion of the detention circumstances would ensue with the responsible U.S. officer and subsequently with the SMLM-F tour officer.

Following a SMLM-F detention, the Soviets would invariably complain to ACS and USMLM that the U.S. detention resolution procedures were too rigid. Whereas the Soviets empowered the local Kommandant to resolve USMLM detentions, which was a relatively quick process, SMLM-F detentions required that an ACS representative travel to the detention location. Whereas USMLM vehicles were usually allowed to resume touring after they were released at the site of the detention, ACS would escort the detained SMLM-F vehicle back to Frankfurt, essentially negating the opportunity to continue a tour. The consistent U.S. response to this complaint was that the Soviet Kommandants were still required to call SERB before the tour was released, and SERB would usually direct the Kommandant to hold the tour for an additional amount of time, often until it became dark.

USAREUR never orchestrated or attempted a detention as reciprocity for USMLM detentions or other objectionable activities; the risk of retaliation against USMLM was simply not worth the benefit. Although USAREUR reserved the right to detain SMLM-F vehicles to make a political statement or as retaliation for incidents that occurred in East Germany involving USMLM members, USAREUR did not have a plan or a process to orchestrate SMLM-F detentions. In 1978, when there was a surge in the number and seriousness of incidents targeting USMLM, CUSMLM informed CSERB that he could not rule out the possibility of asking USAREUR to take retaliatory measures against SMLM-F. This rare threat was likely taken as laughable by CSERB, as in contrast to the demonstrated Soviet and East German ability to orchestrate retaliatory measures on demand, the U.S. never demonstrated the desire or ability to prompt U.S. forces to act in a similar manner.

The relatively few detentions of SMLM-F tours were invariably the result of opportune and aggressive military units acting spontaneously on their own initiative. Although these events could be a great source of morale for the detaining units, unless the vehicle was in a PRA/TRA which would be an exceptionally rare occurrence, USAREUR would invariably direct CACS to effect a rapid release of the vehicle as it did not usually serve a purpose in the larger game of chess at the theater level. After these events, USMLM was alerted and would anticipate (as would always be actualized) that one of their vehicles would be aggressively detained within the next three days. If USAREUR detained a SMLM-F vehicle for six hours, a USMLM vehicle would subsequently be detained for six or more hours.

In comparison to the dynamic USMLM experienced in the Soviet sector, among the factors that made detentions much less frequent for SMLM-F was that of a much lower rate of SMLM-F touring which presented fewer detention opportunities. In addition, SMLM-F tour activity was not generally perceived as a significant threat worth the unnecessary risk to safety, and the reciprocations against USMLM and the impacts on intelligence collection were not worth the benefits of such efforts.

Other Incidents

Other than the sporadic occurrences of detentions, there were no other types of incidents that SMLM-F were subjected to, in contrast with the USMLM operating environment. There was never a preplanned or deliberate collision with or ramming of a SMLM-F vehicle. U.S. soldiers never fired their weapons at or in the vicinity of SMLM-F personnel. Arguably, however, SMLM-F tours never placed themselves in a position wherein they might have been perceived as unidentified aggressors by a sentry guarding his post. A 1978 U.S. protest letter regarding a very serious shooting incident noted that Soviet mission members had never been fired upon in West Germany. As late as 1985, during the post-Nicholson killing negotiations between CINC USAREUR and the CINC GSFG, the CINC USAREUR, General Glen K. Otis, at one point stated that "there were no instances when SMLM members had ever been shot at," to which there was no retort from the well-prepared Soviet general.

Other Monitoring Activities

Telephone Monitoring

As a provision of the Huebner–Malinin Agreement, SMLM-F was provided one commercial West German telephone line. Recordings of all conversations on this line were provided by BfV to Det A for translation and exploitation. This program was called BR 220.

Obviously, SMLM-F personnel were aware (or at least strongly suspected) that the line was monitored and there was never a conversation on this line that was assessed to have been of intelligence value. In fact, mission personnel even made snide comments to ACS personnel regarding Army Intelligence listening to their conversations.

On occasion, mission personnel would have conversations of interest which were invariably assessed to be provocations as attempts to elicit a reaction that would confirm their conversations were recorded. As would be expected on occasion, the Soviet personnel, assuming the line was monitored, would dangle fabricated information of interest to prompt a response which would confirm that conversations were being monitored. For example, they might voice a legitimate quality-of-life grievance in an effort to manipulate ACS to address this issue without it having been officially raised as a concern.

The SMLM-F personnel exercised extreme OPSEC on a constant basis throughout the years. In addition to BR 220, there were more invasive technical collection efforts in the compound which did not develop information of intelligence value, and further indicated that the Soviets did not openly discuss activity of intelligence value at the compound, with the likely exception of the communications room.

The only actionable information (although not intelligence related) derived from the BR 220 monitoring, occurred directly after the Nicholson shooting. Prior to a 25 March meeting between the USAREUR Chief of Staff General C. J. Fiala and the CSMLM-F General Shevtsov, General Fiala was made aware of phone intercepts of threats made to the SMLM-F compound in English and German. Given this knowledge, when Fiala met with Shevtsov, he expressed his concern regarding the safety of SMLM-F personnel and family members, and offered the Soviet general additional security support.

The Observation Post

Det A maintained an apartment across the street from the front of the SMLM-F compound for use as an observation post, referred to as DART. This observation post was of value during periods of heightened tensions such as that following the shooting of Major Nicholson. The observation post was not used as a permanent residence and was only activated when needed. The observation post was detected by SMLM-F during its first two months of use in 1959, and this data point was likely passed along through the years, as SMLM-F personnel were regularly observed giving the location special attention, and even made comments to CACS which strongly suggested that they were aware of DART and its purpose.

Collection of USMLM Biographical Data

CACS and DCACS were Russian Foreign Area Officers (FAOs) with intelligence training. In addition to the standard liaison functions, the FAOs had the responsibility to elicit and report biographical information on SMLM-F personnel. Social functions with relaxed atmospheres and alcohol were the best occasions to collect this type information. The SMLM-F officers were also trained intelligence officers who understood the game, and likely only divulged what they wanted U.S. intelligence to know.

Other Potential Counterintelligence Operations

For the majority of the MLM era, USAREUR made it very clear that it was policy not to accept a SMLM-F defector. Obviously, as this were the case, there would have been no program to actively recruit SMLM-F personnel as agents. The reason for this stand was that if such an event were to occur, it could have jeopardized the Huebner–Malinin Agreement and the intelligence-collection access that USMLM aggressively exploited on a daily basis. This position was relaxed by the mid-1980s, and there was a plan in place to handle a SMLM-F defection.

In 1986, a SMLM-F member was identified to have been using his privileges to shop at the U.S. post exchange to purchase large amounts of audiovisual equipment for resale and profit. Rather than using this as leverage for a possible recruitment, ACS placed restrictions on the amount of equipment SMLM-F personnel could purchase. Some consideration was given to planting technical devices in the equipment sold to SMLM-F personnel, but the risk/gain probability was assessed as too high/low. SMLM-F personnel were also known to profit off of the sale of USAREUR fuel ration coupons. In fact, the most compelling potentially exploitable leverage developed against SMLM-F personnel occurred just as the Soviet Union was laying down its king.

The Strategy, The Narrative, The Enigma

The very few works that memorialize the MLMs are largely anecdotal and presented almost exclusively from the standpoint of the Allied MLMs. Consistent with this perspective, throughout the MLM era, the U.S. generally tended to view the game as one dynamic in the U.S. sector and one very different dynamic in the Soviet sector, with the two only impacting each other when there was a high-level reciprocity issue. However, an informed analysis of how the Soviet and U.S. MLMs played the game, and how this game evolved, is only possible when factoring the actions in the U.S. sector and the actions in the Soviet sector together.

The Cold War was appropriately termed a war. A war is an existential struggle between two states or alliances based on principles or ideologies that prevent the two belligerents from peaceful coexistence. A war consists of multiple battles, which are engagements that are generally limited by area and the commitment of resources. The U.S. sector and the Soviet sector were divergent battlefields on which the MLMs and their hosts engaged on a daily basis. Multiple mutually supporting battles are referred to as a campaign. A review of the MLM era discloses that USAREUR viewed USMLM and SMLM-F as two interrelated but separate battles, while the Soviets viewed them as a campaign.

Although the Huebner–Malinin Agreement and the two agreements establishing the other MLMs were intended to extend the same privileges to each of the MLMs, there was not true quid pro quo among the MLMs—unless the Soviets allowing USMLM to collect aggressively could be considered as "quid pro quo" for having tolerated incidents of surveillance, rammings, and shootings.

One perception that developed over time was that the dynamic in the Soviet sector was tantamount to the "wild, wild west" and the one in the U.S. sector was a relative "sleepy hollow." As this model would suggest, the large majority of the USAREUR and GSFG time, effort, and resources were dedicated to activities in the Soviet sector, and relatively little in the U.S. sector. If it were ever the Soviets' intent to keep the spotlight shining on USMLM and allow SMLM-F to "fly below the radar," then they orchestrated that scenario to perfection.

To USAREUR, the Huebner–Malinin Agreement equated to little more than a unique intelligence-collection opportunity that needed to be sustained at virtually all costs. Although the relationship was one of hosting an MLM and operating an MLM, USAREUR was a largely disinterested caretaker to the former and strong champion of the latter. Perhaps the Soviets helped shape this perspective.

The Focus on USMLM and the SMLM-F Anomaly

During the initial years, SMLM-F operated and collected intelligence very aggressively in comparison to USMLM, which began in a relatively measured manner. This model changed diametrically by 1954, and within the next few years, USMLM developed into an overt intelligence-collection machine, while SMLM-F had settled into a much less active routine of touring. Based on the disparity of operating models, and the fact that USMLM could maintain a "fresh bench" of tour officers and vehicles at its West Berlin sanctuary location, SMLM-F could not sustain the same tempo of operations—even if their intelligence-collection taskings required that level of activity. Over time, SMLM-F established a pattern of touring just enough to demonstrate that they cared, but not much more. By the 1980s, the effort SMLM-F dedicated to overt HUMINT touring was less than 10 percent of the effort relative to USMLM. However, the Soviets tolerated this disparity for various unknown, but conceivable reasons.

The highly disparate risk environments among which the U.S. and Soviets operated essentially ensured that the focus was almost always on the Soviet sector. The Soviets (with East German support) effectively perpetuated a relatively chaotic game of cat and mouse that kept all eyes focused on USMLM, and consequently off SMLM-F through the years. USAREUR allowed high-risk incidents to continue through the years in order to enable USMLM collection access in East Germany to continue, which was obviously apparent to the Soviets. By establishing, through repetition, competitive norms which enabled high-visibility incidents to recur on a regular basis, the Soviets were able to ensure that USAREUR's attention remained almost exclusively on USMLM.

One event that made it very evident that the Soviets understood and accepted this gross inequity was a January 1980 conversation between the CUSMLM and the CSERB regarding a detention of a SMLM-F vehicle while violating a PRA. While discussing the incident the CUSMLM intimated that the USAREUR Chief of Staff was unhappy with the SMLM-F PRA violation and provided a written statement from the Deputy Chief of Staff stating that they had considered escalating the issue but chose not to in the spirit of good relations. The SERB official dismissed the threat as ridiculous and asserted that if the U.S. was attempting to compare the activities of SMLM-F with USMLM, then SMLM-F was "on a scale of one to a hundred as far as activeness," and that SMLM-F would never be able to tour as much and as hard as USMLM. The SERB official concluded by reminding the USMLM official that this had been the first detention of SMLM-F in "ages," which was far from the case as it applied to USMLM detentions: there were 21 USMLM detentions in the previous year of 1979. Further increasing the disparity in "activeness" that the Soviets were willing to accept, the Soviet MLMs were spread among the three Allied sectors (at 96,000 square miles) while the three Allied MLMs were concentrated in the single Soviet sector (at 42,000 square miles).

Once the Soviets allowed USMLM to exploit their West Berlin base of operations to gain a significant advantage in their capacity and capability to conduct tours, there was a tendency to view this as a binary condition that the Soviets simply conceded. In reality, however, the Soviets could have achieved relative equity in a manner for which the U.S. would have had no basis to argue, due to the precedent established by USMLM. SMLM-F could have implemented an operational process similar to the one USMLM employed. If the Soviets had chosen to resource SMLM-F for this type of collection mission in the manner that the U.S. did USMLM, they could have established a base in East Germany along the inner German border across from the U.S. sector. SMLM-F could have launched one-, two-, three-, or four-day tours out of the Frankfurt compound which could have ended by entering into the East Germany compound, where they could simply transfer license plates to another tour vehicle and accreditation documents to a fresh tour officer and tour driver to launch a tour back into the U.S. sector. In fact, if they had employed this similar USMLM methodology and changed their designated inter-sector crossing point farther south toward the Czechoslovakian border, this would have placed their tour start point much closer to the two primary training ranges—Grafenwoehr in particular. The fact that this would have been a feasible option was acknowledged during numerous meetings among USMLM and SERB, wherein SERB regularly complained about the practice of liberally exchanging accreditation documents, to which USMLM responded that this was a "self-imposed" constraint that the Soviets chose to operate under.

Although never considered at the time because they were viewed as binary operations, the Soviets, who significantly overmatched the West in virtually all aspects of HUMINT collection during the Cold War, consciously chose not to do so in the case of their MLMs. Although the Soviets could have chosen to even the odds by resourcing SMLM-F to an equitable level, they did not. This was an anomaly, but it also fed a certain narrative. The Soviets and their East German partners resourced an extensive monitoring and surveillance process against USMLM while placing no importance behind establishing a touring capability anywhere close to the USMLM gold-standard. It was very clear, in retrospect, where they wanted the attention of all involved focused.

Whether orchestrated by the Soviets or simply fortuitous in its development, the highly disparate risk environments among which the U.S. and Soviets operated resulted in USAREUR leadership attention being almost exclusively focused on the Soviet sector, relative to the U.S. sector. Although there are many additional examples, the two fatalities occurring during the 43-year history occurred within nearly a year of each other in 1984 and 1985, and reflected the contrasting risk environments among that in which SMLM-F operated and that in which USMLM operated. As it applied to the divergent risk environments, it was the competitive norms that really got to the game within the game, and could suggest that the competitive dynamics that evolved over time may have been part of a larger Soviet strategy.

The Soviets regularly contended that incidents occurring in the Soviet sector were caused by USMLM instigation and even the extreme measures of gunfire and vehicle rammings were appropriate countermeasures given the "undisciplined" USMLM tour personnel. Therefore, from a legal precedent standpoint, it could be validly argued that the U.S. allowed such dangerous and eventually life-ending incidents to become tacitly recognized norms, by allowing them to continue without a protest that would seriously threaten the sustainment of the Huebner–Malinin Agreement. By establishing a narrative which enabled such high-visibility incidents to recur on a regular basis, attention remained almost exclusively on USMLM. Conversely, even though SMLM-F toured with an understanding that they did not risk being rammed or shot at, or even detained unless they allowed themselves to become vulnerable when blatantly violating a restricted area, this relatively low risk of physical harm did not appear to increase SMLM-F propensity to tour more aggressively, as might have been expected.

Accepting Surveillance

Another aspect that helped to keep the focus on USMLM and not cast suspicions on SMLM-F was the Soviet treatment of the topic of U.S. surveillance as taboo. SMLM-F certainly detected indications of and observed surveillance by U.S. Counterintelligence, but they never protested these actions after the 1952 moratorium. One feasible explanation would be that they did not want to create any perceptions that they had anything to hide.

It is virtually impossible to conduct an extended physical surveillance of a hard target without detection, or at least the target observing indicators of surveillance prior to a surveillance element terminating the surveillance to avoid a complete compromise. Over the course of the years, SMLM-F certainly detected the presence of intended covert surveillance by Det A on multiple occasions. It is also very possible that Det A radio transmissions were detected by SMLM-F SIGINT due to the proximity to the compound when initiating surveillance operations. However, the only surveillance activity protested by SMLM-F as incidents of surveillance were reports of military units conducting overt surveillance of SMLM-F vehicles, which, as CACS would explain to CSMLM-F, did so spontaneously and without any USAREUR direction.

SMLM-F understood that the West Germans did not monitor their travel. Since U.S. Counterintelligence only conducted surveillance of tours, and never surveilled SMLM-F when conducting non-tour activities (until the final year), the Soviets would have never detected any indications of surveillance when on non-tour travels, which must have eventually given them high confidence that their activities in such circumstances were not monitored. However, based on Soviet tradecraft at the time, SMLM-F would not have needed to rely purely on their own instincts regarding the possibility of U.S. or West German surveillance when conducting non-tour travel, usually in the greater Frankfurt area. Had SMLM-F been involved in clandestine or covert activities, the Soviets maintained a vast support infrastructure that would have operated to confirm that SMLM-F was not under surveillance when conducting these activities. Therefore, SMLM-F would have established over the years that there was periodic surveillance of tours and no indications to suggest that their non-tour activities were monitored.

In the spy/counterspy world, being observed being surveillance conscious is tantamount to admitting guilt regarding an act in progress. Similarly, complaining about perceived surveillance may be interpreted as a concern voiced by someone who has something to hide. Although SMLM-F tours would "switch on" and conduct surveillance detection and antisurveillance maneuvers, it would have probably been more conspicuous if they had not done so, and was perhaps an effort to demonstrate that their heart was actually in the game. Again, as it applies to the spy game, one should only be concerned with surveillance if they have something to hide. Perhaps avoiding the discussion of any surveillance concerns by SMLM-F was intended to project the sensing that they had nothing to hide. Perhaps there was little regard for any surveillance detected during touring, because that is not what really needed to be hidden.

Mirror Imaging

One of the more intriguing elements of the USMLM and East German dynamic was the Stasi obsession with detecting USMLM involvement in clandestine intelligence or covert operations. Despite the obsessive and immersive surveillance state efforts against USMLM, as of 1986, the Stasi reported that they found no solid evidence of USMLM conducting "espionage" or other clandestine activities. Although USAREUR was very aware that the Stasi's compulsive belief that USMLM was involved in clandestine activities and "espionage" was unfounded based on reality, USAREUR analysts simply attributed this to Stasi paranoia and never considered that the Stasi might have been guilty of an intelligence analysis shortfall referred to as "mirror imaging." Mirror imaging is the tendency for analysts to fill gaps in their own knowledge by assuming that the adversary is likely to act in a certain way because that is how their side would think and act. In the case of possible Stasi mirror imaging, if they had insights regarding the manner in which SMLM-F was operating in the U.S. sector, they might have assumed that USMLM was operating in a similar manner. A plausible explanation for this was that they were aware of SMLM-F activities being undertaken that would give them similar concerns regarding USMLM "espionage."

If this were a case of mirror imaging, then it was probably not the only one. The USAREUR perspective of the MLM dynamic was based on the USMLM focus on intelligence collection. This apparently led to a USAREUR counterintelligence approach to SMLM-F that tended to mirror image this perspective, simply assuming that SMLM-F was less aggressive in conducting these threat activities due to the perceived limitations that did not similarly constrain USMLM. In reality, 100 percent of the time spent by USMLM in the Soviet sector consisted of multiple 24/7 tour operations, and then the relatively few official engagements. Alternatively, SMLM-F spent no more than 25 percent of their time on tour operations, and generally only dedicated two of its 14 members to that mission at any given time. So, in relative terms, SMLM-F only dedicated a fraction of its effort to intelligence-collection tours and a much smaller fraction of their time to touring in comparison to USMLM—less than 10 percent of USMLM's efforts by even the most liberal calculations. Further factoring in that an eight- to nine-hour SMLM-F tour would only include about two to three hours at the most looking for military activities of interest, it is clear that SMLM-F personnel spent more time off the compound conducting non-tour activity than was actually spent conducting overt collection. Therefore, to apply a tour-only-monitoring counterintelligence approach to SMLM-F because USAREUR had a tour-only collection threat mentality based on USMLM, was the wrong image to mirror.

Refusing Surveillance

The West German BfV was not nearly as immersive and repressive as their Stasi counterpart in East Germany, but had they been asked and authorized to monitor SMLM-F activities when off the compound and to identify visitors to the compound, they would have done so with the same rigor with which they monitored other Soviet presences (e.g., embassy, consulates) on West German soil, which was relatively thorough. The U.S. decision to preclude West German assistance began as one of an occupying power exercising its authority, but eventually became a precautionary position having seen the aggression of the Stasi and wanting to avoid "unleashing" the West Germans on SMLM-F at the risk of the Soviets terminating the Huebner–Malinin Agreement. Ultimately, however, the U.S. decision to deal unilaterally with SMLM-F above the heads of the West German government resulted in a significant information gap regarding the actual activities of SMLM-F. It was also very unfortunate that the West Germans were compelled to acquiesce to the U.S. position that SMLM-F would be a U.S.-only problem, because they very likely assumed that the U.S. was exercising the level of diligence that they would themselves against a known extension of an existential threat on its soil; but this was not the case.

Whereas the East German approach to USMLM was a whole-of-sector counterintelligence methodology, the U.S. approach was to maintain one dedicated counterintelligence capability as the primary action arm. This U.S. approach was the most effective means to ensure that the surveillance of SMLM-F tours remained covert and less detectable, but was not effective in maintaining visibility on SMLM-F activities writ large.

The limitations in not having a larger support capability for U.S. surveillance operations was only marginally mitigated with the implementation of mobile telephone technology in the mid-1980s, which enabled Det A surveillance operations to benefit from near-real-time sighting reports relayed by USCF. This highlights the self-imposed limitations in comparison to the East Germans who employed a nationally integrated monitoring and communications capability throughout the entire MLM era. Det A operated as a single, autonomous element tracking SMLM-F tours throughout the U.S. sector of West Germany, with the various challenges this methodology posed, such as the multiple changes of "socks" for each callsign for every operation. However, this did compel Det A to develop a surveillance capability to conduct covert, independent operations, which would provide a strong basis if Det A ever needed to develop a full-spectrum capability to conduct sensitive counterespionage surveillance operations.

The First Reflections

First and foremost, the evolution of MLM cooperative norms demonstrated that intelligence collection was a mutually accepted practice. The mutual MLM culture even used a bland term (touring) to avoid having to characterize the actual practice of intelligence collection, while accepting it for what it was. However, even with the practice of intelligence collection, the two sides differed significantly. USMLM became among the most prolific intelligence-collection elements in DoD history, while SMLM-F was focused less so on touring, but perhaps more so on something else.

Based on USMLM collection operations and the USMLM/Soviet/East German dynamic in the Soviet sector in general, USAREUR attention was largely focused in this direction, certainly in comparison to the relatively benign SMLM-F. Allowing this mutually recognized level of inequity, which a Soviet representative characterized as "on a scale of one to a hundred," ran counter to how the Soviets did business, unless there was some form of "equity" that was not apparent. The

Soviets (and their East German partners) expended considerable resources in their daily cat-and-mouse games with USMLM, while placing relatively little importance behind establishing a touring capability anywhere near the magnitude of the USMLM gold-standard.

The DCSINT USAREUR, who benefited greatly from the intelligence collected by USMLM, was also the individual and staff element responsible for countering the intelligence-collection activities of SMLM-F. The effectiveness of an intelligence-collection program is very evident in the amount and quality of reporting. A counterintelligence program, on the other hand, is effective when nothing is happening, meaning that it will go relatively unnoticed until something bad happens. This dynamic led to the natural tendency for DCSINT USAREUR to only take actions which would maximize the effectiveness of its most prolific intelligence-collection element, and not take actions that would impact the quantity and quality of USMLM intelligence reporting. This resulted in a perpetuation of the opinion that if nothing "bad" was happening in regard to SMLM-F, that everything was status quo, which was "good" in that it did not need to impact activities on the USMLM side of the curtain. One of the great ironies that emerged was that while the Stasi maintained a compulsive belief that the Allied MLMs were involved in clandestine intelligence activities, they were not; but in contrast—and while long-ignored during the MLM era—there was much more evidence to suggest that the SMLMs were involved in covert/clandestine activities than evidence to the contrary.

Due to USAREUR's recognition that there was a vast inequity of intelligence-collection capability, and the concern that the Soviets would be justified in citing this as the reason for discontinuing MLM operations, the U.S. employed a relatively hands-off approach to SMLM-F. USAREUR placed an obvious priority on USMLM collection over any counterintelligence or other activities that could upset the Soviets and cause a negative reaction that might disrupt the highly effective intelligence collection of USMLM. With the possible exception of the reaction to the Nicholson shooting, which was more political theater than practical measure, USAREUR did very little to reciprocate against SMLM-F for very aggressive and hazardous Soviet and East German actions against USMLM. The U.S.'s relative hands-off approach and refusal to request West German support in monitoring SMLM-F activities resulted in a counterintelligence vulnerability that went unaddressed for 40 years during the Cold War. If there was any benefit that the Soviets might have gained which would justify the inequity of intelligence collection that played out in the overt worlds of the MLMs, it was a graciously granted degree of freedom of movement in the U.S. sector that was a near-polar opposite to what USMLM was subjected to by the Stasi surveillance state methodology. This freedom included access to large urban areas, which was a reflection that was largely lost in the MLM "wilderness of mirrors."

For USAREUR to sheepishly stand by thinking that they were taking advantage of the Soviets' good will to allow USMLM to collect aggressively with no relative reciprocity, was to completely neglect the Soviet mindset. The dichotomy among USMLM and SMLM-F touring activities, which the Soviets continued to allow, always suggested that there must have been some benefit SMLM-F was realizing that would justify such an apparent imbalance of benefits. However, the U.S.'s myopic fixation on USMLM collection enabled the real dichotomy to go virtually unnoticed, because it was so unlike the manner which USMLM operated. Sometimes analysts should compare apples and oranges if it helps them to avoid mirror imaging.

Perhaps the most confounding manifestations was the flawed U.S. perspective that SMLM-F posed the same type of intelligence-collection threat to USAREUR that USMLM posed to GSFG. Looking at this mirror image resulted in a counterintelligence approach that focused 100 percent of the counterintelligence effort on 10 percent of SMLM-F activities, relative to USMLM. In comparison to the 14-person SMLM-F and the other two SMLMs which did not even maintain their fully authorized personnel strengths, the U.S. and Allied MLMs appeared to have drastically overmatched the Soviets in terms of HUMINT collection capabilities. However, had U.S. Counterintelligence considered reflections other than the one in the mirror image, they might have realized that the staffing levels of the SMLMs were actually relatively robust in terms of GRU residencies with highly trained clandestine HUMINT case officers who were in very high-demand globally.

Had the Soviets intended to allow USMLM to prosper while lulling USAREUR into a false sense of counterintelligence security in regard to SMLM-F for a larger purpose, then they succeeded. However, it would have been inconvenient and probably considered delusional to have given the Soviets that much credit for being capable of orchestrating such a "grand strategy." Rather than blindly pushing forward under the belief that the MLMs were somehow uncharacteristic of the larger game, the USAREUR DCSINT and supporting intelligence and counterintelligence elements should have been studying what was going on in the world around them.

PART II

THE WILDERNESS OF MIRRORS

CHAPTER 3

The Strategic Wilderness of Mirrors

To fully analyze and understand the East-versus-West intelligence and counterintelligence battle in Cold War Europe and among the MLMs, it is important to understand the paralleling strategic context of which DoD counterintelligence, intelligence, and the MLMs were a microcosm. A perspective regarding the strategic "wilderness of mirrors" demonstrates how the MLM saga was also its own such wilderness, and how DoD Counterintelligence needed to separate itself from the larger failed system in order to operate effectively. This strategic view also demonstrates how many of the more intriguing episodes involving U.S. and Soviet espionage and disinformation were interwoven and remain mysteries to this day, as do many surrounding the Soviet MLMs.

An examination of the strategic competitive landscape among the U.S. and Soviet Bloc throughout the Cold War demonstrates very clearly who fared best—at least based on what is known history. Although the U.S. had some intelligence and counterintelligence successes during this period, the Soviets won the spy/counterspy battle due to an effective Soviet grand strategy, a failed U.S. strategy, a centralized Soviet system control, the weaker defenses of the U.S., and in some cases, perhaps pure luck. Irrefutably, Soviet intelligence and counterintelligence dominated the landscape until the end of the Cold War. The downside to this for the Soviets, however, was that stealing their way through the Cold War rather than innovating their way through it was ultimately not a winning strategy. Regardless, the tangled web of Soviet espionage and disinformation that should have become very apparent from the initial and most damaging of all compromises—the disclosure of nuclear designs to the Soviets by spies inside the U.S. nuclear weapons program—continued to degrade and deceive U.S. counterintelligence, at least until a brief reemergence in the mid-1980s among DoD counterintelligence elements.

James Angleton, the long-standing CIA Chief of Counterintelligence during the Cold War, is credited with devising the concept of the "wilderness of mirrors," referring to the confusion of the world of intelligence and espionage. The term wilderness of mirrors is a cliché for counterintelligence in general and more specifically an idiosyncratic view of Soviet operations where facts and illusions merge to confuse U.S. counterintelligence activities. According to the originator of the concept, this wilderness was the myriad of stratagems, deceptions, artifices, and all other devices of disinformation which the Soviet Bloc and its coordinated intelligence services used to confuse the West.

When two mirrors face each other, they reflect against each other again and again into infinity. The wilderness of mirrors dictates that when an intelligence service has an agent, it must assume that the adversary has doubled him back, and analyze the information provided as potential disinformation, and if so, what the endgame of the disinformation may be. In turn, the doubling intelligence service must assume that the agent was always intended to be doubled back, or has been doubled back again, and so on. In this wilderness, any defector or volunteer must be assumed to be a potential disinformation agent or agent provocateur, their information must be analyzed from the standpoint of where it is intended to lead the opposing intelligence agency, and what the ultimate objective might be. With each additional mirror added, it then becomes increasingly difficult to know where the next reflection begins, and where that one ends. Against the complex and centrally orchestrated Soviet intelligence, counterintelligence, and disinformation apparatus, in that wilderness of mirrors, it was only known where the first reflection of intrigue began, but rarely where the last one ended. During the Cold War, U.S. intelligence agencies constantly found themselves walking through virtual houses of mirrors.

The Cold War wilderness of mirrors was played out on battlefields best characterized as chessboards. The game of chess has always been symbolic of political and military confrontation, with its gambits, stalemates, sacrifices, and endgames being played out among two opponents facing each from opposing sides of the board. During the Cold War, the chessboard was a metaphor for the battlefields of espionage and intrigue.

The game of chess played a particularly significant role in Soviet society and helped to shape the Soviet world view and its persistent competition with the West. The game had long been a passion of Russia's intelligentsia and elite, but in the Soviet era it was nationalized. The aura of chess epitomized the official image that the Soviet Union aspired to project of a government and military made up of serious, logical, rigorous, and scientifically minded leaders. As one of the only sanctioned, unpoliced arenas of intellectual and creative activity, the game flourished. During the formative 25 years of the Cold War, the USSR produced an unbroken line of 10 chess world champions between 1948 and 1972.

Chess strategy consists of setting and achieving long-term goals during the game, while tactics concentrate on immediate maneuvers to advance toward the endgame objectives. However, these two levels of game play are intrinsically interconnected because strategic goals are mostly achieved by the means of tactics, while the tactical opportunities are based on the guiding game strategy. Chess strategy is concerned with the evaluation of chess positions and with setting up goals and long-term plans for future play. Tactical moves are largely tradeoff decisions based on various factors to include the value of the pieces on the board. As history demonstrated, the Soviets viewed the adversary as rooks, bishops, knights, and pawns on the board, and even viewed their own pieces as expendable assets when the tactical losses supported their larger strategy.

So the games begin.

The Demise of U.S. Counterintelligence

Immediately after World War II, the Soviets were very quick to pick their battles in the intelligence and counterintelligence arenas—which largely became the battlefields of the Cold War. The Soviets set the standard for the wilderness of mirrors through the manipulation of the Western intelligence services during the formative years of that war.

Heinz Felfe was the first, and most impactful example of the Soviets' use of appropriately placed assets to misinform, deceive, and misdirect Western intelligence and counterintelligence on a grand scale. Felfe served as a Nazi intelligence officer during the war, and after working briefly as a British agent, was recruited by the Soviets in 1951. Two months after his formal recruitment by Soviet intelligence, Felfe was accepted into the U.S.-sponsored intelligence agency that was the predecessor to the German Federal Intelligence Service, the Bundesnachrichtendienst (BND). To accelerate Felfe's rise through the ranks of the BND, the Soviet KGB undertook elaborate operations designed specifically to support Felfe's usefulness and credibility in the eyes of his supervisors. In, 1955, Felfe became the deputy chief in charge of counterintelligence operations against the Soviets.

Felfe also became the most knowledgeable West German official regarding CIA operations in Eastern Europe. He personally lobbied for West German involvement in CIA operations during a visit to the CIA Counterintelligence headquarters in the U.S. in 1956. To solidify his bona fides with the Americans, Felfe provided the CIA information regarding low-level intelligence sources deliberately provided by the Soviets as bait. One of the many projects compromised by Felfe concerned CIA operations run from its Berlin station against the Soviet military and intelligence headquarters in East Germany. By 1958, the Soviets, with Felfe's help, planted "dummy" sources in the intelligence headquarters who fed disinformation to their CIA handlers.

Felfe was not the only intelligence hemorrhage impacting U.S. operations in West Germany at the time. George Blake was a British Secret Intelligence Service (SIS) agent supporting the British Army in the Korean War who was captured and became indoctrinated to Communism while in a North Korean prisoner of war camp. Sometime prior to his release in 1953, he volunteered his services to the Soviets. Blake was welcomed back into the SIS as a returning war hero and resumed work at the SIS HQ in London. In 1953, Blake compromised the British intelligence operation in Allied-occupied Austria that covertly tapped into the landline communications of the Soviet Army headquarters in Vienna, which ran from 1949 to 1955. To protect their valued agent, the KGB allowed the operation to continue to collect until the operation was ended when Austria regained full sovereignty in 1955. Again in 1954, Blake compromised a joint operation conducted by the CIA and the British SIS to tap into landline communications of the Soviet Army headquarters in Berlin using a tunnel into the Soviet-occupied zone. In 1955, Blake was assigned to the SIS Berlin office, which was fortuitous for the Soviets but did present some challenges. To protect Blake from becoming a potential suspect for the compromise of the Berlin tunnel operation, the Soviets waited to "discover" the tunnel in April 1956 when heavy rains and flooding provided a plausible explanation for Soviet engineers to happen on the site. In addition to the Berlin tunnel, Blake compromised a well-placed CIA agent, GRU Lieutenant Colonel Pyotr Popov, who was the only other clandestine source for Soviet military information from 1956 until his arrest in 1959. Like the Berlin tunnel project, the KGB allowed Popov to operate while providing highly sensitive information to protect Blake until they could fabricate a narrative to distance Popov's discovery from their valued Berlin SIS agent. In 1960, Popov was executed by the oft-repeated method that Russians euphemistically referred to as "*vyshaya mera*"—the highest measure of punishment—which in the Stalinist tradition the condemned person is taken into a room, made to kneel, and then shot in the back of the head. Until Blake departed the Berlin office in 1960, he was viewed by his supervisors as a highly productive agent, but much of his apparent success was due to the information provided to him by the KGB, which was intended to perpetuate the façade that he was a loyal and dedicated servant to the crown.

In 1959, a volunteer referring to himself as "Sniper" offered his services to U.S. intelligence. In 1960, Sniper reported that he had overheard the KGB chief of counterintelligence boast that two of the six BND officers who had visited the U.S. in 1956 at CIA expense were Soviet agents. This information led to the November 1961 arrest of Felfe.

After Felfe's arrest, his compromises led the West German intelligence and security services to assume that the majority of their sources in East Germany were compromised and under hostile control. Due to Felfe's damage, the West German counterintelligence and intelligence services did not know if any of their spies or other sources of intelligence could be trusted to provide credible information. The CIA estimated in its 1963 damage assessment that Felfe, from his position within the BND, was able to compromise most counterespionage operations against the Soviet intelligence agencies.

The damage that Felfe's treachery inflicted on U.S. counterintelligence and intelligence operations during this formative decade of the Cold War was extremely damaging by itself. As though this were not bad enough, as fate would have it, the Felfe legacy would also have a psychological impact that would essentially cripple U.S. counterintelligence for decades to come.

The Beginning of the End

In addition to exposing Felfe, the source known as Sniper provided information on a three-person ring, referred to as the "Admiralty Ring," that was passing British naval intelligence to the KGB. The British allowed this relatively low-level ring to operate to protect Sniper from any suspicion. This caution was not enough, however, as at the same time George Blake was providing information to the KGB regarding a mole in Polish intelligence with access to KGB operations, which began the intensive hunt for Sniper. In late 1960, Sniper contacted his CIA handlers and informed them that he needed to defect. When Sniper crossed into Berlin in January 1961, he was identified for the first time as Michael Goleniewski, a high-ranking officer in Polish intelligence who had also worked as a Soviet agent reporting to the KGB on anything his fellow Poles might try to hide from their Russian masters—meaning that he had technically been a triple agent. In January 1961, with Goleniewski safely in hand, Scotland Yard rolled up the Admiralty Ring. Also in 1961, Goleniewski provided the lead that resulted in the arrest and conviction of George Blake.

In addition to specific operations Goleniewski reported on, he was also the first to describe the Soviets' grand "strategic deception" apparatus, the aura of which would shape the U.S.'s Cold War psyche. He reported that the KGB had managed a significant disinformation operation since 1953 and that it had formally created a disinformation department by the late 1950s. Goleniewski's revelations regarding the Soviet disinformation methodology was the genesis of the "wilderness of mirrors," which was described as follows: by penetrating the CIA and other Western intelligence services, the Soviets could do far more than just spy on them; the moles would serve a second role as agents of influence, sowing deceptions to enable Moscow to manipulate those services, and by extension, their governments; fake defectors would peddle phony intelligence, support each other's bona fides, backstop operations the West was running unaware that they were bad, and send its spy hunters down false trails; meanwhile, the moles inside would report back on how the false information was being received in the targeted services; Moscow Center would then fine tune the message and continue the cycle. This process came to be known as the "deception theory."

In addition to the elaborate strategy, Goleniewski confided that one of the many objectives of KGB disinformation was the protection of Soviet agents by means of actions designed to mislead Western security services. He listed among the specific objectives and types of disinformation operations those designed to discredit accurate information of significance received by the opposition through sources not under Soviet control, such as defectors, thus casting doubt on the veracity of the source of the true information. Goleniewski attested that in extreme cases, the KGB would be willing to sacrifice some of its own agent assets to enhance the credibility of an agent penetration of a Western intelligence service.

Augmenting this revelatory information regarding the Soviets' grand strategy, Goleniewski injected a germ in the body of the CIA that would become a debilitating disease. He was the first to assert that there was a mole in the CIA, claiming that the Soviets talked as though they had penetrated the agency. Goleniewski was convinced that he was compromised by this mole and that he had barely eluded arrest and a death sentence. Most experts assess that it was the British traitor, Blake, who compromised the asset formally known as Sniper. However, this would not negate the possibility that there was a mole in the CIA as well.

The Deception Theory

In December 1961, a mid-level KGB staff officer named Anatoliy Golitsyn defected to the CIA while stationed in Helsinki, Finland. Golitsyn was the first KGB staffer to defect since 1954 and the CIA had not had a well-placed Soviet source since Popov in 1959. In addition, since the credibility of much of the information Popov provided had come under question, not knowing exactly when he was compromised by Blake, the information provided by Golitsyn was considered valuable in the absence of other comparable (or verifiable) intelligence. However, the reason that Golitsyn was to become such a pivotal figure in Cold War spy/counterspy history was not any specific intelligence he provided, but rather, his professed understanding of the Soviet "grand strategy." Golitsyn's depiction of the Soviet espionage and disinformation system confirmed Goleniewski's characterization, but on a much grander scale. Golitsyn's 1961 defection also occurred just one month after Felfe's arrest, and it was his contention that the Felfe model was characteristic of the Soviets' approach of attacking the U.S. intelligence system that sent a shockwave through the counterintelligence community. This narrative regarding a complex and sophisticated Soviet apparatus resonated with one senior CIA official in particular.

James Angleton, the Director of CIA Counterintelligence for 20 years, from 1954 to 1974, is the most iconic figure in the history of U.S. counterintelligence. During this critical period of the Cold War, Angleton wielded immense authority over operations against the Soviet Union. Angleton became convinced early in his career that the KGB had successfully run major deception operations against the West in general, and against the U.S. in particular, for many years. Golitsyn's description of the Soviet disinformation apparatus served to solidify Angleton's predisposition to believe the KGB had made multiple senior-level penetrations of the CIA, and was aggressively and successfully conducting provocations and major deception operations against U.S. intelligence. Golitsyn elaborated on the espionage work of Felfe and cited his methods of using his high placement in the organization to feed disinformation and protect Soviet intelligence operations as the master Soviet

James Angleton, CIA Counterintelligence Director from 1954 to 1974. (Wikimedia Commons)

model of disinformation and manipulation. He provided analysis of KGB deception operations against the Western allies that meshed completely with Angleton's theories. Golitsyn posited the theory that the Soviets had penetrated all the Western intelligence services and encouraged suspicions that there were high-ranking spies planted in virtually every agency.

As the architect of the wilderness of mirrors concept, James Angleton espoused the deception theory as a key concept of Soviet disinformation and deception efforts. This theory (actually practice) involved the abstract calculus of Cold War double-cross, with the placement of false agents within enemy ranks, and the planting of false information with enemy intelligence analysts. Although referred to as a theory, influence operations consistent with the deception theory had historically been effectively employed by intelligence services—most notably by those of the Soviet Bloc. Central to this theory was that there must be an apparently credible line of communications to the target intelligence service by the one perpetrating the deception and manipulation. Angleton came to view all volunteers and defectors as channels by which the Soviets ventured to establish "credible" lines of communications through which to pass disinformation.

In addition to the first credible line of communications, for the deception theory to succeed, there must be a second channel (verification channel) through which the perpetrating intelligence service receives feedback to confirm that the operation is having the intended result, and ensure that it is not the service being deceived. With this verification and feedback loop, the perpetrating intelligence service can amplify or reinforce the parts of the story the opposing intelligence service is prone to believe, and eliminate or revise those that are doubted. The end effect is that intelligence analysts adopt the narrative that the perpetrating intelligence service intended as the deception. When effectively employed, the "deceived" intelligence agency becomes its own deceiver.

The wilderness of mirrors dictates that a false defector or volunteer will need to provide some credible information to establish their bona fides as a legitimate spy. The credible information may be intended to misdirect the intelligence service or to convince the intelligence service to accept disinformation after it is verified that the agent had in fact provided credible information. Therefore, the challenge with assessing the validity of any defector or volunteer in this wilderness is to determine where their credible (verifiable) information may end, and where their potentially non-credible (non-verifiable) information may begin. As a means of misdirection, an intelligence service may deploy an agent to provide credible information that compromises a legitimate agent/activity to protect a more valuable agent/activity. In addition, the opposing intelligence service may provide information through other sources or undertake activities to bolster the credibility of a given source.

The Felfe model was a severely damaging demonstration of the deception theory in practice. The KGB's protection and bolstering of George Blake was a further demonstration that the agency would surrender valuable information and allow damaging operations to continue to protect its valuable sources, and its deception theory channels of communication.

When Cold War Counterintelligence Was Doomed to Fail

Angleton became convinced that the KGB had penetrated the CIA at high levels and that it had taken advantage of these penetrations to successfully run agent provocations against the agency. In the end, Angleton took the position that virtually every major Soviet defector or volunteer was a KGB provocation, a position that essentially paralyzed CIA operational efforts against the Soviet Union during his tenure, and well beyond. The CIA refused to accept KGB and GRU defectors who were later determined to have been bona fide volunteers. In some cases, the CIA reacted to these efforts in a manner which directly exposed them to the KGB and resulted in their arrests and deaths by *vyshaya mera*. This sent a very clear signal to any potential KGB or GRU volunteer that any attempt to cooperate with U.S. intelligence was a death sentence. In one case, the CIA's negligence not only resulted in the execution of a KGB illegal who attempted to defect, but a subsequent study concluded that the genuine would-be defector would have enabled the U.S. to discover and manipulate an entire network of Soviet agents.

One ironic factor regarding the Golitsyn saga was that he, himself, was a defector. Despite this glaring contradiction, he successfully convinced the highest echelons of U.S. Counterintelligence that no Soviet defectors could be trusted. He further insulated himself from scrutiny by professing that at least one defector would be sent to attempt and discredit his theories. As was destined to eventually feed into the Golitsyn narrative, KGB Lieutenant Colonel Yuri Nosenko volunteered his services to the CIA in 1962 and defected in 1964, becoming the first and most notorious case of Angleton's acceptance of Golitsyn's advice to refuse to accept the bona fides of other high-level Soviet defectors. Of course, Golitsyn advised Angleton that Nosenko displayed all the attributes of a Soviet provocation, and Angleton agreed.

Due to the paranoid and distrustful approach to Nosenko, he was confined and periodically subjected to hostile interrogations for four years. Despite much contradicting evidence, Angleton remained steadfast in his position that Nosenko was a plant, and even concealed many solid leads provided by the KGB defector from CIA colleagues and other U.S. allies. Again, even if a defector is an agent provocateur, he can be expected to provide some accurate information to establish credibility.

Nosenko was released from detention in October 1968, and the CIA eventually accepted his bona fides as a valid defector. Strong arguments continued to be made by experts, to include the CIA agent responsible for Nosenko's investigation, that Nosenko was sent with some good information to make his disinformation more readily accepted. Whether Nosenko was a legitimate defector will likely never be definitively known, but regardless, the defection and its aftermath were largely attributable to 21-year lull in KGB and GRU defections to the U.S. Nosenko's mistreatment certainly sent the message to any KGB or GRU officers who might have considered defecting that the U.S. was inept in such cases and could not be trusted. After Nosenko's 1964 defection, there was not another attempted defection to the U.S. by an agent of either the KGB or GRU until 1985.

The Void in U.S. Counterintelligence Perpetuates

When Angleton's reign as the most powerful person in U.S. Counterintelligence was finally terminated in 1974, the CIA's counterintelligence program went into a different type of tailspin. Several official post-mortems on Angleton's tenure and on specific cases handled under his supervision were exceptionally critical, and soon an anti-Angleton orthodoxy emerged. The CIA overreacted to Angleton's excesses by diminishing the importance of counterintelligence and security. Due to the negative perceptions, the counterintelligence program's staff personnel and budgets were slashed and much of their responsibilities were dispersed among other divisions. New officers on the staff generally had less counterintelligence experience than those who worked there before. The counterintelligence staff was not where up-and-coming officers wanted to work, and enforcement of security rules waned. This negative dynamic had cascading impacts on all U.S. counterintelligence agencies, to include DoD Counterintelligence in Europe. After having been doomed to fail by the Angleton era and its aftermath, U.S. Counterintelligence was never reconstructed during the Cold War.

Leading to the Year of the Spy

After the near collapse of U.S. Counterintelligence during and post Angleton, once the policy of viewing every would-be volunteer or defector as an agent provocateur was discontinued, the intelligence community realized a very intuitive result. In contrast to its counterintelligence program, the CIA began to more quickly and effectively recover its clandestine HUMINT program. With a new perspective, the CIA began developing sources who could do what counterintelligence programs were unable to do, which was to provide actionable counterintelligence leads. However, this short-lived period of success ended abruptly.

During the Cold War, the KGB and GRU transitioned their agent recruitment tactics based on the adapting motivations of their Western targets. During the initial years they very successfully leveraged the ideological attraction of having been the first worker-peasant state and later on the fight against fascism, which were the motivations leading to the recruitment of many high-level spies. However, events such as the crushing of the Hungarian Revolution of 1956 and the 1968 Prague Spring virtually ended the recruitment of idealists who were repelled by the Red Army's violations of sovereignty. This marked a shift in KGB and GRU tradecraft to a reliance on the employment of blackmail and bribery to recruit Western agents, which then transitioned seamlessly to what became the most prevalent motivation to betray one's country, particularly for Americans. By the 1970s and until the end of the Cold War, greed and monetary incentives were the factors that shaped the most damaging spies the Soviets and their partner intelligence agencies recruited.

In 1979, FBI agent Robert Hanssen volunteered to spy for the GRU. Hanssen provided a significant amount of information to the GRU, including details of the FBI's technical operations targeting the Soviets and lists of suspected Soviet intelligence agents. Among the compromised agents was the highest-ever ranking GRU spy, general Dmitri Polyakov, who was quietly retired to his Russian dacha rather than being arrested, likely because the GRU did not want to admit to the KGB to having such a high-ranking Red Army spy. Hanssen's first run of espionage ended in 1981 after his wife approached him regarding his suspicious activities. To convince her that he was not having an affair, he confessed to his efforts to "swindle" the Russians, and agreed with her demand to discontinue the "non-Christian" activity.

In 1984, as part of his duties as a CIA operations officer, Aldrich Ames began meeting with officials of the Soviet Embassy in Washington, D.C. These meetings were authorized by the CIA and FBI, and were designed to allow Ames to assess Soviet officials as possible sources for intelligence information and recruitment. This episode was the most emblematic of how the U.S. counterintelligence perspective had so miserably devolved by dubiously allowing a CIA officer to enter the belly of the beast alone.

The Year of the Spy

On 20 May 1985, John Anthony Walker was arrested for running perhaps the most damaging spy ring in history, spanning 17 years. U.S. counterintelligence history recognizes 1985 as the year of the spy because of Walker and the other spies who were neutralized that year. In reality, a year that was seen in a positive light as a dawning of DoD counterintelligence successes was actually the year that began a 16-year period of counterintelligence ineptness that was unparalleled in counterintelligence annals. In contrast to the counterespionage successes, this was the year in which the counterintelligence services of the CIA and FBI, despite having irrefutable evidence of at least one high-level and highly damaging mole in their ranks, for the most part did not even seem to care.

In April 1985, Aldrich Ames agreed to sell classified information from the CIA and other departments of the U.S. government to the KGB. On 13 June 1985, he disclosed the identities of numerous U.S. clandestine agents in the Soviet Union, at least nine of whom were eventually executed. According to Ames's own account, during his first meetings with the KGB he intended to scam the Russians by feeding them information about their own double agents, but the John Walker arrest in May 1985 compelled him to change his strategy. Ames did not believe the FBI's account that Walker's ex-wife turned him in, and rather calculated that the U.S. was disseminating disinformation to protect the true source who was likely a U.S. agent in the KGB. For this reason, Ames decided that he would need to wipe out anyone who could betray him.

By 1985, the CIA had moved on from the Angleton approach to defectors, but neither that agency nor the FBI was well practiced in handling these cases in a secure and conducive manner, due to a history of not needing to for a period of 21 years. Therefore, it is not surprising that the first such big episode was ultimately botched. On 1 August 1985, KGB Colonel Vitaly Yurchenko walked into the U.S. Embassy in Rome and a day later arrived at Andrews Air Force Base in Maryland before being whisked away to a safe house for debriefing. The first CIA member to meet with Yurchenko when his plane arrived was Aldrich Ames, who had postured himself to participate in the initial CIA debriefings of the defector.

Yurchenko revealed important details about many KGB assets in America. Prior to Yurchenko's defection, the CIA had suspected there might be a KGB mole inside the CIA; not based on Angleton-era paranoia but based on a number of unsuccessful and potentially compromised operations. Yurchenko confirmed this suspicion by providing information that exposed two major spies. The CIA was enthusiastic about the disarray this must have been causing in the upper echelons of the KGB, not knowing what other assets might be compromised by Yurchenko's information. However, the KGB did not need to guess about what Yurchenko was telling the Americans, because they already knew. In what must have been the most ridiculous and sad cases of counterespionage duplicity—from the initial debriefings of Yurchenko in August 1985, Ames was able to provide details regarding the information Yurchenko was providing to U.S. intelligence during his authorized meetings with Soviet officials at the Soviet Embassy. The KGB essentially had ears inside the Virginia safe house where Yurchenko was undergoing eight-hour-a-day debriefing sessions. Whether Yurchenko had been a bona fide defector or an agent provocateur, this information was certainly invaluable to Soviet intelligence. The safe house and all the information provided by Yurchenko, unbeknown to the Americans, was compromised. If Yurchenko had been a disinformation agent, then Ames would have been locked in as the verification channel of communication per the deception theory.

On 1 October 1985, Robert Hanssen began his second phase of espionage when he sent an anonymous letter to the KGB offering his services and asking for $100,000 in cash. In the letter, he gave the names of three KGB agents working for the FBI. Although all three agents he exposed had already been exposed earlier that year by Ames, the information provided to the KGB demonstrated that Hanssen had valuable access. With the FBI involved with the handling of Yurchenko, Hanssen provided the KGB a second source for the Yurchenko debriefings. To ensure that he did not meet the same fate as the agents he compromised, Hanssen never disclosed his identity or met with his Soviet handlers in person.

The fact that Ames and Hanssen compromised the same highly sensitive sources demonstrated a grave shortfall in the U.S. intelligence process for protecting (or not) its sources. Having jurisdiction for counterintelligence activities in the U.S., the FBI had the authority to recruit known or suspected KGB and GRU officers operating out of official residencies in the U.S., such as the embassy, consulates, or the United Nations office. Any recruited FBI assets returning to Russia or being transferred to another country would be transferred to the CIA for continued exploitation. Due to this dynamic, the agencies shared consolidated source lists, which were also being shared with the KGB by at least two spies.

Although Yurchenko had established himself as a credible defector and was providing valuable information, his CIA handlers did not have a guidebook to manage such cases, and made some critical errors along the way. After a series of mishaps, to include a disastrous effort by the CIA to reunite Yurchenko with a former mistress who had been his primary motivation to defect, the defector had a change of heart. On 31 October 1985, three months after arriving in the U.S., Yurchenko slipped away from his CIA handler at a Washington, D.C. restaurant and walked to the Soviet Embassy. On 4 November, Soviet diplomats invited the D.C. press corps to a surprise press conference. This well-orchestrated spectacle gave Yurchenko the opportunity to spin a yarn that was far from what the U.S. government knew to have been the true chain of events. According to Yurchenko, on 1 August, as he sat in St. Peter's Square in Rome, a liquid was splashed on him which rendered him unconscious. He further claimed that the next thing he remembered was waking up in a house where CIA men forced him to take drugs and interrogated him, keeping him there against his will for months. As a result of the drugs, he professed that he could not recall what he had told the CIA, but he was sure he had never willingly revealed any Soviet secrets. After the press conference, Yurchenko was flown back to Moscow where he was welcomed as a hero.

In addition to the Western spies operating in the East he exposed, Ames also compromised two KGB agents who were passing information to the FBI, Valery Martynov and Sergei Motorin. Sergei Motorin had returned to Moscow on normal rotation in January 1985, so his arrest was not immediately known to U.S. intelligence when the Russians acted on the information provided in June 1985. At the time of his compromise, Valery Martynov was assigned to the Washington residency. The final ironic twist to the Yurchenko affair was that Martynov was assigned to the escort detail for Yurchenko's flight to Moscow on 6 November 1985. Normally, such a non-scheduled return to the Soviet Union by a witting spy would have prompted the FBI to consider a defection, rather than risk that the agent was being recalled because his treachery had been discovered. However, the assignment as a "trusted escort" for the high-visibility Yurchenko situation appeared to be a feasible reason for his travel to the homeland. Upon arrival in Moscow, Martynov was unceremoniously arrested after disembarking the aircraft. Mortorin and Martynov were separately sentenced and executed by *vyshaya mera*.

It has been argued that Yurchenko was sent by the KGB with explicit orders to reveal two of its past moles to throw U.S. counterintelligence off the scent of the KGB's active mole. However, even former KGB officers interviewed after the breakup of the Soviet Union rejected the theory that Yurchenko had been a KGB provocateur, and that the KGB handled the publicity the only way they could. The U.S. government assessed that Yurchenko was a bona fide defector and viewed his warm welcome home as part of the propaganda ruse. Logically, publicly punishing Yurchenko would have verified that he had been a genuine defector. Had the KGB arrested Yurchenko rather than publicly agreeing with the fabricated story, the U.S. might have questioned how the KGB was so certain that he was lying, which might have compelled the U.S. to intensify its search for moles who might have provided the Soviets such insights—namely Ames and Hanssen. If Yurchenko had actually tried to convince the KGB that he had been drugged and interrogated, reporting by

Ames and Hanssen confirmed that he was a cooperating source while under U.S. control. Unbeknown to Yurchenko who was spared by dumb luck, the Soviet moles whom he had both met were to thank for his not being publicly branded a traitor and meeting the fate of *vyshaya mera*.

Unheeded Warnings

By the end of 1985, the U.S. government acknowledged that there were grave national security concerns. Security lapses across the intelligence community prompted two congressional investigations that reached damning conclusions about the state of post-Angleton counterintelligence. The findings included that "despite verbal acknowledgment that some espionage losses have been truly devastating and have negated enormous defense investments, top managers remain unwilling to budget relatively modest sums for improved counterintelligence and security measures that would help protect much larger investments." The study concluded that the U.S. government's counterintelligence had "basic flaws" and was "poorly organized, staffed, trained, and equipped to deal with continuing counterintelligence challenges."

Government agencies that placed national interests above institutional hubris would accept such criticism and recommendations for improvement as a mandate for change. In stark contrast, these warnings came at the beginning of the 16-year mole hunt, which demonstrated once again that the CIA and FBI were derelict in their inaction.

The 16-year Mole Hunt

By late 1985, it became increasingly clear to CIA officials that the agency had a major counterintelligence problem. A significant number of CIA sources began to be compromised, recalled to the Soviet Union, and in many cases, executed. A number of these cases were believed to have been exposed by one of the spies Yurchenko identified, which prompted the CIA to initially relax its search, but it became evident that not all the compromised sources could be attributed to him. Still, given this realization that there was an active mole in the ranks, the CIA did not establish a special task force to formally initiate the mole hunt until the fall of 1986—and even then, the task force only consisted of one part-time and two full-time analysts. In addition, the CIA failed to coordinate with the FBI, which was the lead domestic counterintelligence agency and should have been the lead agency for such an investigation. As such, the CIA denied itself robust FBI investigative resources simply to hide the embarrassing possibility that they might have a mole. In addition, such coordination would have helped the two agencies realize they had a common problem.

In 1986, Ames was reassigned to the CIA station in the same Rome embassy that Yurchenko famously walked into the previous year. Content to continue his relationship with the KGB, he took a page from his old playbook and attained approval to conduct regular meetings with the Soviet minister of foreign affairs to Italy, ostensibly to assess him as a potential recruit. In reality, however, the minister would serve as Ames's cutout to pass intelligence to the KGB. By this time, Ames had become very concerned about the non-deliberate manner in which the Soviets were arresting and executing the agents that he compromised. Ames demanded a meeting with his KGB case officer to determine if they had a plan to protect him as the source. On 20 October 1986, Ames met with his KGB case officer and learned why the normally careful KGB handled the information he provided in a manner that threatened to expose him. The KGB officer explained that the information Ames provided went to the very top, and an enraged General Secretary Gorbachev ordered that all of the traitors be immediately executed. Obviously, the KGB would have chosen to handle this in a more secure manner, but in this case, they had no choice. The KGB officer assured Ames, however, there was a plan to protect him, which they immediately put into motion with at least five operations to confound and mislead the CIA over the next five years. Once again, a variation of the Felfe model was in place.

In December 1986, the KGB, knowing that the U.S. was aware that their embassy in Moscow was compromised by U.S. Marine guards bringing Soviet women and their "uncle" into the facility, passed information through a number of sources that technical devices planted in the facility were the source of the compromise of many of the U.S. agents. The KGB also passed source information that at least five of the agents had been discovered by poor tradecraft, and other disinformation was passed attributing some of the compromises to a spy known to have been compromised by Yurchenko. In addition, the KGB launched a "dangle" operation with the source providing disinformation that the agents were compromised by technical intercepts from the CIA's Warrenton, Virginia, switchboard. And as a final measure, the KGB had been able to delay the execution of a few of the agents compromised by Ames to continue their interrogations, and in those cases, the KGB had the agents contact their CIA case officers and report that they were alive but needed to keep a low profile due to all of the other arrests. The elaborate KGB disinformation operation successfully kept the undermanned task force looking in different and misleading directions for years.

Between 1988 and 1990, the CIA mole hunt came to a low ebb as the officers involved concentrated on other counterintelligence matters that were believed to have higher priority. By 1988, the FBI was aware of the significant U.S. agent compromises and recognized that there could be an FBI mole as well. Ironically, when Hanssen was reassigned to the Washington, D.C. FBI headquarters that same year, he was given the task of conducting a study of all known and rumored penetrations of the FBI in order to find the individual who might have betrayed Martynov and Motorin. Since he was obviously not aware that Ames was the one who initially betrayed the two, and knowing that Martynov was not recalled until after he provided the same information to the Soviets, this essentially meant that Hanssen was looking for himself. This amazing turn of events took the Felfe model to a new level of manipulation from within; but Hanssen's identity was not known to the Soviets, so they could not provide information to manipulate and influence on his behalf. In the case of Hanssen, however, this was not necessary because the agency built on the investigation of bank robbers was its own worst enemy when it came to counterintelligence. Rather than recognizing that anyone who had access to the compromised information should be among the suspects, in a classic case of investigative ineptitude, the U.S. government's "premier" investigative agency assigned a fox to guard the henhouse. Obviously, Hanssen ensured that he did not unmask himself with his study, but he did pass the entire study, including the list of all Soviets who had contact with the FBI, to the KGB in 1988.

Ames and Hanssen continued to commit espionage well into the post-Cold War era.

Post-Cold War Epilogue

After a rejuvenation in 1991, the CIA mole hunt special task force established a cooperative arrangement with the FBI and intensified its investigative effort. In August 1992, a financial inquiry found a correlation between bank deposits by Ames and meetings between Ames and a Soviet official that the CIA and FBI had authorized in 1985. This and other information was referred to the FBI in 1993, and after an investigation which found evidence of his communication with the Soviets, Ames was arrested on 21 February 1994. Ultimately, the 1994 arrest was based on a basic evidence lead that dated back to 1985.

From its beginnings in 1985, management of CIA's mole hunt effort that eventually uncovered Ames was deficient in several respects. Management deficiencies contributed to the delay in identifying Ames, who was a careless spy who used sloppy and inattentive measures to conceal his activities, as demonstrated by depositing a large sum of money directly after his meeting at the Soviet Embassy. The mole hunt suffered from insufficient senior management attention and a lack of proper resources. According to the Agency's Inspector General's report, the deficiencies in the Ames investigation reflected a CIA counterintelligence function that had not recovered its legitimacy since the excesses of James Angleton, and that to some extent, the "Angleton Syndrome" had become a canard that was used to downplay the role of counterintelligence in the agency. This conclusion confirmed that the legacy of counterintelligence paralysis and ineffectiveness that began as early as 1954, had endured well into the 1990s.

The compromises of Martynov and Motorin were attributed to Ames following his arrest in 1994, thus ending the CIA-led search that had been a significant risk of detection to Hanssen. However, the FBI was still convinced that they had a spy in their ranks based on the failure of a sensitive investigation and other sensitive operations not attributable to Ames (or others). Therefore, an FBI mole hunt continued until Hanssen was arrested on 18 February 2001. This portion of the mole hunt had dragged on for 13 years after Hanssen was initially given the assignment to find himself. In 2002, it was disclosed that Hanssen was identified as the mole by a former Sluzhba Vneshnei Razvedki (SVR) agent who was paid $7 million by the FBI. Therefore, it was not the FBI's investigative efforts that fingered Hanssen. The SVR was the post-Cold War successor agency to the KGB.

The Department of Justice review of the FBI's performance in detecting, deterring, and investigating the espionage activities that were attributable to an FBI mole was predictably similar to the Ames study from seven years prior. The report concluded that Hanssen escaped detection, not because he was extraordinarily clever and crafty, but because of longstanding systemic problems in the FBI's counterintelligence program and a deeply flawed FBI internal security program. The review of the Hanssen case revealed that there was essentially no deterrence to espionage at the FBI during the 1979–2001 period, and that the FBI's personnel and information security programs presented few obstacles to Hanssen's espionage. The report noted that these deficiencies played a major role in Hanssen's willingness and ability to commit espionage over a more than 20-year period. The Hanssen affair clearly demonstrated that after having the counterintelligence charter to protect the nation from foreign intelligence-collection threats since 1917, the FBI could not even protect the nation from within its own ranks. Although not the same cause as the CIA's Angleton-era paralysis, the FBI was simply ineffective due to a cultural "cop mentality" that never recognized the need to nurture a true "counterintelligence culture."

Why the U.S. Lost the Cold War Intelligence and Counterintelligence Battle

As history substantiates, the Soviet grand strategy and deception theory were effectively employed through the years. The game of chess was certainly played out in the cases of Felfe, Blake, and Ames, and potentially many others to include Popov, Golitsyn, Nosenko, and Yurchenko.

Although Golitsyn and Nosenko were defectors who provided verified information, there are arguments to be made that either or both were agent provocateurs. It will likely never be known if Golitsyn was a bona fide defector who influenced Angleton based on what he viewed as valid analysis, or if he was the most effective disinformation agent in the history of intrigue and espionage. Scholars on the subject argue both sides of the debate, but tend to view Golitsyn as a legitimate defector. Golitsyn's influence on Angleton alone, whether an intended or unintended consequence, was an intelligence coup for the Soviets. The timing of Golitsyn's defection, one month after the arrest of one of the Cold War's most damaging spies, was key to playing on the paranoia resulting from the Felfe legacy. If the

Soviets' intent had been to deploy Golitsyn as an agent provocateur immediately after Felfe's arrest to deceive and paralyze U.S. counterintelligence for the next 20 years, then the operation was the most successful of the Cold War era. Whether Golitsyn was a Soviet ruse or a genuine defector, it is undeniable that his influence over Angleton virtually paralyzed the U.S. counterintelligence community until at least the early 1980s, and had an indirect impact that impaired counterintelligence programs beyond the arrest of Hanssen in 2001.

Nosenko was the first and most notorious case of the Angleton policy of disbelief, but there were others having similar, cascading debilitating effects on the CIA and the U.S. counterintelligence enterprise in general. The fates of individuals in many other mismanaged cases had stifling effects on would-be defectors and volunteers, and certainly impacted the number of volunteers approaching U.S. Intelligence throughout the formative decades of the Cold War. CIA operations against the critically important Soviet target were adversely affected in the 1960s and 1970s as the result of Angleton's insistence that the KGB controlled virtually every source that the CIA handled. This paralyzed efforts to recruit Soviet agents and diminished the CIA's ability to produce intelligence from human sources on the subjects of most importance to U.S. policymakers. Perhaps most significantly during this period wherein Angleton and others were convinced there were high-level moles, the lack of sources in the KGB and GRU ensured that no first-hand information would be developed to help identify them if there were.

Due to the Angleton policy, it will probably never be known the degree to which the Soviets were employing agent provocateurs or the degree to which the U.S. could have benefited from legitimate defectors. Certainly, there were and would have been more disinformation efforts by the Soviets, but the stifling effect that the zero-tolerance policy for defector acceptance had is undeniable. Even that first-again defection in 1985, and its immediate aftermath, demonstrated how badly the U.S.'s national security posture had suffered due to the void of information that could have been provided by legitimate defectors in identifying Soviet Bloc spies. Vitaly Yurchenko was an apparently legitimate defector who provided valid information and would have continued to be debriefed for more, but his mishandling once again stymied counterintelligence efforts, by sending a very public message to any potential defectors that U.S. intelligence had still not learned how to control and protect its assets. When the 21-year gap in defectors to the U.S. ended with the defection of Yurchenko in 1985, a very public message was once again propagated that the U.S. processes for handling such matters remained insufficient.

The downward spiral of U.S. counterintelligence did not end with Angleton. The Angleton philosophy severely crippled U.S. counterintelligence and intelligence until at least 1985, but the threat that Angleton feared most was exactly what completely shut down U.S. counterintelligence and intelligence through the end of the Cold War, and well into the 21st century. At least five current or former CIA employees began spying against the U.S. in the decade after Angleton's departure and the change in counterintelligence philosophy.

At the same time of the Yurchenko defection, Ames and Hanssen (and perhaps another) were beginning a 16-year period where it became immediately obvious that cooperation with the U.S. was a death wish. Ames and Hanssen provided detailed information, and on at least two occasions, complete lists of American double agents. The devastating rollup of spies that began during the second half of 1985 sent the undeniable message to any would-be defectors or volunteers that the U.S.'s security was a disaster and it was simply not capable of protecting its intelligence assets.

The Angleton policy and legacy had a cascading effect on CIA, FBI, and DoD counterintelligence activities. Except for one marginally significant espionage arrest between 1966 and 1975, counterintelligence was non-existent as a U.S. national security capability. The impact this had on Army Counterintelligence in Europe was that it precluded aggressive counterintelligence activities and relegated counterintelligence agents to OPSEC experts, recommending camouflage and telephone security measures, rather than spy-hunting.

Despite the institutional ineptitude of CIA counterintelligence, the CIA maintained a traditional culture of "Ivy League" elitism. Outside of the U.S., counterintelligence activities conducted by any U.S. element were performed under the jurisdiction and authority of the CIA, and DoD Counterintelligence was regularly regarded by the CIA as "blue collar laborers." This unearned elitism and relegation of DoD Counterintelligence to lower-tiered status were factors that compounded the poor state of U.S. counterintelligence during the Cold War. Since a professional DoD counterintelligence capability might challenge the CIA's sense of superiority, there was no motivation to help these organizations succeed where the CIA could not do so themselves. The large majority of Army Counterintelligence agents were non-college-educated enlisted personnel who were relatively much younger and less experienced than their KGB and GRU counterparts, who were selected from a pool of the upper 4 percent of graduates of higher educational institutions and would not even be allowed to operate against U.S. targets in third countries until they were seasoned majors or lieutenant colonels. Due to convergent cultural and institutional obstacles, Army Counterintelligence in Europe was very slow to mature, and to recognize one of the most significant threats that DoD Counterintelligence was ever responsible for countering.

CHAPTER 4

Opportunities Lost Prior to the Dark Era of Counterintelligence

U.S. intelligence agencies developed some valuable sources of intelligence throughout the Cold War period, but as the global wilderness of mirrors demonstrated, U.S. counterintelligence was largely blind to how the Soviet Bloc intelligence and disinformation apparatus was operating against the U.S. in a sophisticated and centrally controlled manner. The U.S. counterintelligence leadership acknowledged that this apparatus existed, was frightened by the notion, and was paralyzed by this fright.

Specific information regarding the conduct or support of clandestine activities out of the Soviet MLMs was very scarce. However, this is not necessarily telling given the shroud of secrecy that the Soviets operated under, and the lack of sources U.S. intelligence developed with this level of information.

Any known or suspected KGB or GRU residency operating in West Germany received intense focus from the West German BfV. The CIA, as the lead U.S. agency for foreign counterintelligence activities, was the lead agency for coordination with the BfV to ensure the protection of U.S. interests. Since the U.S. State Department viewed the Huebner–Malinin Agreement as a protocol managed completely under USAREUR's purview, the CIA did not attempt to exercise counterintelligence authority over SMLM-F, and did not become interested or involved in counterintelligence operations targeting SMLM-F until a series of technical operations was launched in the early 1980s. Essentially, USAREUR directed the BfV and CIA to leave SMLM-F alone so as not to risk taking actions that might damage the Huebner–Malinin Agreement or USMLM intelligence collection in the Soviet sector. The CIA and BfV deferred these responsibilities to USAREUR, likely assuming USAREUR was ensuring that counterintelligence due diligence was enforced against this main enemy element operating in the heart of West Germany.

The KGB and GRU ran known clandestine HUMINT operations out of their residencies operating out of the Bonn embassy and Cologne consulate. Although the majority of embassy and consulate personnel conducted "legitimate" business, all individuals accredited to these platforms were viewed as potential KGB or GRU officers by the BfV (and CIA). Any individuals operating out of these platforms were generally restricted to a 25-mile (40-kilometer) travel radius and were required to submit detailed travel requests with the specific travel plans/routes to the West German government for approval prior to any travel outside that limited 25-mile area. In comparison, SMLM-F exercised complete freedom of movement, with the exception of restricted areas, over an area reaching 130 miles to the north of the sector, nearly 200 miles to the east, and nearly 350 miles to the south. The freedom of movement for suspected KGB and GRU officers operating out of the embassy and consulate was restricted to a less than 2,000-square-mile area, and the suspected KGB and GRU officers were subjected to rigorous BfV surveillance throughout that limited area. In comparison, with an average of 19 percent restricted areas in the U.S. sector over the years, Soviets operating out of SMLM-F had freedom of travel over a nearly 35,000-square-mile area, and were only subjected to sporadic tour surveillances.

USAREUR adamantly leveraged U.S. authorities as an occupying power and the provisions of an internationally recognized agreement (treaty) that was not executed through U.S. State Department channels to restrict the West German government and the CIA from operating against SMLM-F. Therefore, USAREUR accepted risk on behalf of West Germany, NATO, U.S. military forces in West Germany, and all U.S. national security interests in Europe, by assuming sole counterintelligence responsibility for SMLM-F. From the beginning, USAREUR leadership was likely never advised regarding the magnitude and the implications of assuming these responsibilities. The slow maturation of DoD counterintelligence in Europe, and the inability to address the SMLM-F threat during the early years, established a trajectory which enabled perhaps the West's most significant counterintelligence vulnerability to go unrecognized during most of the Cold War.

The Slow Maturation of Department of Defense Counterintelligence in Germany

As has historically been the case with its counterintelligence capabilities, the U.S. perceived a "peace dividend" at the conclusion of World War II and let its guard down against the next opportune threat. The Soviets aggressively exploited this weakness and the result was over 40 years of setbacks. As history repeats itself, just as the counterintelligence community was beginning to develop an actual capability when the Cold War ended, the U.S. once again cashed in the peace dividend and gutted the national counterintelligence enterprise based on the perception of a diminished threat, opening the door to the next series of threats being China and a resurgent Russia. But that's for another story.

Before getting into more cases of early opportunities to unlock the SMLM-F enigma before U.S. counterintelligence (and intelligence) was essentially locked down, it is instructional to examine the evolution of Army Counterintelligence to understand how the larger strategic dynamic stymied its maturation and what needed to be overcome before Army Counterintelligence emerged as the elite U.S. counterintelligence capability.

Development of the Army Counterintelligence Corps (CIC) in Germany

The Army CIC performed admirably during World War II. A prime example was the CIC's support to Allied operations to defend against the late 1944 German surprise counteroffensive through the Ardennes and Alsace region of France—the Battle of the Bulge. To support the operation, the Germans built the 150th Panzer Brigade, which was a unit made up completely of English-speaking soldiers in U.S. uniforms equipped with captured U.S. weapons and jeeps. The unit's mission was to infiltrate the U.S. zone of occupation in France, collect intelligence, commit acts of sabotage, and spread disinformation and sow confusion. Through interrogations and the analysis of suspicious incident reports, CIC agents and analysts were able to anticipate the elaborate German effort and neutralize the 150th by the second day of the battle. In one case, military police who were tipped off to be alert to the threat, apprehended a team of 150th agents who appeared to be "too damn polite," when attempting to pass through a checkpoint. After the interrogation of the architects of the 150th Panzer Brigade operation, it was disclosed that of all the teams sent out only two returned, and only one provided information of any value. In light of such successes, it was unfortunate that Germany would become the next battlefield on which U.S. counterintelligence would not fare as well.

The strategic counterintelligence wilderness of mirrors landscape dominated by the Angleton-era excesses and ensuing anti-Angleton orthodoxy had cascading, stifling effects on DoD counterintelligence during the pivotal decades of the Cold War. The significant vulnerabilities that resulted from these dynamics led to CIA and FBI mole compromises which disrupted U.S. counterintelligence capability during the concluding decade of the Cold War and beyond—while during the same time exposing how inept the U.S. counterintelligence capability had become. Compounded by this overarching shadow, Army Counterintelligence in Germany continually encountered obstacles that further impeded the ability to effectively counter a centralized and determined Soviet Bloc threat.

At the conclusion of World War II, a number of divergent factors degraded the CIC's ability to adjust and counter the primary emergent Communist threat. The termination of the draft eliminated the reservoir of skilled and highly educated personnel with whom the wartime CIC had become identified. The CIC established a policy for security purposes that prohibited agents from marrying foreign nationals, which caused the loss of still more highly qualified individuals, many of whom possessed much-needed language skills. In addition to the decrease in quality of personnel, during the immediate postwar period the CIC was saturated with the denazification program and the screening of displaced Germans, which included a 12,500-a-month case load of immigration requests. Routine background checks and loyalty investigations to screen for Communist elements and other groups considered to be threats to national security suffered due to the other priorities. This much diminished capability could never fully recover in the face of a massive, complex, and well-coordinated Soviet Bloc intelligence and disinformation apparatus.

Further degrading the CIC's Cold War transition was the lack of a unified organization and coordination at the top. The establishment of SMLM-F was a prime example of an intelligence threat that slipped through the counterintelligence cracks due to the inability to address a threat in a centralized and coordinated manner. Although the CIC was aware that Soviet liaison officers were actively engaging in espionage during the period immediately prior to the establishment of the MLMs, there was no strategy to address this threat when SMLM-F was established. Military police detachments, and not CIC elements, were responsible for the surveillance of SMLM-F tours until such activities were suspended per an agreement in 1952.

Army CIC assumed responsibility for the SMLM-F "target" in the latter part of 1955, but was slow to establish a counterintelligence program to address the SMLM-F threat. The CIC headquarters in Germany was an administrative headquarters with no authority to command and control operations. In fact, there was no entity that maintained a strategic, big-picture perspective of operations across the West German zone of occupation because the CIC operated in a completely decentralized, disconnected, and autonomous manner. Throughout the majority of the Cold War era in West Germany, the regional counterintelligence structure persisted with the region that encompassed the Frankfurt area having de facto responsibility for SMLM-F. Consequentially, the SMLM-F counterintelligence coverage mission was primarily addressed as an additional duty which was not consistent with the supported commands' priorities, and competed with other higher counterintelligence priorities such as counterespionage investigations. These factors also explain why national intelligence requirements for information regarding SMLM-F may not have been entered into the system for consideration of tasking assets that may have developed information regarding SMLM-F activities.

In addition to an operational structure in Europe that was not conducive to addressing the most sophisticated threats, DoD Counterintelligence endured a litany of setbacks that impacted priorities and resources. In 1961, the army consolidated all intelligence capabilities under the Intelligence Corps (INTC), thus ending the CIC. The Civil Rights and anti-Vietnam War movements in the U.S. in the 1960s were largely viewed as domestic U.S. issues, but the Soviets viewed all fronts in the global Cold War as opportunities for influence. The Soviet Union allegedly spent more money funding U.S. antiwar movements during the Vietnam War than on funding and arming North Vietnamese military forces, which turned out to be a wise investment as the American people's lack of national will to continue the war became the decisive factor in the humiliating defeat. Soviet support to entities practicing civil disobedience, many of which had their radical fringe groups bent on violence, tested the U.S. government on a scale never before faced. This period of civil disobedience and disturbance resulted in overreach on the part of DoD Counterintelligence which further diminished its capability. Army Counterintelligence stumbled into the mission of collecting information on these groups to fill a void in the ability of the FBI or any other agency to address these domestic issues. This policy of turning DoD Counterintelligence to a mission of spying on U.S. citizens caused a public distrust that essentially shut down DoD Counterintelligence. Although these excesses marked a low point in DoD counterintelligence history, they did eventually result in a major overhaul which finally brought Army Counterintelligence under a centralized control and oversight structure.

DoD Counterintelligence also suffered from perpetual instability throughout the Cold War. By 1974, DoD Counterintelligence in Europe had undergone seven major restructurings, averaging one every four years. Obviously, this lack of continuity cascaded throughout the ranks. Inconsistent mission requirements also impeded a centralized focus on major intelligence-collection threats. The CIC restructure in 1974 placed an emphasis on bringing counterintelligence in step with the rest of the army. In what was termed the "greening" of military intelligence, counterintelligence became focused more on direct support to tactical army units making OPSEC the priority function. This essentially relegated counterintelligence agents who were trained and experienced in counterespionage investigations to advisors to the commands regarding camouflage and communications security practices. This devolution of counterintelligence from a focus on strategic threats posed by the main enemy would have continued had it not been for the Reagan administration's intent to defeat the Communist menace in the 1980s.

Although these were dark years for Army Counterintelligence as a profession, the positive development was the establishment of the U.S. Army Intelligence and Security Command (INSCOM) in 1977, which finally began the process of bringing strategic counterintelligence under coordinated counterintelligence command-and-control structures. Thirty years following the end of the Cold War, DoD Counterintelligence was finally adopting a corporate-enterprise approach to how it addressed the main enemy. By the end of the decade, counterintelligence agents were no longer taking direction primarily from combat unit commanders who viewed the threat from their own very narrow perspectives, and were finally placed under the direction of professional counterintelligence leaders. With this first effective reorganization in nearly 30 years of Cold War setbacks, and a renewed mission focus, the 1980s began with a focus on more proactive counterintelligence measures such as upgrading counterespionage. Although the FBI and CIA counterintelligence capabilities remained in paralysis based on myriad factors, Army Counterintelligence emerged as the elite U.S. counterintelligence capability—but this was still a long time coming.

Lacking a Strategic Vision

The SMLM-F threat slipped through two cracks. Firstly, USAREUR leveraged its occupying forces authority and the Huebner–Malinin Agreement to prevent BfV and CIA involvement in countering the potential SMLM-F threat, which should have been addressed as a strategic and unified concern. Secondly, Army Counterintelligence in Europe was not structured to address a strategic, theater-wide threat that USAREUR had dubiously assumed responsibility for by restricting BfV and CIA involvement. This dynamic resulted in a blind spot that endured through the entirety of the Cold War.

DoD Counterintelligence was a symptom of the larger disease. The U.S. never had a unifying counterintelligence strategy; to use a sports analogy, DoD Counterintelligence "stumbled out of the blocks," in a manner which took decades to recover.

The Lost Opportunity

A vignette that characterized the issues DoD Counterintelligence experienced during the majority of the Cold War due to a lack of centralized coordination and mission focus was the initiative to bug the SMLM-F facilities. This technical surveillance and monitoring effort never matured far beyond the concept stage because it simply did not follow the simple principles of centralized planning and unity of effort.

The Allies undertook some major technical collection efforts as the Soviet Communist system began to materialize as an existential threat. The first, Operation SILVER, was a British intelligence operation in Allied-occupied Austria which ran from 1949 to 1955 that covertly tapped into the landline communications of the Red Army headquarters in Vienna. Although it was considered a success, the details of the operation were passed to the KGB in October 1953 by George Blake, the British double agent. To protect their most valued agent, the KGB allowed the operation to continue to collect until it was ended in 1955 when Austria regained full sovereignty. Operation GOLD was another large-scale technical operation demonstrating great competency and security; again, it only failed due to the British traitor Blake.

In contrast to SILVER and GOLD, the Army Counterintelligence effort to plan and execute a much less complex technical operation targeting SMLM-F was a virtual failure from the technical standpoint. This effort sadly demonstrated how Army Counterintelligence was not structured to operate against centrally controlled Soviet threats throughout the majority of the Cold War era.

Following World War II, counterintelligence in Europe was administered by the 7970th CIC Group. In 1949, all counterintelligence organizations were transferred to the 66th CIC Detachment which was redesignated as the 66th CIC Group in 1951. The 66th CIC Group was primarily an administrative headquarters comprised of six regional commands responsible for counterintelligence operations in their given geographic areas in support of the senior intelligence officers in their regions. The 66th CIC Group Region III area of responsibility included Frankfurt, and was therefore the regional command responsible for counterintelligence coverage of SMLM-F.

The CIC organization structure was such that the regions executed standard decentralized counterintelligence activities in support of their designated regions. However, low-density/high-demand technical capabilities and expertise were centrally maintained at the headquarters levels to provide support to the highest priorities across the regions of responsibility. The Technical Aids Division was the 66th CIC Group element in West Germany that provided technical operations support across the 66th CIC Group area of responsibility. The 902nd CIC Group located at Fort Holabird, Maryland, was the CIC element that provided counterintelligence support to the highest global priorities, and therefore centrally managed elements with the highest degree of low-density capability expertise, to include the most capable technical experts. This is important context because a technical operation requires technical expertise.

On 26 March 1956, HQ USAREUR notified the 66th CIC Group of the plan to construct buildings on a new SMLM-F compound and requested an assessment on the feasibility of planting surreptitious audio devices in the buildings during construction. In April 1956, the 66th CIC Group agreed with the concept of planting bugging devices in the compound, but noted that they did not have the capability or expertise to conduct such an operation, and advised that the 902nd CIC Group would likely have this level of expertise. The project was initially planned for completion by September of that year; however, due to project delays the compound was not made ready for occupation until July of 1959. Despite this extended timeline, the lack of centralized management and focus led to a miserable failure in the face of this only such counterintelligence exploitation opportunity. Ultimately, this one-time counterintelligence exploitation opportunity was lost, which enabled a blind spot and a gaping counterintelligence vulnerability to persist until the end of the MLM era.

DART I

There was a series of delays to the SMLM-F compound construction project during 1956 and 1957 due to ongoing negotiations between USAREUR and GSFG. The Soviets placed two primary demands on the USAREUR-proposed plan, which were that the facility not be "in the woods" and that it be located within the city limits of Frankfurt and in the area of Niederrad. The request to not be in the woods was obviously so the facility could be leveraged as a SIGINT platform, and not be interfered with by high-standing trees. The Frankfurt-Niederrad location provided ready access to downtown Frankfurt and both of the main highways out of the area, and was centrally located between the two primary U.S. military activities in the area, the V Corps headquarters and the Rhein-Main Air Base, for SIGINT collection.

In late 1957, the sides agreed to the project plan and the construction plans were finalized in January 1958. At this juncture, USAREUR asked the 66th CIC Group for the status of planning. Inexplicably, there had been no progress in planning for the technical surveillance of SMLM-F compound buildings over the extended period of project delays. Compounding this two-year gap in effort, when the ground breaking for the new buildings on the compound took place on 25 April, the 66th CIC Group had not attained a copy of the construction plan, nor had they begun to plan for the technical surveillance operation. The 66th CIC Group finally attained a copy of the construction plan on 9 May 1958, and after the USAREUR DCSINT staff once again expressed their concerns regarding a lack of a plan, the 66th CIC Group directed its Technical Aids Division to provide a feasibility assessment regarding the installation of clandestine listening devices in the SMLM-F compound. This was the first time that technical experts became involved in planning for the operation. On 4 June, the Technical Aids Division provided a report stating that the appropriate equipment was available and the CIC had technical experts who were qualified to perform the installation. The report specified that the "take" would need to be transmitted by wires embedded on telephone cables which would need to run from the compound to a nearby "stakeout" location. Albeit much later than it should have been, the requirement to acquire a stakeout location in the vicinity of the SMLM-F compound to receive the take was specified in the report.

The project to bug the SMLM-F compound was assigned the codename of Project DART on 8 July 1958. There were a series of technical meetings during the months of August to October 1958 to discuss the operation. The 66th CIC Group Technical Aids Division representatives specified that the project plans provided by Region III were not sufficient and that they would need detailed blueprints for the planned construction. However, the key components of the technical surveillance plan were known and the planning should have been able to proceed while the detailed blueprints were acquired. Technicians supporting the project determined the equipment best suited to lower the risks of detection and reduce maintenance requirements. The four sites identified for the devices to be implanted were a large room that was likely to be used as a meeting room, a small room adjoining the radio room, and the living rooms of the living quarters likely to be used by the chief and deputy chief. Although the basic parts were coming into place, one key component was not.

It is very likely that the 66th CIC Group leadership and Region III were not made acutely aware that the stakeout location was in fact the pacing component for the entire operation. Technicians could not finalize any plans until they identified the location of the junction box that would transmit the take from of the compound.

The wiring schema from the listening device needed to be configured based on the location of this box, and the location of the box could not be determined until the stakeout location to which the wiring would run was identified. So again, a component of the plan that could have been determined much sooner was that the only suitable stakeout location would be a unit in one of the apartment complexes in the vicinity of the compound.

On 30 October 1958, the 66th CIC Group finally authorized Region III to begin the process of acquiring an apartment. Region III determined that all the apartment complexes in the vicinity of the compound were occupied and could not be sublet, so agents began the process of conducting background checks on all occupants to identify a suitable candidate to approach with an offer to cooperate. This lengthy process of vetting potential candidates in a secure manner continued for nearly four months. On 24 February 1959, Region III agents approached a German family occupying the desired apartment with a generous offer to relocate them to another apartment in the Frankfurt-Niederrad area, to which the family agreed. The Region III agents then negotiated new occupancy terms with the landlord, and by 10 March 1959, all contracts were signed and money paid to facilitate an occupancy date of 1 May.

The fact that Region III did not attain the apartment until March 1959 with an occupancy availability of May, demonstrated that they never appeared to understand the devastating impacts that delays in gaining this critical component would have on the overall project. In addition to delays in obtaining an appropriate apartment, the ultimate failure of Project DART was that Region III was responsible for monitoring the progress of the construction, but did not have the resident expertise to do so from a technical perspective. Technical Aids Division representatives, who had been disengaged from the project while the apartment issue was being resolved, returned for a site assessment on 1 March 1959. As it turned out, no site assessment was required, because the team only needed to take one glance out of the DART window to see that that the construction had progressed beyond the point where listening devices could be installed. After this assessment there was a flurry of activity to salvage the project and then conduct damage control, but the fact remained that the opportunity for this once-only counterintelligence opportunity was lost. On 25 March 1959, USAREUR officially canceled Project DART. As a face-saving gesture, the 66th CIC Group contended that the apartment remained an important asset and that it would be retained and used for visual and photographic observation of the SMLM-F compound. Although the project was canceled, the apartment continued to be referred to as DART.

During the three-year trajectory to failure, USAREUR assumed that the 66th CIC group, as the technical experts, were working the problem smartly. The 66th CIC Group, however, did not take any proactive measures and only acted during the planning process when prodded. Although it was known that a new SMLM-F compound would be constructed as early as March 1956, the 66th CIC Group did not get the true technical experts involved in the process until May 1958—over two years later. Granted, the Technical Aids Division did need the construction plans before planning the technical surveillance operation in detail, but technical experts could have advised in 1956 that the plan would eventually require a nearby stakeout location to receive the take.

When the USAREUR DCSINT announced the final decision to terminate Project DART, he provided his candid observations of the project during a 25 March 1959 meeting with the project leadership team. The DCSINT concluded that the project ultimately failed because no clear-cut responsibilities had been assigned or delineated. The DCSINT expressed his frustration that during a recent visit to Fort Holabird, Maryland, he had been shown "innumerable" clandestine listening devices that could have been leveraged to make the project a success. The DCSINT accepted a share in responsibility because he admittedly assumed the 66th CIC would understand that a project of this complexity would require that it "pick the best technical brains" available in the U.S. He concluded by stating that the Soviets were installing bugs all over the world and in the U.S., and "it seemed mighty strange" to him that U.S. Counterintelligence could not bug an installation for which the U.S. Army controlled the construction.

DART II

The failure of Project DART was immediately perceived by the 66th CIC Group as a "black eye." This sense of failure also likely led to an overreaction in the employment of the newly acquired observation post (OP). Region III began continuous surveillance of the SMLM-F compound on 29 June 1959 while the compound was in the final stages of preparation for occupancy. The OP operation required six dedicated agents operating in two-person teams conducting 24-hour shifts, while entering and departing DART at 3:00 AM to minimize the risk of detection by neighboring residents.

Region III employed several fully vetted German nationals to support aspects of their counterintelligence investigations and operations. One German national employee was identified to occupy the apartment with his wife on various nights and weekends to establish an appearance of normalcy for the apartment. The couple further maintained the bona fides of the apartment by meeting neighbors and providing a cover story for their irregular occupancy that he was a traveling salesman and his wife preferred to join him while away on his very frequent business trips. Due to the amount of time the German national was required to spend at the apartment, Region III gained approval and agreed to pay an additional salary and to pay his wife to regularly clean the apartment.

SMLM-F personnel completed their move to the compound between 6 and 9 July. The focus of the initial surveillance was to observe activities immediately prior to and after occupancy that would disclose any enlightening OPSEC measures such as digging around the buildings, window blanking, or activities indicative of sweeping for technical surveillance devices. Other specific observations of interest were items entering the compound that might contain radio or other technical electronic equipment. During an ensuing two-month period, the SMLM-F compound remained under continuous observation.

The first indication that SMLM-F personnel were actively attempting to identify an OP in the vicinity of the compound was on the night of 24 July 1959, when a SMLM-F officer was observed scanning the surrounding apartment complexes through binoculars. After visiting the SMLM-F compound on 20 August 1959, ACS personnel reported that a pair of binoculars was seen mounted on a window sill oriented in the general direction of DART. On 21 August, SMLM-F personnel were observed in the compound yard looking at DART and gesturing as though asking the occupants to come down and talk. Later in the day, counterintelligence agents manning the OP observed the deputy chief, Colonel Vlasov, looking out of a compound window directly at the apartment window with binoculars. When the manning agents attempted to photograph this activity, Vlasov waved in their direction. Also on 21 August, Vlasov informed ACS personnel that the compound was being observed by persons with a telescope and pointed out the apartment he suspected of being an observation post. He further queried whether any Americans lived in the area. ACS personnel subsequently sketched a diagram of the location identified by Vlosov which was confirmed by Region III as DART. Agents assessed that the location was compromised by the reflection off the camera when attempting to photograph Vlasov, but circumstances would suggest that Vlasov was aware of (or at least suspicious of) that specific location before the attempt to take photographs. In late August 1959, Region III was authorized to terminate 24/7 observation of the SMLM-F compound.

DART III: Successes Lost in Failure

The DART apartment was compromised within the first two months of operations, which may suggest how long the technical operation may have remained secure. Plausible explanations for the compromise included poor Region III agent tradecraft, countersurveillance diligence on the part of SMLM-F members, or sources within the West German government who may have been aware of the U.S. vetting process. Most telling was the question posed to ACS regarding the "Americans" living in the area, which would suggest that it was simply an apartment complex resident (or perhaps even the landlord) who tipped the Soviets off, understanding that the Americans were not always well liked among the West German people at the time. In any case, the root cause for compromise of what would have likely been a very expensive technical surveillance operation would have been the rushed apartment acquisition process. An alternative argument could be made that had the 66th CIC

Group not felt compelled to save some face by showing that the apartment was a valuable asset when the Soviets began occupying the compound, that the apartment would have been brought into the technical surveillance operation in a more deliberate and discreet manner, and, therefore, not be as readily compromised. In addition, it was the use as an "observation" post, rather than as a "listening" post, that was the most likely cause of compromise.

Although Project DART was perceived as a monumental failure, this short-lived activity actually provided what could have been the most enlightening window into SMLM-F operations during the entire MLM era. Perhaps everyone involved was too busy looking for the big observables to focus on the lesser ones.

There were many observations that should have been flagged as being of counter-intelligence interest, but only two stood out as remarkable observations of activities of potential counterintelligence interest. The only observation of truly suspicious activity occurred when a SMLM-F member known to have the rank of captain departed the compound in a private's uniform and later returned to the compound wearing his captain's uniform, accompanied by an unidentified individual wearing a private's uniform. The other noteworthy occurrence was the detection of antennae masts and wires on top of the building housing the communications room on 9 July 1959. The interesting point of this event was that it was not observed by the counterintelligence agents manning the OP until daylight. This confirmed that the Soviets performed the work during the hours of darkness in a clear effort to avoid observation—an effort that proved successful. This would suggest that there was something they wanted to conceal in the installation of the antennae equipment, and may have indicated that the Soviets were already aware that (or suspicious that) the compound was under observation.

Those two anomalous observations aside, the true value in the observation post surveillance that should have been taken away was the identification of a counterintel-ligence vulnerability that was never redressed during the remaining 30-plus years that SMLM-F operated out of the Frankfurt-Niederrad compound. In general, there was a considerable amount of activity at the SMLM-F compound during the two-month period of continuous observation. Although much of this activity could be attributed to the establishment of the new facility, there were many visitors to the compound who did not appear to be associated with these activities. Men in business dress were observed being allowed into the compound without escort, greeted on the grounds by SMLM-F officers, escorted into the operations building, and subsequently departing the compound after varying periods of time. Men visited the compound carrying briefcases bearing papers that were regularly taken onto the operations building. Well-dressed women who were not associated with the support staff regularly visited and were escorted into the operations building or living quarters, and in some cases, were driven onto or off the compound in SMLM-F vehicles. Given that the SMLM-F compound was not monitored on a regular basis after the brief period in 1959, these observations demonstrated that SMLM-F personnel felt free to welcome "guests." The Soviets may have (falsely) assumed that their compound was being monitored throughout the years and that efforts were made to identify individuals visiting the compound, but in reality, individuals could enter the compound, conduct secure meetings with SMLM-F officers, and depart without being identified or even without U.S. Counterintelligence knowledge that a meeting had taken place. And this was even when the compound was under constant surveillance. The surveillance of the SMLM-F compound also disclosed that SMLM-F personnel regularly departed the compound by vehicle and by foot in civilian clothing, and not always in uniform which was the agreed-upon rule/norm.

The DART Aftermath

The Project DART debacle had lasting effects on the Army Counterintelligence perspective of SMLM-F. Due to the failure, SMLM-F was recognized as a sore spot and the CIC became very much less inclined to see it as one of their primary targets. Army Counterintelligence observed the SMLM-F freedom and volume of activity out of this potential GRU residency nestled in the heart of the U.S. sector, and recorded these observations for analysts and leaders to assess. Apparently, the scars from the failures outweighed the successes in identifying the potential vulnerability, which led to a propensity to cut the SMLM-F losses. USAREUR's sensitivities regarding actions that might antagonize the Soviets for fear of retribution against USMLM also provided Army Counterintelligence some top cover for adopting a relatively hands-off approach to this main enemy element operating in the U.S.'s backyard. See no evil, hear no evil, speak no evil.

On 1 October 1959, USAREUR reorganized the CIC in West Germany yet again, dividing the counterintelligence and field intelligence operations between the 66th CIC Group and another CIC group. This reorganization gave the 66th CIC Group responsibility for the southern portion of Germany, which did not include the Frankfurt area or SMLM-F.

Although Project DART was officially canceled in 1959, the apartment continued to be referred to as DART until it was finally returned to its landlord in 1990. DART was employed in support of various operations over the years, but it was not until 1985 in the wake of the Major Nicholson shooting that it was manned again on a 24/7 basis to support overt surveillance operations canvassing SMLM-F vehicles leaving the compound.

Every month from March 1959 until October 1990, a German national employee would be given the rent money out of the Army Intelligence Contingency Fund, drive across the river to the Frankfurt-Niederrad apartment complex, and render payment, in cash, to the DART apartment landlord. Every month for over 30 years, Army Counterintelligence paid for an observation post that had been compromised within two months of operations, and regularly went years between operational usages. Apparently, keeping DART on the books served to give some leaders the false perception that Army Counterintelligence was actively addressing the SMLM-F issue.

Lost Sources and Lost Leads

The only methods possible to develop information regarding SMLM-F clandestine intelligence collection or other covert activities were by immersive surveillance and monitoring of SMLM-F activities, or through intelligence sources with access to credible information regarding such activities. Project DART was the opportunity to establish the first step in a comprehensive surveillance and monitoring regime. Following this lost opportunity, the SMLM-F enigma became an issue more easily ignored than addressed.

Since U.S. (or West German) Counterintelligence did not concentrate substantial efforts on surveillance and monitoring of SMLM-F, the only available source would have been individuals with insider knowledge. Perhaps the only period wherein the U.S. might have developed information regarding SMLM-F clandestine activities was prior to the dark age of counterintelligence, which was triggered by the Golitsyn defection in 1961, and imposed by CIA Counterintelligence Director James Angleton.

The Lost Sources

There were only two productive sources of Soviet military information applicable to the GSFG prior to the "dark ages." These were perhaps the best, and last, opportunities to understand, from first-hand sources, how the GRU employed SMLM-F, for many years.

Operation GOLD

The first opportunity to gain insights regarding SMLM-F operations was the complex technical collection operation named Operation GOLD by the U.S., and Operation STOPWATCH by the UK. This was a joint operation conducted by the CIA and the British SIS in 1955 to tap into landline communications of the Red Army headquarters in Berlin using a tunnel into the Soviet-occupied zone. The KGB was informed of the operation before digging of the tunnel began by their mole George Blake, but in an effort to protect the true source of the compromise, waited to "discover" the tunnel during a major rain and flooding event in April 1956. The short-lived, 11-month operation collected very valuable information from the unwitting headquarters staff.

The technical surveillance operation intercepted phone conversations from multiple lines averaging 405 hours of conversation per day to be transcribed and translated. Over the 11-month period of the intercepts, the operation netted

50,000 reels of tape, 443,000 fully transcribed conversations, 40,000 hours of telephone conversations, and 6,000,000 hours of teletype traffic, which resulted in the production of 1,750 intelligence reports.

The Best and Last Source

Probably the best, and perhaps last, opportunity to develop specific information regarding SMLM-F operations was through the GRU officer, Pyotr Popov, who was assigned to the GSFG in the late 1950s. Popov was a lieutenant colonel in the GRU stationed in Vienna during the Soviet occupation of Austria after World War II. On New Year's Day 1953, Popov dropped a letter into the car of a U.S. foreign service officer offering to trade information for money, and subsequently became an agent for the CIA. After the withdrawal of Soviet occupation forces from Austria in 1955, many GRU officers, including Popov, returned to Moscow for leave and reassignment. The CIA briefed Popov on their intelligence requirements in the Moscow area and other communications arrangements needed to reestablish contact in Moscow. However, the CIA lost contact and did not realize that Popov had been assigned to the GRU element supporting the GSFG in East Germany in the summer of 1955.

On 10 January 1956, Popov made contact with a BRIXMIS tour that happened to be touring at the port of Stralsund, East Germany. Popov passed the tour officer a letter with a notebook containing intelligence information addressed to the CIA case officer who had handled him in Vienna. The BRIXMIS tour officer had the presence of mind to arrange for Popov to be met again in Stralsund two weeks later. BRIXMIS passed the information to the Berlin SIS office who in turn passed it on to the CIA. The CIA, having verified Popov's bona fides, requested that the CUSMLM arrange for a tour to visit Stralsund on 24 January to meet Popov and pass him contact instructions. A USMLM tour made contact with Popov, who simply handed the USMLM tour officer a notebook with 58 pages of intelligence reports and four pages of instructions regarding future meetings.

Popov met regularly with his CIA case officer and provided valuable intelligence on the Soviets' knowledge of U.S. military organizations and tactics, state-of-the-art Soviet military equipment, and one highly sensitive strategy report that might have been the known leak that enabled the KGB to pinpoint him as a spy. After a short but productive run as an asset inside the GRU office supporting GSFG, Popov was discovered by the KGB. While under KGB control he continued to pass information to the CIA, likely while the plan to protect the source of his compromise was put in place. Popov was arrested on 16 October 1959 and executed by *vyshaya mera* in 1960.

There are a few theories regarding how Popov was compromised. Blake confessed to compromising Popov and it is known that the information provided from the first brush with BRIXMIS was passed between Blake's SIS office and the CIA, but this information likely did not identify Popov by name. Additionally, it was likely that a highly sensitive document that Popov provided the CIA was reported to the KGB by Blake, which was assessed to be the likely compromise that enabled the KGB to close in on Popov. Until Blake's confession in 1961, there was information to suggest that Popov's compromise could be attributed to one of two potential causes which were the result of poor security measures the CIA employed to protect its valuable sources, and in one case compounded by the FBI's disregard for the security of a CIA source. After Blake's confession, however, both of these potential causes of compromise were then assessed to have been disinformation efforts to obfuscate the root compromise and again protect the well-placed asset, Blake.

Even after Blake's arrest, the KGB apparently attempted to provide disinformation to support the theory that Popov was compromised by poor security, likely to confuse the CIA's assessment of when he was actually compromised and what intelligence provided by Popov was actually disinformation between the time of his compromise and the time he was arrested. Although the circumstances of the KGB's discovery and neutralization of Popov may never be known, he was likely the best potential source of information regarding SMLM-F prior to the U.S. entering the dark era of intelligence and counterintelligence. Popov was a career GRU case officer with experience throughout Europe, and would have known about the existence of every GRU residency. The most likely reason why he did not provide information regarding SMLM-F is the simplest one—he was not asked.

USAREUR should have had the most immediate interest in information Popov may have been able to provide regarding SMLM-F. However, the fact that USMLM assisted the CIA with the initial U.S. contact with Popov does not equate to USAREUR knowing about Popov being a well-placed agent in the GRU. Since the CIA requested USMLM assistance with the initial Popov meet directly, there is no information to suggest that USAREUR was aware of USMLM involvement. Based on USAREUR's sensitivities regarding taking any actions that might impact USMLM collection activities, it is likely that USAREUR would not have authorized USMLM to conduct the covert meet. In fact, this was the only recorded incident of USMLM providing support to covert or clandestine activities.

A Threat of Little Concern

Although Popov was probably the best prospective source of information regarding potential SMLM-F clandestine activities, the fact that he did not report any such information does not strengthen any arguments that they were not involved in such activities.

Not only did the U.S. have very few sources of intelligence who might have been able to develop access to SMLM-F intelligence of interest, SMLM-F did not appear to be a priority intelligence-collection requirement. At the time, the counterintelligence elements with the responsibility to monitor SMLM-F as a tertiary responsibility were not integrated into the national strategic collection process, so it is understandable why sources which might have been able to develop information on SMLM-F activities were not tasked to collect and report on this type information. However, in retrospect, Popov was a fleeting opportunity that proved to be the best and probably the last one for over the next 25 years. GOLD was another that, likely, simply was not queried.

Other GRU assets over the years were valuable sources of strategic information regarding military plans and technologies, but all of the intelligence-related documents provided were "finished" intelligence products, and not intelligence-source-specific. Therefore, they did not appear to have access to information regarding GRU intelligence collection and covert activities in denied-area Western countries, which would have been the type of reporting associated with SMLM-F.

The Lost Leads

The Soviets established their disinformation department as early as 1953, but it was not until the defection of Golitsyn in 1961 that the seeds of distrust and paranoia were planted, either intentionally or simply fortuitously, by the Soviets. Golitsyn's portrayal of the Soviet grand strategy of disinformation and deception was based on the model of the notorious Heinze Felfe, the Soviet agent who had penetrated West German intelligence for over 10 years ending in 1961, six of which were as deputy chief of the section responsible for countering Soviet KGB espionage. Felfe's legacy and methodology of treachery formed the basis for Golitsyn's theory which ignited institutional paranoia and created the blind spot that was perpetuated through the policies exercised by Angleton. This began a long void in credible intelligence for the U.S., and is perhaps why the only credible information regarding SMLM-F involvement in covert intelligence operations to emerge prior to the final decade of the Cold War preceded the Golitsyn/Angleton era.

One remarkable case with a Soviet MLM nexus illustrated how the Soviets were able, through Felfe, to monitor the U.S. and German intelligence agencies' attempts to induce the defection of an apparently inept GRU case officer named Pyotr Sokolov. The Sokolov case was one of the more extensive examples of how Felfe used his high-level placement and influence to lead West German and U.S. Counterintelligence away from KGB operations.

The Case of the Inept GRU Officer

Sokolov was a GRU major operating out of Erfurt, East Germany, who purportedly ran multiple networks of agents collecting military information on U.S. army and air force bases in West Germany. One of Sokolov's primary operations involved a network of low-level West German agents whose targets were airfields between Frankfurt and Kaiserslautern, West Germany. In 1954, one of Sokolov's agents, Karl Heinz Kiefer, was recruited as a double agent by the U.S. Army CIC. Through Kiefer and other sources, the CIC developed information on the Sokolov ring, but eventually assessed that the threat did not warrant the time invested, and turned the case over to the West German BfV in 1959, with the recommendation that the case be terminated and the network rolled up.

When the BfV received the case, agents took interest due to the opportunity it presented to double Sokolov against the GRU. Kiefer was directed to become more active and increase his contact with Sokolov. As a result, Sokolov provided communications equipment and instructions that would have been of high interest to the CIC, which by this time was completely out of the case. Sokolov provided Kiefer with state-of-the-art communications equipment and provided instructions for emergency communications, which involved a radio in a Soviet MLM in West Germany. Kiefer was also directed to set up a dead drop for the passage of bulky materials, which would also be serviced by personnel of this MLM. Since the Sokolov network included collection against U.S. Air Force targets, the BfV brought the Air Force Office of Special Investigations (AFOSI) into the case, but also asked the CIA to act as the coordinator for the U.S. agencies involved due to the rapidly expanding number of agencies becoming involved—which also included, on the West German side, Felfe's BND.

The Sokolov operation was run under the GRU, but at the time, Felfe had wider access to West German operations to counter KGB activities. Based on information provided by Felfe, the KGB took particular interest because the agency viewed this as an opportunity to learn how the U.S. and German intelligence services were conducting double-agent operations, by observing how they operated against Sokolov and members of his network. Therefore, while this was a GRU-run operation, it was in the best interests of the centralized Soviet intelligence machine that the operation be seen by the West German Counterintelligence Service as at least having a KGB nexus, so that Felfe would have full visibility. Given this, he could report on the progress and obscure the facts to divert attention as necessary. To serve its purposes, the KGB fed information that identified individuals associated with the Kiefer portion of the Sokolov network as KGB agents. This effort succeeded and Felfe was able to monitor all aspects of the case.

With seemingly credible information that the suspected network agents were KGB assets, Felfe had jurisdiction to deploy BND agents to investigate and ostensibly double them back and get closer to the ultimate target, Sokolov. It was not uncommon for agents to "double-dip" and work for two intelligence services of the same country or alliance such as the GRU and KGB, but the degree of overlap in this case should have raised some red flags; but Felfe was there to keep them down anytime one began to be raised. It was this very duplicity of a contrived joint GRU/KGB operation that enabled Felfe to make demands on the investigation, allegedly on behalf of his agency.

Felfe unilaterally represented the BND position that the Kiefer portion of the Sokolov network should be allowed to operate as long as necessary to recruit Sokolov.

This approach was contrary to the CIA's position, which was to force Sokolov's defection by arresting his agents. Felfe contended that it was the BND insistence that if the BfV arrested Kiefer, the action should be taken in such a way that none of the BND sources was impacted. At the behest of the KGB, Felfe endeavored to delay any network arrests to allow them to continue as KGB diversionary assets for as long as possible. With his access, Felfe was able to warn the KGB when the arrests were to begin, so the GRU could be notified to recall Sokolov before he had the opportunity to defect. By July 1960, Felfe's BND could no longer justify a delay and the network rollup began with a simultaneous effort to deliver a letter to Sokolov with an offer to defect. Sokolov, however, had already been recalled to Moscow, never to seen or heard from again.

The Sokolov network case was an excellent illustration of Soviet manipulation of circumstances and events without the opposition's knowledge, in a manner that came to be framed by James Angleton as the "deception theory." Specific Soviet tactics included throwing away seemingly valuable agents and equipment; dangling attractive, or potentially attractive, tidbits of information; and prolonging the case by causing it to suddenly take a new and intriguing turn—usually just when the opposition's interest seemed to be lagging or when it appeared that the operation was about to be terminated. Although the KGB effort ultimately enabled the agency to isolate an inept and potentially treasonous GRU officer, the Soviets also succeeded in tying up the investigative assets of two German and several U.S. services. They effectively manipulated the case to involve a service (the BND) that was not originally connected with the case to leverage a penetration agent (Felfe) who could monitor the case. Finally, the KGB and Felfe were able to influence the Western services to create an interservice liaison task force, which created the illusion of a collaborative investigative effort among the services, while actually enabling the KGB to monitor the activity of all Western services involved in the case.

The Sokolov case was hailed at the time as a Western success, but this was not the actual result. In the end, of all the 200 agent leads, only five individuals were arrested. The CIA and AFOSI learned that most of their double agents provided information regarding the size of the network that had been significantly exaggerated by Sokolov. It was only after Felfe's arrest that U.S. agencies learned (from Felfe himself—a man who could not resist bragging occasionally) that the KGB had paid him a rare 1,000 deutsche mark bonus for his contribution to this Soviet "failure." The KGB viewed the effort as a successful diversion of American and German resources on nonproductive activities.

Two Lost Leads

One of the more intriguing aspects of the Sokolov case, from the SMLM perspective, was his apparent lapse in security of informing Kiefer that a Soviet

MLM would service his dead drop. Sokolov, as an agent handler, would have no reason to disclose where communications were going and who was servicing a dead drop. In fact, this would be extremely poor tradecraft in violation of compartmentalizing information in HUMINT operations. Alternatively, there is no plausible explanation why he would fabricate such a plan. Sokolov was inept and a drunkard, so it is likely that he carelessly disclosed accurate information. This opens an intriguing possibility, as it would suggest that use of the MLMs at the time was GRU tradecraft, and that this fact was only disclosed by this one, singularly inept GRU officer.

The SMLM that would service the dead drop or provide communications support was not specified in Sokolov's instructions to Kiefer, but SMLM-F would have been the most feasible SMLM to provide either form of support. Kiefer collected on U.S. army and air force installations in the vicinity of Kaiserslautern and Wiesbaden. Kaiserslautern was in the French sector but was much closer to Frankfurt than the SMLM (MMS) located in Baden-Baden (110 miles in comparison to 170 miles). The more feasible location to establish a dead drop to be serviced by a SMLM would have been in the vicinity of Wiesbaden, which was just over 20 miles from the SMLM-F compound and in the U.S. sector, making it within the SMLM-F freedom of travel area.

Probably the most intriguing aspect of the Sokolov case, from the SMLM perspective, was the instructions to Kiefer for emergency communications involving a radio in a Soviet MLM. Although the reporting of these instructions to Western intelligence was unique and never again repeated, there is no rational reason why Sokolov would have provided these instructions if this were not an aspect of GRU tradecraft, at least at the time. Although it was never known whether Kiefer or any other agents were instructed to provide information to a SMLM compound, if they had been, then they might had been the only agents to actually be observed by U.S. counterintelligence agents visiting the SMLM-F compound. In the same year of 1959 in which Sokolov provided Kiefer instructions for emergency communications involving a radio in a Soviet MLM, construction was completed on the new SMLM-F compound, which was occupied in early July of that year. The compound was under continuous observation during the first two months of occupation which confirmed patterns of activities that likely continued throughout the duration of SMLM-F. There were many visitors to the compound for whom there were no obviously apparent reasons for the visits. Individuals could freely and anonymously visit the SMLM-F compound and meet secretively with SMLM-F officers in the operations building where the secure communications room was located. Any of these visitors could have just as well been agents anonymously visiting the compound to provide documents or other materials for provision to GRU-central in Moscow. And this was when the compound was under observation. It was not again for the next 30-plus years.

The Missed Connection

There is no information to indicate that USAREUR or the CIC were ever made aware of the GRU/SMLM nexus reported during the Sokolov affair. Supporting the likelihood that this was the case, is the fact that it would be difficult to conceive how U.S. Counterintelligence would not have made the connection between this information and the observations of the SMLM-F compound that very same year. The detailed analysis of Felfe and the Sokolov case was conducted during the paranoid and insular Angleton era, so it is very likely that this information was not made available to the DoD, to include the USAREUR DCSINT staff officers responsible for the SMLM-F problem. The information regarding the GRU employing SMLMs to service dead drops and transmit agent communications was not included as a key finding in the CIA analysis, and was therefore either assumed to be common knowledge, or simply overshadowed by the CIA focus of studying the larger Felfe model and Soviet deception theory.

The failure to connect various dots at least as early as 1959 began a 25-year period of relative ambivalence in regard to the SMLM-F intelligence-collection threat. Given the lack of concerted effort the U.S. expended to understand the potential SMLM-F threat, and in light of the opportunities the U.S. failed to exploit, it should not have led to any arbitrary conclusions regarding what the threat may have been. However, by the 1960s and the dark age of counterintelligence, there was no known information or analysis to implicate SMLM-F as anything other than an overt collection "OPSEC" threat, which then became the widely held assumption without any effort for nearly three decades to confirm or deny that supposition.

Even if analysts did not have the benefit of the Sokolov case information, had they proceeded under the assumption that SMLM-F was a GRU residency supporting clandestine operations, they would have found that there was more evidence to support this assumption than to deny it. For starters, simply the risk of a potential GRU residency being run out of a denied-area mission that could freely host and securely meet with potential agents at their compound and whose personnel exercised unparalleled freedom of movement throughout a large part of West Germany, should have been inherently concerning. In addition, the tendency to assume the problem away was to simply ignore the data and its applications to known tradecraft.

As it applied to the ability of SMLM-F to service a dead drop, every year there were days in the tens to hundreds that the Soviets departed the compound for four hours or less, in what was assessed to be non-tour/non-official travel, for which U.S. Counterintelligence had no idea what the destination or purpose of the travel had been. They would often make a quick appearance at the post exchange, where they knew their presence would be observed and reported, which might feed analysts an (deceptive) explanation for the short departure from the compound. The extraterritoriality privilege of SMLM-F vehicles was always recognized and there was never an occurrence of a SMLM-F vehicle being entered or searched, with the exception of one isolated technical surveillance effort that did not develop evidence of suspicious activities.

The volume of non-tour departures from the SMLM-F compound in comparison to the number of tours they conducted was in stark contrast to USMLM activities. From a clandestine operations tradecraft perspective, this should have raised more concerns. It would be standard tradecraft for a GRU case officer operating out of a residency on foreign soil to depart the residency on a regular (if not daily) basis to establish a pattern of travel that would appear routine and mundane to a surveillance effort, if present. This routine activity is conducted initially to facilitate passive surveillance detection to identify indicators of surveillance coverage, but regardless of whether surveillance is detected or not, the case officer will always operate under the assumption that he is under surveillance. Over time, this standard tradecraft is employed to make the many times the case officer departs the residency for mundane purposes blend with the very few times (perhaps three or four a year) that the case officer conducts operational activity such as to meet with an agent or service a dead drop. By establishing a routine and mundane pattern of activity, the case officer identifies those times and places where a surveillance effort, if present, may be lulled into a false sense of security and relax coverage, which the case officer would thereby exploit to lose the surveillance for the short time the case officer takes to conduct the operational activity. As soon as the operational activity is completed, the case officer would travel in a manner that best enables the surveillance effort to reestablish contact, to give it the false sensing that nothing of interest could have occurred in the short period of lost contact.

If it were not so sad that it was allowed to happen non-deterred for decades, it would be almost comical to imagine that SMLM-F officers may have conducted this rigid security precaution day after day after day, for over 40 years, based on the possibility they may have been under surveillance—which they were not.

CHAPTER 5

The U.S. Military Liaison Mission Microcosm

The wilderness of mirrors involves the organizational culture of the secret services wherein deceptions are false, lies are truth, and the reflections can be both illuminating and confusing. In this wilderness, the mirrors are comprised of information from agents and defectors, disinformation from the opposing sides, deviously covered false trails, and facts thought to be valid (but perhaps incomplete).

What U.S. Counterintelligence failed to recognize, until perhaps very late in the Cold War game of chess, was that the big players on the board in the strategic wilderness of mirrors were not the only players with license to dabble in the diabolical. In fact, given what is known about the centralized intelligence and counterintelligence approach, it is clear that the Soviets always enforced unified objectives and associated narratives that were aligned from the highest levels down to all mission managers and operators on the ground.

The MLMs not only paralleled the strategic wilderness of mirrors in theory, they also did so in practice in several circumstances. Unlike the U.S., the Soviets viewed this as a unified global war, and it is likely that they viewed the USMLM/SMLM-F dynamic as just one of the many campaigns/battles they centrally managed as a part of the larger war effort. In addition to understanding the dynamics of and among the MLMs and their hosts, it is also important to view them as they fit within the larger strategic landscape. Sometimes they were pawns, sometimes they were knights, and sometimes they were bishops; but the MLMs were always pieces on the board and in play.

The U.S. failed to exploit the fleeting opportunities to develop information regarding SMLM-F. After these opportunities passed, the U.S. did not develop intelligence sources to determine what type a threat the Soviet MLMs might pose for nearly the duration of the Cold War. This lack of institutional will to develop insights on the Soviet presence on third-country soil, for which the U.S. was responsible, is only made more discouraging when compared to the information the Soviets possessed in regard to USMLM activities during this time. As would be eventually discovered, the damage to USAREUR interests (to include USMLM) caused by

Soviet Bloc clandestine HUMINT agents demonstrated how valuable just one or two well-placed sources could have been for the U.S.'s understanding of SMLM-F. But that was not the chess strategy the U.S. chose to play by.

The Chess Strategies

The USMLM was very likely the most productive U.S. intelligence element, per capita, during the Cold War. It was certainly the most productive collector of first-hand information on Soviet Bloc military organizations, equipment, and tactics. USMLM reporting was widely disseminated and consumed by analysts and defense leaders from Europe to the Pentagon. The dynamics shaping the U.S. intelligence strategy and national collection efforts serve to explain why USMLM HUMINT collection was of such high value to U.S. consumers—particularly in comparison to the relatively lower value the Soviets placed on SMLM-F touring and reporting, given its equally unique freedom of movement and access in West Germany.

The CIA and the Small-Guy-in-Charge Mentality

Throughout the Cold War, the Director of the CIA also served as the Director of Central Intelligence (DCI). The DCI was established to be the senior advisor to the president on matters of national intelligence, and to be the central coordinator of all intelligence activities. However, the DoD, as the largest collector, producer, and consumer of intelligence in the U.S. government, always opposed the concept of any other entity controlling its intelligence priorities. The DoD resisted DCI efforts to control its intelligence activities and independently developed programs to ensure intelligence support to the defense effort. The growth of intelligence organizations within the DoD served to accentuate the relative lack of DCI authority over the rest of the community. During the 1950s and 1960s, the DoD established the National Security Agency (NSA) to conduct national SIGINT, the Defense Intelligence Agency (DIA) to conduct HUMINT and produce intelligence analysis, and the National Reconnaissance Office (NRO) to procure and operate satellite collection systems.

Although the DCI was technically the head of the intelligence community, the Secretary of Defense controlled three of the four most powerful and influential intelligence organizations. In addition to the NSA, DIA, and NRO, each of the military services maintained substantial intelligence organizations at the departmental and tactical levels. The ranks of intelligence personnel in the DoD dwarfed the capabilities of the CIA, which promulgated a "small guy in charge" mentality within the CIA, and a legacy of tensions between the CIA and DoD. A series of setbacks in the 1960s and 1970s, beginning with the ill-conceived Cuban Bay of Pigs invasion in 1961, further degraded the CIA's influence over the larger intelligence community's budget and operations.

The functions which the CIA maintained strong control over throughout the Cold War were foreign HUMINT and counterintelligence. This led to a tendency for the CIA to exert control over and limit the efforts of DoD HUMINT and counterintelligence programs, as though punishing those programs for its lack of control over the other DoD intelligence programs. This also set the course for how HUMINT was conducted during the Cold War, which limited the effectiveness of clandestine HUMINT, and thus increased the value of tactical HUMINT such as that collected by USMLM.

U.S. Cold War HUMINT

As the central coordinator, the CIA had jurisdiction for all U.S. foreign HUMINT activities. As such, any U.S. government agency conducting HUMINT operations targeting another country was required to coordinate with, and gain approval from, the CIA. The CIA operated essentially all clandestine HUMINT programs throughout the Cold War, and resisted efforts by the DoD to build such programs. The few attempts by DoD services to delve onto clandestine HUMINT were in reaction to a perceived lack of support by the CIA in meeting their requirements. With the exception of two relatively short-lived programs, the DoD was not able to make significant progress. In fact, U.S. Army Special Forces maintained a program to recruit and operate agent networks in denied areas that was much more robust than any other DoD clandestine HUMINT program. Despite the limitations to the levels and types of sources to employ, army programs were the most prolific producers of U.S. HUMINT throughout the Cold War.

Although the CIA did run some effective clandestine HUMINT operations against the Soviet Bloc, the primary source of HUMINT for U.S. intelligence was DoD overt HUMINT. In addition to USMLM collection, the large majority of the HUMINT collected against the Soviet threat during the Cold War was through the U.S. Army Joint Interrogation Centers (JICs) in West Germany. The DoD's primary focus on HUMINT was preparation for tactical-level battlefield interrogation and debriefing operations, for which JICs were the best HUMINT collection and wartime preparation capabilities. The JIC system leveraged the dynamic of the increasingly oppressive Soviet Bloc regimes which incentivized their citizenry to escape to the West for various reasons. JIC sources consisted of a steady flow of migrants, refugees, asylum seekers, and defectors, most of whom could only provide information regarding Soviet Bloc military activity observed where they lived and during their treks to the inner German border, so the information each of the very many sources provided was just one small piece in a very large intelligence picture puzzle.

The CIA maintained a presence in the JICs and reserved the authority to take over sources for debriefing or to recruit as agents to be returned to their Eastern Bloc countries of origin. Although far from a sophisticated clandestine HUMINT capability, DoD elements were authorized to recruit low-level sources from the JIC system and dispatch them back to their Eastern countries of origin as HUMINT assets.

The Differing Chess Strategies

While HUMINT was the intelligence-collection means that was most emblematic of Cold War spy/counterspy intrigue, there were other highly valuable intelligence-collection disciplines. The other two primary intelligence-collection disciplines were signals intelligence (SIGINT) and imagery intelligence (IMINT) (previously termed photographic intelligence or PHOTINT). SIGINT is the category of intelligence comprising either individually or in combination all communications intelligence, electronic intelligence, and foreign instrumentation signals intelligence. SIGINT is most commonly associated with voice communications intercept. IMINT is the technical, geographic, and intelligence information derived through the interpretation or analysis of imagery and collateral materials. Cold War imagery analysts were facetiously referred to as "squints" because of the time they spent studying reconnaissance aircraft or satellite imagery (overhead photography), squinting through a magnifying glass to identify details of intelligence interest.

During the initial years of the Cold War, technical collection capabilities did not adequately provide long-range, denied-area standoff collection capabilities. This initially rendered HUMINT as the primary denied-area intelligence capability. Unlike the U.S. and NATO, however, the Soviets did not have the advantage of thousands of HUMINT sources coming to them from the denied areas in the form of line-crossers willing to provide intelligence, as was leveraged by the JIC system. Therefore, the Soviet KGB and GRU needed to establish forward-based, international HUMINT networks to actively develop the information necessary to plan for and fight a war with the West. In addition to the fact that HUMINT sources were fleeing to the West, another dynamic that largely shaped the distinction between U.S. and Soviet HUMINT operations was the difficulties and risks of running denied-area operations in repressive/restrictive Communist countries in comparison to relatively open democratic countries.

As the Cold War progressed, the U.S. maintained an advantage in standoff and overhead IMINT and SIGINT, which further decreased the need for denied-area HUMINT sources relative to Soviet Bloc intelligence services. The limitations of conducting HUMINT operations on the eastern side of the Iron Curtain also increased the sense of urgency to develop standoff technical collection capabilities. In fact, senior U.S. policymakers were generally enamored with technical collection, and dedicated a relatively limited amount of resources in support of HUMINT programs. The Soviets, on the other hand, did not develop such technological advancements as rapidly and remained largely dependent on clandestine HUMINT collection for intelligence on NATO plans and military capabilities for the majority of the Cold War. The U.S.'s technology monopoly resulted in a false sense of intelligence capability superiority. Ironically, the most significant advances in Soviet technical capabilities such as satellite platforms was from information provided by spies recruited and controlled through clandestine HUMINT, which demonstrated the effectiveness of their programs, but also demonstrated that the Soviets always remained at least one step behind the West in the technology race.

All methods of intelligence collection enable a country to understand what their adversary is doing, but the most valuable intelligence is that which tells a country what its adversary is planning (or intends) to do. A complete perspective of a country's military organization, equipment, and doctrine is important, but an understanding regarding the strategic and operational plans they intend to execute in the time of war is the intelligence that would prove most decisive. For example, it is important for a country to develop information regarding what capabilities and technologies an adversary has today, but it is even more important to understand and anticipate what capabilities the adversary intends to develop and the plans to employ over the next five to 10 years. This enables the country to begin planning/preparing for the future rather than remaining stagnant and then reacting to some capability or event when it is first observed at some point in the future. During the Cold War, clandestine HUMINT was far and away the most consistently reliable source of information regarding an adversary's intent—days, months, and years into the future.

IMINT was a very effective intelligence-collection capability, but generally, it could only tell analysts what was happening or had happened. SIGINT was a valuable intelligence-collection capability, but it rarely developed the fidelity of information provided through clandestine HUMINT. In addition, to counter this intelligence-collection threat, capabilities to encrypt and decrypt sensitive and classified discussions/transmissions were practiced and improved upon by both sides throughout the Cold War. The U.S. and UK excelled in "code-breaking," but this was an ongoing cycle of breaking the latest Soviet encryption, exploiting the vulnerability for the short period until the Soviets realized they were compromised and implemented the next generation of encryption, and then the cycle began again. The Eastern Bloc was not as successful at code-breaking, largely because the U.S. and UK employed more sophisticated encryption methods. However, the Soviets demonstrated that an effective clandestine HUMINT program was an effective alternative to sophisticated research and development programs. In short, an intelligence service does not need to expend resources developing decryption (code-breaking) technologies when a spy is giving them decryption codes.

Making USMLM a Valuable HUMINT Source

The constrained operating environment in the East, the fact that HUMINT sources were coming to the West, and the tradeoffs provided by technical collection capabilities, converged to incentivize the U.S. to adapt a rather lazy approach to clandestine HUMINT. In addition, while the DoD would have been willing to dedicate substantial assets to provide the U.S. a holistic clandestine HUMINT program, the CIA demonstrated bureaucratic hubris and leveraged its authorities in that area to restrict such efforts, essentially limiting the U.S.'s ability to collect predictive intelligence. The overt HUMINT programs the DoD did manage, to include the USMLM collection effort and the JIC system, were highly effective in collecting intelligence as designed. However, these programs collected and reported observations from the past, with relatively less insights into the future.

In contrast to the DoD, there were no restraints imposed on the Red Army and its GRU HUMINT-collection programs. Essentially, the Soviets had two robust and aggressive clandestine HUMINT programs in the KGB and GRU, and the U.S. had a single, much less capable clandestine HUMINT program in the CIA. Ultimately, the U.S. approach to HUMINT collection developed an abundance of tactical intelligence, but it also relegated the large majority of the U.S. HUMINT effort to collecting on past observations with relatively much less effort focused on developing the intelligence regarding future plans and intent that would have been of the most value during the Cold War. Again, these limitations were largely imposed by the CIA.

Alternatively, the British SIS did maintain a very capable clandestine HUMINT program, which was the best among the Western alliance, and helped to mitigate what was a large gap in capabilities between the U.S. and the Soviets. In addition, had foreign HUMINT authorities not rested under the CIA since the National Security Act of 1947, and had clandestine programs been established more widely by the DoD, then U.S. intelligence might have avoided the debilitation that the clandestine HUMINT program suffered during the Angleton era.

The GRU ran a clandestine HUMINT residency out of all Soviet legal residencies worldwide, just as the KGB did. In the majority of its legal residencies, the GRU ran its clandestine HUMINT programs out of its defense attaché offices. The DoD would have had the same platforms from which to conduct clandestine HUMINT operations, had it been given the authorities to do so. In every country of interest, the DoD ran a defense attaché office out of the same embassies and consulates that the CIA ran their clandestine HUMINT programs out of (stations), but the defense attachés were limited to collecting overt HUMINT which was further limited to reporting only on observations during authorized travels and information developed during conversations with foreign counterparts.

As the U.S. continued to learn throughout the Cold War, the imperative for the KGB, GRU, and Stasi to collect HUMINT forward in denied areas, with a primary focus on West Germany, resulted in those services having vast networks of sources they could task for intelligence. In contrast, the relative lack of HUMINT sources that could be tasked by U.S. agencies for denied-area intelligence was a factor that made USMLM a valued source of first-hand, denied-area HUMINT for U.S. intelligence analysis and production agencies/elements. In comparison, SMLM-F did not appear to be as highly valued to the Soviets—at least not for the type of intelligence that USMLM was collecting.

They Knew All

Intelligence reporting is classified based on the sensitivity of the information (i.e., Confidential, Secret, Top Secret). Intelligence reporting is further compartmented for limited distribution based on the sensitivity of the source of the information (e.g., Sensitive Compartmented Information (SCI), Special Category (SPECAT), Limited Distribution (LIMDIS)). The more sensitive the source, the more highly classified and compartmentalized the information will be. The reason for the more stringent classification controls is that if the information is compromised, the intelligence agency receiving the information may be able to identify and neutralize the source based on the details of the compromised information. As such, reporting based on information from a well-placed mole or highly specialized technical collection capability will be much more highly controlled than information provided by a known, overt collection platform.

HUMINT collection reporting from USMLM was generally classified Confidential or Secret with no specific restrictions on distribution, which meant the USMLM reporting was very widely disseminated. Although there was still a "need-to-know" restriction, this was a relatively low threshold, and there was a broad appetite for any information involving Soviet military organization, equipment, and operations. Any element in the DoD, and particularly in USAREUR, responsible for collecting intelligence on or planning operations against the Soviet military, was a steady consumer of USMLM reporting. This was one reason why they were considered among the very most prolific sources of intelligence—because their intelligence reporting was among the most widely disseminated and consumed.

Another principle of intelligence is that information collected on an adversary is only completely valuable as long as that adversary does not know the information has been collected/compromised. When the adversary is made aware that information has been collected/compromised, the information becomes less valuable; and, if the information is damaging to the adversary, it will likely be rendered of no value over time due to actions taken to mitigate the damage/risks associated with the compromised information. Unfortunately, all of the intelligence that USMLM collected for at least the final two decades of the Cold War lost its value as it applied to this intelligence principle.

In contrast to the absolute void of insider-type information regarding SMLM-F, the Soviets (or their surrogates) had multiple sources who were known to have access to all USMLM reporting, and who were proven to have provided everything they had access to. Although the known spies are recognized for significantly more damaging compromises than USMLM intelligence and collection activities, the fact remains that they provided comprehensive information applicable to USMLM for at least a 20-year period from 1969–88.

Perhaps there were even more, but there were three known spies who had access to USMLM reporting who were known to have compromised all of the information they ever had access to. Therefore, unequivocally, the Soviets knew all.

George Trofimoff: 18 Years of USMLM Intelligence and a Legacy of Compromised Sources Thrown Back over the Wire

George Trofimoff was raised in Germany by Russian émigré parents, enlisted in the U.S. Army in 1948 after his family moved to the U.S., became a U.S. citizen in 1951, and was commissioned as an officer in the U.S. Army Reserve in 1953. In addition to his status as a reserve officer, Trofimoff, worked from 1959 to 1994 as a civilian at the U.S. Army 66th MI Group Joint Interrogation Center (JIC) in Nuremberg, West Germany; an element that debriefed or interrogated Eastern Bloc migrants, refugees, asylum seekers, and defectors. Trofimoff held a Top Secret security clearance as he rose to the position of chief of the center's U.S. Army Element, where he had access to documents outlining Allied knowledge of the military organizations and capabilities of all Soviet and other Warsaw Pact armed forces.

In 1969, Trofimoff was recruited into the service of the KGB by his boyhood friend, Igor Vladimirovich Susemihl, a Russian Orthodox priest who at the time served as archbishop of Austria. Trofimoff saw espionage as a way out of his financial problems and betrayed the U.S. purely for money. He removed classified documents from the JIC, photographed and returned the originals, and then passed the film to Susemihl or other KGB agents during meetings in Austria or southern Germany. It is believed that he turned over more than 50,000 pages of classified documents over an 18-year period.

The U.S. and Allied partners operated interrogation and debriefing facilities throughout West Germany. These facilities, referred to as JICs, were primary sources of Soviet forces intelligence. The initial component of the interrogation and debriefing process was source screening. In this initial phase, a source would be screened to determine if they possessed information of intelligence value, and if so, whether the information was of interest to the U.S. Army or another agency. If the information was of value to the army, the source would remain at that JIC or be processed to a more appropriate facility in West Germany. If the source was of interest to another agency, the source would be processed as appropriate. In general terms, the farther west and away from the inner German border a source was processed, the more valuable the source was assessed to be in terms of strategic intelligence, with the most valuable making it all the way west to the CIA HQ in Langley, Virginia.

The JICs in West Germany were primarily focused on tactical military intelligence—much the same focus as the Allied MLMs. All JICs had the latest and most detailed intelligence holdings on Soviet Bloc military equipment, organizations, and order of battle, to guide the interrogators to seek the most relevant information and to validate the credibility of the information provided by a given source. These documents detailed the whole of the U.S.'s knowledge of Soviet Bloc military capabilities, much of which was collected by USMLM. Since USMLM was a widely known collection element and not considered a sensitive source, it was cited as the source of the information in the documents when applicable. Therefore, not only was Trofimoff providing the Soviets the most up-to-date and comprehensive intelligence regarding what the U.S. knew about their military forces, they were also able to discern the information of relevance that USMLM had collected over the period of the latest reporting. Even the latest breaking intelligence that USMLM collected would be disseminated on a priority basis in the effort to have JIC sources augment the information. This meant that Trofimoff's treachery enabled the Soviets to understand all of the Allied MLMs' intelligence successes and the entirety of the information provided on GSFG and East German equipment and military force disposition from 1969 to nearly the end. Had Trofimoff been the only source of USMLM reporting, then information detailing the U.S.'s intelligence holdings on the larger Soviet military would have been of much greater value than the multitude of debriefing reports derived from the low-level and often inconsequential sources he was also providing.

In addition to the wealth of intelligence provided by Trofimoff, his access to the identities of the individuals entered into the interrogation and debriefing process was also of significant value to the Soviets. The desperate people making their way through the process were the epitome of expendable pawns in the game. The methods that Western agencies used to extract information from refugees, asylum seekers, and travelers included emotional manipulation based on bonds to family, colleagues, friends, and lovers. This was one of the darkest aspects of the Cold War spy business, and most of the individuals caught up in this game of chess were the lowest of pawns on the lowest of boards. Collateral damage.

The assessments of the intelligence agencies often proved decisive in determining whether an individual would be granted asylum in the West or sent back to a potentially tragic fate in the East. Often, they were recruited and given the opportunity to earn their way into the West by returning home and working as low-level U.S. intelligence assets. This was commonly referred to as "throwing them back over the wire." The U.S. and Allies haphazardly "threw back" East German and other Eastern European refugees for dangerous and often suicidal intelligence operations and other covert actions behind the Iron Curtain. Unfortunately for them, Trofimoff provided the names of individuals whom the Soviet Bloc intelligence services could screen for as returning Western intelligence assets. The number of assets compromised in this manner will never be known, but it must have been substantive, as there was no shortage of compromised assets that the U.S. continually dealt with throughout the Cold War and beyond.

In the Cold War spy business, it was important that the spies operating for the U.S. or Soviets understood that their sponsors would try to take care of them when they needed safe haven, or even after they had been caught. This is a reason why the Glienicke Bridge, also referred to as the "bridge of spies," is one of the most iconic Cold War fixtures. Not only was it the launch route for USMLM tours, it was also the site of many spy exchanges throughout the years. These spy exchanges were symbolic of the fact that the powers would negotiate for the freedom of their spies even after they had been arrested and sentenced. Not taking these extraordinary measures would send the message to would-be spies that there was not this loyalty that they could depend on, which might dissuade them from entering into the risky business in the first place. And while it was the high-level spy exchanges that received all the notoriety, the same principles applied at the lower levels of espionage. The 66th CIC Group and later the 66th MI Group had a long-standing program to address long-lost agents who climbed back over the wire and came in from the cold.

When agents thrown back over the wire or any other agents working for U.S. intelligence failed to report, it was assumed that they had been arrested and their details were recorded in a final report. These reports made their way to an elderly gentleman with a trench coat and a pipe hanging from his mouth, who worked in the deep dark recesses of the 66th MI Group HQ in Munich, West Germany. This gentleman, referred to as the "bag man," sat in an office lined with cabinets full of final reports. Occasionally, he would get a phone call, normally from the Berlin Counterintelligence Detachment, informing him that an individual claiming to have been arrested as an agent of the U.S. wanted their compensation. The bag man would pull the applicable report to confirm the assertion, and then pull out his formula sheet and calculator to determine the amount of compensation to be provided to the individual based on various factors to include intelligence reported prior to arrest and the number of years in confinement. The bag man would then take his black satchel bag (hence his name) to the Intelligence Contingency Fund custodian and draw the money (in deutsche marks) that would be provided to the individual. He would board a train to the applicable meet location, render payment and express the appreciation of the U.S. government, gather a receipt for the payment, and then return to Munich to file the final, final report. It is apparent that the bag man had Trofimoff to thank for much of his job security.

In 1986, an East German citizen made his way to West Berlin in an effort to defect and get his family safe passage to the West. After quickly being filtered through the West German agencies and then to the CIA, Army Counterintelligence was given the final opportunity to speak with him before he was turned away. The man was an academic who claimed to occasionally work for the Stasi as an English translator. He wanted help getting him and his family out of East Germany, but did not have any valuable information to offer at the time. The Army Counterintelligence agents explained that he would need to provide "something significant" to justify this level of support. When asked what would qualify as significant, the agents handed him a small slip of paper with a phone number on it and said, "Bring us an American traitor." The would-be defector, now codenamed CANNA CLAY by Army Counterintelligence, was thrown back over the wire. After nearly two years of not being heard from, CANNA CLAY was assumed as destined to become just one more file in the bag man's endless wall of file cabinets.

In 1987, Trofimoff was directed by the KGB to terminate his collection activities. It is assumed that this was due to improved U.S./Soviet relations and a Soviet desire to avoid the possibility of such a long-serving and devastating spy being discovered, but his espionage activities could have been terminated for a variety of other reasons. Trofimoff continued working at the JIC until his retirement in 1994, at which time he relocated to the U.S.

The Szabo/Conrad Ring: Another 16 Years of USMLM Intelligence

Zoltan Szabo was a naturalized U.S. citizen whose parents fled Hungary with him after the 1956 Soviet invasion to put down the Hungarian revolution. Szabo enlisted in the U.S. Army, was selected for officer candidate school, rose to the rank of captain, earned a Silver Star for valor in Vietnam, was ordered to separate from service after a postwar reduction in force, and was allowed to rejoin the army as a sergeant. In 1971, Szabo was approached by Hungarian intelligence service agents while vacationing with his German wife and children in Hungary. With the offer of money and the opportunity for his parents to be comfortably repatriated to Hungary, Szabo agreed to become a spy.

In 1972, Szabo was assigned to the 8th Infantry Division (ID); the 20,000-man U.S. Army organization that would have been critical to the defense of West Germany against a Soviet Bloc attack. As a part of the larger defense plan for West Germany, the 8th ID planners were provided access to all major war plans for the defense of West Germany. Szabo worked in the 8th ID G3 (Operations) War Planning section and became the first steady source of USAREUR and NATO war plans that made their way to the KGB via the Hungarian intelligence service. All war plans from NATO down to the lower echelons needed to be aligned, so elements such as the 8th ID needed all of the higher war plans to ensure that their plans were "nested" with the higher plans. Throughout the Cold War, USMLM reporting was essential to all USAREUR war planning efforts, and major elements such as the 8th ID were on the mandatory distribution lists for all USMLM reporting. In addition to standard tour collection information, USMLM regularly received taskings from USAREUR to conduct route and deployment location reconnaissance in support of all USAREUR plans, to include all corps and division planning efforts.

Until his retirement in 1979, Szabo was recognized by Hungarian intelligence as their most productive agent ever. At the time of his retirement from the U.S.

Army as a staff sergeant, he was also a colonel in Hungarian military intelligence. To expand his access to classified information and prepare for his eventual retirement, Szabo endeavored to grow his network, and in 1975, he found his prized jewel. Clyde Conrad was assigned to the 8th ID as the classified documents custodian, responsible for the accountability of all classified documents to ensure that none of them could be taken from the secure facility.

In 1975, Conrad began delivering information from the vaults housing the Top Secret documents he was supposed to be protecting. Szabo introduced Conrad to Hungarian brothers Imre and Sandor Keresik, who would serve as couriers between the two. With their help, Conrad was able to set up a spy ring that passed more than 30,000 documents over the course of a 13-year period. The documents involved were among the most valuable in the world to the Eastern Bloc and included NATO wartime general defense plans which disclosed where all U.S. and other NATO forces would be deployed and the areas they would defend in the event of war. They also included NATO strategies and nuclear weapon sites. All of the intelligence Conrad provided worked its way through the Hungarian intelligence service to the KGB. In return, he received payments reaching into the millions of dollars.

As Szabo had done before him, Conrad began preparing for his retirement by putting in place the third generation of the spy ring with access to all the war plans. In 1983, Conrad recruited Roderick Ramsay, a young soldier with a genius-level IQ as his prodigy. Conrad pulled some strings and was able to get Ramsay a position in the 8th ID G3 Plans section as his assistant classified document custodian. Here, Ramsay was able to access everything Conrad could, and even broadened his access through some innovative efforts. As a result of Ramsay's espionage, Conrad provided Hungarian intelligence perhaps the most damaging information of the entire Cold War—Top Secret COSMIC nuclear deployment codes and the locations of tactical nuclear weapons.

The Conrad ring was among the biggest spy rings since World War II. After his retirement from the army in 1985, Conrad continued to run his network from his home in Bosenheim, West Germany. Unknown to Conrad, his agent in the 8th ID G3 Plans office, Ramsay, had recruited two additional agents, Sergeant Jeffrey Rondeau and Sergeant Jeffrey Gregory. Ramsay consolidated the take from the three agents and delivered the "mother lode" to Conrad—a flight bag filled with over 20 pounds of documents. In 1985, Conrad's retirement plan hit a snag when Ramsay failed a drug test and was released from the army. Having been given the "mother lode," however, Conrad was able to convince his Hungarian handlers that he still had an agent in the 8th ID G3 Plans division, and provided information from the "mother lode" stockpile in smaller bits as though they were all newly acquired documents from his agent. In 1987, Conrad recruited a young female clerk-typist working in the 8th ID G3 Plans section, Private First Class Kelly Warren, who allowed Conrad to come to her office and copy documents until her transfer in 1988, making her the last active member of the 16-year espionage enterprise.

James Hall: Inside Insights on USMLM Intelligence Collection

In June 1982, James Hall III, a U.S. Army signal intelligence NCO, dropped a letter volunteering his services in the mailbox at the Soviet consulate in West Berlin. Hall started passing documents to Soviet agents in 1982 while serving as a communications analyst monitoring Eastern Bloc communications traffic from the NSA Field Station Berlin. In 1982, Hall was also recruited by an East German Stasi agent, so from 1982 to 1985, he passed the same information to the Soviets and East Germans and was paid by both. Hall provided large volumes of documents, intercepts, and encryption codes, exposing many operations. Like the JICs and the army divisions, the field station maintained the most current and comprehensive intelligence holdings regarding Soviet Bloc military, to include USMLM reporting.

In addition to his daily duties when assigned to Field Station Berlin from 1982 to 1985, Hall represented the field station at periodic meetings of the various U.S. intelligence collectors operating in or out of West Berlin. The forum was an analytic exchange of information to help "tip off" fellow agencies of collection opportunities. Each of Berlin's intelligence collection elements attended the exchanges, to include the field station and USMLM. Among other discussions, this venue provided USMLM analysts an opportunity to detail USMLM collection priorities and techniques.

At one meeting in early 1984, the USMLM analyst boasted of his unit's most sensitive collection success, proudly displaying a series of close-up interior photographs of a modified Soviet T-64B tank. The pictures could only have been taken by someone actually inside the tank. The analyst described how the USMLM tour officer photographed the tank on New Year's Eve, when Soviet sentries were not manning their posts. In addition to all other USMLM reporting which he had access to, Hall provided this information to the Stasi and KGB, to include the report that specified when and where the embarrassing compromise had occurred.

Intelligence analysts understand that the exchange of relevant information among fellow analysts is important because it is necessary to increase the amount of data available to be analyzed, therefore resulting in more informed and complete analysis products. DoD intelligence analysts had the highest security clearance possible, conversed in secure facilities, and were therefore very liberal in the information they were willing to share with each other. The analytic exchange that Hall attended with USMLM analysts was conducted for this very purpose. The information that Hall brought to the exchange was based on Top Secret and highly sensitive technical collection capabilities and was much more sensitive than the information overtly collected by USMLM tour officers. Therefore, as analytic exchanges go, Hall would have appeared to be bringing more to the table than the USMLM analysts, so USMLM analysts were likely to appreciate it when they could highlight their more remarkable successes, such as the T-64B episode. Although Trofimoff and the Szabo/Conrad ring members provided the KGB the same USMLM intelligence products they were able to receive from Hall from 1982 to 1985, his participation in the analytic exchanges with USMLM analysts gave him additional insights regarding their collection methods and future intentions to provide his Soviet and East German handlers.

In 1985, Hall was assigned to a military intelligence unit in New Jersey, where he maintained contact with his Stasi handler. Hall discontinued contact with the KGB after his KGB handler confronted him regarding his duplicity in receiving payments for reporting the same information to two agencies. After a year state-side providing whatever he could to the East Germans, Hall volunteered to return to West Germany in 1986 where he was assigned to a sensitive military intelligence unit in Frankfurt. Based on his continuous access to the most sensitive Top Secret information, Hall was able to pass "massive amounts" of highly classified data on communications intelligence. According to U.S. officials, Hall's espionage inflicted serious damage on U.S. electronic intelligence activities in Europe. Arguably his most damaging action was compromising Project TROJAN—a capability that would have allowed, in the case of war, the U.S. and its allies to target Soviet armored vehicles, missiles, and planes by tracking their communication signals. Since Russia had the clear advantage in armored warfare at this point, the success or failure of TROJAN was viewed as a deciding factor in the event of a conventional conflict with the Soviets. Hall gave the East Germans, and in turn the Soviets, what could have been a deciding factor. Hall departed West Germany in 1988 to attend warrant officer candidate training in the U.S.

The Implications of Large-scale U.S. Intelligence Compromises

USMLM was regarded by intelligence experts to be among the most, if not the most, prolific intelligence collector on Soviet and East German military organizations, equipment, and tactics.

The last known compromises of intelligence collected and produced by USMLM ended in 1988. By this time, but unbeknown to USAREUR, USMLM intelligence was verging on irrelevance. On 9 November 1989, the Berlin Wall began to crumble. On 3 December of that year, the U.S. and Soviet leadership declared an end to the Cold War. On 1 October 1990, USMLM was disestablished. What was not known until after their intelligence-collection mission was no longer relevant, was that all of their reporting had been compromised to the Soviets, by multiple sources, during the 20 most critical years of the Cold War.

The Soviets were keenly aware of what (and likely when) USMLM collected and reported on Soviet (and East German) forces. Stasi elements demonstrated a keen understanding of the touring patterns of specific tour officers, and it is likely that analysts developed detailed pattern analysis based on the fusion of tour officer tour dates, sighting reports, and the compromised USMLM reporting. USMLM did not recognize areas marked by MRSs as restricted areas, but the East Germans did. SERB regularly used restricted-area violation data provided by the Stasi to either support a protest of USMLM or in response to a USMLM protest. USMLM invariably dismissed these claims because the numbers presented were always much too high to have been compiled by Stasi surveillance and unit/citizen sighting reports alone. Stasi analysis of compromised USMLM reporting would explain how the Stasi developed the restricted-area violation data that they provided to the Soviets and stood behind as valid. Had the USAREUR intelligence staff ever considered the alternatives rather than dismissing the Stasi claims as fabrications, they might have concluded that such statistics could only be developed through the analysis of detailed, compromised USMLM reporting.

Cold War spies are notorious for the types and amount of information they compromised, and not necessarily based on an understanding of how or whether the Soviet Bloc intelligence services exploited the compromised information. There is no conclusive evidence that has been declassified and released by the U.S., German, or Russian governments to disclose the degree to which the Soviets and East Germans exploited USMLM intelligence reporting compromised by Trofimoff, the Szabo/ Conrad ring, or Hall. However, this is no different than virtually all of the intelligence that was compromised to the Soviet machine during the Cold War. It is known that Trofimoff and the Szabo/Conrad ring provided everything in the JIC and 8th ID classified document vaults, which definitively included the USMLM reporting. Any USMLM reporting provided by Hall may have been considered much less valuable in comparison to the highly sensitive information provided, based on his access to technical collection activities, but in his post-arrest debrief, he did confirm providing USMLM reporting to the KGB and Stasi. Therefore, to conclude that the KGB, GRU, or the Stasi did not exploit the USMLM reporting, would be to conclude that it was of little value given the other information available.

A principle of intelligence is that information collected on an adversary is only completely valuable as long as that adversary does not know that the information has been collected/compromised. As for USMLM collection, they knew all.

The Deception Theory and Narratives

Although liaison and direct communication between the occupying forces commands was the stated purpose of the MLMs, the ironic truth was that the large majority of communication between the MLMs and their hosts was about MLM activities. In other words, rather than simply being the channel of communications, they became the primary reason for the need for a channel of communications. The large majority of formal engagements and informal face-to-face discussions among the senior leadership were to protest the actions of the accredited MLM or hosting elements, and to then argue, debate, negotiate, and reconcile the issues. Logistical issues regarding the support and maintenance of the MLMs such as fuel rations and facility maintenance were the next most pressing issues requiring direct interface. Again, had the MLMs not existed, there would have been no reason for these discussions.

Shortly after the MLMs were established, the relatively few discussions regarding non-MLM issues/incidents such as official visits, congratulations, and condolences were no justification to maintain a permanent mission for the purpose of direct liaison. There were certainly no discussions regarding the welfare of the German states or engagements of concern regarding their return to international normalcy, as was the original purpose for their cooperation. Since this dynamic continued in kind year after year after year, there was obviously a value to both sides that was well beyond an overt channel of communications for purely liaison purposes. Much like the current paradigm, most "liaison" functions can be handled through a single liaison officer or a small office, unless there is the need to build an artificial reason for a larger presence, as is the case in many military/defense attaché offices. By 1952, neither of the MLMs were even collocated with the CINCs to which they were accredited, but they remained intact as "liaison" organizations despite this disparity.

The MLM dynamic was a strategic, operational, and tactical game of chess that both sides accepted and excelled at along different trajectories. Although practical and relevant information was regularly exchanged, the MLMs provided the mechanisms to exchange information when it benefited one of the members to push out information (or disinformation). The MLMs also provided among the most effective means to verify the information in many cases. Exchanges among the MLMs and their hosts enabled the sides to establish and reinforce the narratives that they wanted to have resonate. In most cases, liaison channels among the MLMs also provided an effective means to assess how well the narratives were being accepted and how the messaging needed to change to more effectively communicate the narrative.

Information exchanged through liaison channels was invariably reported to senior leadership for understanding and evaluation. Just as practices that were allowed to continue by both sides eventually established precedents that made them acceptable under international law, practices that were discussed but not objected to could also be considered acceptable practices after being reinforced through multiple official engagements.

Intelligence is not a substitute for communication between adversaries, but rather, a confirmation thereof, and an additional safety catch against a possible escalation into war. Intelligence collection is a risk-reduction tool, and in many cases, the U.S. recognizes and even appreciates that adversaries collect information that can confirm that intentions are consistent with messaging delivered through diplomacy. Particularly during the tense Cold War years, information received through diplomatic channels was accepted with open arms, but never believed until verified through intelligence. Therefore, any information received by either side immediately triggered an intelligence-collection requirement to verify the information as true or false.

In many cases, the MLMs provided the most expedient collection assets available. The MLMs were unique in that they not only provided an official means to exchange information, but also to verify the information provided. For example, the Soviets might find value in knowing that the information they provided through SMLM-F could be readily verified as accurate by USMLM intelligence collection. Alternatively, they refrained from providing information that might be proven false by USMLM (or other sources of) intelligence collection. This dynamic was one aspect of the wilderness of mirrors labyrinth that made it a game within a game. These mutually accepted procedures that were allowable based on a liberal (and again mutual) interpretation of the agreement made the MLMs emblematic of the Cold War dynamic of diplomacy, intelligence collection, and counterintelligence.

The Deception Theory

The traditional paradigm of the wilderness of mirrors is a strategic deception campaign based on feeding information/disinformation through a range of sources to include spies, double agents, defectors, and agent provocateurs. The deception theory (in practice) involved the abstract calculus of Cold War double-cross with the placement of false agents within enemy ranks and the planting of false information with enemy intelligence analysts. Although referred to as a theory, influence operations consistent with the deception theory have historically been effectively employed by intelligence services—most notably by those of the Soviet Bloc.

For the deception theory to succeed, there must be two distinct channels of communications to the target intelligence service. The first channel must be an apparently credible line of communications to the intelligence service by the one perpetrating the deception. There must also be a second channel through which the perpetrating intelligence service receives feedback to confirm that the operation is having the intended result, and ensure that it is not the service being deceived. With this verification and feedback loop (verification channel), the perpetrating intelligence service can amplify or reinforce the parts of the story the opposing intelligence service is prone to believe, and eliminate or revise those that are doubted. When effectively employed, intelligence analysts adopt the narrative that the perpetrating intelligence service intended as the deception, and the "deceived" intelligence agency becomes its own deceiver.

The dynamic of the MLMs did not directly mirror this traditional construct, but it did provide processes through which potentially deceptive (or true) narratives could be developed through liaison contacts, actions on the ground, official complaints or demarches, and quid pro quo or reciprocity reactions. In fact, this was the dynamic through which the competitive norms were established and mutually recognized without either side officially negotiating or acknowledging their viability as acceptable practices.

The East/West MLM dynamic actually provided a very streamlined, interactive process that could be exploited to enable the key element of disinformation (or other narrative) delivery, and perhaps even facilitate both channels necessary for the deception theory process. Since it was mutually understood that all liaison interactions were documented and provided to each other's intelligence services, the MLM liaison channel provided a conduit that enabled either side to deliver information directly to the other's intelligence services without elaborate ruses such as false defectors or volunteers.

The MLM communication channel also provided a potential channel for the verification and feedback loop by simply asking questions, observing reactions to information, or through other forms of interpersonal elicitation. Other than this direct channel, information could be developed by activity monitoring through central call centers, physical surveillance, technical surveillance, or other methods of information development.

Among the many examples throughout the years, the Poland crisis in the early1980s was one of the more obvious of which the USMLM was leveraged to both deliver and verify a narrative. On 1 July 1980, a crisis began when the authorities of the People's Republic of Poland raised the prices of certain types of meat. Polish workers reacted with work stoppages beginning that day, sparking a wave of strikes throughout Poland. As the labor union protests continued, the Soviets began to perceive the movement as a serious threat to the Communist Party rule in a key Soviet Bloc partner country. As the world had witnessed in Hungary in 1956 and Czechoslovakia in 1968, the Soviet military began to posture to intervene in Poland, if necessary, to put down the popular unrest. To mask preparations for an invasion, the Soviets established a TRA along the East German and Polish border area from 30 November to 9 December 1980. The Soviets ultimately decided not to invade, but they needed to sustain pressure on Poland through the threat of a military intervention to compel the Poles to put down the uprising on their own, to avoid a Soviet intervention. To ensure complete transparency in sending this message to the U.S., 1981 was an unprecedented year in the history of the MLMs in that the Soviets did not issue a single TRA. This served to send a message to the U.S. that the Soviets had nothing to hide and that they were not building up forces for an invasion of Poland. In addition to sending this narrative through the official USMLM channel of communications, USMLM was able to confirm the narrative through intelligence collection and observations on the ground.

As this and many other examples demonstrated, although named the deception theory, the same concept applies to communicating a true narrative and ensuring that it is also having the desired manner of influence.

Strategic Landscape

It is important to view the MLM dynamic from the perspective of the strategic wilderness of mirrors and within the context of the strategic espionage and counter-espionage landscape. This devious and often nasty business was still generally played by tacitly understood "gentlemen's rules" that both sides recognized. Based on the strategic wilderness of mirrors, the U.S. and Soviets had established "norms" that served to bound the spy/counterspy dynamic.

Although every country considers espionage a high crime, there is no international law that precludes countries from collecting intelligence or even recruiting or emplacing individuals to commit espionage. The U.S. and Soviet Union may have purported that espionage was unlawful, but elaborate codes of behavior govern their actions in regard to this delicate topic. Spying activities are obtusely regarded as falling within the category of "unfriendly acts" between states. Generally, discovered episodes of espionage among the U.S. and USSR were only raised to the level of a demarche, which is a petition or protest presented through diplomatic channels.

Despite all the episodes of state-sponsored espionage directed against each other, the sides very rarely accused the other of committing espionage in formal or public channels. The only individuals imprisoned for collecting intelligence against the U.S. or Soviets are those who were paid or otherwise incentivized to do so, and not the representatives of those countries who actually directed the espionage activities of those individuals. Even agents referred to as "illegals," although technically emplaced by a foreign power, are on their own and "officially" disavowed if captured. Related to this concept is the reason why intelligence officers operate out of official establishments, such as embassies, with official diplomatic status. If their espionage-related activities are detected, the worst that could happen is that they are expelled as persona non grata with a demarche being issued to the sponsoring government. For example, when a Russian diplomat is expelled from the U.S. for known or suspected espionage activities, the official State Department explanation is normally an ambiguously worded statement such as that the individual was expelled for "taking actions not consistent with the duties they were accredited to perform"—which is diplospeak for conducing espionage. The Soviet defense attaché who was expelled from the U.S. in response to the Nicholson shooting was selected because he had been "very active" in his duties.

Legal scholars may debate the point in general, but as it applied to the U.S. and the Soviet Union during the Cold War, espionage was tacitly acknowledged as an acceptable norm. Espionage has never been cause for either country to discontinue diplomatic relations, and was certainly not an issue that either side would go to war over. The acts may be protested and potentially strain relations, but they never rose to the level of being a deal-breaker, and were therefore ultimately recognized as establishing an acceptable precedent under international law. Obviously, if one side were to actually declare espionage a deal-breaker, then they too would need to be committed to discontinue the practice, or face the consequences of no longer allowing the game to be played by the gentlemen's rules. Even in the case of Gary Powers, who was shot down by the Russians in 1958 while conducting a U-2 spy plane overflight of Russia, he was not charged with collecting intelligence, but rather, for violating Russian airspace.

The U.S. did unilaterally place restrictions on the use of certain organizations and occupations as spy platforms, such as the Peace Corps and missionary work, but the Soviets appeared to employ all of their forward foreign presences as clandestine intelligence-collection platforms. With espionage established as an accepted norm under international law, either the U.S. or Soviets could have used this as a defense had either of their MLMs been accused of an act that legitimately qualified as espionage. The Soviets, however, did not simply rest on this legal international standing, as they ventured to ensure that this was a narrative that was delivered redundantly through their primary and secondary MLM channels of communications.

Espionage Narrative

Among the many narratives developed over the years through Soviet rhetoric as they applied to the MLMs were that all dangerous incidents were caused by undisciplined USMLM tour officers, that a sentry was required to protect his post by any means necessary, and that the Soviet sector of East Germany was a "wild, wild west" while the U.S. sector of West Germany was a relative "sleepy hollow." USMLM did not appear to follow such a strategy of consistent messaging through the years to establish or reinforce norms, but there were isolated examples. The Allied MLMs presented a unified front in reinforcing that MRSs were not recognized as valid restrictions under the provisions of the Huebner–Malinin Agreement. And while this narrative did not appreciably impact Soviet and East German actions on the ground, at the SERB level, this narrative was accepted in that tour officers were expelled for violating a PRA or TRA, but never for the very many "violations" of MRS marked areas. One Soviet narrative propagated over the years which was established under the context of USMLM activities, but could very conceivably have been promoted to enable a "mirror image" scenario, was the espionage narrative.

Espionage is defined as intelligence activity directed through clandestine means towards the acquisition of information that a competing nation holds secret. The term "clandestine means" is defined as any activity or operation sponsored or conducted by governmental departments or agencies with the intent to assure secrecy or concealment. Intelligence collection is defined as the acquisition of information or intelligence information for provision to processing and/or production elements. Overt intelligence collection is defined as intelligence activities with the ultimate goal of intelligence information collection which are not designed or executed to conceal sponsorship, collection activity, identity of operators, or methodologies employed. Based on this lineage of definitions, overt intelligence collection, with which USMLM was openly associated, does not fall under the definition of espionage or clandestine activities. The act of intelligence collection is more generic, and could fall under the definition of espionage if practiced under certain parameters.

USMLM had two specified missions—liaison and intelligence. The official USMLM mission statement specified that the "secondary and confidential mission of USMLM is to exploit its liaison status and attendant access for collection of intelligence information in the German Democratic Republic (GDR)." The intelligence mission remained classified until long after the MLMs ceased operations. Since it is known that reports including this classified mission statement were compromised to the Soviets as early as 1969, knowing that the U.S. acknowledged that they leveraged their "attendant access" for the "collection of intelligence" would have provided the Soviets a range of claims of reciprocity had SMLM-F ever been accused of an act legitimately falling under the rubric of espionage.

Although intelligence collection was never officially agreed to as an acceptable practice under the provisions of the Huebner–Malinin Agreement, intelligence collection in the form of "tours" was never brought into question. Just as the two countries recognized that espionage and other covert activities were run out of the embassies in each other's country, the MLMs were extraterritorial, so the concept of collecting intelligence on foreign soil applied. The U.S. allowed the Soviets into their sector of West Germany and SMLM-F actively collected intelligence against U.S. military and other interests, as did USMLM as an accredited guest of the Soviets. Like the international norms that were established among the two superpowers as they applied to espionage and other methods of intelligence collection, MLM intelligence collection was mutually recognized as a norm with the only limitation being mutually agreed to restricted areas.

The Soviets and East Germans consistently repeated the narrative that USMLM was engaged in espionage. When Akts (incident reports) were produced after detentions, they regularly stated that the USMLM tour had been engaged in espionage. This espionage narrative continued throughout the duration of the MLMs. In 1959, a USMLM tour was detained by Stasi agents and the USMLM tour equipment was seized. Following the process of the East German agents turning the tour personnel over to the local Soviet Kommandant, a report was written accusing the tour of carrying espionage equipment for the purpose of conducting espionage against East German and Soviet forces. The incident Akt stated that "Processing of the items picked up in the search revealed that the Mission members were carrying espionage equipment, including long-range photographic equipment and maps, for the purpose of conducting espionage against the East German and Soviet Army."

The tour officer was subsequently declared persona non grata and expelled from East Germany. The PNG action with no further reprisals served to "legitimize" the espionage claim, and could have been referenced in the future as the standard, established response to MLM acts of espionage by either side. As another example, following a 1983 detention in which USMLM equipment was confiscated by the detaining East German forces, CUSMLM called for a meeting with CSERB to demand the return of the equipment. In response to the USMLM demand, CSERB asked CUSMLM, "When in the history of espionage, has an apprehended spy ever had his tools returned?"

Coincidentally, the entity that appeared to be most vested in the espionage narrative was the Stasi. The most rational explanation for their compulsive approach to USMLM was that they had insights regarding the manner in which SMLM-F was operating in the U.S. sector, which led them to assume that USMLM was operating in a similar manner (mirror imaging).

Espionage as an Accepted Norm

The Huebner–Malinin Agreement had standing as a treaty between the U.S. and the Soviets, and was therefore binding under international law. When two countries enter into a treaty, all actions taken under the provisions of the treaty are legitimized if they are allowed to continue without becoming cause to break the treaty. Again, just as practices that were allowed to continue by both sides eventually established precedents that made them acceptable under international law, practices that were discussed but not objected to could also be considered acceptable practices after being reinforced through multiple official engagements. The consistent narrative that USMLM was committing espionage, and the fact that the U.S. never officially challenged this contention, essentially established espionage as an acceptable norm.

The practice of acknowledging USMLM intelligence collection as an acceptable norm while repeatedly accusing USMLM of espionage may have appeared on the surface as being competing narratives, but they were not. This narrative served to expand the range of the meaning of the term "intelligence collection," that was generally associated with overt HUMINT, to eventually include clandestine HUMINT and espionage as well. Although the U.S. never accused SMLM-F of "espionage," if it was tacitly acknowledged as a common practice by one MLM, then it would be considered fair game for the other. Therefore, if SMLM-F had been discovered conducting activities consistent with the true definition of espionage, they could have leveraged the on-the-record espionage narrative to justify their actions as consistent with an established USMLM precedent. It is very possible that the Soviets deliberately established the "espionage" narrative over time in the case of an eventuality for which they may have needed a legal precedent justification, but which never came to be.

Entering the Final Decade

The MLMs were traditionally viewed by the U.S. as USAREUR responsibilities that operated on their own unique and isolated battlefields, that were insulated from the outside world. In reality, however, they were microcosms of a larger strategic framework with which they were intrinsically connected. The U.S. tendency was to view MLM activities as decentralized efforts with their own parochial purposes and objectives. In contrast, the Soviets always operated with a big-picture perspective which took all of the players into account, to include the MLMs.

The two-year period between December 1979 and December 1981 provided a very enlightening case study of how at least three episodes which U.S. military history would have depicted as isolated and unrelated—if even remembered at all—were actually viewed by the Soviets as interrelated components of a grander strategy.

A Point of USMLM Pride, or an Anomaly

A point of pride which USMLM association members and historians espouse is that USMLM was the only U.S. intelligence agency operating out of Berlin that was not penetrated in some manner by the Soviets, the East Germans, or any other Soviet Bloc intelligence service. This assertion is based on what may be incomplete information, but if true, it adds one more mirror to the wilderness.

Although this contention may tend to reflect well on the quality of the USMLM personnel throughout the years, it really raises more questions than the one it portends to answer. Notably, the implication of this argument is that USMLM personnel were impervious to any such efforts, whereas the other agencies were not. Therefore, to suggest that the 40 years of USMLM personnel were infallible in comparison to those who were successfully exploited by Soviet Bloc intelligence, is probably not the reason for this legacy if it is in fact the case. Alternatively, the true counterintelligence professional would attribute this legacy to other factors that were certainly controlled by the Soviets at the higher levels of the KGB and GRU.

The Soviets and East Germans retained files on USMLM members that contained the types of biographical and other personal information typically contained in dossiers intended to develop exploitable information. For example, two days following the Nicholson shooting, the Stasi provided a report to the KGB with a summary of information that was obviously contained in the dossier the Stasi maintained on Nicholson, which was indicative of the dossiers maintained on all USMLM personnel. The report included information regarding Nicholson's prior military education and performance while at USMLM. The report specified when he attended intelligence officer training and Russian language training, and summarized his record of restricted area violations and other questionable activities to include offering to pay an East German citizen to not notify VOPO about an accident for which the USMLM driver was at fault. Any potentially exploitable information, such as Nicholson's attempt to bribe a citizen to disregard the law, would be retained in the USMLM personnel dossiers. So while the Stasi did maintain files containing potentially exploitable information on USMLM personnel, there was never an indication of a sophisticated effort to recruit a USMLM member.

The USMLM record of infallibility assumes that there was not a recruitment of a USMLM member that was never discovered. There are many spies who will go to their graves never having been discovered, but as time passes without incriminating details, the likelihood that USMLM was not penetrated increases. However, with the Soviets and their East German surrogates, things were often not as they appeared

Pawns in the Game

On 27 December 1979, the Soviets conducted a successful takeover of the Afghanistan government. That event marked the beginning of the most significant decline in U.S./Soviet relations during the Cold War.

On 29 December 1979, the CUSMLM accompanied by DCUSMLM, Lieutenant Colonel James Tonge, USMLM tour officer, Lieutenant Colonel Bill Burhans, and USMLM tour officer, Major John Goff, attended the annual gift exchange hosted at the SERB HQ. The usual vodka, mineral water, salmon, and sardines were served. CSERB concluded the event with a toast stating that he looked forward to increased social contact during the new year and hoped to keep things on an "even keel." After the conclusion of the event, CUSMLM departed in his vehicle driven by a tour NCO, and Tonge, Burhans, and Goff departed in a USMLM vehicle with Burhans driving.

After driving the three-block route from SERB to the Glienicke Bridge, Burhans expertly threaded the serpentine barriers, stopped at the guard post to present credentials, and then proceeded toward the USMLM facility. Shortly after clearing the guard post and passing into West Berlin, Burhans lost control of the vehicle which sideswiped two cars, careened up an embankment, and slammed into a bus. When the vehicle came to a stop, Tonge told Burhans to move the car to the shoulder, but Burhans sat unresponsive and motionless, except for his trembling hands. After helping Burhans into the back seat, Tonge moved the car himself. Several bottles of vodka they had received from their Soviet "friends" were broken in the accident, making the vehicle reek of alcohol. U.S. Army military police were called to the scene of the accident. By the time of their arrival, Tonge too had become impaired.

Burhans and Tonge were certain that the only explanation for the vehicle accident was that they had been drugged by the Soviets at the gift exchange. USMLM personnel were under the jurisdiction of the U.S. Army Berlin commander for what the military refers to as non-judicial punishment. A hasty investigation of the incident ensued: Burhans was found guilty of driving while intoxicated and ordered to pay for the damages, and Tonge was found guilty of driving while intoxicated for the brief instance that he drove the vehicle to a safe position following the accident. Burhans underwent a drug test two days after the event and was found to have Bromazepam, a drug with similar side effects as Valium, in his system. A drug test administered to Tonge five days after the accident found traces of drugs that he had not been prescribed or taking. However, the medical staff had no way of confirming that Burhans or Tonge had not ingested the medications after the accident to support their side of the story. The two officers were expeditiously removed from USMLM.

Stasi documents discovered in 2019—40 years after the USMLM officers were sent away in disgrace—disclosed that the Soviets plotted to target and discredit the men. According to the documents, the Stasi had opened a dossier on Burhans when he first served as a USMLM tour officer from 1971 to 1975, characterizing him as a bold officer with a propensity for eluding Stasi surveillance. The Soviets continued to monitor Burhans after he returned to the U.S. in 1975, with intercepted mail and HUMINT source reports thickening the dossier. A source report in the file from 1979 informed the Stasi that Burhans would be promoted to lieutenant colonel and returning to USMLM, which did occur in July of that year. The dossiers on both Burhans and Tonge reflected extensive monitoring of the two by codenamed informants including East German cooks, cleaning women, and maintenance workers who eavesdropped on conversations, followed their movements, and read their private mail. Tonge's and Burhan's files documented that they regularly eluded surveillance for long periods of time, ignored signs marking restricted areas, and that the Stasi was convinced they were spies. The Stasi files included an "action plan" put into place as a "targeted measure to discredit" the USMLM officers. The case was closed in 1980 with the entry by a Stasi lieutenant colonel stating that on 29 December 1979 "the friends" had successfully carried out a measure to "discredit Tonge as well as his intended successor, Burhans." The term "friends" was an obvious reference to the Soviets.

One month prior to the drugging incident, on 30 November 1979, Tonge and Burhans attended a promotion ceremony for the Deputy CSERB (DCSERB). This was the first time the MLMs were invited to such an event, which could have conceivably been staged to assist in planning for the fateful event less than a month later. Noting who preferred to drive among the officers when attending such events would have served that purpose. Present at the 29 December gift exchange was the alleged newly assigned supply officer, a Soviet captain who was never referenced in a USMLM report after that event. A relatively low-ranking captain attending such a senior event was uncommon. Perhaps he had special skills and was there to "mix the drinks."

Although the "action plan" had the intended result of ridding the Stasi of its two nemeses, the plan was most likely intended to have the accident occur on the

Soviet sector side of the Glienicke Bridge, which would have given the Soviets more propaganda and leverage to complain that the officers were unfit and should be expelled. Ironically, the U.S. reaction served this very same purpose. As such, the incident likely served to reinforce to the Soviets the lengths the U.S. would go to in order to avoid casting a shadow over the MLMs. This reflection on the USAREUR, U.S. Army Berlin, and USMLM leadership at the time demonstrated the collateral damage they might be willing to accept so as not to disrupt the balance that enabled USMLM to continue its intelligence-collection mission. Just as the aftermath of the Nicholson shooting would demonstrate five years later, the U.S. side would accept exceptional wrongs by the Soviets in order to maintain the status quo of the USMLM collection capability in East Germany. If this were a drugging incident, it would not have been lost on the Soviets that they could take the most extreme measures and the U.S. would not only turn a blind eye, but would even eat their own to avoid contention.

The 1979 USMLM Unit History report, which was written after the suspicious circumstances of the vehicle accident that was documented by the Stasi to have been a Soviet "targeted measure," recorded the gift-exchange event in the annals of USMLM history as having an "atmosphere that was relaxed and friendly." USMLM reporting after the 29 December 1979 event does not address the accident, as though it was consciously expunged from the record. The 1980 USMLM Unit History report does not list Burhans or Tonge as members of USMLM during that year, or among the officers departing the mission that year. Like the event, the two officers were erased from the record. Even Major Goff, who was simply a backseat passenger, was expeditiously and quietly transferred to another unit in West Berlin. The officers at issue were very possibly treated as expendable pawns in the larger game, with their careers being rapidly derailed.

The potentially glossed-over Soviet drugging event in December 1979 could have been a demonstration that as the MLM era entered the 1980s, the Soviets were not playing by the same rules, or even the same game, as the U.S. In USMLM's haste to disregard the claims of two of its officers and avoid a potentially serious international incident that might have raised senior-level questions regarding the viability of the MLMs, analysts and leaders may have been deprived of a key alarm that may have resonated throughout USAREUR, the U.S. intelligence community, and the U.S. State Department. Instead, the details of this incident remained buried in Stasi files for decades while it took counterintelligence analysts and leaders an additional eight years to come to a conclusion regarding the Soviet threat that the details of this incident may have hastened.

USMLM members assigned to the unit during the period of the alleged drugging event claim that Burhans and Tonge were appropriately charged with driving while intoxicated, and that their reputations were belatedly and fortuitously bolstered by Stasi opportunism. It is questionable why the Soviets would have assisted the

Stasi at that time and in a manner with little plausible deniability had the officers been proven to have had drugs in their blood systems. The Stasi report refers to "targeted measures to discredit" but does not specify what those targeted measures were. A plausible alternative, as contended by some former USMLM members, is that the Stasi seized on the fact that two USMLM officers were unceremoniously transferred out and claimed credit for conspiring with the Soviets to orchestrate the positive outcome. The only two individuals who could truly make the distinction if this were the case, benefit from the version of the Stasi report, and are going to hold with that one.

If the USMLM officers were found to have been drugged in 1979, it would have been the first acknowledged incident involving a Soviet drugging of a U.S. government representative since 1968. Had the U.S. accused the Soviets with such an act, it would have been a major international incident, which may have raised questions regarding the continued viability of the MLMs. Therefore, regardless of whether it was intoxication or a malicious act, the impact to the USAREUR collection effort and any risk of the MLMs being terminated were minimized by ensuring that the investigation of the incident was handled as an internal USAREUR issue. Given the demonstrated USAREUR propensity to protect the USMLM collection mission in spite of substantial and persistent risks such as shootings, rammings, beatings, and then a possible drugging, ensuring that the vehicle accident incident was administratively handled rather than entertaining a more high-visibility examination into the alternative would have been consistent with this propensity.

On 30 December 1980, the SERB-sponsored gift exchange was a tri-mission event with senior officers from SERB and each of the Allied MLMs. The event included a three-course, sit-down dinner establishing a completely different atmosphere from the previous year. This event also served as a final demonstration that both the U.S. and Soviets were content to let the events of the previous year be buried in the past. Despite the holiday decorum of the event, however, this was another period of high-stakes brinksmanship and intelligence interest.

Warning of Another Soviet Invasion

As the labor union protests in Poland continued during September 1980, U.S. intelligence agencies began to monitor army movements in the western military districts of the Soviet Union. The U.S. intelligence community quickly reached a consensus that the USSR might undertake military intervention in Poland with a force of up to 30 divisions.

The CIA had an exceptionally well-placed source to confirm Soviet intentions, so the agency was confident that they would know the Soviet plan in advance. Colonel Ryszard Kukliński was an officer in the Polish People's Army who had progressed to senior staff positions which included assisting with the preparations for the Warsaw

Pact's invasion of Czechoslovakia in 1968. Coincidentally, it was in the wake of this invasion to put down the popular uprising, and the subsequent massacre of Polish workers in Gdańsk by Polish security forces in December 1970, that compelled Kukliński to question the legitimacy of Communist rule and the USSR's control over Poland. Kukliński ultimately volunteered to spy for the U.S., and from 1972–81, proved to be among the CIA's most productive assets. Therefore, the agency was confident that Kukliński would bring clarity to the ambiguity surrounding the possible Soviet invasion of Poland.

In November 1980, SERB delivered a notification to USMLM for a TRA along the East German and Polish border area from 30 November to 9 December, which gave rise to the speculation that its purpose was to conceal the movement of forces into Poland. Simultaneous to this TRA notification was an event viewed as an ominous pretense for a potential Soviet intervention—the *Soyuz 80* maneuvers for the Soviet, East German, Czechoslovak, and Polish armies which were scheduled to begin in Poland and elsewhere. The maneuvers were planned to take place in two stages with the first consisting of training on the territory of the participating states, including Poland, and the second stage consisting of military and command training that would bring foreign troops onto Polish territory. Five to six Soviet divisions, four Polish divisions, two Czechoslovak divisions, and one East German division were to take part in the maneuvers. The training was anticipated to begin on 8 December, but no end date for the exercise was known. CIA analysts emphasized that these activities were similar to those which took place immediately preceding the invasion of Czechoslovakia in 1968.

When Kukliński's reporting reached Washington, it appeared to confirm the worst. In addition to what was already known regarding this planned, large-scale exercise, Kukliński informed the CIA that the maneuvers of the Soviet, East German, Czechoslovak, and Polish armies were a cover for an intervention and that 15 Soviet divisions would be involved. Although Kukliński had always been a reliable source of intelligence, the information he provided was technically "single source," so the U.S. intelligence community was anxious to confirm the information through other sources. Unfortunately for U.S. intelligence, atmospheric conditions degraded the effectiveness of intelligence satellite coverage during the first two weeks of December 1980. However, during this period of degraded satellite imagery, USMLM and the Allied partners were on the ground collecting intelligence that contradicted Kukliński's warning of an imminent invasion. In fact, it appeared that the activity that had been planned for the TRA had been canceled, or that the TRA had been implemented as either a contingency or a deception measure.

Also during this period, USMLM collected information through "liaison" channels that provided some context to the ambiguity. On 11 December 1980, the Polish military attaché to Berlin invited the CUSMLM to join him for dinner. The attaché asked CUSMLM for his opinion as to whether the Soviets would invade Poland, and provided his opinion that they would not because they understood that the Polish people would not allow it. The Polish attaché's message, which was certainly one from Warsaw that was intended to go directly to Washington, DC, was that the Polish army would defend the nation against Soviet aggression.

When atmospheric conditions improved in mid-December and intelligence satellites could be used, it became apparent that Kukliński's information was erroneous and that only three mobilized units were stationed on the eastern border of Poland, and not the 15 Soviet divisions Kukliński had reported. USMLM had proven to be a valuable source of intelligence during a critical period of ambiguity regarding Soviet intentions, but USMLM operating west of the Polish border was not the only collection element receiving tasking to develop intelligence regarding Soviet intentions to invade Poland.

More Pawns in the Game

With the circumstances of the potentially drug-induced 29 December 1979 vehicle accident essentially expunged from the record at the local USMLM level, the opportunity to connect that reflection with the other related reflections in the wilderness of mirrors was lost. An episode that occurred just over a year later with a USMLM nexus, demonstrated just how important it is to illuminate, and not cast shadows on, this type of information.

In an effort to get as close as possible to observe for signs of a military buildup in the Polish border area, the U.S. Defense Attaché Office (DAO) in Moscow submitted numerous requests for authorization to travel in December 1980 and January 1981, which were all summarily rejected. This daily routine of proforma request and rejection was unexpectedly interrupted with a Soviet approval for the DAO to travel as requested on 13 January 1981. Although the immediate Polish border area remained restricted to the DAO, the travel area that had been authorized was assessed as sufficient to allow the attaché team to observe for indications of a military buildup, assuming that they would be able to make it as far as intended. In their excitement for the opportunity to travel and report on priority intelligence requirements, no one stopped to consider why the sudden change in bureaucratic processes, when it should have been well understood that the Soviets did not do anything without a reason.

On 13 January, Army Lieutenant Colonel Thomas A. Spencer and Army Major James R. Holbrook departed on a mission that would take the military attaché officers through the Ukraine toward the Polish border region. The plan was to travel by train to Kiev where they would pick up an attaché vehicle and drive to Rovno, Ukraine, and then continue forward the following day to the area of the Soviet Armed Forces Carpathian Military District Headquarters in Lviv, which would get them within 50 miles of the Ukrainian/Polish border.

The officers, who both spoke fluent Russian, traveled by train to Kiev in civilian clothes. After taxiing from the Kiev train station to the "secured" parking lot where an attaché vehicle had been parked for them to pick up, they found that the vehicle had a slashed tire and a broken windshield wiper. The attachés drove the hobbled vehicle to an auto mechanic shop with a vehicle following their every move. They received good service at the shop but were not able to see everything that was done with the vehicle. With the same blue car following their departure from the shop, the officers made the last leg of the day's journey to Rovno, where they began to experience vehicle problems just as they arrived at their hotel.

After the attachés checked into their rooms, they went to the hotel restaurant for dinner. It had not occurred to the officers when they began their travels that 13 January is the Orthodox Russian New Year's Eve. As such, the hotel bar was very festive, and after a couple of drinks, the Americans were joined by two attractive Ukrainian women. What ensued was the classic honey-trap scenario. During the course of the evening, Spencer would be drugged and become incapacitated, leaving Holbrook who was the obvious target of the operation intoxicated and alone with a woman in a hotel room. In the middle of the dalliance, KGB officers busted into the room, pictures were taken, and Holbrook was confronted with the hard, cold facts. A married man, a military intelligence officer, and a U.S. defense attaché entrusted to use good judgement when traveling throughout the Soviet Union would be made the center of an international incident.

On the morning of 14 January, Holbrook and Spencer tried to make a quick getaway, but their vehicle was completely inoperable. This was not, however, the first time that the U.S. Army officers had dealt with adversity as strangers in a strange land. Spencer served as a USMLM tour officer from 1973–6 and Holbrook served as a USMLM tour officer from 1976–7. Holbrook was Spencer's replacement, arriving the month following Spencer's departure from USMLM. Although the two tour officers' time at USMLM did not overlap, they did both work at USMLM during the period when Colonel Igor Kanavin was the DCSERB and then CSERB from December 1975 to January 1979. Holbrook recalled Kanavin favorably as a very polished and socially astute officer who would discreetly help Holbrook find the right Russian words during his senior-level translation duties. When Holbrook departed USMLM in 1977, he and Kanavin parted on very amicable terms. With Holbrook being an army intelligence officer who was fluent in Russian, and Kanavin being a GRU officer who was fluent in English, it was not uncommon for these types to cross paths more than once during the course of their careers. However, their next encounter was not common by any measure.

After finding that the vehicle was inoperable, Holbrook returned to the hotel to contact the embassy and advise them that he and Spencer were stranded in Rovno. When Holbrook entered the lobby, he noticed Colonel Kanavin dressed in civilian clothes standing conspicuously by the elevator. Holbrook approached Kanavin who immediately recognized Holbrook as well. The two spoke briefly and Kanavin suggested that they meet for dinner to catch up. Holbrook, knowing that he would not be able to get out of Rovno that day, agreed.

That evening, Holbrook arrived at the hotel restaurant to find Kanavin seated and waiting. As soon as the two finished exchanging pleasantries and were seated, Kanavin lit a cigarette which prompted the waiter to remind him that smoking was not allowed in the restaurant. Of course, a GRU officer in the Ukraine could smoke anywhere he wanted, but that was not the point. Kanavin acknowledged the waiter and commented that he recalled that Holbrook smoked a pipe, and asked Holbrook to step outside and join him for a smoke.

As the two walked and smoked the discussion quickly turned to the events of the previous night. A predictably sympathetic Kanavin assured Holbrook that he could protect him from the KGB and that he could ensure that Holbrook's "people" would never hear of what happened. Holbrook had some lapses in judgement the previous night, but he was able to see how the KGB shakedown was the precursor to Kanavin's recruitment effort. Holbrook made very clear that he did not accept the GRU officer's offer to assist.

Holbrook returned to the Moscow embassy on 15 January, reported the events of the previous two days, and was on a plane back to the U.S. on 17 January. Counterintelligence professionals understand that an individual caught in a honey trap and then ensnared in the "bad cop extortion" and "good cop throw in a lifesaver" routine simply needs to call the bluff and walk away. In the end, the KGB would never actually provide the incriminating information to U.S. officials, because it would simply disclose the fact that the KGB had undertaken the elaborate effort to recruit a source; so, Holbrook and Spencer probably could have left Rovno, never mentioned the incident, and it would have gone away forever. Whether Holbrook wittingly or fortuitously called the KGB bluff, he obviously did the right thing by reporting the incident. Holbrook understood that in his case the stakes had been a little higher. At the time of the 13/14 January 1981 incident, Holbrook was being vetted for a position as a military advisor to Vice-President George H. W. Bush.

On 16 February 1981, a story broke in *The New York Times* that was clearly based on information provided by a source with first-hand knowledge of Holbrook's account of the episode. The U.S. State Department had obviously chosen to weaponize the event for use in the realm of information operations. The article lent credibility to the contention that at least one of the attachés had been drugged by the KGB to help orchestrate the incident. The Soviet-controlled TASS news agency immediately responded with a news release accusing two American military attachés of drunkenness and sexual misconduct during a visit to the Ukrainian town of Rovno, near the Polish border, in mid-January. The careers of Spencer and Holbrook stalled after their assignment as military attachés, but they both retired under honorable conditions, so their careers technically survived the ordeal. Holbrook's marriage, however, did not. Data from the DIA's Office of Security Records cites that approximately one-third of the U.S. defense attachés relieved from training or duty in 1981 were removed because of family problems, with one-fourth of those being for marital problems involving alcohol or sexual indiscretions. Therefore, Holbrook was not the anomaly. As an unfortunate pawn on the board, Holbrook went from an up-and-comer competing for among the most exclusive assignments to a Russian language instructor waiting out his time.

The effort to recruit Holbrook was an elaborate and well-orchestrated operation, one which the KGB obviously undertook because they assessed it would have a high probability of success. The circumstances were too well interwoven to have been coincidental. The Soviets, knowing that Holbrook could very possibly be an insider with the U.S. executive branch, uncharacteristically approved a travel request that named him as a member of the traveling party. When the officers arrived in Kiev, their vehicle was damaged, requiring that it be taken to a repair shop where the mechanic could be directed by KGB agents to manipulate the vehicle. The vehicle began to experience mechanical problems just as they reached their stop location in Rovno, ensuring that they would in fact stop there, and making the fact that the vehicle did not start the following morning less conspicuous. The travel was approved on a date that would provide a festive atmosphere that would more likely entice the Americans to take advantage and enjoy the opportunity to mingle with the populous. The honey trap and subsequent entrapment was simply classic KGB "sexpionage." The vehicle being inoperable and Holbrook having to remain at the hotel allowed for the "chance" meeting with Kanavin. And finally, delivering the pitch (way out of a bad situation) by a known individual with whom Holbrook had shared a sense of fellowship in the past was intended as the coup de grâce. Perhaps Kanavin recalled from four years previously that Holbrook smoked a pipe, but if not, that little piece of biographical data would have been in Holbrook's GRU dossier. This episode also demonstrated cooperation among the KGB and GRU to achieve a higher interest.

The episode in Rovno served as further confirmation that the Soviets collected information on USMLM officers and kept track of those officers who had established relations with their Soviet hosts. What was now new to the landscape was that the Soviets would use this information and these relationships as leverage when the need reached a threshold. The threshold in the case of Holbrook was the Soviets' obvious understanding that he was in line to become a military advisor to the executive branch of the U.S. government. Although this is the first and only recorded case of such a Soviet recruitment effort associated with USMLM, there is no way of knowing if this were the only one. In the case of Holbrook and Spencer, they could have probably walked away without reporting the incident and it would have been their (and the KGB's) dirty little secret to take to the grave. If Holbrook, or any other former USMLM officer in that situation, had fallen prey to such an entrapment effort, it could have forever remained a Soviet secret.

Prior to the incident in Rovno involving the incapacitation of Spencer, the last known major recorded drugging incident involving the Soviets and the U.S. occurred in 1968 when a British and an American officer were drugged during a trip to Moldavia. A key word there being "recorded." It could not possibly have been lost on the USMLM leadership that after they chose not to more aggressively explore the officers' claims of drugging the year prior, two of their own alumni had been the victims of a similar incident with implications that reached directly back into the intrigue that was the MLMs.

The First Rip in the Curtain

Although the 13–15 January 1981 DAO mission did not reach the intended destination, they were able to report that as far west as Rovno there were no indications of a large-scale Soviet force buildup. The U.S. collectors in East Germany and the Ukraine confirmed during the pivotal period of December 1980 and January 1981 that the Soviets were not posturing for an immediate intervention in Poland. As it happened, the Soviets had planned to invade on 8 December 1980, but decided against that option just days prior to execution. Polish government officials persuaded the Soviet leadership that a Soviet Bloc intervention in Poland would initiate internal and international forces that would certainly lead to the end of Communism in Poland. The Soviets agreed with this assessment, but were also convinced that this meant that only a Polish government internal crackdown could preserve the Communist system in that country. Therefore, the invasion plan that Kukliński provided the U.S. was accurate at the time he provided it. Unfortunately for Kukliński, the details of the high-level U.S. warnings to the Soviets to not go through with the intervention made it clear to the Soviet and Polish intelligence services that there was a high-level mole in their midst.

During the ensuing months, Kukliński provided details regarding the Polish planning for the potential imposition of martial law, which did not include a plan for direct external support. USMLM was instrumental during this period in confirming that there were no indications of a plan including GSFG. However, the Soviets sustained the appearance of a potential intervention to exert pressure on Polish policymakers to take measures into their own hands to avoid the alternative. The March 1981 *Soyuz* exercise was again planned to include large maneuvers of Warsaw Pact troops on Polish territory. For USMLM, however, this exercise was an anomaly in that it was the first time that an exercise of this nature had not been protected under a TRA. In fact, 1981 was an unprecedented year for USMLM in that no TRAs were issued for the entire year. The reason for this was assessed to be twofold. In the first place, refraining from issuing TRAs was a form of self-imposed penance for having issued the TRA in December 1980 for the obvious purpose of being able to hide hostile military movements—which was a blatant abuse of the mutually accepted rules/norms. Secondly, during a period when the Soviets were sustaining pressure on Poland through the threat of an intervention, by not issuing a TRA, the Soviets were signaling complete transparency to convince the U.S. that they did not, in fact, intend to invade. Ultimately, this level of transparency was of no additional consequence because as the Soviets and Poles knew, there was a high-level mole in the Polish military with access to all high-level plans.

Even though Kukliński learned in September 1981 that the Polish Ministry of Internal Affairs had begun searching for a CIA spy in the upper levels of the Polish military, he continued his clandestine work for another two months. In November 1981, the Soviets devised a scheme to leverage their knowledge of the existence of a mole while at the same time weeding him out. The Soviets assessed that the U.S. would view an internal crackdown by the Polish government as the lesser of two evils relative to a Soviet invasion of Poland. To confirm this assessment, Soviet and Polish officials updated the plan for the Polish crackdown, with the understanding that it would be passed to the U.S. by the mole. The plan to leverage the mole as a channel of information directly to senior U.S. leadership to gauge their reaction (or lack there of), was quickly verified through the vast KGB agent network.

During the period of unrest in Poland, the pope was the widely revered, Polish-born John Paul II. The U.S. was courting the Vatican to leverage the pope in support of the anti-Communist movement in Poland. When Kukliński provided the latest plan for the crackdown in Poland to the CIA in November 1981, the CIA provided it to the Vatican as proof of the Polish government's intent to suppress the Polish people. Nearly immediately thereafter, a KGB source in the Vatican reported that the CIA had acquired the full plans for martial law in Poland. This was a very interesting play on the deception theory in that Kukliński served as the credible line of communication to deliver the desired message, and the KGB asset in the Vatican served as the second channel to verify that the operation had the desired result.

After receiving confirmation that the plan had been compromised to the CIA, the KGB promptly alerted the Polish authorities who embarked on a much more intensive investigation for a spy in their midst. Because Kukliński was one of the few Polish officials who had access to all final planning, he realized that it was only a matter of time until the investigators settled on him as the culprit. Using a CIA-provided encrypted communications device, Kukliński urgently notified his CIA case officers that he and his family needed to leave Poland as soon as possible. An intricate exfiltration operation ensued, and the CIA successfully relocated Kukliński and his family to the U.S. in December 1981, just days prior to the imposition of martial law in Poland.

At the time of the crackdown there was a general public perception that the events had caught the U.S. government by surprise, but this was not the case. The American administration was aware of the details of the crackdown and were aware of the date of imposition at least a week before it actually happened. The mole, who the Polish government learned was Kukliński after his defection, was effectively employed as a channel of information regarding Poland's true intent. Given the confirmation that the U.S. was aware of the plan and chose not to warn against a crackdown, the U.S. was perceived as tacitly signaling that this action was acceptable as the better of the two alternatives in comparison to a Soviet military intervention. The leader of the Polish regime who implemented the plan, General Wojciech Jaruzelski, asserted that he knew the U.S. had information on his intentions and that he interpreted Washington's silence as signaling acceptance of his internal crackdown as a "lesser evil" than the otherwise "inevitable" Soviet intervention.

Although the Soviets may have gotten the better of that particular endgame, it was also actually the gambit in another game that would not end well for the Communist empire. The imposition of martial law in Poland marked a Cold War paradigm shift. As a reversal to the "domino theory" of Communism as professed by U.S. President Dwight D. Eisenhower in 1954, history views the Polish crackdown of 1981 as the first domino to fall in the opposite direction in the leadup to the collapse of the Soviet Union 10 years later.

The Nicholson Negotiations: I

The 24 March 1985 killing of Major Arthur Nicholson began a nearly 13-month period in which the U.S. attempted to gain Soviet reparations and concessions as penance for the tragic event. What actually transpired, however, was a classic example of the Soviets turning a crisis into an opportunity.

There were circumstances surrounding the Nicholson shooting that lent credibility to the argument that it was an intentional incident sanctioned at the top, but the totality of evidence does not support that position. There is no basis to suggest that this incident was orchestrated for this (or any other) purpose—and to so assert would be to give the Soviets far too much credit for the possibility that they orchestrated such a fortuitous cause and effect. However, it did ultimately prove to serve the Soviets' operational objectives.

There was a contentious period immediately preceding the Nicholson episode involving restricted-area disputes that established some important context prior to the fateful day. In May 1984, during a very low period in U.S. and Soviet relations, GSFG issued a PRA map that restricted USMLM freedom of movement at an unprecedented level of 39 percent. In response, USAREUR finally retaliated for a legacy of GSFG PRA maps that were much more restrictive than those imposed

Major Nicholson (right) at the site of a 1984 accident/detention. (USMLM Association)

upon SMLM-F. In August 1984, USAREUR delivered a PRA map that restricted SMLM-F movement through West Germany to an unprecedented level, nearly doubling the amount of restricted territory. To increase the percentage of PRAs, USAREUR arbitrarily placed blanket PRAs over large urban areas in the sector, significantly expanding the range of restrictions in and around the city of Frankfurt and other large cities. Although there had always been PRAs covering portions of Frankfurt and other cities, the Soviets considered these latest urban-area restrictions excessive.

After a series of Soviet protests regarding the latest restrictions, on 13 March 1985, CSERB met with CUSMLM and warned that a new GSFG PRA map would be delivered "soon" that would result in the closure of Potsdam and other urban areas unless the Soviets were once again granted unimpeded access to the urban centers. Although the GSFG complaint was directed at the latest map in general, the specified primary concern was restricted movement in the large urban areas which the SMLMs were located, and the other urban centers throughout the country. Interestingly, the Soviets' rhetoric did not reflect a high degree of concern regarding the restrictions that would reduce SMLM-F's ability to collect intelligence on U.S. military units. Eleven days after the SERB issued the latest protest regarding the PRA map, Major Nicholson was killed.

The Nicholson Negotiations

When studied from the perspective of the wilderness of mirrors, the senior-level talks which began soon after the Major Nicholson shooting and continued for 12 months disclosed a number of potential clues to the Soviet enigma and the strategy which drove how they played their intelligence game of chess. Although the Soviets entered the post-incident negotiations from a position of weakness having been the party at fault for the lethal incident, they effectively leveraged the negotiations to achieve the very objectives they intended to achieve by threatening to issue a highly restrictive PRA map. By either Soviet ingenuity or serendipity, the shooting incident ultimately enabled them to achieve objectives that they were not attaining through standard deliberations prior to the incident.

After a flurry of high-level maneuvering and a series of statements from the U.S. executive branch, the Defense Department, and the State Department—and retorts from the Soviets—the U.S. determined that USAREUR would take the lead in negotiations consistent with the framework of the Huebner–Malinin Agreement. When General Otis, CINC USAREUR, was given authorization from the Pentagon to hold CINC-to-CINC talks with General Mikhail M Zaytsev, CINC GSFG, he sent a letter on 11 April requesting that the meeting take place no later than 12 April. When the CUSMLM delivered the letter to the CSERB, Colonel Pereverzev, the initial response was that it would be unrealistic to expect a response within one day, highlighting the Soviet proclivity for doing things by numbers since their system did not encourage improvisation and spontaneity. On 12 April, when it was beginning to appear as though the Soviets would not respond to the letter, and much less meet the deadline, the CSERB delivered a midday letter replying that General Zaytsev had agreed to meet with General Otis between 5:00 and 6:00 PM that day in Potsdam. The response was apparently timed to minimize any additional time Otis may have needed to prepare prior to flying to Berlin. General Otis arrived in Berlin at 4:50 PM and arrived at the GSFG Potsdam officers' club, where the initial discussions were to take place, at 6:00 PM.

During the initial talks between the CINCs, the U.S.'s primary going-in position was to attain an official apology and compensation for Nicholson's family. In addition, the U.S. held two MLM mission-related objectives, which were the implementation of measures to preclude recurrences of violent incidents by compelling the Soviets to produce an appropriately worded MLM instruction card for GSFG soldiers, and to increase intelligence-collection access by negotiating a reduced and equitable percentage of PRA coverage. However, the initial meeting demonstrated the Soviets' unwavering approach to negotiations that would remain consistent throughout the process. It was also the beginning of a drawn-out negotiation process that would continue for a year.

Following the initial CINC-to-CINC talks, a period of U.S. and Soviet talks ensued which incrementally cut away at the U.S. demands. The senior U.S. officers involved in the series of negotiations were always well prepared when entering talks, but their approach was in stark contrast to Pereverzev's depiction of the Soviet way of doing business. Whereas the U.S. officers tried to apply logic and reason, the Soviets dogmatically adhered to the talking points approved in advance by the Politburo, and never strayed, regardless of whether they were being complimented, insulted, invalidated, or otherwise enticed to go off script.

Despite the U.S.'s honorable intentions, it was clear from the beginning and immediately acknowledged that the Soviets would not acquiesce to the first two fundamental demands of an apology and compensation. After the Soviets initially demonstrated that they would not budge from their fundamental positions and the talks proceeded with little progress, USAREUR became more desperate for a victory to gain concessions from the Soviets to demonstrate that Nicholson's death was not without consequence. Therefore, the two primary demands were decoupled from the follow-on negotiations, and USAREUR shifted the focus of the talks to their two mission-related objectives. The two potential wins that USAREUR grasped onto were a Soviet commitment to produce an instruction card for all personnel and to produce PRA maps that were equitable in percentage to the Allied MLM PRA maps. The second and third rounds of general officer-level negotiations centered around these topics.

The instruction card was the secondary subplot which demonstrated the Soviets' unyielding position on affixing fault for the Nicholson shooting. The U.S. insisted that the Soviets produce and issue an instruction card that specifically restricted any Soviet soldier from using violence against USMLM personnel. The Soviets countered that a sentry guarding his post had standing orders to take whatever actions necessary to protect his post. This reflected the Soviet position that the sentry who shot Nicholson was justified because he was protecting his post against an unidentified intruder. Despite the strong U.S. protests to all shooting incidents throughout the years, the Soviets had been very consistent in their sentry guarding his post position as policy. Interestingly, the HQ USAREUR order dating back to 1959 basically recognized that this was a valid argument, and that the litany of shooting incidents involving USMLM after which the Soviets continued this line of reasoned justification, would favor the Soviet argument that such responses to USMLM agitation were the norm. Strengthening this Soviet argument was that, as with all USMLM tour personnel, Nicholson was wearing a camouflaged uniform which the Soviets contended gave him the appearance of an aggressor.

Following the third round of talks, CUSMLM and CSERB were authorized to conduct "away from the table" negotiations to finalize the details of the instruction card and PRA maps. The instruction card issue provided the Soviets a smokescreen to frustrate and prompt the U.S. to rush to the PRA map issue, which was clearly the endgame strategy victory that the Soviets had orchestrated from the beginning. Although CUSMLM was very interested in resolving the safety issue, his primary parochial interest was increasing intelligence-collection access for USMLM. As the resolution to the instruction card issue became increasingly problematic, and even threatened to undermine a successful transition to the PRA map topic, the U.S. defaulted to the negotiation strategy that was almost singularly focused on maximizing freedom of maneuver in the Soviet sector to maximize USMLM intelligence collection. Given that this approach was immediately obvious to the Soviets as well, it is noteworthy that they chose not to use the historic disparity of collection aggressiveness and violations as negotiating leverage against the U.S. who began the negotiations with the moral high ground.

With USAREUR clearly focused on the objective to attain a "balanced and mutual reduction of restricted areas," the challenge was to convince the Soviets to meet the Allied objective to exchange maps that were limited to PRA coverage of no more than 25 percent of the sectors. In the "spirit of good faith," the Soviets agreed to attempt to meet this mark but contended that it would be impossible if they did not eliminate the PRAs canvassing large urban areas. The Soviets contended that to effect this change while demonstrating to Soviet and East German leadership that they had received some quid pro quo for this significant compromise, the Allies would need to remove restrictions of the base cities of the Soviet MLMs and other large urban areas throughout West Germany. USAREUR, perhaps desperate to demonstrate a win by negotiating what would be the least restrictive PRA map in the history of the MLMs, and which in turn would increase USMLM intelligence-collection access, immediately seized on the opportunity. In fact, CUSMLM, who remained the U.S. lead for the third and final round of negotiations, expressed that he wanted to conclude the negotiations as soon as possible to secure the "considerable benefits to the missions" of the new PRA map. He thought that these benefits would result in "a perceptible improvement to the [USMLM's] collection environment." This contention, as well as this entire stage of the negotiations, clearly demonstrated that the U.S. side was purely focused on the benefits to USMLM and not the counterintelligence implications for USAREUR in regard to SMLM-F.

The mentality to preserve the political status quo and maximize intelligence collection above all else was shared across the Allied MLMs. During the negotiations in which the U.S. obviously needed to present a public face of championing MLM safety, but in coordination with their fellow MLMs, the British and French MLMs placed a priority on intelligence collection over safety and security considerations, and did not want any measures implemented that altered the existing balance. The British, in particular, wanted to continue their position of not recognizing MRSs and accept the risks associated with Nicholson's death, rather than the U.S. pushing the issue and risk having the Soviets transfer more MRS areas to PRAs.

On 11 April 1986, USAREUR and GSFG general officer representatives signed the accord affirming the sides' commitment to continuing operations under the terms of the Huebner–Malinin Agreement. The two U.S. priorities of USMLM safety and operational access were specifically addressed, but the issue of the sentry on his post remained a potential deal-breaker to the very end, with the U.S. technically conceding the issue. The final agreement specified that "mission members will be continuously briefed on the special procedures which apply to a sentry at his post." Ultimately, this qualifying wording implied that the fault for Nicholson's shooting had been his own and his USMLM leadership for not having ensured that he was aware of this ever-present risk. Although the agreement was signed, the safety issue would not be finally resolved until the Soviet instruction card was produced for dissemination to all GSFG personnel, as agreed to.

The Soviet "Concessions"

There were two sanctions imposed after the shooting incident which endured throughout the negotiations: a moratorium on official and social contacts, and a restriction on SMLM-F interzonal travel. The interzonal travel restriction prevented SMLM-F from traveling directly to the Soviet Embassy in Bonn or the other two MLMs, and required that they travel to East Germany and then reenter the British Sector of West Germany to travel to these locations. The restriction on interzonal travel was a sore point for SMLM-F throughout the process for which SMLM-F and SERB regularly argued for relief from the sanction. USAREUR, understanding that this was a particularly aggravating restriction on SMLM-F, kept the restriction in place after the negotiations were concluded as leverage until the Soviets produced their instruction card.

The agreement document adequately addressed the U.S. priority to reduce restrictions by specifying that the sides would "reduce on a mutual basis the PRAs and open for free movement by mission members along autobahns and roads which border restricted areas." However, the more prominent caveat in the freedom of movement agreement section was that "with the introduction of new PRA maps abolish the existing restrictions on movement by mission members the cities which the missions are located and the roads which provide entrance to and exit from."

On 9 June 1986, new PRA maps were exchanged, both of which totaled 25 percent PRA coverage in the sectors. For the first time, the U.S. had attained parity with a significant reduction in Soviet restricted areas. Also noteworthy was that for the first time in 30 years, the PRA along the East German coast was eliminated, enabling extensive collection against naval targets. This was an unrequested concession with no apparent quid pro quo other than increased freedom of movement in urban areas, which did little to increase collection opportunities for SMLM-F against militarily significant targets.

On 22 August 1986, four months following the conclusion of the negotiations, CSERB provided CUSMLM copies of the new Soviet MLM instruction card. The card was publicly recognized by USAREUR as a Soviet concession and the restriction on SMLM-F interzonal travel was immediately lifted. In reality, however, the card included the caveat that the instructions on the card did not extend to the actions of a sentry on his post. This inclusion on the card reinforced the position that the sentry who shot Nicholson was justified, and that it was Nicholson's negligent actions that resulted in his death. As the Soviet instruction card demonstrated, the Soviets refused to concede on that issue to the very end. Once again, by retaining wording on the MLM procedures card that essentially authorized sentries to shoot, this specific point of contention was not definitively resolved during the talks. In addition, there was never any confirmation that instruction cards were actually distributed to GSFG personnel.

In July 1986, less than three months after the conclusion of the Nicholson negotiations, a USMLM vehicle was deliberately rammed by an East German vehicle belonging to the same unit responsible for the Mariotti murder. In June 1987, two East German teenagers were shot and killed by Soviet sentries when attempting to climb a wall into a Soviet army barracks, demonstrating that it was still extremely dangerous to be an unidentified intruder near a sensitive Soviet military site. On 17 September 1987, Soviet military personnel fired at a USMLM tour vehicle while attempting a detention, slightly wounding one USMLM member, and demonstrating that the Nicholson negotiations did not effectively end this lethal risk to USMLM personnel.

The Pawns in the Game and Acceptable Collateral Damage

In the end, the negotiations to elicit Soviet concessions and restore normalcy to the MLMs did little to affix mutually agreed-upon responsibility for Nicholson's death. Despite the gravity of the situation, it was apparent from the beginning that neither side wanted the Nicholson episode to alter the MLMs' mutually accepted norms or bring color to the gray areas that had existed for so long. Despite the demands for public apologies and compensation for the Nicholson family, the only discernable concession that the U.S. attained was a parochially perceived improvement to collection operations that might have actually conceded more to the adversary. In either case, this was the only tangible concession to honor the legacy of a fallen comrade.

Although USAREUR did attempt to stress the positive outcomes of the talks, the summary of the negotiations appearing in the USMLM close-out report was far from laudatory. The report ultimately deferred any final conclusions by stating in an almost submissive fashion that "History will inevitably judge the results." This was the appropriate tact, as to have concluded that the final results were even marginally effective in meeting the initial U.S. objectives would have been a disingenuous attempt to rewrite history.

The Nicholson negotiations were the strongest admission that the U.S. placed maintaining the status quo of the MLMs above any other consideration. As with the many life-threatening shootings and vehicle rammings of the past, as with the expeditiously adjudicated fault for the vehicle accident in December 1979, and as with the Mariotti murder the preceding year, the post-Nicholson shooting negotiations once again demonstrated that the U.S. and Allies would accept an extreme amount of collateral damage to continue its intelligence-collection mission.

If the U.S. would accept this degree of risk, it begged the question of how much the U.S. would concede in counterintelligence vulnerabilities to achieve the same. Even USMLM tour officers, knowing that they only conducted overt ground collection and never conducted covert/clandestine intelligence activities, regularly opined that the reason the Soviets would tolerate USMLM's brazen intelligence-collection methods was that they must be conducting important activities out of SMLM-F, such as "running agents."

And finally, the Soviet "concessions" on PRA coverage were largely mitigated by circumstances that were unknown to the U.S. at the time. Trofimoff was still compromising USMLM reporting provided to the JIC system, the Conrad ring (at least as the Soviets thought at the time) was still delivering, and if that were not enough, James Hall was returning to West Germany just as the Nicholson negotiations had concluded.

CHAPTER 6

Reflections in the Soviet Military Liaison Mission, Frankfurt Wilderness

By the onset of the Cold War, the Russian mentality was hardened by a national history of hardship which dated back to the Mongol invasion and occupation of 1223, the Ottoman invasion and destruction of Moscow in 1571, the devastating French invasion of 1812, the German invasions of 1914 and 1941, and other setbacks in between. The Cold War era was largely defined by the Soviet propensity to take whatever actions were necessary to ensure that NATO did not become the next invading force in a legacy of human loss.

Over the years, Soviet diplomats of all ranks, from ambassadors to administrative personnel such as library employees, translators, and clerks, were accused of espionage and other active measures, and expelled from the foreign countries to which they had been assigned. The most thorough study conducted by the U.S. State Department covering the period of 1970–86 reported that nearly 700 Soviet officials were expelled from at least 57 countries. These numbers did not reflect the actual totals as many countries did not publicize such actions, and there were years with incomplete data for other reasons. Still, those numbers are significant, as they would represent but a fraction of the activities taking place that were not identified.

The Soviets did not limit the use of their forward foreign presences for espionage and other covert and clandestine activities to official government entities. Individuals in occupations operating under non-official cover were also expelled, including press correspondents, banking and industry representatives, trade union officials, UN employees, employees of other international bodies such as the International Labor Organization and the International Civil Aviation Organization, and the state-run merchant marine fleet and airline enterprise. Many of the expelled individuals ostensibly working for these entities were publicly identified as KGB and GRU officers.

Given the legacy of aggressively and ruthlessly leveraging every possible venue to advance its global objectives, it is only intuitive that the Soviets would leverage their three extraterritorial MLM legal residencies in large Western urban areas to aggressively further their intelligence objectives. Not doing so would simply be inconsistent with the Soviet (and GRU) mentality to leverage any possible legal platform—particularly ones in the heart of first battlefield of the next war for Russian survival. At a point, this became an inconvenient truth.

Suspicions Finally Confirmed

Although it could be assumed that the information regarding SMLM contact procedures reported by Kiefer in 1959 based on GRU officer Sokolov's instructions would have eventually been reported to U.S. Army Counterintelligence, there is no record to confirm that this did occur. Regardless, the Project DART observations of 1959 should have confirmed to USAREUR leadership that there was a forward Soviet presence for which they were responsible and which, while not under observation or any other monitoring measures, provided the Soviets a forward presence to conduct or support clandestine or covert actions with very little risk of detection. Although USAREUR would contend over the years that they allowed this permissive environment to continue in strict adherence to the Huebner–Malinin Agreement, the reality was that they valued USMLM collection in East Germany above any counterintelligence concerns in West Germany, and accepted the counterintelligence risks rather than taking any actions that might cause repercussions impacting USMLM operations.

In addition to the standard conduct of espionage activities out of their residencies, the GRU (and KGB) had a long and well-documented legacy of conducting other clandestine and covert active measures to destabilize the West and prepare the battlefield for that ultimate engagement. It was long known that SMLM-F members were GRU personnel and widely assumed that the mission served an operational purpose beyond their basic tour activities. However, with the exception of the failed Project DART, there were no serious efforts to confirm or deny this perspective over the initial three decades into the Cold War.

Denial is not an effective intelligence analysis technique, but it is an easy one to employ when the alternative is a legacy of wishing away the threat. USAREUR leaders mortgaged the counterintelligence security of NATO and West Germany to enable USMLM to flourish. But all debts eventually come due. As the U.S. entered the fourth decade of the MLM era, the first credible source to confirm that the SMLMs were GRU residencies walked into the British Embassy in Switzerland.

Three GRU Residencies Identified

In 1978, a GRU officer named Vladimir Rezun defected to British intelligence. Rezun had considerable information regarding the Soviet army and military intelligence organizations and doctrine. Beginning in 1980, British intelligence authorized Rezun to write a series of books under the pseudonym Viktor Suvorov, in an effort to both embarrass the Soviets and to inform the public of some very real threats. The British incrementally cleared Rezun to write about topics he reported to British intelligence which were originally classified due to sensitivity.

Almost overlooked among the volumes of information provided by Rezun was the disclosure to the British that the GRU referred to the SMLMs as residencies, which by definition meant they were sophisticated intelligence-collection platforms. This confirmation meant that the SMLMs made up the majority of the GRU residencies in West Germany, with the other two of their five residencies being collocated with the KGB residencies in the Bonn embassy and Cologne consulate. This very matter-of-fact disclosure was not widely realized until the 1984 publication of a Suvorov book titled *Inside Soviet Military Intelligence*.

By the time of his defection, Rezun had served 13 years in the Red Army, but only spent his last four years in the field as a GRU HUMINT officer. Rezun was stationed as an intelligence officer in the GRU residency operating out of the Soviet mission to the United Nations Office at Geneva from 1974 until his defection in 1978. During this time, he coordinated intelligence operations with other GRU residencies in Western Europe. Based on this access, Rezun provided the only evidence of SMLM clandestine intelligence-collection activities since Heinz Kiefer reported on the Sokolov network contact procedures in 1959. Rezun reported on two episodes involving one of the SMLMs conducting agent operations.

The first case involved a U.S. Army sergeant who approached the mission, was admitted, and provided a component of a cipher machine and offered to provide the other component for money. The Soviets agreed and the sergeant provided the other component to the cipher machine which then enabled the technical services of the GRU to decipher thousands of U.S. radio communications that had been intercepted earlier but remained undeciphered. GRU technicians were also able to use the cipher components to study the latest cipher techniques used by the U.S. and its allies. Although it had not been his immediate intent, once the U.S. service member provided the cipher for payment, he had no option but to continue to support the GRU as a recruited agent. This episode demonstrated once again, that an intelligence service does not need to expend resources developing decryption technologies when a spy is giving them decryption codes.

The other episode was also a walk-in to the same SMLM by a U.S. Army major proposing to sell an atomic artillery shell. To establish his bona fides, the major provided detailed plans of the atomic depots and instructions on checking procedures and standing orders for work with atomic equipment. These documents by themselves were of great value, but the major's primary agenda was to provide an atomic artillery shell for a very large sum of money. The major's proposal was that a shell would be provided to be studied for a two-month period and then returned, which appeared to be a credible plan to enable the Soviets to examine the munition without U.S. officials ever knowing that it had been removed from storage. Arrangements were made and the exchange of the shell and a briefcase full of cash was made. However, after the shell was transported to Moscow, the GRU discovered that the U.S. officer had provided an intricately detailed copy of a shell casing containing radioactive waste that was apparently removed without accountability from the U.S. munitions depot to give the copy a radioactive reading. As the GRU subsequently discovered, the U.S. major had timed the exchange just prior to his reassignment to the U.S., and he apparently, fortuitously and correctly, calculated that the GRU would choose to minimize the visibility of this embarrassing operation and not seek retribution.

In addition to the disclosure that the SMLMs were GRU residencies, Rezun provided detailed information regarding the inner workings of the GRU that was recognized at the time as being highly sensitive and universally accepted as credible. However, the information regarding the SMLMs being GRU residencies was presented in his British intelligence debriefs and his follow-on publications as though this was already widely known information, with the information of higher interest being the perhaps first-told details regarding the two isolated examples of SMLM espionage-related activities. Although Suvorov may have sensationalized some of the content of his books for entertainment value, British intelligence approved the information for release and would not have allowed the publication of information, such as that regarding the SMLMs as GRU residencies, if it were blatantly incorrect. Although it was over three decades into the MLM era, a credible source had finally confirmed that the SMLMs were managed by the GRU as denied-area residencies.

One That Would Have Remained Forever Unknown

The only other known episode involving SMLM clandestine activity was reported in the West German press in 1981. Reiner Paul Fulle was arrested in 1979 after a Stasi lieutenant defected and identified him as being a Stasi agent who had been passing secrets from a nuclear research center in Karlsruhe, West Germany since 1964. In 1979, Fulle escaped from his guard detail while being transported to a state prison in Karlsruhe, and made his way to the State Art Gallery in Karlsruhe where he hid for the night. The following day, Fulle made the over 20-mile trek to Baden-Baden where he was given refuge at the SMLM in the French sector. Eight days later, Fulle was driven to East Germany hidden in a ventilated wooden box in the trunk of a SMLM vehicle.

Fulle left a wife and daughter in West Germany, which was likely his motivation for contacting the BfV in 1980 with the offer to provide information on the Stasi officers he regularly associated with in East Germany. Had Fulle not contacted the BfV and reported the SMLM complicity in his escape from West Germany, this would have never been known, at least not during the MLM-era.

It would not have been unusual for any long-time resident of Karlsruhe to know there was an official Soviet presence in Baden-Baden, but the fact that Fulle went directly to the mission after his escape may suggest that this was a contingency option when he was an active Soviet Bloc agent. Although this was the only such episode discovered in the first 34 years of the MLM-era, Fulle's actions were very consistent with the emergency contact procedures provided to Heinz Kiefer by GRU officer Pyotr Sokolov in 1959.

The Fulle episode was another example of SMLM activity that could have very well remained forever unknown, making it very unlikely that this was simply an isolated episode of SMLM involvement in clandestine activity over the years. The Soviets took eight days to plan the exfiltration and likely made at least one trial run to ensure they were not under suspicion and that the West Germans would not violate the extraterritoriality rights of their vehicles. The use of a specially configured wooden box with holes for ventilation would suggest that this was not the first time they had executed such an operation.

Preamble to the Darkest Fears

Rezun did not specify which SMLM the two episodes of the of U.S. military walk-ins involved, but there are various reasons which would lead to the conclusion that SMLM-F was the more likely one to be approached by U.S. service members. In either case, the fact that one SMLM readily accepted the overtures demonstrated that the SMLMs were at least in the business of accepting volunteers as intelligence sources. Due to Rezun's position in Geneva and the Soviet propensity to compartmentalize intelligence operations, it is likely that he became aware of these two episodes tangentially due to their notoriety and not as a part of his operational focus at the UN. Therefore, Rezun's visibility on these two episodes during his tenure in Switzerland would not suggest that these were the only two isolated cases of the SMLMs managing espionage-related activities over that four-year period, and certainly not over the decades-long period of SMLM operations.

Among the information provided by Rezun that was most illuminating, was the realization that mirror imaging the GRU SMLM-F officers with the USMLM tactical MI officers was likely a grave miscalculation. Rezun confirmed that the KGB and GRU HUMINT case officers were trained under the same program so their operational tradecraft was identical. SMLM-F officers were trained and experienced clandestine HUMINT case officers.

Even after it was credibly asserted that the SMLMs were GRU residencies by at least the mid-1980s, there was an inertia to disregard the threat that had been wished away for nearly four decades. Again, this tendency was perpetuated by a reluctance to take any measures against SMLM-F which might have negative ramifications on USMLM collection operations in the East. Also, at least initially, the information regarding the SMLMs being GRU residencies with specific examples of agent operations was largely overshadowed by the most alarming information Rezun provided, which appeared to confirm another of NATO's darkest fears.

Unclear and Present Danger

The Cold War earned its name because the East and West were constantly in a "phase zero" of the next big engagement. The Soviets were incredibly active in shaping the environment for that next world war. The full arsenal of the measures taken to proliferate Soviet influence worldwide were referred to as "active measures"—a term for the actions of political warfare conducted by Soviet agents to influence the course of world events.

Active measures were largely comprised of subversive measures to weaken the West in preparation for the war to establish the Communist world order. The primary objectives of these efforts were to sow discord among the Western allies and to weaken the U.S. in the eyes of the people of Europe, Asia, Africa, and Latin America. In addition to espionage and other forms of intelligence collection, active measures ranged from other "soft measures" such as disinformation and propaganda, to "wet operations" such as assassination. The Soviets endeavored to legitimize active measures as support to third-country liberation movements, but this category of support included taboo practices such as support to terrorist and criminal organizations.

In addition to the litany of Soviet expulsions for espionage-related offenses, Soviet officials were declared persona non grata for activities consistent with subversive Soviet active-measures techniques such as plotting to foment religious and sectarian strife; maintaining contact with and financing leftist rebel movements, Communist parties, and other anti-government groups; dissemination of hostile propaganda; manipulation of local media; and, infiltrating and influencing local exile communities and ethnic émigré groups. Other Soviet officials were expelled for actions deemed hostile or threatening by foreign governments, which included infiltrating agents for the purpose of sabotage; conspiring to kidnap and murder local officials; involvement in narcotics smuggling; and, maintaining contact with suspected terrorist and violent paramilitary organizations.

The Soviet mentality during the duration of the Cold War was driven by a strong national resolve to avoid another devastating invasion of Russia—one which would inevitably include nuclear weapons. They leveraged any and all potential assets in a concerted effort to achieve this vital national objective. Although it was recognized that there were international mores that they needed to overtly project, behind the scenes, the Soviet Bloc was ruthless in the methods employed to protect their national interests. The Soviets leveraged virtually any foreign presence—official or unofficial, overt, covert or clandestine—as platforms for the employment of active measures.

Most active measures were executed in a decentralized manner, but were always conducted consistent with the centrally orchestrated Soviet masterplan. The most dangerous active measures, as far as the U.S. and NATO forces in Europe were concerned, were those which directly supported Soviet Bloc preparations for war.

Spetsnaz: Myth and Legend

The Russian military umbrella term for special operations forces is Spetsnaz, which is the abbreviation of special (*spetsialnovo*) purpose (*naznacheniya*). Although Spetsnaz forces were controlled by other Soviet government elements (to include the KGB), the large majority of Spetsnaz elements operated under the GRU. Spetsnaz were specially trained and equipped to operate behind enemy lines—which during the Cold War was anywhere in the West—with West Germany being the most immediate of the denied-area territories. Spetsnaz doctrine specified that they would infiltrate enemy territory prior to the initiation of hostilities by means such as airborne (parachute) insertion, long-range reconnaissance, and water approaches by frogmen or mini-subs, or in preparation for hostilities by establishing sleeper cells. Networks of sleeper agents, or sleeper cells, were alleged to have been established throughout Western Europe, waiting for the signal to activate.

Although Spetsnaz doctrine was known to Western intelligence services well into the 1970s, it was largely considered to be exaggerated tales of Soviet super-soldiers who were considered as almost mythical figures due to how unrealistic many of their professed tactics appeared to be at the time. In the ever-deceptive wilderness of mirrors, there was a wide perception that Soviet Spetsnaz doctrine was intended to perpetuate the myth among NATO of the 10-foot-tall Soviet soldier. However, this perception began to shift entering the final decade of the Cold War.

In addition to the information confirming the SMLMs as GRU residencies, Rezun provided the first comprehensive and detailed account of Spetsnaz organization, equipment, and tactics. These revelating details had a profound impact on the NATO perception of the Soviet threat, by transforming the enigmatic Soviet Spetsnaz from myth to legend. This perception was crystalized in reality as the world witnessed Spetsnaz lethality during the 1979 Soviet invasion of Afghanistan.

As British intelligence was still processing the alarming details about the Red Army's elite forces being provided by Rezun, the 27 December invasion of Afghanistan validated his depictions of how Soviet attacks were doctrinally executed with Spetsnaz conducting surgical missions to establish preconditions for success. Spetsnaz personnel performing as military advisors, trainers, translators, and security support personnel, or working in unrelated positions such as services contracting personnel, were hiding in plain sight in Afghanistan while waiting for the orders to unleash their violence. As invasion forces began to move on Kabul, several hundred key Afghan officers who had been invited to a reception celebrating "Afghan–Soviet friendship" were locked in the dining hall and killed by Spetsnaz forces detonating explosives that collapsed the structure. Simultaneously, Spetsnaz forces wearing Afghanistan army uniforms attacked the presidential palace from three sides, fought their way inside, and killed Afghan president Hafizullah Amin and his entire family. Everything that Western intelligence agencies saw in the Afghanistan "decapitation" operation confirmed the remarkable specifics they were beginning to realize were real and serious threats. USAREUR and other NATO commands were recognizing for the first time that the enemy had been operating in their backyards, undetected for years.

Spetsnaz were prepared to operate in NATO countries, speaking the native language and wearing the military uniforms of the indigenous forces. Staffs at Soviet embassies and consulates were augmented by fit, military-aged men acting as guards, chauffeurs, and groundskeepers. Spetsnaz also operated out of the range of non-official foreign presences in NATO countries, and were prepared to create chaos in NATO's rear areas with a primary focus on destroying high-value capabilities such as command and control elements and nuclear weapons or delivery systems. They would also destroy national infrastructure such as electrical and railway systems that NATO would depend on for military operations.

Spetsnaz agents were emplaced or recruited in place as agents referred to as *zamorozhennye* (frozen), or sleeper agents. Spetsnaz recruits included military personnel serving and living in NATO countries, and depending upon their access, civilians living in the vicinity of targets. Some 5,000 "frozen" agents were claimed to reside in West Germany alone.

Assassination was key to the Soviet blitzkrieg planning. In the event of a Soviet attack, the rapid and total political collapse of key NATO governments was seen as essential. Since NATO's nuclear weapons could only be released by political leaders, the preemptive, simultaneous assassination of national decisionmakers would delay decisions to retaliate with nuclear weapons. To facilitate sabotage and assassination missions, specially trained and equipped Spetsnaz teams were prepared to infiltrate with small portable nuclear charges with a trinitrotoluene (TNT) equivalent ranging from 800 to 2,000 tons. U.S. special forces commonly referred facetiously to these type missions as "one way" missions or "dip" (die in place) missions.

Senior U.S. leaders and top military strategists assessed the new revelations regarding the Spetsnaz as a strong indicator that the Soviets were preparing for offensive actions. By the mid-1980s, the Spetsnaz phenomenon was viewed as among the most serious threats to NATO and U.S. national security. One senior leader commented that the development of the Spetsnaz phenomenon had been remarkable and the U.S. had been very late in recognizing the magnitude of the threat they posed. Just as the British government allowed Suvorov (Rezun) to publish books in order to raise the public consciousness, in 1986, the CIA released previously classified information for an article that was published in *Reader's Digest* magazine and another later in the year in *The Washington Post*. The articles raised the specter of Spetsnaz living among the friends and neighbors of the citizens of Europe, and even the U.S. Obviously, the U.S. government viewed this as a credible threat to the point where it actively ensured that the public was aware of the threat potentially living among them.

Weapons and Equipment Caches

Central to the Spetsnaz doctrine was that there would be established agent networks and operations support infrastructures in countries the Soviets had plans to invade. Key to their operations support infrastructure and any plans for Spetsnaz infiltrators or sleeper agents to initiate their rear area attacks was the forward placement of caches. Cache is a term derived from the French word *cacher*, meaning to hide. A cache is a hiding place for munitions, equipment, documents, or other items to be recovered when needed. Common cache techniques were submersion in water, encasement in structures, or the use of natural hide sites such as caves. The most common cache technique was to bury the contents underground in hermetically sealed plastic or containers. Typical containers were large suitcase-sized containers with suitcase-type handles for ease of recovery and carrying. Although cache sites were generally smaller sites that were less susceptible to detection/discovery and could be serviced by one or two persons, there were isolated, larger sites containing the materials to equip 10–15-man units.

Beginning as early as 1955, the GRU began emplacing arms caches in many countries for use in the event of hostilities. Similar caches were also established for equipment such as shortwave radio receivers and cryptographic materials for use by sleeper cells based in West Germany to support clandestine activities. The caches were established for use by infiltrating GRU Spetsnaz or sleepers. In support of sleeper agents, caches were established in the vicinity of their domiciles, which were proximate to the target locations. The KGB ran a separate program to cache arms, munitions, and other equipment to support operations throughout Western Europe, but they primarily employed their own assigned Spetsnaz forces to perform these tasks, so the methods employed were the same as those of the GRU cache program. Since West Germany was envisioned to be the initial main effort of any Soviet or NATO aggression, this was the country with the most such caches.

The Spetsnaz sleeper cell and weapons cache concept should not have been difficult for USAREUR leadership to grasp, given an understanding of their own go-to-war plans. The only major combat force in West Berlin was the Berlin Brigade, which was comically referred to as "the speed bump," as its impact in deterring what would have been a massive Soviet Bloc military offensive would have been somewhere in the range of negligible to none. Therefore, West Berlin would very rapidly become Soviet-occupied territory. Given this understanding, USAREUR maintained a 100-person special forces unit, also coincidentally named Det A, with the mission to melt into West Berlin when the Soviets overran it and begin attacking high-priority rear-area targets just as the Spetsnaz sleeper agents servicing cache sites would do in the West. USMLM regularly collected information on targets that were planned objectives for Det A (special forces) rear-area missions.

In 1985, Oleg Gordievsky was compelled to defect to Britain after being compromised to the Soviets by Aldrich Ames. Gordievsky was assessed as an impeccable source who provided critical information regarding the Soviet mindset during a period of high ambiguity that enabled the U.S. to reduce tensions and avoid what experts regarded as the closest the two sides ever came to a nuclear exchange. During debriefings with British SIS, Gordievsky confirmed the weapons cache information provided by Rezun following his 1978 defection. This information confirmed that the Spetsnaz threat, to include the weapons cache program, could no longer be debated or ignored. In addition to providing specifics regarding the GRU and KGB cache programs, Gordievsky provided information regarding another dire threat.

Suitcase Nukes

Gordievsky detailed a GRU program involving the prepositioning of a relatively smaller number (less than 100) of cached suitcase nuclear devices. According to Gordievsky, who again was viewed as an impeccable source based on the litany of credible information provided, a nuclear suitcase would be placed in a hide site in the vicinity of a target in preparation for a contingency in which a Spetsnaz team would extract the device, travel to and emplace it on the target, and set the device for timed detonation.

Establishing a nuclear suitcase cache was a very complicated procedure. The device required a connection to a continuous power source, such as a nearby facility with power or a utility electrical power transmitter, to keep it active. The device had a reserve battery system that would activate if the power supply was interrupted for any period of time. When a battery system was activated, the device transmitted a signal to a GRU residency, which would initiate a recovery or repair mission.

The Soviets maintained a covert action support infrastructure to enable the forward deployment of nuclear suitcase caches in West Germany, which was unique, but the concept of employing man-portable nuclear devices behind enemy lines was not the sole purview of the GRU. Beginning in the 1960s and continuing until at least 1985, select U.S. Army soldiers were trained and prepared to parachute into Soviet Bloc countries in teams of two with one of the soldiers carrying a special atomic demolition munition (SADM). Once on the ground, the SADM team would conduct a small-yield nuclear attack against a target, similar to the mission that was to be performed by Spetsnaz after infiltrating with small portable nuclear charges or unloading nuclear suitcases from caches in West Germany. Again, "dip" missions.

Occasional USMLM and Spetsnaz Interaction

Since USMLM was very active throughout East Germany, they had their brushes with the GRU's most elite special forces. In 1978, a tour vehicle was detained by a platoon-sized element of Soviet soldiers in camouflaged uniforms with hoods and no service, nationality, or rank markings. The vehicle tires were slashed and the tour members were forced out of the vehicle at gunpoint. The detention was resolved, but only after the CSERB rushed to the scene of the detention. This incident demonstrated how dangerous it could be to stumble upon an element of Spetsnaz. One of the element members spoke fluent German, which was indicative of Spetsnaz elements training to infiltrate into West Germany in preparation for, or in response to, East/West combat.

Another of the many such engagements over the years occurred in March 1984 when a USMLM tour stopped at an isolated location to examine a known training site. The site contained no signs of recent use and there was no military activity initially observed in the area. While the tour officer was out of the vehicle examining the area, four soldiers emerged from the brush without warning, approached the vehicle without detection, and slashed three of the tour vehicle's tires. The soldiers were wearing two-piece hooded green camouflage suits with no insignia of rank or nationality, black lace-up boots with the pants tucked into the boots, and camouflage paint on their faces and hands. Also noteworthy was that the soldiers did not appear to carry any communications equipment, and rather than wearing standard backpacks to carry equipment, carried brown satchels slung diagonally across their chests. The tour driver was able to maneuver around the soldiers, pick up the tour officer, and depart the area without further incident. The soldiers made no further effort to stop or chase the vehicle. The tour vehicle traveled to a nearby town and telephoned for a recovery team to come and replace the damaged tires. Under these type circumstances, the USMLM tour team would find a hide site knowing that the Soviet and East German forces would be alerted to the presence of a damaged USMLM vehicle in area and intensively search the area for the USMLM vehicle to detain. Although the hiding tour team did observe military vehicles passing through the area, it did not appear that there were any military, Stasi, or VOPO actively searching for the vehicle. This would suggest that the training mission the USMLM team stumbled upon was more important than contacting authorities to detain a USMLM vehicle. The satchels worn by the Spetsnaz were the type used to deliver man-portable special munitions such as high-explosive, chemical and biological agents, and even nuclear munitions. A lack of communications equipment may have contributed to USMLM presence not being reported, but it was also indicative of training for denied-area missions that were so sensitive that the use of communications equipment was considered to be an unacceptable risk of detection and mission compromise.

Dangerous Cadre

Based on what was known regarding Soviet global intelligence collection and active measures, and what was beginning to crystalize around the SMLM-F enigma, the notion that the Soviets would not leverage the SMLM residencies to support the range of GRU operations had been exposed as an utter contradiction of logic.

As GRU assets, it became increasingly difficult to conceive that the SMLMs did not actively support the GRU cache and suitcase nuke programs. The Soviet Embassy in Bonn and Consulate in Cologne were known GRU residencies, but unlike the other Western European countries, the GRU had three additional residencies at the SMLMs. Although the Cologne consulate provided good cover for GRU operatives, it was actually the school facility for the children of personnel stationed at the Bonn embassy, so the two were located very close to each other. Latitudinally, they were located in the center of the country, but far to the west near the Dutch and Belgian borders. Therefore, the SOXMIS residency in Bunde provided a capability farther north and east, the MMS in Baden-Baden provided a capability much farther south, and SMLM-F provided a capability over the eastern central region which was known to be ground-zero for a Soviet Bloc attack.

Among the many advantages the SMLMs could have provided by being spread over West Germany, was that they provided the capability to more widely receive suitcase nuke distress signals. It is very feasible that the SMLM communications facilities were equipped to receive these signals as well. Again, the SMLM-F communications facility was never seen by non-Soviet eyes. It is also logical that the SMLMs, at a minimum, would have been employed to leverage their freedom of movement throughout West Germany to inconspicuously travel through the general area of cache sites to ensure that there were no signs of planned excavation or other activities that might uncover the cache sites or disrupt identifying landmarks.

A Point of Inflection

In 1959, U.S. Counterintelligence failed to connect two dots that could have placed their operations on a trajectory to effectively address the potential SMLM-F threat. This failing led to a 25-year period of relative ambivalence. By 1986, USAREUR had finally made the analytical judgement, based on confirmations that the SMLMs were GRU residencies and new insights regarding the GRU Spetsnaz phenomenon, that SMLM-F was likely conducting clandestine activities, which in a worst-case scenario was support to Spetsnaz activities that could prove detrimentally decisive in any future conflict.

Most of the information regarding Soviet covert actions did not come out until after Rezun's defection to the British in 1978, and even then, the implications as they applied to SMLM-F did not appear to resonate until after Gordievsky's 1985 defection. And while these unrelated sources confirmed the same information regarding the deadly games the Soviets were playing, the fact that they were able to conduct such operations until this information emerged well into the fourth decade of the Cold War demonstrated that the Soviets were able to effectively operate while protecting their secrets. SMLM-F was a traditionally suspected, but never verified, clandestine intelligence-collection threat that USAREUR acknowledged by 1986 was likely an even greater threat as it applied to the support of other operations. SMLM-F transcended being viewed as solely an intelligence threat and was by that time viewed as very possibly being an active component of the Soviet unconventional warfare and active-measures threat.

By 1986, USAREUR analysts were studying operations outside their area of responsibility (AOR) as they could apply to a future conflict with the Soviets. Any lingering doubts that Spetsnaz could have been establishing and maintaining cache sites in West Germany over the past 30 years were dispelled after an examination of the petri dish that was Afghanistan. In addition to the sleeper network that was established to facilitate the decapitation of leadership and a flawless coup de main, Spetsnaz capabilities were increasingly on display throughout the occupation. By 1986, Spetsnaz presence in Afghanistan accounted for 20 percent of the ground troops—up from 5 percent at the beginning of the war. As such, Spetsnaz forces were immersed in deep reconnaissance and covert operations in a hostile environment. The Afghanistan conflict was providing Spetsnaz forces "live environment training" that would make them highly proficient adversaries in the event of a Soviet Bloc invasion of Western Europe. The long-held opinions regarding the feasibility of complex preparations such as establishing weapons caches began to shift when viewed from the perspective of the relative ease of planting caches (to include suitcase nukes) in the West German countryside in comparison to these type activities that were ongoing in the rugged mountainous terrain and hostile environment of the Afghanistan war zone.

The Nicholson Negotiations: II

The largely symbolic negotiations to establish Soviet responsibility and attain concessions as reparations for Nicholson's death, rapidly digressed to little more than a USMLM-led effort to leverage Nicholson's death to gain greater collection access for USMLM operations. After the Nicholson negotiations were concluded and the process was analyzed, the Soviet negotiating strategy and endgame victory was one of the compelling and growing number of divergent dynamics shaping USAREUR's concerns regarding the nature of SMLM-F intelligence activities.

From the USMLM perspective, the Soviets made significant concessions in the percentage of restricted areas as a result of the negotiations. However, it simply was not the Soviet approach to give away so much while gaining so little in what was operationally relevant given the traditional and known MLM missions. This would suggest to the counterintelligence analysts negotiating their ways through the wilderness of mirrors that there was in fact something operationally relevant that the Soviets gained in the end. As a sudden flash of the obvious, the lack of Soviet concern over restrictions around areas of military interest relative to the high level of interest in unrestricted, unmonitored, and unhindered access to urban areas, would become an undeniable issue of counterintelligence concern.

The MLM Intelligence Collection Norm

The first key point that U.S. counterintelligence professionals should have taken from the Nicholson negotiations was that intelligence collection was a mutually recognized and accepted norm. Throughout the negotiations, the U.S. and Soviets effectively preserved the gray area associated with MLM intelligence collection, and sustained the legitimacy of MLM intelligence activities. Since the very beginning of the MLMs, the Soviets stressed the principle that a sentry was required to obey orders and protect his post. By continuing this theme in the negotiations, the Soviets were able to avoid the sacrosanct topic of intelligence collection. Although the Soviet press did make reference to U.S. "espionage" as instigating the shooting, the Soviets never contended during face-to-face negotiations that Nicholson had penetrated a restricted area to conduct illicit/clandestine intelligence-collection activities. Rather, they contended that Nicholson was in a restricted area, was not readily recognizable by the sentry as an MLM member, did not respond to the sentry's orders, and was shot as an "unidentified intruder."

The very avoidance of the topic of intelligence demonstrated that this was an acceptably practiced norm which was beyond being entered into the debate. The Soviets (and East Germans) had a legacy of citing USMLM for "espionage" in Akts and other exchanges conducted within the bounds of the Huebner–Malinin Agreement, but never made this charge in a formal protest or reply to a protest. The continued avoidance of the topic during the negotiations implied that such intelligence-related activities were long-standing norms that were above the discussion of procedural issues such as instruction cards and PRA maps. By tacitly acknowledging that such practices were considered acceptable norms for USMLM, the Soviets could certainly argue, or use as a defense if necessary, that these were acceptable practices for SMLM-F as well.

The Nicholson negotiations once again served to establish the MLMs as a microcosm of the larger U.S./Soviet spy-versus-counterspy dynamic. Throughout the Cold War, and in parallel with the ever-eventful MLM dynamic, the Soviet Union and U.S. tolerated a considerable amount of legation-based espionage. The U.S. and Soviets allowed these norms of espionage and other forms of intelligence collection to develop and persist for their own related purposes. The MLM norms emerged in a manner that could be considered an element of their respective nations' norms for intelligence-collection activities, which could then extend to all such activities to include clandestine intelligence activities associated with espionage.

Had the Soviets ever chosen to raise the disproportionality of intelligence-collection activities through the years, the Nicholson negotiations would have been the opportune time. But rather than use this disparity as leverage at a time when they were obviously entering the negotiations from a defensive standpoint, they very consciously chose not to play that card. For decades, the Soviets built the espionage narrative through a steady cadence of messaging that must have been preparing the battlefield for some eventuality. Ultimately, this narrative was so effectively delivered that USAREUR planned to turn the tables during the Nicholson negotiations, if the Soviets raised the issue of aggressive intelligence collection, by arguing that from the legal standpoint, the practices of both Soviet and U.S. MLM personnel legitimized the clandestine collection of intelligence inside restricted areas. Again, when the deception theory is effectively employed, intelligence analysts adopt the narrative that the perpetrating intelligence service intended as the deception, and the "deceived" intelligence agency becomes its own deceiver.

Soviet Access to Urban Areas

Freedom of movement in large urban areas had long been an objective of the Soviets, but they were never able to sufficiently negotiate this point due to a lack of acceptable rationale. After years of frustration in their attempts to gain complete freedom of movement in the cities, for whatever their ultimate objective may have been, the Nicholson talks presented them with the unlikely opportunity to achieve this objective while acting the loser. The Soviets leveraged the negotiations to get this long-sought objective of freedom of movement while making it appear as though they were the side making the concessions.

As a possible precursor to the eventual endgame, during the initial round of CINC-to-CINC meetings between CINC USAREUR and the CINC GSFG, General Zaytsev asserted that while there had been no formal changes to the Huebner–Malinin Agreement in regard to restricted areas, the standards that had been established by exchanging PRA and TRA maps established this practice as a recognized point of agreement under international law. This contention solidified the notion at the very highest level that travel in unrestricted areas was a basic privilege under the agreement and that MLM activities in non-restricted areas could not be monitored or hindered in any manner. When the final maps were exchanged in June 1986, this unmonitored and unhindered freedom of movement included the entirety of Frankfurt and the other urban areas in the U.S. sector. Until SMLM-F ceased operations, they realized an unprecedented degree of mutually recognized freedom to operate in these areas. And while this finally gave SMLM-F the authorization for complete freedom of movement in these areas, in reality, their access had never been monitored or challenged.

There is no information to suggest that USAREUR or INSCOM counterintelligence leaders voiced concerns or were even consulted regarding the counterintelligence risks associated with the emergent PRA map framework. The Allies were consulted throughout the negotiations, but the only counterintelligence consideration was a French concern that more so applied to the risks to their personnel due to the fact that such access in East Germany for Allied MLM personnel increased the risk that they could be subjected to or entrapped in compromising situations. This singular counterintelligence concern demonstrated the nearly complete disregard for consideration of any SMLM-F-related counterintelligence implications.

The CUSMLM advocated for a speedy conclusion to the negotiations due to his perception that the Soviets' willingness to compromise on PRA coverage would result in an appreciable improvement in USMLM's collection environment. The results of the negotiations disclosed that they were conducted purely from the perspective of improving USMLM interests, without regard to the counterintelligence implications of what was being ceded, although these concerns were acknowledged in retrospect.

A portion of the USMLM report written by the CUSMLM, who led the majority of the negotiations, readily acknowledged that in retrospect the Soviets had a clear agenda to increase SMLM-F access to Frankfurt and other large urban areas in the U.S. sector, rather than what would be seen as improving military-related collection access. Specifically, the USMLM report stated that it was apparent that the "SMLMs require access to medium and large-sized urban areas to do their work, whatever its nature." The report continued with an assessment that "by analyzing GSFG's proposals for new PRA guidelines, a visceral Soviet attachment to both the seats of mission (Frankfurt, Baden-Baden, Bunde) and other major cities became apparent." The report concluded this observation by noting that the "likely use of embassy facilities for the exfiltration of acquired material, replenishment of stocks, and receipt of instructions also cannot be discounted. Thus, a substantial—but still circumstantial—case can be built around the suspicion that the SMLMs support clandestine operations in some unspecified manner." What is not as vividly stated in the report, but is a matter of historical record, is that the CUSMLM-led negotiations gave the Soviets exactly what they wanted in this regard. In retrospect, it was rather duplicitous for the CUSMLM to issue such a warning after having been the one to make the concessions resulting in these counterintelligence risks.

The embassy reference in the report points to another nuance that developed over the course of the negotiations. The restriction on interzonal travel was an inconvenience to SMLM-F during the negotiation period, which primarily impeded the frequency at which they were able to travel to their Bonn embassy. During the many appeals for the U.S. to rescind the sanction, the only specific rationales provided were the need for specific foods and new movies available from the Bonn embassy. While it was recognized that the restriction was a legitimate imposition on the Soviets, many, such as the CUSMLM in his final analysis of the negotiations, viewed the Soviet complaints over the restrictions as indicative of a more vital, operational link between SMLM-F and Soviet Embassy in Bonn.

Another enlightening observation from the Nicholson negotiations was the high sensitivity to publicity noted on behalf of the Soviets. Whereas USAREUR had long accepted the risks of a Soviet presence in its backyard due to the benefits of USMLM collection, the existence of these occupation-era relics may have raised questions regarding the efficacy of this continued arrangement. Although a bit of an analytical leap, the CUSMLM assessment of the negotiations noted that "the desire for discretion cannot fully explain the Soviet reactions," and that "such secretiveness does track with the needs of an organization engaged in true clandestine activity."

The Urban Battlefield

The Nicholson talks provided the Soviets the ironic opportunity to manipulate the negotiations in a manner that achieved, for whatever their ultimate rationale may have been, complete freedom of movement in the cities. The Soviets leveraged the negotiations to gain this long-sought objective of freedom of movement while making it appear as though they were the ones making the concessions.

However, this was the first time in the nearly 40 years that the Soviets potentially overplayed their hand and exposed an aspect of their surreptitious agenda. The Nicholson negotiations finally brought the political theater of the MLMs that was tit-for-tat debates over PRAs and TRAs—which were ultimately about the OPSEC of tactical units and not among the more strategic counterintelligence concerns—into view for the counterintelligence leaders and analysts who had a true adversarial intelligence service perspective. When it became apparent that freedom of movement in large urban areas had long been an objective of the Soviets, but was one that they were never able to sufficiently negotiate due to a lack of acceptable rationale, these counterintelligence professionals began to isolate the individual reflections as the litany of concerns continued to mount.

There were a few cities that epitomized the key battlegrounds in the spy-versus-spy intrigue of the Cold War. The neutral spy zone of Vienna, Austria, provided a permissive environment for Eastern case officers to securely meet with their Western agents. The divided city of Berlin was a cloak-and-dagger hotbed where Eastern and Western spies anonymously operated among each other. But like no other city, Frankfurt was recognized as the "gateway to the West" for all bad actors—spies and terrorists included.

Traditional espionage and other clandestine activities require that a case officer (handler) meet with an agent or another network asset of some type. Large urban areas were commonly used by case officers to conduct meets in densely populated and trafficked areas where they and their assets could blend in and disappear. Referred to as "hiding in plain sight," large urban environments enable handlers and assets to "clean off" from possible surveillance before the meet, and even meet in an innocuous manner in case surveillance coverage were still possible.

The U.S. CIA, the British SIS, and the Soviet KGB and GRU (among many others) ran their stations, bases, and residencies out of embassies and consulates in foreign urban centers because they provided legal operational platforms and were immersed in large cities which provided the urban fabric in which to operate. By 1952, GSFG consolidated its HQ in Wunsdorf and the USAREUR HQ was established in Heidelberg. Wunsdorf was exclusively a Soviet military city which was referred to as "the forbidden city" and "little Moscow," so USMLM had pragmatic reasons for not relocating due to its West Berlin sanctuary facilities and the diametric quality of life that a vibrant West Berlin offered USMLM personnel and their families. Alternatively, SMLM-F had no discernable reasons for not relocating to Heidelberg to facilitate liaison with USAREUR, other than that Frankfurt was marginally closer to the Bonn embassy and the inner German border. However, as it applied to the urban fabric at the time, Heidelberg was not among the 50 largest cities in West Germany with a population of less than 123,000, whereas Frankfurt was West Germany's fourth largest city with a population of over 530,000. Even when planning was initiated in 1956 to move SMLM-F to upgraded facilities, there was no apparent consideration to moving the mission to Heidelberg at that opportune juncture.

The Game Was Already On

By connecting the dots in 1986, to include insights from the Nicholson negotiations, USAREUR was beginning to realize that the inexplicably docile SMLM-F contingent may have actually been a much more dangerous cadre. Adding to the concern was the realization that when the U.S. did attempt to attack the SMLM-F target, they were probably prodding a highly sophisticated GRU residency in a relatively amateurish manner.

Department of Defense Counterintelligence Begins to Evolve, but Stumbles along the Way

In December 1981, President Ronald Reagan signed Executive Order (EO) 12333 (Intelligence Activities) as a step toward fulfilling his campaign promise to revitalize America's intelligence capabilities. The EO directed that "Special emphasis should be given to detecting and countering espionage and other threats and activities directed by foreign intelligence services against the United States Government, or United States corporations, establishments, or persons."

The 1980s are referred to as the decade of the spy. During this period, U.S. Counterintelligence arrested or neutralized over 60 Americans who attempted to or actually committed espionage. This relatively high number is somewhat skewed by the number of individuals who did not recognize the peril in volunteering their services by phoning or walking into the Soviet Embassy or one of their consulates in the U.S. Although there may be no detailed analysis regarding the cause and effect of 12333 and the arrests during the decade of the spy, the correlation is difficult to dismiss. And while the decade began with this and other aggressive policy measures to counter Soviet espionage efforts, with each of those over 60 arrests, the pressure for counterintelligence elements to press even harder escalated. EO 12333 and other counterintelligence-enabling policy initiatives essentially "took the gloves off" and facilitated much more aggressive counterintelligence activities. In addition to the great successes realized during this period, this newfound mentality resulted in some now well-documented excesses.

The New DoD Counterintelligence Mentality

The CIA held the authority to approve all counterintelligence investigations and operations overseas. The CIA historically operated with a cultural hubris toward DoD Counterintelligence, treating those services as disadvantaged stepchildren. During the period of increased pressure to perform in the interests of thwarting Soviet activities, the army became frustrated with a perceived lack of covert operations support from the CIA and began to undertake many of these activities on its own. In response to this threat to its covert mission ownership, the CIA began providing support to army operations that did not always follow the deliberate and risk-averse approach traditionally associated with these types of operations. In addition, as the army developed sophisticated counterintelligence capabilities in a range of areas, the CIA tended to approve and partner with the army so as not to miss out on claiming credit for any successes. This dynamic manifested in a generally more aggressive approach to operations in the early 1980s and beyond.

In 1980, USAINSCOM established the quick reaction team (QRT), which was among the Army Counterintelligence capabilities that convinced the CIA to adopt a more cooperative approach. Technical surveillance countermeasures (TSCM) is the counterintelligence practice of conducting technical inspections of facilities that are cleared for classified discussions and transmissions, commonly referred to as "sweeping for bugs." The army had been out of the "bugging" business since the 1960s, so the most qualified technicians to conduct offensive technical operations were the technicians who were trained and qualified to discover such operations. The QRT was established under the INSCOM TSCM program manager as the army agency providing highly specialized technical support to army operations, primarily in the form of technical surveillance. The QRT quickly recognized that the Det A SMLM-F target presented an opportunity to apply their capabilities.

The early 1980s was the lowest point in the history of the MLM relations, largely due to the dangerous Soviet and East German actions against USMLM. In addition, the Reagan doctrine was pushing the community for wins against the Soviets, and the senior leadership in USAREUR was aware that the 66th MI Group was investigating reports of war plans being compromised to the Soviets. These and other convergent factors led to a dynamic that was rife for miscalculation and overreach.

Operation LANKY MISS

During the early 1980s, Det A, with QRT support, coordinated a series of technical operations targeting SMLM-F vehicles codenamed LANKY MISS. In the first "successful" effort, Det A agents gained access to a SMLM-F vehicle while at a repair shop and clandestinely replaced the gas tank of the Soviet vehicle with a specially prepared tank with an embedded tracking device. In a follow-on effort, Det A learned that a SMLM-F official ordered a vehicle through the U.S. military exchange system as one of the quid pro quos the U.S. provided the Soviets. QRT agents in the U.S. gained access to the vehicle before it was shipped and emplaced tracking transmitters. In the most daring such operation, INSCOM discovered that the Soviets ordered a fleet of diplomatic vehicles from an Opel plant in Russelsheim, West Germany, and devised an elaborate plan to leverage the opportunity. A recruited source working inside the plant notified INSCOM agents when the vehicles were ready for delivery, ensured that a selected vehicle was ready for quick access, and ensured that that night-shift guards were paid to turn a blind eye. QRT technicians spent a night in the factory inserting devices into the chassis and ceiling of the vehicle.

The QRT was disestablished in 1983 after they were found to have been supporting unauthorized special operations, primarily in Central America. The QRT was rebranded as the Technical Analysis Team and continued to support technical operations, but on a more closely governed basis. In 1988, a book was published providing details regarding the LANKY MISS efforts targeting SMLM-F. Either due to faulty sources or the author's own literary license, some details of the operation were erroneous, and the outcomes sensationalized. Regardless, the information was in the public domain, so the U.S. braced for the Soviet reaction—but the Soviets did not complain, inquire, or even comment about the book's content.

It is likely that the Soviets became aware of the LANKY MISS efforts early on, but even after they became public in 1988, the Soviets did not express any outrage. There are a number of reasons for this, among which was that they did not have any moral high ground themselves as it applied to technical espionage against the U.S. In 1982, an NSA team inspecting the construction site of the new U.S. Embassy in Moscow assessed the location to be "honeycombed with insecurities." After parochial infighting among the State Department and the intelligence community, the construction project was suspended in August 1985, not to be reinitiated until 1991 and not to be completed until 1997. In 1983, the U.S. discovered highly advanced keylogger technology devices planted inside the IBM Selectric typewriters that were delivered to the U.S. Embassy in Moscow between 1976 and 1983. The electromechanical implants were cutting-edge technologies that recorded every key press and transmitted the keystrokes to Soviet transcribers in real-time. In December 1986, a U.S. Marine Corps embassy guard confessed to allowing Soviet agents to implant technical listening devices in the U.S. Embassy in Moscow the previous year. Given these and other examples, USAREUR and U.S. diplomats were prepared to retort to any Soviet protest regarding the tampering with their vehicles, but it never came.

LANKY MISS and the Principle of "Control"

A key principle that all intelligence services understand, as it applies to countering technical surveillance and monitoring, is to never lose "control" of the potential target of a technical operation. Also, as any intelligence service would know, the three primary SMLM-F technical targets would have been facilities, vehicles, or personnel in the form of items they would commonly carry (or wear, such as watches). As it applies to facilities, a competent, security-conscious entity would never allow unobserved individuals to have access to the facilities or accept into the facilities any items that they did not control the manufacture of through trusted providers. As it applies to vehicles, a competent entity would never accept a vehicle that they were not able to control the production of through trusted agents, and once in their possession, would not allow a vehicle to leave their control unless it were given to trusted agents. In each case of the LANKY MISS operations, it would appear that the Soviets violated this key principle of control in countering the potential for technical attacks. So it would appear.

In these days prior to the proliferation of Global Positioning System (GPS)-enabled technologies, vehicle monitoring and voice-collection capabilities emplaced in a vehicle required that a receiver be within range of the vehicle when occupied and traveling to effectively track vehicle location and collect communications. As U.S. Counterintelligence discovered, bugging a vehicle that was purchased by a SMLM-F officer through the U.S. post exchange for personal use in the East served no intelligence purpose, at least not for the U.S. In the case of the third LANKY MISS operation, assuming that the Soviets would not disregard the principle of control, they would only have ordered vehicles from the Opel plant if their support infrastructure had agents who could either confirm that the vehicles were not tampered with, or inform them if they were. If they did not have such a source, then standard security procedures would dictate that they assume that the vehicles were manipulated.

In each of the incidents of U.S. Counterintelligence exploitation of Soviet vehicles, the Soviets certainly understood the risks involved in not having control of vehicles that were vulnerable to technical exploitation. This strongly suggests that these instances of lack of control were consciously undertaken with the understanding that U.S. Counterintelligence would attempt to exploit these opportunities. The attributes of the West German vehicle repair business which was frequented by SMLM-F, and was where the first technical exploitation episode occurred, exemplifies Soviet tradecraft.

In accordance with known Soviet intelligence support processes, SMLM-F would not have taken part in any of the efforts to develop or identify a secure location to take their vehicles. It was Soviet tradecraft that the GRU infrastructure in West

Germany would establish a secure establishment and direct SMLM-F where to take their vehicles for service. The only West German business where SMLM-F took their vehicles for service was on the outskirts of Frankfurt, but in a PRA. This was the location where the first LANKY MISS exploitation effort occurred. ACS gave SMLM-F special approval to travel to the shop along a designated route when requested in advance. Although well after the LANKY MISS efforts were terminated, the aftermath of 1985 Nicholson shooting provided a glimpse of the exclusivity of this business for SMLM-F. Less than a month after the Nicholson shooting, SMLM-F presented USAREUR with three grievances regarding the sanctions imposed on SMLM-F as a result of the incident. One of these concerns was that SMLM-F was not able to take its vehicles to its long-favored repair shop located in a PRA. In the grievance letter, SMLM-F stated that they would even be willing to travel with a U.S. Army military police escort if that was what would be necessary for them to patronize their favored facility. This SMLM-F insistence to patronize a specific vehicle maintenance business is indicative that the establishment was a "trusted agent" for which they did not consider that they were "losing control" of their vehicle when using it. The fact that this business was in a PRA indicates that SMLM-F personnel were not involved in establishing the garage as a front or trusted business, and that this function was conducted by a larger GRU support infrastructure.

The security diligence exercised in the case of the business SMLM-F used for vehicle maintenance should be seen as indicative of the diligence they would take in all cases regarding control of their vehicles, unless the loss of control served another purpose. Based on the control principle of countering technical exploitation, it would have been negligent incompetence had they not considered the risks when leaving a vehicle overnight for repair, ordering a vehicle through a U.S. government-owned exchange system, or ordering vehicles through a West German manufacturer under the jurisdiction of the BfV. Given this understanding, it is likely that during the first operation in 1981 the Soviets had safeguards in place to confirm or deny whether their vehicle had been covertly tampered with. This would lend credibility to the theory that the Soviets were complicit, or at least witting, in the technical operation against their own vehicle. In fact, the true counterintelligence professional would question why SMLM-F would relinquish control of their vehicle if they were not doing so as a dangle. The only rational explanation for all three cases of Soviet "incompetence" was that they correctly calculated that U.S. Counterintelligence would take the bait and provide the Soviets with its state-of-the-art technical surveillance capabilities.

The principle of control in technical surveillance operations also cuts both ways. In the case of LANKY MISS, at the point wherein U.S. Counterintelligence emplaced technical devices on vehicles that were returned to Soviet control, they lost a degree of control because the Soviets then had opportunities to detect the technical surveillance device(s) without U.S. Counterintelligence knowing. Again, a receiver needed to be within the transmission range of the monitoring device to receive any transmissions.

Therefore, when the Soviets drove a SMLM-F vehicle that was suspected to have been tampered with to GSFG HQ, they would have been out of the range of receivers, and therefore the technical devices could have been detected and tampered with unknown to U.S. Counterintelligence.

In all probability, the vehicles associated with the LANKY MISS operation were three more mirrors the Soviets added to the wilderness.

Why Them and Not Us?

Sometimes mirror imaging can lead to analytical bias, but in other cases, it is appropriate to look in the mirror and ask, "Why not?" By every measure, the Stasi was exceedingly more aggressive in regard to their coverage of USMLM than was the U.S. side toward SMLM-F. Since USMLM acquired their vehicles from trusted sources and maintained control of all vehicles in their West Berlin motor pool, there was never any consideration regarding sophisticated technical efforts targeting their vehicles. But should there have been?

For political reasons, USMLM only used U.S.-made vehicles until 1975. By that point, it was assessed that American-made Fords and Chevrolets were inferior to the European models that were designed and built for East German roads and terrain. In addition, the American vehicles were slung too low and had wide bodies, and were very distinguishable which made the USMLM tours stand out in relation to European models.

By 1981, the entire fleet of USMLM vehicles was comprised of West German-manufactured Mercedes 350SE sedans and Mercedes 280GE jeeps. Based on the U.S.'s post-Cold War analysis and understanding of how deeply penetrated and compromised every West German institution was by Soviet Bloc intelligence services during the 1970s and 1980s, it is very plausible that USMLM vehicles could have been compromised with monitoring devices during manufacturing and production.

The Soviets had a multitude of opportunities to observe and document USMLM vehicle upgrades to assist in determining where best to emplace technical monitoring devices. Despite the U.S. Counterintelligence awareness of the technical efforts targeting SMLM-F, there was no record of TSCM inspections of newly acquired USMLM vehicles. In addition, as the 1983 Selectric typewriter discovery demonstrated, the Soviets' technical monitoring devices had progressed well beyond the capability of U.S. TSCM equipment of the time to detect. There were many instances of Stasi elements detecting and converging on hidden USMLM vehicles in a manner that could only otherwise be explained as "dumb luck."

LANKY MISS and the Espionage Narrative

The Soviets did not address the LANKY MISS accusations before or after they appeared in a widely publicized book. Whether it factored into their reasoning for protesting the incidents or not, Soviet knowledge of the LANKY MISS effort fed into the MLM espionage narrative. If SMLM-F were ever to be discovered conducting or supporting clandestine activities in West Germany, LANKY MISS provided the Soviets the justification to argue that such activities had been tacitly accepted as norms among the MLMs.

This was the first "smoking gun" of clandestine espionage-related activity among the MLMs in the nearly 40-year history. When the time came, perhaps the Soviets intended to keep it as a card up their sleeve in case they needed to defend their own similar or equally intrusive actions. After years of building the espionage narrative, by remaining silent on the LANKY MISS issue, the Soviets now had this card to play if they were ever discovered conducting related activities. It was also very possible—if not likely—that the Soviets had complete knowledge of the technical operations and had secured the evidence long before the disclosures in the 1988 book.

Stumbling into Competency

Even though the LANKY MISS operation was a proactive effort to put together some pieces to the SMLM-F puzzle, this was more of an example of Det A initiative and INSCOM's desire to demonstrate its technical capabilities to target the Soviets writ large, rather than a demonstration of USAREUR resolve to solve the SMLM-F enigma. However, it was likely two steps forward and one step back due to any lingering perceptions that the SMLM-F problem could be addressed by technical solutions alone.

The 1980s was a dawning of high-fidelity technical collection capabilities, and in many cases, new technologies were viewed as operational expedients that could replace the manpower-intensive and time-consuming methods of old. LANKY MISS was an example of U.S. Counterintelligence employing a technical solution and assuming a false sense of progress in truly addressing the fundamental threat. Even had the technical surveillance and monitoring effort been an unmitigated success, it would have only provided a half-measure in addressing the SMLM-F threat—which would have likely only prolonged the refusal of counterintelligence leaders to employ the measures necessary to effectively confront the threat.

Whatever activities SMLM-F was conducting that U.S. Counterintelligence would have been interested in, it is likely that they were using their vehicles to initiate those activities. As is the case in any classical clandestine espionage activity, after an agent uses a vehicle or takes public transportation to reach the vicinity of planned operational activities, virtually all operational activities will be conducted while on foot after the agent has conducted extensive surveillance detection and antisurveillance before arriving at a preplanned location that provides optimal cover and security. Therefore, technical tracking of a vehicle may lead a surveillance team to the general vicinity of the potential operational activities of interest, but unless the team has the capability to effectively transition from a vehicular to a foot surveillance and then sustain foot surveillance coverage of an agent conducting surveillance countermeasures techniques, the surveillance operation will fail. As such, a comprehensive physical surveillance capability was the only means by which DoD Counterintelligence would be capable of developing the necessary insights into SMLM-F activities. USAREUR and INSCOM would eventually agree to this realization.

LANKY MISS can be seen as DoD Counterintelligence incompetently stumbling into a period of unprecedented and never-again-equaled competence. Perhaps never before or after had U.S. intelligence given away its most advanced technical capabilities by emplacing them in vehicles that could then be driven deeply into a denied area far out of reception or control, and examined with Soviet technical equipment that was assessed to be the most advanced in the world. What can be viewed in retrospect as relatively amateurish and doomed efforts, can also be seen as the first signs of a true commitment to address the SMLM-F enigma.

All Reflections Lead to Soviet Military Liaison Mission, Frankfurt

The Cold War era of international intrigue, espionage, intelligence collection, and counterintelligence was characterized by a very calculating and deliberate Soviet machine. Every single piece on the strategic chessboard was planned and orchestrated based on the larger objectives and narratives that each of the pieces was compelled to dogmatically adhere to. Therefore, given what is known about the Soviet mentality and the strategic landscape, it would have been counterintuitive to deduce that the Soviets would allow USMLM to aggressively collect on their elite forces in East Germany for decades if they were not realizing a reciprocal or even greater benefit.

Unlike U.S. democratic-based institutions which encouraged decentralized leadership and initiative, Soviet institutions were rigidly and centrally controlled at the senior levels in an autocratic manner to ensure that all elements were operating in accordance with common narratives and objectives. This often resulted in organizations that did not always operate in their own best interests, but often had to sacrifice those interests to serve the larger centralized cause. One example in the strategic wilderness of mirrors was that the Soviets were known to have compromised sensitive sources and operations to protect other more valuable agents and operations. Therefore, as would be expected, SMLM-F and USMLM's hosts and monitoring counterintelligence entities would respond to the centralized direction from their chess-masters, in many cases, in a manner that did not necessarily serve their immediate interests.

The SMLM-F quandary was a circular argument in that there was a predisposition that SMLM-F did not conduct clandestine activities, because there was no solid evidence that SMLM-F conducted clandestine activities, although there were no actions taken to definitively confirm or deny whether SMLM-F was conducting clandestine activities. The U.S.'s relative hands-off approach and refusal to request

West German support in monitoring SMLM-F activities resulted in a counterintelligence vulnerability that went unaddressed for 40 years during the Cold War.

The Problem with Bureaucracies

Cooperating Western intelligence services did not have any sources with direct access to SMLM-F operations, and the ones with potential access prior to 1959 were apparently never asked the question. By the 1970s and 1980s, the counterintelligence staff officers responsible for the programs to monitor SMLM-F had no cognizance regarding the pre-dark age information regarding Sokolov and the GRU tradecraft of the time to establish dead drops to be serviced by a SMLM and to deliver communications through a SMLM. Also lost were the two months of observations in 1959 that revealed a permissive base for the conduct of Soviet clandestine operations in the heart of West Germany. The general sensing among the USAREUR counterintelligence staff was always that "yes, SMLM-F is probably up to something no good," but in spite of this general sensing, USAREUR leaders refrained from committing the resources necessary to see what they were "up to," to avoid any risk of a potential backlash against USMLM had they been detected trying to do so. At least not until it was too late.

A systemic problem with the U.S. military bureaucracy is that officers are required to move up and out of positions to gain diverse experiences and continue to earn promotions. The common comment is that an officer will finally master a job just when it is time to rotate out. This continuous turnover in leadership is widely recognized as a negative but necessary strain on organizational effectiveness. To mitigate the dysfunction, large staff elements in the army had civilian personnel to provide "continuity" to offset the rapid pace of officer turnover. As with any bureaucratic organization, however, there is a tendency for personnel who remain in the same position or staff element for many years to become set in their ways and even vested in their (and their organization's) perspectives. This regularly results in an entrenchment and inertia to resist change if it requires admitting that past perspectives or ways of doing business may have been wrong. Probably the greatest flaw in all bureaucracies that adopt institutional perspectives is the tendency to dismiss information that does not agree with "conventional wisdom." This is a tendency that practitioners of the deception theory certainly exploited.

Every two or three years, a new USAREUR DCSINT would arrive, be briefed on the criticality of USMLM collection to the USAREUR intelligence mission, be briefed on the relatively benign threat posed by SMLM-F based on what was known, and be cautioned regarding the delicate reciprocity balance between the MLMs that mitigated against a more rigorous examination of SMLM-F activities. Basically, they would receive the bureaucratic warning that "you" do not want to be the one who takes actions that put at risk the effectiveness of the DoD's most renowned collection capability operating against the main enemy. This was the perspective that perpetuated over the years, but was finally changing as the MLMs were concluding their fourth decade of operations.

The prospect that the GRU would employ the SMLM compounds as denied-area clandestine intelligence platforms should have been intuitive from the beginning given the Soviet use of other official forward presences for such activities. However, the lack of definitive evidence to support an argument that they did, perpetuated the general conclusion that they did not. The evidence to support the argument that they did so was very scarce and perhaps even lost over time, but in reality, there was no credible information to support an argument that they definitively did not. Since SMLM-F was a GRU organization, it was only feasible that the GRU would leverage this capability to support its operations as needed.

The Nicholson negotiations exposed the Soviet objective to ensure freedom of movement in large West German urban centers. This was the first strong, undeniable demonstration that the Soviets would readily incur sacrifices in their sector to further the interests of SMLM-F. Coming into focus was a realization that, had analysts examined U.S. and Soviet sectors based on the assumption that SMLM-F was a sophisticated intelligence collection threat, they would have found that there were many other data points to support this assumption that had been apparent for decades. Although the revelations regarding urban centers was the inflection point from the USAREUR counterintelligence perspective, as the counterintelligence analysis autopsy was conducted, it was discovered that in all likelihood, virtually everything the Soviets made or allowed to occur in the Soviet sector could be tied back to shaping the environment for SMLM-F in the U.S. sector.

All Reflections Lead to SMLM-F

SMLM-F displayed three tendencies which should have been viewed as supporting a deliberate effort to maintain a low profile. They did not tour aggressively or instigate incidents that would warrant increased attention. They did not protest any suspected or detected occurrences of tour surveillance so as not to suggest that they were surveillance conscious and might therefore have something to hide. Even though they were likely aware of the LANKY MISS technical operations targeting their vehicles before they were detailed in the 1988 book, the Soviets chose not to raise the issue, even after it was in the public domain, which served to avoid a debate around an issue involving SMLM-F. Avoiding this issue also likely served to provide the Soviets with an example of U.S. clandestine operations in the event they needed this data point as a counterargument at some future time. The stable of Soviet Bloc spies also provided information that negated the need for SMLM-F to conduct aggressive overt HUMINT on U.S./NATO capabilities in West Germany, further enabling a low profile. By all accounts, SMLM-F operated in a manner that appeared to intentionally maintain a low profile. What was not as apparent was that, arguably, more was done in the USMLM sector to facilitate the relatively low SMLM-F profile, reduce the tendency for the U.S. to view SMLM-F with a suspicious eye, and to shape the narrative in case SMLM-F were detected conducting clandestine activities.

Of course, the concession of a (relative) 35 percent increase in USMLM freedom of movement and collection access to enable SMLM-F freedom of movement in large urban areas was the most ominous signal of the overriding priority on SMLM-F interests in relation to the Soviets' and East Germans' interests in the Soviet sector. This appeared to many involved in the MLM game to have been the first instance in which the Soviets had placed SMLM-F interests above their interests in repressing USMLM collection. However, a holistic examination of the U.S. and Soviet sectors over time demonstrated that this was not the case, and that there were other narratives that extended throughout the entire MLM era.

An issue that confounded intelligence analysts and leaders alike for decades was why the Soviets tolerated the highly disproportionate amount and aggressiveness of USMLM intelligence collection. They tolerated an intelligence analysis and production capability that was continually analyzing incoming intelligence and directing intelligence-collection requirements; they tolerated a rotating bench of tour officers and vehicles to sustain a relentless pace of operations that they chose not to attempt to replicate; and, they tolerated aggressive collection methods and brash measures to evade detention efforts. With no clear rationale, the follow-on concern became whether this vast disparity was allowed in order to serve a higher purpose—a more sophisticated endgame. The highly disparate risk environments among which the U.S. and Soviets operated essentially ensured that the focus was almost always on the Soviet sector. The Soviets (with East German support) effectively perpetuated a relatively chaotic game of cat and mouse that kept all eyes focused on USMLM, and consequently off SMLM-F through the years.

The Soviets allowed and even reinforced the narrative that intelligence collection was a norm, although in doing so, they were allowing their own forces to become more vulnerable to collection while not realizing any noticeable degree of reciprocity in the U.S. sector. The Soviets even reinforced the steady narrative which associated acts of espionage with the acceptable norm of intelligence collection. Although these narratives were delivered during meetings wherein the two sides sat collegially debating who was to blame for the latest incident, the narrative was so consistent that it must have had a conceived purpose. Certainly, had the Soviets needed to defend any SMLM-F actions associated with clandestine espionage, they could have cited the multitude of "espionage" claims against USMLM that were never reconciled.

There was one other narrative (a legacy per se) that developed on the USMLM side of the curtain that was, with the exception of the urban areas issue in the Nicholson negotiations, perhaps the most daunting demonstration of how the Soviets placed their interests on the SMLM-F side of the board above those on their own side.

Counterintelligence professionals should be in the business of constantly observing for anomalies. Apparently, one anomaly went unnoticed.

A USMLM Infallibility Legacy (Myth) From the Counterintelligence Perspective

A point of pride which USMLM association members and historians espoused is that USMLM was the only U.S. intelligence agency operating out of Berlin that was not penetrated in some manner by Soviet or East Germans intelligence. This would have made USMLM the anomaly, which essentially confirms that this point of pride for the "infallible" USMLM personnel was clearly a reflection of the Soviets' restraint, and very likely, part of the larger grand strategy. It is highly unlikely that USMLM's legacy of not having a recruited spy was attributable to the ability of USMLM to insulate themselves from exploitation as individuals and an organization. The restraint by the Soviets and the East Germans was obviously calculated.

USMLM spent 43 years traveling among the East German populace to include frequent overnight hotel stays. In addition, off-duty USMLM personnel regularly

Soviet-provided Potsdam House workers would only socialize with USMLM if directed to do so by the Soviets. (USMLM Association)

patronized and socialized throughout West Berlin, which was known to have been a hornets' nest of Soviet Bloc intelligence activities. However, there were never reports of indications of hostile intent to recruit USMLM personnel through traditional Soviet Bloc intelligence methods such as a honey trap or the orchestration of an arrest for alleged illegal activities to facilitate cooperation through blackmail.

It would be easy to jump to a conclusion that the explanation for why the Soviets may not have needed to recruit a source in USMLM was because they already knew what USMLM was collecting through existing sources. Again, they knew all: between Trofimoff, Szabo, Conrad, and Hall, the Soviets had absolute visibility of what USMLM tours were collecting and reporting. However, despite what they did know, the USMLM hosts, and the Stasi in particular, maintained a persistent paranoia that USMLM was involved in clandestine intelligence-collection activities. And even knowing what they did about the USMLM tour collection, it was not in the Soviet (or Stasi) mentality to assume that they knew the worst and relax on their defenses. In fact, they only needed to look west into the U.S. sector to see the flaws in such a counterintelligence approach. In either case, USMLM was the most active and persistent threat in East German territory, so the restraint in not taking more active clandestine measures to penetrate USMLM must have been based on additional calculus.

The KGB and Stasi had an agreement of cooperation protocols between the two agencies that addressed the recruitment of East German citizens to operate against members of the MLMs, but did not mention recruitment activities targeting MLM personnel, indicating that it was understood that these elements were off limits. The attempted 1981 KGB recruitment of a U.S. attaché and former USMLM officer in the Ukraine demonstrated that USMLM personnel had vulnerabilities that the Soviets chose not to attempt and exploit while associated with USMLM. KGB tradecraft would suggest that the honey-trap method of manipulation and recruitment was selected for Major James Holbrook because he had previously been identified, perhaps when at USMLM, as having demonstrated a propensity to be vulnerable to such a situation. As the post-Nicholson incident Stasi report revealed, the Stasi maintained detailed dossiers on USMLM personnel which included potentially exploitable information.

Another feasible explanation for Soviet restraint is that they did not want to risk undertaking actions that might damage relations and bring the viability of the MLMs into question. However, if this were the motivation for restraint, then again, it would have been for some unrecognized benefit they were gaining with SMLM-F, as there was certainly not an equitable situation in the East. Which touches on the obvious reason for exercising restraint in not targeting USMLM for penetration.

While competitive and cooperative norms had established intelligence collection as a mutually accepted practice, the Soviets did not want to push the bounds in the Soviet sector, and perhaps give the impression that they might be pushing the bounds in the U.S. sector as well. Essentially, the conduct of clandestine activity with little restraint in the Soviet sector might lead to the conclusion that SMLM-F was operating in a similar manner in the U.S. sector—just as the Stasi were very likely mirror imaging their suspicions of USMLM clandestine activities. Further, in the gentlemen's tit-for-tat game of espionage, the Soviets chose not to unilaterally escalate the intelligence-collection threshold given the potential consequences. Once either side detected that the other was attempting to recruit MLM personnel as intelligence agents, this may not have been seen as a deal-breaker by either side, but would likely have prompted the other to up their game and respond in kind. Therefore, the most feasible reason for such restraint against USMLM was consideration of the potential consequences to SMLM-F—again, placing their interests in SMLM-F above those of theirs in the Soviet sector. By exercising restraint in not attempting to penetrate USMLM, they may have been depriving themselves of potentially valuable insider information, but this likely served more important purposes for SMLM-F interests. As such, this Soviet and Stasi restraint served to ensure that no additional attention was shifted to SMLM-F.

The development and recruitment of an agent, particularly in a hard target like one of the MLMs, would be a resource-intensive operation. The amount of information that must be developed to accomplish this type of operation would require that the targeted MLM personnel be examined in detail. Given the relatively hands-off approach practiced by USAREUR against SMLM-F, and the relative freedom from counterintelligence and security scrutiny that SMLM-F enjoyed, the last action the Soviets would want to take if SMLM-F were conducting clandestine activities would be one that placed SMLM-F under the microscope. If SMLM-F were exploiting their freedom of movement and general lack of supervision to conduct or support clandestine or other illicit activities, any provocative attempt by the Soviets to penetrate USMLM by recruiting an agent might have had stifling consequences for SMLM-F. This was another way to divert the focus away from SMLM-F.

The Deception Game

Arguably, the Soviets orchestrating the apparently chaotic game of chess in the Soviet sector did more to shape the operating environment in the U.S. sector and to enable the potential for SMLM-F clandestine operations than SMLM-F did for themselves. The Cold War was over four decades old when the undeniable optic of placing freedom of movement in urban areas above the long-held propensity to maximize the percentage of restricted areas emerged. This epiphany shattered long-perpetuated perceptions and deceptions, and superseded them with the realization that there were consistent, narrative-reinforcing activities that were occurring nearly every day of every year spanning the MLM era.

The Soviets established their disinformation department as early as 1953. During the initial years, SMLM-F operated and collected intelligence very aggressively in comparison to USMLM, but this model changed diametrically by 1954. From this point forward, Soviet actions in the U.S. sector and the Soviet sector (with East German support) appeared to reinforce a strategic narrative that the Soviet sector of East Germany was a "wild, wild west" while the U.S. sector of West Germany was a relative "sleepy hollow." Among the long litany of examples, in 1980, a SERB official responded to an admonishment from the USAREUR deputy chief of staff by asserting that SMLM-F was "on a scale of one to a hundred as far as activeness" in relation to USMLM, knowing that this response (narrative) would be reported directly back to the USAREUR DCSINT and other USAREUR leadership. This was the narrative that bureaucratic USAREUR intelligence staff analysts conveyed to the incoming DSCINTs throughout the years. When the deception theory is effectively employed, intelligence analysts adopt the narrative that the perpetrating intelligence service intended as the deception, and the "deceived" intelligence staff becomes its own deceiver.

The Soviets had so effectively ingrained these narratives and deceptions throughout the years that there was even institutional resistance to accept a refreshed perspective of the threat after the evidence was staring them in the face. The information from at least two confirming sources that the SMLMs were GRU residencies and the GRU was operating covertly throughout West Germany should have been the "break-glass moment," but it was not. In addition, there is no information to suggest that USAREUR altered its approach to SMLM-F after being informed by the BfV that the French-sector MMS had exfiltrated the Stasi agent Reiner Paul Fulle to East Germany. And while there were other damaging yet enlightening episodes just around the corner, the counterintelligence analysis of the Nicholson negotiations should have sounded the call to arms, but it very nearly did not, because to sound the alarm at that point would have been to admit how adroitly the U.S. had been once again played by the Soviets during those talks. Probably the greatest flaw in bureaucracies that adopt institutional perspectives is the tendency to dismiss information that does not agree with "conventional wisdom."

The 40-Year Mirror Image

Perhaps the most effective reflection cast into the U.S. sector was the mirror image of USMLM. Through the years, USAREUR analysts perpetuated the hypnotic notion that SMLM-F was a relatively benign threat because the Soviets appeared content to tour with a limited staff of 14 members; whereas USMLM operated as a 70-person intelligence-collection machine. The persistence of this institutional mirror-image mindset was blind to the amount of damage a 14-person GRU clandestine HUMINT residency could do if left unimpeded for four decades. One Walker, one Conrad, one Hall, or one Trofimoff, was more valuable than any number of tour officers and supporting intelligence analysts.

A New View and Negative Intelligence

The Soviet employment of the deception theory was focused on strategic narratives, and not day-to-day overt collection activities as was the focus of USMLM, or the sporadic counterintelligence effort against SMLM-F. Throughout the MLM era there was the propensity for the U.S. to view the USMLM and SMLM-F problem sets as two diametric issues that did not work in close coordination. USMLM was managed out of one DCSINT staff directorate and SMLM-F out of others. This was a time wherein HUMINT and counterintelligence were viewed as two distinct, compartmentalized disciplines.

By the summer of 1986, a new USAREUR DCSINT and Counterintelligence Division leadership had taken over, and unlike many before them, they were unwilling to double down on the baseless assumptions of the past simply to protect the legacies of those who proceeded them.

A new breed of counterintelligence leadership was left to question why the SMLM-F threat had been allowed to persist with no true understanding of how it operated. The operating assumption for so long had been that since SMLM-F was less active than USMLM in regard to touring, that it was much less of a threat to USAREUR than USMLM was to the Soviets. Latently, USAREUR leadership recognized that this was only an assumption, and not supported by facts. The counterintelligence approach to SMLM-F had been woefully inadequate over the years, and by 1988, there was a commitment to address that national security shortfall.

Based on the information provided by Rezun and Gordievsky, and then finally the Nicholson negotiations revelations, the USAREUR DCSINT finally determined that the SMLM-F enigma needed to be addressed. The Nicholson negotiations endgame was clearly to advance SMLM-F interests while making sacrifices in the Soviet sector. Clearly, SMLM-F were not the expendable pawns as had long been the perception.

This new perspective convinced USAREUR counterintelligence leaders that there may have always been an ultimate endgame that was based on sleight of hand and deceptions, and that the seemingly spontaneous and unrelated events that had played out over the years may not have been as they were perceived. The staggering history of mirroring observations made, assumptions perpetuated, narratives received, deceptions accepted, and self-ordained myths of infallibility espoused, exposed a counterintelligence-analysis house of cards that appeared to fall layer by layer

General Charles ("Chuck") Eichelberger was the USAREUR DCSINT from 1986–8, and went on to become the army's senior intelligence officer (Army DCSINT). Prompted largely by the Nicholson negotiations, Eichelberger was the first USAREUR DCSINT to truly take seriously the potential that SMLM-F was a real rear-area threat. The SMLM-F enigma fit squarely into an intelligence tenant that Eichelberger had long espoused, referred to as "negative intelligence." Consistent with the prudent military intelligence assumption that "the enemy is everywhere we are not," in many circumstances, negative intelligence could be as valuable as "positive intelligence." The concept is simple: it is often just as important to confirm where an adversary is "not" and what they are "not" doing, as it is to confirm where they are and what they are doing.

Although Eichelberger came to adopt this concept over his career as it applied to tactical combat operations, as DCSINT USAREUR, he applied this concept to the lack of "negative intelligence" regarding SMLM-F activities. The concept of negative intelligence dictates that we can only assume that an adversary is not doing something until we confirm that they are not. In combat, to assume that the enemy will not do something, but then take no action to confirm that assumption, would be an unacceptable and potentially devastating risk. This is why in combat operations, a large part of the intelligence-collection plan is centered around collecting intelligence that either confirms or denies assumptions, by disproving a given assumption or by confirming the assumption as a fact.

As it applied to SMLM-F, if the U.S. had credible observations that confirmed clandestine activities then this would have been "positive intelligence." However, since the fundamental assumption (conventional wisdom) had been that SMLM-F was not conducting these type activities, then this was the assumption that long needed to be confirmed with "negative intelligence," if nothing else.

As the time-honored maxim professes, "absence of evidence is not evidence of absence." At this point, USAREUR needed a capability by which to confirm or deny.

On a Collision Course with Destiny

While the illuminating reflections regarding the MLM dynamic were shaping a new perspective and trajectory for the USAREUR approach to the SMLM-F mystery, there was an Army Counterintelligence trajectory that had emerged in the 1980s that would synergistically intersect with the point of need for a capability to confirm or deny. This was the counterintelligence trajectory that would lead to the final showdown.

PART III

THE FINAL DECADE AND THE BATTLE THAT TIME FORGOT

CHAPTER 7

The Rapid Maturation of Department of Defense Counterintelligence in Europe

During the Cold War, the CIA was responsible for the coordination of foreign counterintelligence activities and the FBI was responsible for the coordination of domestic counterintelligence activities. Therefore, DoD counterintelligence activities conducted outside the U.S. were under the authority and direction of the CIA, and DoD counterintelligence activities conducted in the U.S. were under the authority and direction of the FBI. Due to the competing cultures, priorities, and budgets among the CIA and FBI, there was no effort to develop a holistic national counterintelligence strategy, and neither agency developed a unifying framework to find synergies among the counterintelligence elements operating under their jurisdictions.

It was very apparent from the beginning of the Cold War, in 1945, that the Soviets had a centrally orchestrated, deliberate, and comprehensive counterintelligence grand strategy.

In 1986, the U.S. Senate Select Committee on Intelligence held a review of the U.S. counterintelligence and security programs which recommended that an interagency group for counterintelligence be established, with representatives from the CIA, FBI, and DoD, to frame national counterintelligence objectives and an associated strategy (or "masterplan") to further those objectives. The committee cited the need to establish a first-ever national counterintelligence strategy to ensure that agencies shared best practices and learned from each other's experiences. The strategy as recommended by Congress was never developed under this Select Committee finding. 1986 was also the second year of the 16-year mole hunt. Fifteen years later, the institutional inertia which prevented the CIA and FBI from coming together on the issue of a unifying counterintelligence strategy was found to have contributed to the counterintelligence and intelligence failures of the 11 September 2001 terrorist attacks in the U.S. There was also a realization that same year that overcoming institutional barriers, although as a latent and rare occurrence, was a key element that facilitated the two major arrests resulting from the 16-year mole hunt. To finally address this perpetuous counterintelligence deficiency, the U.S. Counterintelligence Enhancement Act of 2002 established the Office of the

National Counterintelligence Executive (ONCIX) to act as the central coordinator of priorities for counterintelligence collection, investigations, and operations across the U.S. government. The Act directed ONCIX to produce, on an annual basis, a strategy for counterintelligence programs and activities of the U.S. government. The first-ever U.S. national counterintelligence strategy was signed by the president of the U.S. on 2 March 2005—60 years after the start of the Cold War.

By 1986, as the DoD was witnessing the poor state of U.S. national counterintelligence, and grasping the fact that the two lead agencies would never defer their parochial interests to the betterment of the larger whole, Army Counterintelligence decided to forge its own sword and shield.

Historically, the largely decentralized counterintelligence structure in Europe had an inherent weakness in that counterintelligence capability was spread equally and thinly across the theater. As such, DoD Counterintelligence did not adhere to the basic military combat tenet of "massing forces at the decisive point." Instead, seasoned KGB and GRU field-grade officers overmatched the small groupings of U.S. Army agents, many of whom were in their early to mid-twenties.

In the clandestine spy/counterspy business, technical operations generally consisted of technical surveillance and monitoring, typically referred to as bugging operations, or planting surreptitious audio devices (bugs). Initially, the CIC marshaled its technical experts at the headquarters levels because there was simply no other way to effectively manage these low-density capabilities. Over time, the CIC and then INSCOM recognized that the concept of centralizing expertise and deploying it against highest priorities applied to all investigative capabilities. In the early 1970s, the Special Operations Detachment (SOD) was established to centrally manage the highest-priority counterespionage activities globally under teams of the army's most experienced and capable special agents. This element worked under a "pros from Dover" model in which the most capable case officers would deploy to the location of an investigation and run the case with the support of the counterintelligence office responsible for the area in which the case jurisdiction would have otherwise been. In 1982, the SOD was designated as the INSCOM Foreign Counterintelligence Activity (FCA).

All Army Counterintelligence special agents received surveillance training in their basic agent training course, and were considered "qualified" to conduct surveillance operations. However, conducting a discreet and sustained counterespionage surveillance operation requires highly skilled surveillance operators beyond the abilities of the agents in the decentralized counterintelligence elements. Every year, a select few special agents attended the Advanced Foreign Counterintelligence Training Course (AFCITC), which included three weeks of intensive, specialized surveillance training. However, it was acknowledged that even the surveillance skills acquired in AFCITC were highly perishable if not practiced regularly. To address this issue, for the first time in 1987, FCA established a surveillance team with the most qualified surveillance operators to deploy globally in support of priority espionage investigations.

By 1987, Army Counterintelligence had finally established a centralized, dedicated, and sophisticated approach to confronting the most capable foreign intelligence services.

To Catch A Spy

The backlash that emerged as an overreaction to Angleton's legacy resulted in slashes to Counterintelligence staff personnel and budgets in agencies across the U.S. government. This led to a period of relaxed enforcement of security rules which made it possible for spies to thrive. The Ames and Hanssen cases are the most notorious as emblematic of this period because they demonstrated how the agency with responsibility for domestic counterintelligence and the agency responsible for international counterintelligence failed so drastically within their own organizations. Ames was able to endure despite his sloppy nature because the CIA refused to dedicate resources to what was a known problem, and the KGB was able to keep the small effort that was dedicated to the investigation chasing Soviet disinformation. Hanssen was able to endure in part because he kept his identity from the KGB, but largely due to the absolute lack of a counterintelligence culture within the FBI, as demonstrated most vividly by his assignment to find the mole when he should have been among the suspects being investigated. Ironically, the 1980s was coined the decade of the spy for the many counterintelligence successes before Ames's and Hanssen's legacies of damage were disclosed as having begun in the year of the spy.

Although the decade of the spy is renowned for counterintelligence successes during the period, it also exposed the counterintelligence failures during that and the previous decades. If the 1980s was the decade of the spy, 1985 was the year of the spy. Although 1984 actually had more reported espionage cases (12) than 1985 (11), 1985 provided the first major arrest in a series of spiraling discoveries which illuminated just how badly the disposition and vulnerabilities of U.S. forces in Europe had been compromised to the Soviets.

Three of the major espionage arrests during the decade of the spy were of particular importance to USAREUR—both from the standpoint of the advantage lost to the Soviets, and the unknown regarding what potentially equally damaging collection activities may have still remained. The first major shockwave in the decade and year of the spy was the 1985 arrest of John Anthony Walker for running perhaps the most damaging spy ring in history. Vitaly Yurchenko acknowledged during his short-lived defection that same year that the Soviets regarded the Walker operation to be the most important operation in KGB history. Among the many damaging and costly compromises, Walker and one of his network agents provided the Soviets the capability to decrypt DoD classified communications transmissions for well over a decade. Once again, an intelligence service does not need to expend resources developing decryption technologies when a spy is giving them decryption codes.

1985 was the year of the spy, and ironically, the year in which the 16-year mole hunt began. It was also the pivotal year in which DoD Counterintelligence demonstrated that it would not simply ignore the challenges. Army Counterintelligence netted the next two major espionage arrests, demonstrating that it had pulled away from the pack and was posturing for the next level.

The Counterintelligence Window of Opportunity

In light of the near collapse of U.S. Counterintelligence post-Angleton, there were some very positive developments which helped DoD Counterintelligence uncover some of its most devastating leaks. Once the policy of viewing every would-be volunteer or defector as an agent provocateur was discontinued, the intelligence community realized a very intuitive result. In contrast to its counterintelligence program, the CIA began to more quickly and effectively recover its clandestine HUMINT program. With a new perspective, the CIA began developing sources who could do what counterintelligence programs were unable to do, which was to provide actionable counterintelligence leads. As Viktor Cherkaskin, one of the KGB's leading spymasters, noted in his memoir, "almost all the spies in the Cold War were exposed by other spies."

The Soviet espionage approach that resulted in a long legacy of Soviet counterintelligence successes was now being adopted as a U.S. model. For the first time since Felfe and Blake were identified by Goleniewski prior to the Angleton zero-tolerance policy, the U.S. was developing counterintelligence leads from HUMINT sources, and the DoD was the greatest benefactor. Unfortunately, these newfound accomplishments turned out to be too little too late, as for the most part, they were uncovered after the severe damage had already been inflicted. However, if not for these late-breaking wins, the degree of damage would never have been known, which also leads to more questions and the conclusion that the full degree will likely never be known.

The window of opportunity opened after Angleton's 1974 termination as chief of CIA Counterintelligence and closed again after the Aldrich Ames compromises of 1985.

CANASTA PLAYER

In 1979, U.S. sources in the East began reporting that all of the major USAREUR and NATO war plans were compromised to Moscow, and that this was a trend that had begun in the early 1970s. Based on this revelation, the 66th MI Group began an investigation, but with nothing more to go on than the information provided, they were not able to make substantive progress identifying the alleged mole. Into the early and mid-1980s, intelligence sources continued to warn of a significant leak, and in 1984, a source reported that the NATO and USAREUR war plans updated that year were on the shelf in Moscow as soon as they were published. One of the plans alone earned the spy who provided it $50,000. The source, a GRU officer named Vladimir Vasiliev, also reported that the steady stream of plans was being provided to the KGB by the Hungarian intelligence service.

Consistent with the DoD counterintelligence model of marshaling the highest technical and investigative expertise at the higher levels, USAINSCOM maintained its elite counterintelligence investigative element, the Foreign Counterintelligence Activity (FCA), at Fort Meade, Maryland. In 1985, the DCSINT of the army, frustrated with the lack of progress on the 66th MI Group investigation into the compromises that were known to be coming from a DoD element in Germany, directed INSCOM to establish an FCA-run investigation team to find the mole. The investigation was named CANASTA PLAYER.

Understanding that Hungarian intelligence service modus operandi was to recruit ethnic Hungarians, the FCA CANASTA PLAYER investigators began the search for an ethnic Hungarian in one of the corps-level or division-level G3 plans and operations divisions. Although this approach did not lead them directly to a suspect, they did eventually come across a personnel file in early 1986 that fit the other profile indicators they had developed. Clyde Conrad had spent most of his career in Germany and most of that in the 8th Infantry Division, in Bad Kreuznach, West Germany. The team learned that he rose to the position of NCOIC of the G3 War Plans section, where he earned the name of "Mr. Plans" out of respect for his unequalled knowledge of the army's war plans. A 1983 efficiency report on Conrad noted that "SFC Conrad controls and is responsible for approximately 1,000 Top Secret, Secret, and Confidential documents of the G-3 section." One of his much earlier efficiency reports was signed by his then-supervisor, Zoltan Szabo, which provided investigators the ethnic Hungarian nexus they had profiled. Conrad had retired from the army in July 1985, but remained in the Bad Kreuznach area and continued to frequent the 8th ID army base.

The investigation took very stringent measures to conceal Vasiliev as the source of the crucial information to ensure that if the effort eventually resulted in arrests, there would be no evident connection that would compromise the CIA's GRU agent. However, Vasiliev was arrested by the KGB in December 1986 and executed by *vyshaya mera* the following year. The CIA agent who provided the pivotal lead that would help bring down one of the most damaging espionage rings in history was among the U.S. assets compromised to the KGB by Ames.

In 1986, FCA made a bold move. After many interviews of past associates of Conrad, they discovered an army master sergeant who served with Conrad at the 8th ID and maintained sporadic contact over the years. Danny Wilson was cryptically pitched by Conrad 10 years earlier to "make some easy money," but Wilson, a religious family man, assumed that it was the type of petty crime that many army members were involved in at the time, and declined the offer. Wilson had since become a counterintelligence special agent and agreed to support the investigation. When Wilson arrived in Germany in early 1987 and reunited with Conrad, he provided the cover story that he was there on a three-month temporary duty assignment to help the primary counterintelligence unit in Germany update its war plans. Despite the dubious reemergence of a colleague from the past turned counterintelligence agent arriving at his door to have a beer and catch up, Wilson had Conrad when he mentioned "war plans." As planned, the two rekindled their relationship and Conrad "recruited" Wilson within three months. FCA coordinated to have Wilson permanently assigned to West Germany, and with Wilson in play, the investigation progressed rapidly, as counterintelligence investigations go.

In 1987, FCA established a dedicated surveillance team to support priority counterespionage investigations, and CANASTA PLAYER was that priority. By spring of 1988, the FCA surveillance team was providing blanket coverage of Conrad, having emplaced a tracking beacon on his vehicle and employing a surveillance aircraft referred to as *Sky King*. A surveillance operation of this nature requires up to 50 agents at a time to provide 24-hour coverage and to rotate operators in and out as their "heat states" reached a certain threshold, meaning that they had been close enough to Conrad that he might recognize them if seen another time in a different, unrelated location. The core FCA team was augmented by agents from across the globe who had attended the Advanced Foreign Counterintelligence Course, which included specialized surveillance training. Among the many specially trained agents who augmented the FCA surveillance team were Det A agents, who were familiar with operating in Europe, and many of whom where German speakers. Det A also had the established infrastructure to securely lease German vehicles and attain the license plates (socks) to enable the vehicles to appear indigenous to the areas which Conrad traveled among.

Based on the testimony that Wilson was prepared to provide, and the recorded and photographic evidence of Conrad meeting with his couriers and traveling to Hungary, the time had come to put Conrad out of business. Neither the U.S. military nor the FBI had jurisdiction to arrest Conrad in Europe, so the CANASTA PLAYER team examined options to entice Conrad to travel to the U.S. so he could be arrested and tried in U.S. courts. The investigation team was hesitant to bring the Germans in on the operation for security reasons and based on a history of being very lenient in the sentencing of such cases. However, in an unfortunate twist in the case, the German option became the only option.

In June 1988, the U.S. Department of Justice (DoJ) refused to prosecute the case based on a technicality involving the sensitivity of some of the "passage material" provided to Wilson to pass to Conrad. In the event of a trial, had Conrad's defense asked for associated material during discovery, this would have presented some difficult security issues, but not insurmountable in the view of the DoD. This was a very unfortunate development, because at a time when the FBI and CIA knew that they had at least one mole among them, this would have been the opportunity to send a strong message to current or would-be traitors that the consequences were severe. Ultimately, the DoJ informed FCA that they would not arrest or prosecute perhaps the most damaging U.S. spy in history if he were to arrive at JFK Airport "the very next day." At this point, Conrad would only face justice if the West Germans agreed to accept the U.S. evidence against Conrad and charge him with espionage.

After an uncomfortable disclosure to the Germans that a long-running investigation had been ongoing on their soil for years without their knowledge, the West Germans agreed to prosecute Conrad in German courts. On 23 August 1988, West German federal criminal police agents stormed the Conrad household and arrested the spy. On 6 June 1990, Conrad was sentenced to life imprisonment, which was virtually unheard of in the West German court system for a crime that could not be demonstrably proven to have caused a loss of life. In passing the sentence, the chief judge asserted that Conrad enabled the real possibility that "If war had broken out between NATO and the Warsaw Pact, the West would have faced certain defeat." He further asserted that "NATO would have quickly been forced to choose between capitulation or the use of nuclear weapons on German territory," and concluded that "Conrad's treason had doomed the Federal Republic to become a nuclear battlefield."

The Return of CANNA CLAY

On 22 August 1988, the day before the arrest of Conrad, the source known as CANNA CLAY called the West Berlin Army Counterintelligence source line requesting a meeting. Nearly two years after having been thrown back over the wire, CLAY was ready to provide what Army Counterintelligence agents characterized as "something significant." The meeting arranged with CLAY became one of the most important events in U.S. counterintelligence history.

CLAY was used by the Stasi to translate during two meetings with an American service member, and based on the details provided, it was clear that CLAY's information was impeccably credible and that the service member had done very serious damage over the previous six years. Four days after the arrest of Conrad, FCA was given the investigation. The details provided by CLAY enabled the FCA investigators to quickly develop a profile which made it relatively easy to identify the only service member who matched the profile exactly. The volunteer who might have been dismissed as a provocateur during the Angleton era had taken the challenge presented nearly two years earlier, and served Army Counterintelligence one of its biggest "traitors" of all time on a silver platter.

After completing his warrant officer training in July 1988, James Hall was assigned to the 24th Infantry Division at Fort Stewart, Georgia (U.S.), in July of that year. As an officer in the G2 (Intelligence) section of one of the army's key combat elements in support of the DoD's war plans worldwide, Hall had access to information that would be extremely damaging in the hands of Soviet Bloc intelligence. CLAY had reported that Hall and his Stasi handler agreed to meet in East Berlin six months after Hall was assigned to his unit in Georgia, so the investigation was up against a timeline.

The FCA surveillance team, now operating on more friendly Georgian territory, conducted the surveillance of Hall with the support of *Sky King*. The team was able to observe Hall transferring a classified document from his office to his home and having a very surprising meeting with the individual who was determined to have been Hall's courier when in West Germany and when stationed at Fort Monmouth. In addition to Hall's unreported plane travel to West Berlin and CLAY's testimony, by December 1988, there was sufficient evidence to move to the arrest phase. However, to make the case airtight, FCA added one last act to the play.

The plan was for CLAY to travel to Georgia to contact Hall and arrange a meeting with his "new" KGB handler. The plan was complex with many moving parts, but the trickiest aspect was exfiltrating CLAY and his family from East Germany and getting CLAY to the meeting before the Stasi discovered his defection. With CIA support and dedicated U.S. Air Force aircraft, CLAY was able to meet the FBI-provided "role player" to prepare for execution. With the Days Inn hotel meet room prepared with video and audio surveillance monitoring to be conducted from adjacent rooms, the stage was set for the "false flag," sting operation. Other than Hall arriving home much later than anticipated to receive the call from CLAY asking him to come to a meeting at the hotel, the sting went as planned.

When surveillance confirmed that Hall had finally arrived at home, the call was placed and when Hall answered the phone, CLAY used some security phrases and convinced Hall it was payday. Hall rushed to the hotel where CLAY met him in the parking lot and escorted him to the room. The FBI agent posing as a KGB officer was able to convince Hall to familiarize him with his past espionage activities, paid Hall for the documents he provided, paid Hall for the services he would provide in the future, and acquired signed receipts from Hall for both of the payments. Hall and his new "KGB handler" made arrangements for the next meeting, and as CLAY and the FBI agent left the room ahead of Hall, FCA agents stepped in and made the arrest.

During debriefing sessions conducted following Hall's December 1988 arrest, a vital revelation regarding the Nicholson killing emerged. An event that became a story of USMLM legend occurred on New Year's Eve of 1983, when a USMLM tour officer bypassed Soviet sentries, who were drinking and not manning their posts, to gain first-time access and close-up interior photographs of a modified T-64B tank. During Hall's assignment in West Berlin, he represented his unit at collaboration meetings that were regularly held among Berlin-area intelligence professionals to share intelligence and analytical views. The forum was an analytic exchange of information to help tip off fellow agencies on collection opportunities. At a meeting in early 1984, USMLM analysts proudly shared the high-quality photos from the

New Year's Eve achievement and the accompanying report that specified when and where the embarrassing compromise occurred. Ironically, the analytic exchange was of great value to Hall as he appreciated the tip-off, knowing that his Stasi and KGB handlers would be very interested in information regarding the exact location where the poorly guarded equipment was compromised, and the quality of the intelligence collected by USMLM. Hall was keenly aware that Major Nicholson was killed in the same general location of USMLM's New Year's Eve collection accomplishment the year after he provided the details to the East Germans and Soviets. Hall, who knew the Soviet mindset better than most, became depressed after Nicholson's death, believing himself responsible for the killing.

They Knew All

USMLM is cited by reputed sources as the most effective U.S. intelligence-collection capability during the Cold War. USAREUR was never aware of Trofimoff's treachery dating back to 1969 during the MLM era, but by 1988, USAREUR had become aware of the Hall compromises, and most concerning in regard to USMLM, the Conrad/Szabo compromises dating back to 1972. Until this point, USAREUR acknowledged that the Soviets understood that USMLM was its most prolific collector, but had no idea that the Soviets had absolute visibility on what USMLM had collected over the years.

By 1988, USAREUR clearly understood that through much of the MLM era, the intelligence collected by USMLM lost much of its value because the Soviets were aware of the information that had been collected/compromised. In particular, the realization the Soviets were aware of the highly successful SANDDUNE trash collection and exploitation program and did not take any noticeable actions to mitigate this OPSEC vulnerability, demonstrated that this was acceptable damage in relation to protecting their well-placed sources. The realization that "they knew all" contradicted the long-held perception that the U.S. had been leveraging the Huebner–Malinin Agreement to its disproportional benefit by taking advantage of the agreement privileges relative to its under-resourced Soviet counterparts.

Despite being completely aware of the volume of intelligence USMLM was collecting, the Soviets made the calculated decision to allow these vulnerabilities to persist for what must have been some higher purpose. Due to aggressive collection methods employed by USMLM and the constant East German complaints, the Soviets had ample justification and opportunities to terminate the MLMs based on the perceived disparity of collection, without casting any suspicions on assets such as Trofimoff, Conrad, or Hall. Therefore, USMLM collection was acceptable damage. This could have been explained away had the Soviets needed the SMLMs as a source of information regarding U.S./NATO plans and capabilities, but this was not the case.

They Knew All Again

Not only did the Soviets know all regarding USMLM collection, they also possessed intelligence in substantive detail that SMLM-F could not have possibly attained through standard tour intelligence collection. The known damage caused by Walker, Conrad, and Hall, among others, aptly demonstrated that the Soviets did not need the overt collection of their MLMs—they could not have possibly collected information that would have added value to the level of intelligence the Soviet Bloc had been receiving. The Soviets had the latest war plans, the latest U.S. military organization and equipment details, communications codes, and knew everything the U.S. knew about the Soviet Bloc militaries. With one war plan alone worth $50,000 that detailed all of the NATO forces to be employed and the scheme of maneuver for the anticipated epic confrontation with the Soviet Bloc militaries, there was no need to know what units were training on which days at the training ranges in West Germany. Unless the U.S. had sources of this nature—which would have most certainly become public knowledge but did not—it is clear why USMLM collected aggressively out of necessity while SMLM-F did not.

In contrast to USMLM, there was clearly not a high demand for SMLM-F intelligence on USAREUR ground order of battle. It can only be assumed, based on the relatively lower SMLM-F overt collection efforts, that they were not receiving high-demand intelligence requirements from the GRU—at least for intelligence that could be collected by standard tour activity. As SMLM-F touring reached its steady-state, it appeared that they went through the motions of touring just enough to demonstrate that they were playing the game, whereas they were likely not providing information other than what U.S. military units were training and when. If nothing else, perhaps they toured simply as an attempt to demonstrate that they did need to collect in an effort to convince U.S. Counterintelligence that they did not have other sources. Just as the KGB would continue to allow known agents to operate to protect the sources who compromised them, the Soviets could have just as likely directed SMLM-F to tour for similar reasons. In other words, SMLM-F touring may have been another illusive reflection; another false narrative.

Army Counterintelligence Reaches the Zenith

The Conrad case demonstrated the small window in which the CIA was able to recover its clandestine HUMINT program between the Angleton era and late 1985 when Ames's and Hanssen's treachery once again shut it down. Sources began providing information leading to Szabo and Conrad in the late 1970s, and Vasiliev implicated the Hungarian intelligence service in 1985, just before the black cloud fell on the program. Ames admitted that he compromised every spy he possibly could for the very purpose of precluding any of these assets from identifying him as a KGB spy. Ames compromised the GRU agent who provided the golden nugget, and two other CIA assets who provided additional information regarding the plans that Conrad compromised, all of whom met the same fate of *vyshaya mera*.

The U.S. Department of Justice refusal to prosecute Conrad was another demonstration of a U.S. government bureaucracy refusing to tackle the hard challenges to protect the U.S. democracy from espionage at the time. Although it would be non-democratic to take it to the other extreme, we know the punishment agents who did far less damage to the Soviets would receive in their justice system.

The CIA was the first among several intelligence agencies to vet and pass on CANNA CLAY before Army Counterintelligence chose to recruit him and throw him back over the wire. Had the CIA opted to recruit CLAY, it is most likely that his name would have appeared on one of the many lists of agents compromised by Ames and Hanssen, and Hall would have continued with his espionage work.

CANASTA PLAYER was the greatest U.S. counterintelligence success during the Cold War. It also demonstrated the difference in resolve between Army Counterintelligence and the CIA and FBI at the time. The number of individuals with access to the information the Conrad ring was compromising was much higher than the number of individuals with access to the information Ames and Hanssen were providing the Russians, so the army had a much larger challenge in narrowing the number of suspects. Whereas the CIA and FBI knew there was at least one mole in their ranks compromising their most sensitive operations and did basically nothing, the DoD leadership knew they had a serious problem and pushed Army Counterintelligence to a point where it could execute such an effective operation. Army Counterintelligence was on its trajectory, while the CIA and FBI program ineptness had led them into a new dark era wherein it was plain to see by all would-be collaborators that cooperation with those agencies was a death wish. By the conclusion of CANASTA PLAYER, Army Counterintelligence had the most effective counterintelligence capability in U.S. history, and it was posturing to improve upon this capability in its most active threat area—West Germany.

The loss of the Walker ring, the Conrad ring, and Hall, and the information they provided which would have given the Soviets a decisive military advantage, may have factored largely in the calculus which eventually led to the dissolution of the Soviet Union. This also made the KGB and GRU more desperate in those waning years.

Although seemingly unrelated to the MLM problem set, the CANASTA PLAYER case had the second-order effect of illuminating concerns on the USMLM and SMLM-F sides of the board. Obviously, the legacy of compromised USMLM reporting was a blow, but it also made the approach to solving the SMLM-F enigma more evident.

A Wartime Mentality

When assessing the extreme damage caused by Conrad and then again by Hall, USAREUR finally recognized how badly they had been outplayed in the intelligence/counterintelligence battle of the Cold War. And while this entire "battle" played out, a little-recognized Soviet presence had been operating in its backyard out of a compound in Frankfurt. Again, it was an epiphany that this may have been a game of chess that they were losing without even knowing they were playing. After over four decades, the U.S. realized that while its MLM was a prized intelligence-collection element, it had no idea what commensurate value SMLM-F might be to the main enemy.

In the closing years of the 1980s, the USAREUR leadership, to include the DCSINT and counterintelligence leadership, were not going to be beholden to the sins of the past. With absolute clarity that "they knew all," these leaders had inherited the humiliating prospect that for over the past 40 years the DCSINT had accepted unacceptable risk to USAREUR, NATO, and the West Germans by ignoring the threat and exercising the proclivity to not take actions against SMLM-F that might impact USMLM operations. At this point, USMLM collection was largely supplanted by national technical collection capabilities, and was no longer the primary source of understanding regarding the GSFG posture. Alternatively, the damage that had been done by SMLM-F, and what might still be ongoing, was an absolute unknown.

Although history reflects that the end of the Cold War was but years away, the mindset of the time strongly supported the decision to go to combat with SMLM-F.

Cold War at Its Hottest

In the years leading up to 1989, virtually no Western expert, scholar, or official foresaw the impending collapse of the Soviet Union. When Mikhail Gorbachev became general secretary of the Communist Party in March 1985, the Soviet Union was at the height of its global power and influence, both in its own view and in the view of the rest of the world. Despite its occupation of Afghanistan, dropping oil prices, and the expensive arms race with the U.S., no government of a major state appeared to be as firmly in power, with its policies as clearly set in their course, as that of the USSR. Most credit Gorbachev with having the vision to build a more moral Soviet Union, but in the end the Communist system could not be reformed and collapsed under the weight of its enormous span of control and its reliance on coercion, corruption, and cronyism. Up until the historic events of November 1989, and for at least the next two years, U.S. Counterintelligence remained "at war" with the Russian bear. Despite the official government policy of reform, the KGB ran a shadow government and controlled the country's intelligence priorities until after the failed coup of August 1991.

U.S./Soviet relations had come full circle by 1983—from confrontation in the early postwar decades, to détente in the late 1960s and 1970s, and back to confrontation in the early 1980s wherein Europeans were declaring the outbreak of "Cold War II." French President François Mitterrand compared the situation that year to the 1962 Cuban Missile Crisis and the 1948 faceoff over Berlin. Soviet President Mikhail Gorbachev commented in 1986 that never in the postwar decades had the situation in the world been as explosive, difficult, and unfavorable, as in the first half of the 1980s.

One dynamic that became very clear in the years following the Cold War was that the KGB was very cognizant of the fact that their power during the Cold War correlated directly with the U.S. threat. Only through the fear of the threat of a confrontation with the U.S. was the KGB able to remain the most powerful agency in the Soviet Union. One dynamic that emerged during the 1980s and became more intense with each passing year was the KGB narrative that the U.S. was an existential threat intent on eliminating its Cold War adversary. The bellicose Reagan administration rhetoric, although ultimately effective, served to support this narrative into the final years of the Soviet Union. Understanding that an ultimate peace would end the KGB's legacy of global power, the KGB committed rogue actions that undermined the central government and sent other mixed signals to the U.S. regarding the Soviets' true intentions. This was the dynamic that largely kept U.S. intelligence and counterintelligence on a wartime footing with the Soviet Bloc until the dissolution of the Soviet Union could be confirmed as definitively irreversible.

Soviet intelligence services went on alert in 1981 to watch for U.S. preparations to launch a surprise nuclear attack against the USSR and its allies. This alert was accompanied by a new Soviet intelligence-collection program, named Operation RYAN, which was a Russian acronym for "Surprise Nuclear Missile Attack," to monitor indications and provide early warning of U.S. intentions. Every two weeks, a RYAN report was sent to top political and military leadership on the indicators of nuclear war. This program is known to have continued at least into the 1990s, after the end of the Cold War.

Soviet intelligence services were sent into a frenzy when, on 23 March 1983, President Reagan announced the Strategic Defense Initiative (SDI), which was dubbed by the media as "Star Wars." SDI was a plan for a ground- and space-based, laser-armed antiballistic missile system that, if deployed, would create a shield for U.S. land-based missiles. Soviet paranoia regarding a U.S. nuclear first-strike reached a fever pitch in November 1983 with the NATO command post exercise ABLE ARCHER, an annual exercise with which the Soviets were familiar, but for the first time in that year's iteration, included NATO forces simulating a full-scale release of nuclear weapons. When a well-placed CIA source, Oleg Gordievsky, reported how seriously the USSR perceived the U.S. threat and how close ABLE ARCHER brought the world to a nuclear war, the U.S. leadership was surprised by the Soviet mindset and its paranoia over the U.S. threat. Unfortunately, Gordievsky had to be extracted in 1985 after being compromised by Aldrich Ames, eliminating the best source of information regarding USSR leadership thinking, and creating a period of uncertainty that remained until the very end of the Cold War.

Based on these and other convergent dynamics, the 1980s was the most intensive spy/counterspy period in history. For example, West German authorities documented at least 1,500 attempted recruitments of West German officers and NCOs by East German intelligence between 1983 and 1989. Most of those pitched were asked to report on weapons developments, troop strengths, mobilization plans, and/or alert procedures.

The U.S. and Soviet intelligence services' mindsets moving into the final years of the 1980s were as intensely competitive as at any time during the Cold War. At the time of Nicholson's death, it would not have appeared conceivable to the warriors on the ground that this most tense period was actually the twilight of an era. Although the U.S.'s senior leadership was effectively cutting off the head of the snake, and the Soviet senior leadership was aware that the Communist system was rapidly spiraling into failure, the foot soldiers in this spy-versus-counterspy dynamic were fixing bayonets.

One of the many vignettes that exemplified that the end of the Cold War was unforeseen was that in 1988, USMLM completed the upgrade of their communications room to a sensitive compartmented information facility (SCIF). An SCIF is constructed in accordance with the most stringent security specifications to receive and store the highest levels of U.S. government classified information. By this time, the complete coverage of overhead satellite imagery was rendering USMLM collection less critical and they were examining other areas of intelligence support that would require a facility to process the most sensitive information. In addition, access to the highest level of intelligence information provided more timely tip-offs for tour collection. The fact that the very expensive, upgraded SCIF did not begin operations until 1989 demonstrated that USAREUR did not see the events of November 1989 coming. Det A and the CIA launched technical operations targeting SMLM-F in 1989 that also demonstrated there was no sensing on the front lines that the Cold War was ratcheting down.

In addition to the decade of the spy beginning with a renewed charter to conduct aggressive counterintelligence activities, with each revelation regarding severe damage that potentially tipped the military balance, there was increased pressure to find the next big compromise. Although the eventual end of the Cold War was only a few years away, within the strategic context of the Afghanistan war, in the aftermath of the Nicholson murder, and after the arrests of Walker, Conrad, and Hall, 1988 felt like the dawning of a much more intense version of the Cold War.

The Paradox of the Final Five Years

Another aspect that obscured the wilderness, particularly during the Gorbachev years, was that the Soviet intelligence services were not always supportive of the Soviet foreign policy. During the majority of the Soviet era, the Soviet Central Committee of the Communist Party of the Soviet Union (CPSU) ran the government and the union. As such, the party was the government and the general secretary of the CPSU was the Soviet leader (often referred to as president). This structure remained in place until reform-minded Mikhail Gorbachev was elected as the general secretary in 1985, and embarked upon a set of constitutional changes to try and separate party and state, and thereby isolate his hardline CPSU opponents. Gorbachev's reforms were an existential threat to the CPSU and its nearly 70-year control over the vast Soviet empire. In addition to a threat to the CPSU, reforms that degraded the party's grip on power were a threat to the institutions whose power was derived from the CPSU. The KGB had always operated as an arm of the central government and any efforts to weaken the party and implement reforms friendly to the main enemies in the West were a threat to the KGB's immense institutional power. As a rule, officers in the Red Army were members of the CPSU. By the point at which Gorbachev implemented his policy of *glasnost* ("openness") in 1986, a schism had formed wherein the KGB and GRU leadership remained loyal to the Marxist-Leninist hardliners intent on undermining the new central government and sustaining CPSU control. In July 1988, Gorbachev gained the backing to create a new supreme legislative which finally supplanted the CPSU as the decision-making power in the Soviet Union.

There were many incidents during the Gorbachev era that ran counter to the reform efforts and even reflected efforts to derail them. This trajectory of strong resistance to change began in 1985 and culminated with the failed KGB-led coup attempt of 1991.

One event that demonstrated this paradox, as well as Soviet Bloc intelligence and security apparatus complicity in international terrorism, was the 5 April 1986 bomb attack at a West Berlin discothèque that killed two U.S. service members and a Turkish woman, and injured 229 others. Tensions between the U.S. and Libyan governments were high at the time of the attack, and Libyan responsibility for the attack was confirmed immediately following the bombing through SIGINT. Libya at the time was one of the Soviets' biggest military client states, but when the U.S. conducted punitive air strikes against Libya in response to the disco bombing, the Soviets withheld critical intelligence. In addition, the Soviet advisors, who were vital to the operations of the Soviet-made Libyan air defense systems, remained in their underground bunkers, rendering the systems ineffective. U.N. sanctions imposed on Libya in 1985 were constraining Libya from paying its military equipment debt to the Soviets, so the lack of Soviet support in 1986 began a 25-year decline in Soviet/ Libyan relations. What was also known directly following the Berlin disco bombing, but less publicly asserted, was that it would have been inconceivable that such an activity could have been planned and executed without Stasi (and therefore KGB) knowledge—and at least tacit support. Not only was supporting (or allowing) this attack in direct contradiction with the Soviet policy toward Libya, it contradicted the policy of demonstrating Soviet reform to gain U.S. goodwill. The fact that the KGB sanctioned the operation targeting U.S. persons was among the many instances of involvement of factions within the Soviet "shadow" government in activities that ran counter to the central government's direction.

Another likely example of this divergence was the first shooting incident after the Nicholson talks, which concluded with both sides agreeing that measures were in place to prevent future incidents. On 17 September 1987, a group of individuals dressed in black, civilian-style clothing, but demonstrating all other attributes of Soviet military personnel, attempted to detain a USMLM tour. As the USMLM vehicle attempted to depart the area it was fired on and the tour NCO was superficially wounded in an area close to several vital organs. The timing of this incident could not have been worse as the U.S. and Soviet Union were jointly announcing an agreement in principle to a treaty limiting intermediate-range nuclear forces (INF) in Europe. In contrast to the Nicholson incident, Soviet Foreign Minister Eduard Shevardnadze immediately apologized for the incident. The black clothing worn by the group ambushing the tour was indicative of Spetsnaz forces. Among the incidents that could have been orchestrated by the KGB-supported shadow government with the support of the GRU to derail Soviet reforms with the U.S., this was likely one of their more achievable options. Another USMLM killing in the short timespan could have resulted in a U.S. backlash and damage to the Gorbachev government, and therefore, could have supported the interests of the rogue elements. By this point, USAREUR analysis of SMLM-F had evolved, and this episode supported the assessment that SMLM-F were also directed by the same hardliner camp, and could be responding to extraordinary GRU taskings during this period as well.

The Wartime Mentality

Although an era-ending change was approaching, the decade of the spy began with the mindset that the Cold War was destined to go on forever, and until the very end, this mindset persisted. A review of the Nicholson negotiations, an examination of the real and perceived implications of the Conrad and Hall cases, and a critical analysis of the MLM dynamic over the years, merged to form an assessment of the SMLM-F threat that pushed SMLM-F to the forefront as one of the most glaring known unknowns that had been allowed to perpetuate for decades.

The immediate hindsight and second-guessing following the Nicholson negotiations only served to intensify the hysteria surrounding the GRU Spetsnaz phenomenon and potential SMLM-F nexus. The negotiations endgame that gained SMLM-F broad urban-area access came as an epiphany to counterintelligence intellects who by then realized that the SMLMs were very likely GRU residencies supporting the full range of Soviet dirty tricks—clandestine intelligence and other covert active measures. Hall's late 1988 admission to compromising embarrassing USMLM photographs which he surmised had cascading effects which resulted in Nicholson's killing fed an additional emotional desire to retaliate against the Soviets in some manner.

The major compromises in the Conrad and Hall cases provided myriad complex implications for counterintelligence analysts to obsess over. In the wake of the

Walker, Conrad, and Hall era, it became embarrassingly obvious why SMLM-F demonstrated a relatively benign sense of mission in regard to collection of troop dispositions. In fact, analysts looking back began to second-guess themselves as to whether they should have raised red flags regarding SMLM-F's lack of intelligence focus—which certainly could have been assessed as an indicator that Soviet intelligence was satisfying their intelligence requirements elsewhere. A comparison of USMLM intelligence-collection efforts was likely enough to have reached such conclusions. Even the drug-induced entrapments of current and former USMLM members should have demonstrated that the GRU was playing at a different level that could only have applied to SMLM-F as well, but these may have been lost to USAREUR analysts for unfortunate reasons.

Culminating with the most illuminating counterintelligence alarms—the Conrad and Hall arrests, the recognition of the SMLMs as GRU residencies, the Spetsnaz threat, and the Nicholson negotiations—the litany of retrospective data-points appeared to expose another great counterintelligence failure of the Cold War. Once the fundamental assumption regarding SMLM-F collection activities came under serious scrutiny, the multitude of reflections in the wilderness were able to be isolated and analyzed.

It was finally time to engage SMLM-F on the battlefield of the U.S. sector.

Divide and Conquer

There are spies who were discovered and doubled back against the KGB, GRU, or other foreign intelligence services during the Cold War; most of these cases will remain unknown until everyone involved is dead, or there is no one else left alive who cares. The known major spies who betrayed the U.S. during the Cold War and operated long enough to inflict damage, were placed under investigation because another source reported on their compromises, or their compromises became intuitively obvious, as in the cases of Ames and Hanssen. Even Johnny Walker was betrayed by his wife (or so the story goes). Therefore, with the exception of the lost souls who thought calling or walking into the Soviet Embassy or a Soviet Consulate in the U.S. was a wise entrée to espionage, U.S. defensive counterintelligence programs were relatively ineffective. In contrast, although the KGB did attribute many of their spy arrests to their defensive counterintelligence programs to protect the true sources of the compromise, their suffocating and ruthless defensive counterintelligence efforts did uncover many of the spies they neutralized.

The Hall episode wherein Army Counterintelligence deployed an agent who eventually returned with the counterintelligence lead was perhaps the only perfect counterintelligence operation/investigation, but arguably, the agents who threw CANNA CLAY back over the wire had no real expectation that he would return with information of value. Overall, the only truly effective counterintelligence model has been to receive a lead from an external, sensitive source, identify the likely agent, and then place the suspect under investigation until evidence of espionage can be obtained. In successful counterintelligence counterespionage investigations, physical surveillance was an essential investigative capability.

By 1988, USAREUR was fully aware that within a three-year period the Soviets had lost assets they relied on for information that was assessed to have tipped the balance in the event of war. With the loss of the Walker ring, the Szabo/Conrad ring, and Hall to provide intelligence on European war plans and troop dispositions, USAREUR was desperate to develop information of increased intelligence-collection efforts by the Soviets to suggest that the hemorrhaging was now stopped, and that the Soviets' key sources of intelligence had been neutralized. Alternatively, a lack of a discernable increase in intelligence-collection emphasis might be the worst-case indicator that there were more like Hall and Conrad still operating and compromising secrets to the enemy. In either case, USAREUR assumed that the actions of SMLM-F might be indicative of which scenario was likely the case.

During this period of heightened tensions and paranoia, any unknowns were pursued with a fervor, and SMLM-F remained the longest-standing unknown. SMLM-F had long operated in a manner to avoid attention, perhaps in an effort to obfuscate their true purpose. Although the Soviet central government appeared to be intent to maintain the political peace, the insights regarding GRU residencies and Spetsnaz operations in West Germany, and understanding that SMLM-F could be responding to extraordinary taskings that would not be consistent with the polices of the Gorbachev government, added another element of concern that needed to be proactively addressed.

The pressure to improve counterintelligence processes and realize immediate results increased with each successful arrest of an espionage agent, because the circumstance of the most damaging cases increased the U.S.'s understanding of the enemy's knowledge and reduced confidence in the military balance. If nothing else, LANKY MISS represented the aggressive (yet covert/clandestine) approach U.S. Counterintelligence was willing to exercise. As the aggressive counterintelligence approach was manifesting itself in Det A, there were simply too many unknowns that needed to be confirmed or denied. As General Eichelberger would say, positive or negative intelligence—but there was a compelling need for one or the other.

SMLM-F Tour and Counterespionage Surveillance Operations

Throughout the years, intelligence leaders would occasionally ask what it would take to determine if SMLM-F were involved in clandestine or other activities that they would not want disclosed. The answer was always the same: either unleash the West Germans to conduct a comprehensive surveillance of SMLM-F travels, or resource Det A to conduct that level of covert surveillance. Since ceding any jurisdiction of

SMLM-F to the West Germans was out of the question, the invariable follow-on query would be, "What would it take to enable Det A to conduct a comprehensive surveillance of SMLM-F?" This then led to a recurring explanation of surveillance operations.

Det A was minimally resourced to conduct surveillance operations based on the tour patterns established by SMLM-F over the years. Det A developed a purpose-built surveillance capability based on SMLM-F tour tactics and patterns, and no other U.S. surveillance capability could match Det A's ability to operate against the SMLM-F target when on tour. This capability was developed to conduct surveillance of eight- to nine-hour tours along highways and other roads with occasional stops along the way. SMLM-F tour personnel rarely exited the vehicle, and when they did, it was only to check the trunk, stretch their legs, or urinate, and they never left the vicinity of the vehicle or let the vehicle out of their sight. For this reason, Det A surveillance operations never required foot surveillance operations, with the exception of the occasional situation wherein an operator would grab the go-bag and hike through the woods to observe a tour vehicle that had stopped, normally at a roadside rest area.

Det A was well equipped, trained, and capable of conducting surveillance operations against SMLM-F tour activities. However, the Det A surveillance capability tailored to SMLM-F did not translate well to counterespionage operations. The level of capability required for counterespionage surveillance operations, wherein the target is likely to conduct operational activity in a large urban area, is more faceted than the surveillance of a single vehicle. Generally, such operations require that the surveillance team effectively transition from a vehicular surveillance to an extended foot surveillance, and vice versa.

Unlike the Det A vehicular surveillance of SMLM-F tours which were generally conducted on highways and less densely trafficked roads, counterespionage vehicular surveillance operations generally occur in densely trafficked urban areas where team tactics and communications practices require a higher degree of team coordination. An espionage agent preparing to conduct operational activities will usually travel by vehicle (or public transportation) to the general area where the operational activity will take place, and then travel by foot to the location where the operational activity is conducted. Therefore, a counterespionage surveillance requires that the entire team possess a high degree of tactical and technical expertise to ensure an effective and discreet transition between vehicular and foot surveillance.

As the target transitions from vehicle to foot, the surveillance team must also do so while simultaneously maintaining observation of the target and avoiding exposure. It is during these periods of transition that the team experiences the greatest difficulty maintaining contact due to the sudden shift in the operation. Foot surveillance operations require that the team coordinate effectively to maintain observation of a target—one who may also be conducting passive or active surveillance detection or antisurveillance—and effectively transition observation responsibilities among operators to minimize the team profile and reduce the exposure of individual operators to the target. Public locations such as large stores, nightclubs, and restaurants require special team tactics to coordinate control and avoid exposure in locations that are natural intrusion points which facilitate logical surveillance detection measures on the part of the target and provide natural obstacles to facilitate antisurveillance. The team must be able to transition back to the vehicular (or public transportation) follow while maintaining contact with the target, or be capable of transitioning to another target, as may be the case when the target meets with an individual and the surveillance team needs to determine the identity of that second individual. This level of surveillance would be further challenged by the fact that SMLM-F personnel operating in an urban landscape would be a hard (likely surveillance-conscious) target, which would require a surveillance effort with the highest level of sophistication and expertise.

These discussions regarding why Det A was not resourced to confirm or deny SMLM-F clandestine activities invariably ended in the same manner. Although the tutorial on surveillance operations always ended with the same decision to "think about it," the conversation did occur often enough that the concept of surveillance of SMLM-F non-tour travel came to be characterized by the term "downtown ops." Downtown ops was an aspirational term that was usually included in a sentence ending with the words "will do someday." Until that day, USAREUR would never be aware of the activates SMLM-F was conducting during those hundreds of thousands of departures from the compound for which the destination or purpose were never known.

Although USAREUR had never pushed INSCOM to establish a comprehensive SMLM-F surveillance coverage capability, they could not completely ignore the threat, and the Det A capability was the bare minimum necessary to not completely ignore the risk of SMLM-F violating their freedom-of-movement privileges. While the surveillance of SMLM-F vehicular tours did not require the same expertise and resources of a comprehensive combined foot and vehicular surveillance, they were still relatively resource intensive. The CIC/USAINSCOM perspective during the MLM era was that every agent dedicated to the SMLM-F problem was an agent that was not available to support priority counterespionage investigations. Although being marginally manned to perform the SMLM-F surveillance mission, Det A was the largest counterintelligence detachment in West Germany with 21 agents and two local national investigators. This was always a point of contention in that INSCOM regularly campaigned for relief from the SMLM-F mission, while USAREUR refused to relent and occasionally threatened to increase the capability requirement to that "someday" level. This dynamic continued through the years, and then CANASTA PLAYER and the Hall case happened, with cascading effects.

USAREUR and INSCOM Agree to Divide and Conquer

In the early 1980s, a CIA source provided specific details regarding a mother and son team of KGB support agents who both worked for the U.S. Europe Army and Air Force Exchange Service (AAFES) headquarters in Munich. The lead was passed to Army Counterintelligence who quickly identified the duo, who were believed to be KGB couriers. In addition to the AAFES headquarters, the other primary tenant command on McGraw Kaserne in Munich was the 66th MI Group headquarters and a number of its more sensitive subordinate activities.

With support from the West German BfV, it was determined that the mother and son team traveled by vehicle to Austria at least once every weekend, and in some cases, on both Saturday and Sunday. The time they spent in Austria during these frequent trips ranged from two to four hours. The local counterintelligence detachment ran the investigation but was unable to develop information other than their anomalous travel pattern, which was assessed to be one of establishing a pattern of frequent travels to Austria in order to obfuscate the few trips in which they actually carried materials to their meets with KGB officers. Limited surveillance was conducted by the Munich counterintelligence detachment, but there was no other dedicated surveillance capability in Europe other than Det A, and Det A did not have the capability to conduct combined foot and vehicular surveillance as was required for a counterespionage surveillance operation.

Although it was slow to develop, this investigation, codenamed LANCE BLADE, was one of the main impetuses for USAINSCOM to form a dedicated surveillance element to support priority counterespionage investigations. In 1987, INSCOM's elite counterespionage organization, the Foreign Counterintelligence Activity (FCA), established a dedicated surveillance team with a global support charter. However, LANCE BLADE would need to wait as the surveillance team's first major operation was CANASTA PLAYER, which kept the team decisively engaged from early 1988 until Clyde Conrad's 23 August 1988 arrest. During CANASTA PLAYER, USAREUR and the 66th MI Brigade (which transitioned from a Group to a Brigade in 1986) were assured that LANCE BLADE would be the next priority for FCA surveillance support. However, on 22 August, the day before Conrad's arrest, CANNA CLAY emerged to initiate the Hall investigation, which again kept the FCA surveillance team continuously engaged until Hall's 21 December 1988 arrest.

After the details of the Hall investigation were disclosed, neither USAREUR nor the 66th MI Brigade would have argued that the shift in priority was not appropriate. However, when they were notified in August 1988 that they were no longer the priority for support, it made evident that while they had important investigations that could not move forward without dedicated surveillance support, they could not rely on support from a single surveillance team with a global mission that they did not own.

CANASTA PLAYER was a significant accomplishment for FCA and INSCOM in general, but it was an embarrassment for the 66th MI Brigade which had essentially failed to protect the army theater command for which it was responsible. When the army DCSINT tells the INSCOM commander to fix it, and the INSCOM commander sends in the professionals from higher headquarters to take over, it was basically taking the investigation out of the hands of the 66th MI Brigade and relieving the USAREUR DCSINT from significant oversight of the investigation. The fact that the USAREUR CINC allowed the investigation to be run in this manner represented a lack of confidence in his staff and the 66th MI Brigade to manage it effectively. Although the 66th MI Brigade did play a large part in the investigation, the perception was one of failure, and the 66th MI Brigade, with USAREUR's endorsement, committed to not let such a failing repeat itself.

The FCA surveillance team augmented with agents from around the globe operated admirably during CANASTA PLAYER, but there were some shortfalls that could only be overcome with a core team of surveillance operators that were immersed in the German culture. Only an operator who spoke native-level German could be completely discreet and able to operate under any circumstances. The large majority of operators did not speak passable German and would therefore need to avoid any situation where the target or a third person might observe that the operator was an American trying to pass as a German. Particularly at the time, there were nuances to the European culture that needed to be understood to operate discreetly as an operator. Germans wore a style of clothing that was different from the standard American style, and there were many other cultural distinctions such as that people wore wedding bands on their right hands, handled a knife and fork differently, and counted and signed numbers with their fingers differently. Females generally did not shave their armpits and would stand out as peculiar if they did not go topless while sunning by the river. Surveillance operator safety was a significant concern during CANASTA PLAYER because there were no speed limits on German highways, and Conrad regularly drove in excess of 100 miles per hour. The Det A operators attended high-speed driving training every year and were accustomed to driving at dangerous rates of speed, but many of the other operators were not comfortable driving in this manner, which impacted operations.

As CANASTA PLAYER, and the Hall case with its origins with the KGB and Stasi in East Germany demonstrated, USAREUR and the 66th MI Brigade had by far the most subversion and espionage cases due to the direct counterintelligence engagement with the prolific and aggressive Soviet Bloc intelligence services. In the late 1980s, the 66th MI Brigade established the Special Investigations Team (SIT) to employ the FCA "pros from Dover" model in the European theater, but there remained one capability gap.

USAREUR and the 66th MI Brigade did not have a surveillance capability to conduct downtown ops against SMLM-F. USAREUR and the 66th MI Brigade did not have a surveillance capability to support its priority counterespionage investigations. In September 1988, USAREUR and the 66th MI Brigade cut a deal.

CHAPTER 8

The Final Reflections in the Cold War Wilderness of Mirrors

The Sophisticated Adversary

In 1988, USAREUR and INSCOM agreed to resource the army's second dedicated counterespionage surveillance capability to support priority counterespionage investigations in Europe. As agreed, this elite element would also operate against SMLM-F.

In early December 1988, the newly handpicked U.S. Army officer traveled from Munich to Frankfurt to assume command of Detachment A. En route, the U.S. Army captain and counterintelligence special agent with highly specialized training and experience met with the USAREUR Chief of Counterintelligence at the USAREUR headquarters in Heidelberg. The USAREUR Chief of Counterintelligence was a seasoned colonel who was brought in specifically to attack the hard problems that had perpetuated for decades. The colonel wanted a face-to-face with the new commander to remind him that, while the 66th MI Brigade priority for his organization would be counterespionage investigations, a primary reason USAREUR advocated for enhanced resourcing and mission authorities for Det A was to help solve the SMLM-F enigma. Following their discussions, the two parted ways in violent agreement.

Building the Capability

In late December 1988, a U.S. Army Counterintelligence special agent warrant officer was assigned to Det A as the surveillance controller (Sierra Charlie). A surveillance team Sierra Charlie is essentially the "quarterback" of the team, responsible for planning and executing surveillance operations. The newly assigned Sierra Charlie was the top surveillance operator in the army and handpicked by the 66th MI Brigade director of operations to be diverted from Fort Meade, Maryland, to Det A. The title "Q" is surveillance speak for equipment expert. In February 1989, the top Q in the counterintelligence community was assigned to Det A. With the key personnel in place, the 527th MI Battalion provided a revolving door of surveillance-trained Advance Foreign Counterintelligence Training Course (AFCITC) graduates for interviews. By May 1989, the core team of 12 surveillance operators was assembled to complete preparations to go operational. The core surveillance team element was branded with the nondescript title of the Operations Support Team (OST).

The operating concept for the OST was to maintain the core team of 12 highly skilled surveillance operators that would be augmented as needed by additional AFCITC surveillance-trained special agents identified from throughout the 66th MI Brigade. The OST maintained an on-call "bench" of 30-plus surveillance operators to augment operations and ensure the OST could sustain months-long 24/7 surveillance operations.

During the first six months of 1989, Det A conducted an intensive training and equipping phase to develop the capability to conduct sustained, covert surveillance operations. Det A already had vehicles with cover license plates and state-of-the-art equipment, so they were well on their way there. The Q worked with his apprentice to configure each of the surveillance vehicles (callsigns) with foot push-to-talk buttons on the passenger-side floors and microphones embedded in the dashboard for completely hands-free broadcast communications capabilities. Det A also acquired one new vehicle—a specially configured OP van (callsign Lima)—that could be parked to observe a fixed location, such as a residence, while appearing to be unoccupied in areas where vehicles with occupants parked for long periods of time would stand out as conspicuous.

During the training and equipping phase, Det A conducted periodic surveillance operations of SMLM-F tours to meet their obligation to USAREUR and support the continued analysis of SMLM-F intelligence interests.

In April 1989, USAREUR and INSCOM approved the downtown operations plan and authorized the 66th MI Brigade to initiate downtown ops against the SMLM-F target when ready. USAREUR required that they be notified when downtown ops were planned in order to be aware in case there were an incident.

By August 1989, the Det A OST completed training and was prepared to conduct counterespionage operations and focused downtown ops against SMLM-F. It was time; the Det A commander declared the OST fully operationally capable. Forty-two years after SMLM-F began operating in the U.S. zone of West Germany, the U.S. had finally developed a capability to develop evidence regarding suspected SMLM-F covert/clandestine activities.

A Warm-up Event

In August 1989, the Det A OST was ready and itching for a fight. Det A antic-ipated an immediate order to execute SMLM-F downtown ops. However, when that fateful day had appeared to arrive, Det A was directed to begin planning for its first counterespionage operation. As an initial step, all agreed that it was prudent to conduct the OST's first operational surveillance against an individual suspected of being a relatively low-level agent, rather than against SMLM-F tour officers—each of whom were trained intelligence officers, making them "hard" surveillance targets.

The subject of the investigation, codenamed MONDOON RACE, was a Polish national who worked at a U.S. military equipment storage facility in Mannheim, West Germany. The subject was suspected to be providing equipment components to Polish intelligence who in turn were certainly passing the components to the GRU. After a few weeks of sustained surveillance, the OST confirmed the suspicions and the investigation was concluded as many such cases were. The subject was discreetly detained and given the options: either go to jail or become an asset for U.S. intelligence. The subject became a double-agent asset, and the OST had successfully completed its first counterespionage surveillance operation.

Understanding the Sophisticated Adversary

The reason why it was a prudent measure to initially operate against a low-level agent as opposed to a hard target such as SMLM-F, was that there were broad implications for operating against such a sophisticated and hard Soviet target.

During the Cold War, the Soviets maintained a robust espionage support infra-structure throughout Western Europe. Any Soviet elements conducting espionage or other clandestine activities would receive support from this vast network of capabilities. Had SMLM-F been conducting or supporting clandestine or covert operations, they would have been given priority for operational support. This would have invariably included countersurveillance support to ensure that they were not under U.S. or West German surveillance.

Countersurveillance is the most effective method of surveillance detection, and is practiced by the most sophisticated intelligence agencies. Countersurveillance involves a team of specially trained and equipped operators who observe the activities of a potential surveillance target to detect surveillance of that target. Countersurveillance may be conducted as a mission-enabling security measure or as a periodic security practice to observe for surveillance presence when the potential target is conducting standard activities. Countersurveillance is more specifically employed when a potential target is preparing to conduct sensitive activities to determine if the individual is under surveillance, and then signal to either proceed with or abort the operation. Countersurveillance is also commonly practiced during agent meets to observe for surveillance of the meet, which would confirm that the agent is either compromised or a double agent.

Had SMLM-F been conducting activities that would warrant countersurveillance support from the vast Soviet network in West Germany, countersurveillance support provided as both a standard periodic security measure and in support of specific sensitive activities would have definitively determined that SMLM-F was not under surveillance during all previous non-tour, off-compound travels. Regardless of how certain the Soviets may have become over the years that SMLM-F had not been under surveillance, countersurveillance support would have been employed as a standard, periodic security precaution. Certainly, if SMLM-F were to detect indications of surveillance while conducting operational activities, or otherwise, they would coordinate for countersurveillance support to confirm or deny their suspicions.

Det A was very aware of this Soviet espionage support capability, and knew it could emerge when least expected.

The Moment of Truth

With winter approaching, it was not the best time for SMLM-F downtown ops, but it was the 66th MI Brigade's turn to hold up its end of the bargain with USAREUR, and the holiday season was considered a worthwhile opportunity to identify SMLM-F contacts. And anyway, the SMLM-F enigma was unfinished business.

Decades of unanswered questions and undeniable indicators were finally to be confronted, illuminated, and resolved—one way or the other. There was a decades-long Cold War kinetic energy that was finally pressing Det A to engage SMLM-F in an unparalleled spy/counterspy covert battle for the ages. The "re-engineered" Det A was finally primed and postured to unleash on SMLM-F the U.S.'s most elite counterintelligence shadow warriors. The date was set: downtown ops would begin on 15 November and continue until 23 December 1989. There was no one who was professionally vested in reaching this moment of truth who could have imagined any scenario that could possibly stop the inevitable.

On 9 November 1989, a few sections of the Berlin Wall were opened, resulting in thousands of East Germans crossing freely into West Berlin and West Germany for the first time in nearly 30 years.

Downtown ops were put on a pause until USAREUR, and the world, could figure out what had just happened.

LANCE BLADE

Although the events of 9 October 1989 began a period of great uncertainty, one aspect that played in the 66th MI Brigade's favor was that the OST was now available to support the LANCE BLADE investigation two months sooner than had been planned.

LANCE BLADE was a perfect example of how U.S. Counterintelligence allowed a known threat to persist by simply not dedicating the resources necessary to neutralize the threat. The source reporting on the subjects of the investigation and other information available made it undisputable that the mother/son team were KGB couriers.

Based on information developed by the Munich Counterintelligence Detachment, the couple had a long history of traveling to Austria at least once and often twice a weekend. West Germany and Austria had an open border in that vehicles could travel freely across the border in both directions, but the West Germans had a relatively sophisticated system of recording all vehicle license plates entering and exiting, which is how the BfV was able to identify the duo's many travels to Austria. It was confirmed that they had no relatives or official business ties in Austria, so it was apparent that their frequent travels were intended to establish the pattern that they regularly spent their leisure time dining or shopping in Austria. Given this established pattern, it was assessed that they were transferring materials to a KGB officer or cutout in Austria, probably during a select few of their many trips to Austria.

As was the case for the Hall and other espionage investigations, U.S. Counterintelligence received information for LANCE BLADE that undeniably implicated the mother/son team of espionage, but the investigation still needed to develop the information necessary to secure a conviction in a court of law. In such cases, when the incriminating evidence was derived through "sensitive sources and methods," alternative evidence needed to be developed because the sources and methods could not be disclosed in a public trial; and even if they were, it would likely be regarded as hearsay evidence and not admissible. Therefore, the information would need to be developed through surveillance to observe and record the individuals in the act of committing espionage, or the subjects would need to be manipulated into confessing to the act while being covertly recorded. By 1989, the investigation had not developed enough information to establish a pretense to have an agent pose as a KGB officer and elicit a confession. Therefore, surveillance was the only investigative method that would progress the case.

LANCE BLADE Phase One

The surveillance operation was planned with the objectives of observing the subjects receiving (presumably classified) material from an agent or by servicing a dead drop, and then transporting it to Austria. After this occurred, the West Germans would be brought in and arrangements made to detain the subjects at the border the next time they were known to be carrying materials which they acquired by the previously observed, or another, means. This initial phase of the operation was constrained by legal direction to meet the objectives of the operation without continuing surveillance into Austria. The 1955 Austrian State Neutrality Treaty established a demilitarized Austria and included Article 319 which prohibited all military intelligence operations on Austrian soil. The FCA surveillance team had conducted a hot-pursuit surveillance of Conrad into Austria during CANASTA PLAYER, but was able to genuinely plead ignorance for the violation, which USAREUR knew it could not plausibly do a second time in just over one year.

By early December 1989, the OST was "on bumper" and ready to begin the first phase of the surveillance operation. During the investigation, the mother was referred to as "Lance Blade" and the son was referred to a "Son-of-Blade." In surveillance speak, Lance Blade was "Zulu 1" and Son-of-Blade was "Zulu 2." Zulu 1 was a heavyset woman in her early sixties who wore a bulky fake fur coat, a full-bodied dark black wig, and heavy makeup with distinct false eyelashes, dark mascara, and bright red lipstick. Zulu 2 was in his early forties, slightly overweight, and bald. The two lived in the same apartment and had one car ("X-Ray 1") which Zulu 2 invariably drove. INSCOM provided technical support to the operation by installing hidden video monitoring equipment in the offices of Zulu 1 and Zulu 2. An OP was established in a storage facility that enabled agents to observe X-Ray 1 when parked on McGraw Kaserne during the work day and observe the entrance to the building they worked in.

The surveillance became very mundane during the work weeks in that the two Zulus spent virtually all of their time either at home, at work, or traveling back and forth between the two. They were together when they departed their residence in the morning and when they came home after work. They only stopped occasionally on the way home to shop for groceries or put fuel in the car. They walked from their vehicle into the headquarters building together and departed together. The only time the surveillance team observed them apart was through the video feeds from their separate offices.

The only action for the OST during this initial phase of the operation was on the weekends when the mother/son duo traveled to Austria. However, this was a standard highway follow of a vehicle that traveled painfully slowly on the West German highway with no speed limit. Intentionally or not, this slow rate of travel could have served a surveillance-detection purpose as it did compel the OST to employ tactics to avoid mirroring in a "convoying" profile over long observable stretches of highway. Based on direction from higher, the OST would terminate the surveillance when X-Ray 1 passed into Austria and establish positions to pick them back up when X-Ray 1 passed back into West Germany later in the day. When X-Ray 1 with the Zulus were picked up after returning to West Germany, it would lead the team directly back to Munich where they would stop to gas up the car before returning home.

It is a common joke among U.S. counterintelligence agents that Soviet spies observe the Christian Orthodox calendar and do most of their work on the most commonly recognized 25 December date of Christmas, knowing that U.S. counterintelligence would never work on their sacred holiday. Staying true to this edict, and having not accomplished much in terms of moving the investigation forward, the OST was directed to terminate the first phase of the LANCE BLADE surveillance operation on 24 December 1989.

The most informative aspect of this phase of the operation was what the OST did not observe—"negative intelligence." A trained and surveillance-conscious agent, as would be expected of a driver who has been a KGB courier for years, would normally establish a standard pattern of travels to facilitate surveillance countermeasures (surveillance detection and antisurveillance) prior to conducting operational activities. Normally, an agent will establish a broad pattern of travels that a surveillance team, if present, would observe and become familiar with. By establishing this broad pattern, when the agent does need to conduct surveillance countermeasures, they will do so in a manner that would appear consistent with the travel patterns the surveillance team would have observed. This enables the agent to integrate surveillance countermeasures activities into standard travel patterns and make them appear close enough to the norm to discourage suspicion on the part of the surveillance effort. If an appropriate travel pattern has not been established in advance, any significant alteration of established activity patterns will result in enhanced caution (and interest) on the part of the surveillance effort. Such alterations in patterns serve to confirm to the surveillance team that the target does indeed have something to hide—and will probably result in continued and enhanced surveillance coverage.

The travel patterns of Son-of Blade (with Lance Blade accompanying) established a travel pattern to provide cover for the act of delivering material to a contact in Austria by establishing regular travel to Austria as their standard pattern. However, they had to receive the materials as well by a means such as a covert meet or by servicing a dead drop. Surveillance confirmed that they were not stopping along the route to Austria for any such activities. It was peculiar that the subjects' travel pattern, other than travels to Austria, was very narrow and routine. Since they had established such a limited pattern of travel and activities, any deviation would have been readily perceived as anomalous and resulted in intensified OST coverage. Therefore, the OST assessed that based on their observations of travel patterns in the Munich area, it was very possible that material might be loaded into X-Ray 1 or somehow delivered to their residence by an unknown asset.

LANCE BLADE Phase Two

The 66th MI Brigade was becoming frustrated with the circumstance of the investigation, knowing that it was surveillance intensive and it depended on the subjects receiving or acquiring materials for transfer, which could be a monthly, six-monthly, or even yearly occurrence. This was an unknown that could make the surveillance operation unsustainable. Worst case, the subjects could be in a dormant phase. USAREUR and the 66th MI Brigade agreed to conduct at least one more phase of surveillance operations, and then evaluate the way forward.

The next phase of the LANCE BLADE surveillance operation began in mid-January 1990. This phase placed an emphasis on ensuring that the vehicle was observed from the OP at all times that it was parked during the workday, as this was assessed as one of the more likely locations where a third party would load items into the vehicle. Although it would have been ideal to observe the subjects' residence 24/7, the streets around the residence had restricted parking so there was no discreet location to position the OP van (Lima) for this purpose.

Knowing that this phase of the investigation might be the final effort to observe operational activity, the decision was made to go for broke and authorize the OST to follow X-Ray 1 into Austria.

The operation was very standard, and mundane, until the first Saturday, when the subjects departed their residence by vehicle and traveled as anticipated to Austria. Although West Germany and Austria shared an open border, to be completely safe, the OST sanitized two callsigns from any special configurations such as communications equipment and license plate quick-change brackets to continue the surveillance into Austria, using only car phones to communicate in a nondescript manner. The surveillance continued smoothly into Austria where about 20 miles into the trip the subjects stopped at a restaurant to eat. Two OST agents sat, ate, and observed the subjects as they sat and ate, just the two of them. The subjects were obviously known by the establishment staff but there were no suspicious interactions during the stop. When they finished their meal, they paid the check, got in their car, and returned home. This was clearly a "decoy" day.

Lance Blade (Zulu 1) and Son-of-Blade (Zulu 2) lived on a square (equilateral) city block that was adjacent to a four-lane, main thoroughfare. To reach their residence from the main thoroughfare, they would take a right turn onto a small one-way road, take a left on the next small road which was a one-way, and then turn left into the enclosed garage of the residence on the opposite side of the block from the main thoroughfare. The block they lived on was a typical urban West German landscape, lined with two-story structures, with shops on the ground floor and residences above. Since there were residences above, the ground-floor shops were required to be closed by 5:00 PM.

During the initial phase of the surveillance operation, it became quickly evident that when following X-Ray 1 home from work every evening, it was highly conspicuous for a callsign to follow them down the two small roads close enough to confirm when they entered the residence garage. As was common in such circumstances, the OST implemented a procedure to minimize the risk of exposure while incurring negligible risk to the operation. To mitigate exposure and the risk of detection, when it became apparent that X-Ray 1 was returning to the residence, a callsign would maneuver ahead to drop off a foot operator who would take a concealed position in a park area to observe X-Ray 1 enter the parking garage, and inform the team when this occurred. This procedure enabled the callsign observing X-Ray 1 turning right off the main thoroughfare toward the residence to inform the team of the turn and then continue straight to avoid turning down the small street and risking exposure to X-Ray 1. With this process, X-Ray 1 could be seen by the foot operator as soon as it turned onto the road to the residence, so the only time the vehicle was not under observation was the few seconds it was on the first road it would turn down off of the main thoroughfare. This was assessed as very acceptable risk.

The Final Reflection

By the middle of the second week of the operation, the OST was going through the mundane daily motions and largely looking forward to the upcoming weekend's surveillance into Austria. But there would be no more ventures into Austria, as this day in late January 1990 was destined to be the final day of the operation, and for the most part, the LANCE BLADE investigation.

That evening, the subjects departed work at 5:00 PM, which was well after sunset for that time of year. On their way home they stopped at two stores, which was not normal, but none of the OST operators observed anything unusual during these stops. It was a clear winter night with relatively good illumination for visibility. By this time of evening, the side streets in the subjects' neighborhood were very lightly trafficked by vehicles or pedestrians. As was the standard practice when X-Ray 1 appeared to be in its final approach to the residence, a foot operator was dropped to confirm when X-Ray 1 had entered and parked in the residence's enclosed garage. But this was no standard night.

After a callsign notified the team that X-Ray 1 had turned right down the first side street, an unusually long pause in communications followed. X-Ray 1 did not reach the intersection to turn left toward the residence. Knowing something was amiss, the Sierra Charlie directed a callsign to clear down the road X-Ray 1 had turned onto. The clearing callsign notified the team that X-Ray 1 was stopped on the side of the road prior to the turn toward the residence, unoccupied. At this point, suspicious of this anomalous situation, the OST callsigns discreetly dropped foot operators to begin searching for the Zulus.

The OST foot operator who had been dropped to observe X-Ray 1 enter the garage, had it arrived, noticed a pedestrian walking in his direction and moved from his position to avoid appearing suspicious by loitering in a static position. As the operator began clearing down the road toward the main thoroughfare on the side of the block opposite of where X-Ray 1 had stopped, he noticed a figure at the other end of the block walking in his direction on the opposite side of the street along the street-side shops. The shops were all closed and the street was not well lit, but it was a relatively clear winter night. The OST operator peered back to notice that the pedestrian, whose approach compelled him to move, was now loitering in the same location where the OST operator had been. When the "pedestrian" noticed the operator looking back at him, the individual immediately became animated, looking at his watch and pacing in a small square, as though anxiously awaiting someone to meet him or a vehicle to pick him up. This glimpse of overacting by the individual in an apparent effort to project a plausible reason for having stopped at the same location where the operator walked away from, was the first suspicious observation in an unfolding scene that could only have been imagined in spy movie drama.

As the OST operator and the individual on the other side of the road were nearing recognition range, the unidentified individual stopped and turned toward a shop as though looking into the window. As the operator moved closer and the figure came into view, he recognized a heavyset woman wearing a bulky fake fur coat and a full-bodied wig who was undeniably Lance Blade (Zulu 1). The operator, however, was not able to discreetly notify the team until he had passed by the location of Zulu 1, but that quickly became irrelevant. As the operator approached a position nearly paralleling Zulu 1 from across the road, he could see the figure on the other side of the street looking at him through the reflection in the glass, and for a fleeting moment, they were looking at each other in the eyes through the reflection. What the operator saw were the eyes, the skin, and the slender face of a much younger woman than Zulu 1.

As the operator passed the individual who was obviously intended to be a Zulu 1 lookalike, she turned and began walking back toward the main thoroughfare, paralleling the operator. At the same time, the operator heard footsteps behind him and peered to see that the individual who had been loitering at the other end of the block was now following the operator and quickly closing distance. The operator, by now knowing that he was in the middle of a countersurveillance hornets' nest, walked more rapidly to the main thoroughfare, notified the Sierra Charlie regarding the confirmed countersurveillance, and then briskly moved away from the operational area conducting surveillance detection and antisurveillance maneuvers. The hunter had become the hunted. The Sierra Charlie, who had received reports of three additional suspicious individuals from other operators, immediately terminated the surveillance operation and coordinated the secure extraction of foot operators from the operational area.

The following day, the chief of the CIA Munich station confirmed with the Germans that they had not conducted any type of operation in the area that night. The KGB countersurveillance operation was clearly an elaborate effort requiring coordination among the two Zulus and at least five countersurveillance operators. During the OST's operational debrief that night, it was confirmed that it would have been impossible for a Zulu 1 to have walked from the location of the parked X-Ray 1 and the location where the decoy Zulu 1 was first and last seen, without having been seen by OST operators. Therefore, the decoy Zulu 1 was inserted into the operational area in a location that would surprise and confound the surveillance effort.

In virtually all cases, a countersurveillance operation is intended to detect surveillance without the surveillance element ever having known that it was under countersurveillance observation. The LANCE BLADE countersurveillance was uniquely peculiar in that X-Ray 1 stopped in an illogical location, the Zulus must have quickly exited the vehicle and "disappeared," the decoy Zulu 1 first appeared in a location that the team could determine she could not possibly have arrived at without prior detection, and there was increased pedestrian traffic relative to the norm which alone would have appeared suspicious to the surveillance team. This operation was intended to detect U.S. surveillance and make it known that they had done so. There were even some in the leadership who wanted to dismiss the detected countersurveillance as sleep-deprived surveillance operators seeing ghosts. This would be the only other explanation to those who would rather not consider how their investigation had been compromised so thoroughly as to have walked their elite surveillance team into a waiting ambush. The blatantly obvious decoy Zulu 1 alone made the presence of countersurveillance coverage that night indisputable, so there was only one feasible explanation for why the Soviets chose that counterintelligence battlefield on that crisp Munich winter night.

By January 1990, hardliners in the central Communist Party of the USSR were feverishly trying to reverse President Gorbachev's policies of *glasnost* which he was pushing to establish a more free and open government. Aligned with the party hardliners was the KGB leadership, who understood their power and influence depended on the ability of the central government to maintain power through the perception of the U.S. as a continuing existential threat. Therefore, the KGB needed a bellicose and 11th-hour level of tension between the USSR and U.S. to survive. This turn-of-the-decade mentality compelled the KGB to depart from the central government's policies and perpetuate confrontations with the U.S. on all fronts. It appeared that having KGB assets stalking the streets and standing in the shadows on that January evening was one of these efforts.

What the events of this surreal Cold War skirmish actually revealed to USAREUR, Army Counterintelligence, and the CIA, was how capable and confrontational the Soviets remained. This had been the most sophisticated, elaborate, and unorthodox countersurveillance effort ever observed and recorded. The fact the Soviets were able to conduct such a sophisticated and robust countersurveillance operation in the heart of Germany was remarkable. As opposed to what would usually be the case with a countersurveillance operation, the operation against the OST was an aggressive and overt message. The more measured approach upon learning that there was a new counterespionage capability in Europe would have been to "sniff it out," but what the Soviets chose was more like a "punch in the nose." This sensing that the Soviets were still in the mood to pick a fight was viewed by many as a cavalier display of disrespect and confrontation.

Although the brazen Soviet countersurveillance on the U.S.'s turf during LANCE BLADE did support the case for a more aggressive approach in the form of downtown ops, USAREUR was not ready to authorize such a response, yet.

CHAPTER 9

The Last Counterintelligence Battles of the Cold War

Tying up Loose Ends

When the OST returned to Frankfurt, one of the Det A local national investigators informed the commander that he had something to show him. Crime, corruption, and cronyism were the three Cs of the Soviet system.

One provision in the Huebner–Malinin Agreement specified that "The respective missions or individual members of the missions may purchase items of Soviet or United States origin which must be paid for in currency specified by the headquarters controlling zone where purchase is made." This stipulation was interpreted to mean that the MLMs were allowed to shop at the post exchanges of their hosts. This was a considerable privilege for SMLM-F members, of which they took full advantage. AAFES was U.S. government subsidized and provided products to service members tax-free and at a much better price than products on the heavily taxed West German economy. Western clothing, movies, and entertainment technologies were the favored items of purchase for SMLM-F members at the Frankfurt AAFES post exchange. There was no specified limit for purchases, and the Soviets clearly made purchases for themselves, families, friends, and likely for personal gain. In addition to alcohol and tobacco products which the SMLM-F members were also able to purchase at significantly reduced prices, the AAFES products could make a substantial profit on the East European black market. SMLM-F members spent money that was well above their means, which meant that they were purchasing items with other people's money, making money from their post exchange purchases, or making additional money through other methods. PX management regularly complained that the volume of purchases by SMLM-F personnel made items unavailable for U.S. service members. On occasion, the latest of which was October 1986, USAREUR prohibited a SMLM-F member from shopping at the PX due to his suspected "speculation" with purchases of audiovisual equipment, meaning he was accused of exploiting the privilege for personal gain. Despite a history of SMLM-F members exploiting their Huebner–Malinin Agreement privileges for personal gain, there was never a concerted effort to record and compile incriminating evidence that could be used as exploitable leverage—until 1990.

There was another Huebner–Malinin Agreement provision stipulating that the "necessary rations, P.O.L. supplies and household services for the military missions will be provided for by the headquarters to which accredited, by method of mutual compensation in kind, supplemented by such items as desired to be furnished by their own headquarters." POL is an abbreviation for the class of military supplies referred to as petroleum, oil, and lubricants. USAREUR and GSFG exchanged an agreed-to amount of gas on a reciprocal basis. The way that USAREUR provisioned fuel to its service members, and to SMLM-F, was with gas coupons.

Petroleum (gasoline) was highly priced and highly taxed in West Germany, making the cost a hardship for U.S. service members serving in West Germany. To offset the relatively high price of gas on the West German economy, the Germans agreed through the U.S. status of forces agreement to not tax the fuel provided to U.S. military personnel. Gas coupons were sold to service members in a rationed manner for roughly half the price of the cost of gas at the pumps. USAREUR provided gas coupons for purchase to military members and other authorized DoD-affiliated individuals. The gas coupons purchased by the liter at a much lower price were exchanged for gas at stations throughout West Germany.

Gas coupons were stringently controlled and rationed per service member and per authorized vehicle to prevent black marketing. Gas coupons could be sold on the black market at a 25 percent profit or a service member could work directly with a gas station to profit from gas coupons. A service member could collude with gas station personnel to accept coupons without pumping any gas, and the gas station personnel and service member could share the profit from the unpumped gas that would then be sold to a tax-paying West German at full price. For example, the gas coupons a service member would pay $30 for were worth $60 of gas paid for by others at the pump—a $30 savings. Assuming an even split, the gas station would give the service member $15 and keep $15 in profit.

Although these opportunities for abuse existed, the distribution of coupons was controlled to prevent such actions. The coupons were referred to a gas "rations" for a reason, as they were only provided in amounts that an individual or family would be expected to reasonably use on a monthly basis; if service members had a justifiable need for additional rations, this would be addressed on a case-by-case basis through their chain of command. On an individual basis, the profits that could be made by black marketing gas coupons were generally not worth the risk of penalties to the service member and gas providers, so the abuse of gas coupons was a relatively minor issue. However, if an entity had the ability to abuse the privileges on a larger scale, it could be highly profitable.

By reciprocal agreement, SMLM-F and USMLM received a monthly quota of gas coupons. USMLM filled their vehicles and auxiliary tanks at their West Berlin facility prior to every tour and then used fuel coupons to continue ongoing tours while in East Germany. Demonstrating how little SMLM-F toured in relation to USMLM, SMLM-F only fueled their vehicles with the gas coupons provide based on the reciprocal agreement. Even with this significantly lower amount of travel capacity, SMLM-F was never assessed to travel enough to expend all of their fuel rations. The U.S. coupons were good for at least two years after they were issued.

On 3 May 1984, CUSMLM sent a letter to SERB advising that the 2,500 liters of gasoline provided on a monthly basis to USMLM was 500 liters less than that provided to the SMLM-F, and asked that USMLM's allocation be raised to 3,000 liters. The letter further advised that should this increase not be possible, parity would be achieved through a reduction in SMLM-F's gas coupons. The letter was never directly answered but USMLM immediately began receiving the additional 500 liters per month. Although SMLM-F's level of effort did not warrant a ration equal to USMLM's, and this request for additional fuel provided the opportunity to constrain USMLM activity, the Soviets chose to increase USMLM rations rather have a reduction in SMLM-F's rations. By the time of the Nicholson shooting in 1985, SMLM-F was not touring or traveling at nearly a level to expend the fuel coupons they received. After the shooting, there was a discernable reduction in touring, and the year-long restriction on interzonal travel also significantly reduced the amount of SMLM-F travel. Once again, this appeared to be a reflection leading back to SMLM-F that placed their operational interests, whatever they may have been, ahead of this opportunity to constrain USMLM touring and intelligence collection.

In August 1988, USMLM requested that their POL rations be increased from 3,000 to 4,000 liters per month. In December 1988, USMLM began receiving the increased rations, and that same month, the SERB requested a reciprocal increase of 1,000 liters per month for SMLM-F. Although this was the standard quid pro quo game that the MLMs played, based on SMLM-F's relatively low level of activity, the increase in rations was not an operational imperative. Conversely, the USMLM request was based on the operational rationale that their new vehicles got fewer miles per liter and were outfitted with smaller auxiliary tanks, which warranted a 1,000-liter increase per month to sustain touring tempo. For SMLM-F, this increase in coupons amounted to roughly $4,000 worth of gas coupons per month and an additional $1,000 worth of gas coupons above the amount they already could not have possibly used. U.S.$1,000 in 1988 had the purchasing power of $5,000 in the USSR.

Gas coupons provided to SMLM-F were marked with a distinguishing stamp and were made available each month to the "USCF" to monitor for any suspicious activities and to study SMLM-F gas-station usage to support their pattern analysis. Det A and the USAREUR DCSINT were aware that SMLM-F personnel were likely making some side cash off of the coupons due to the size of some isolated exchanges. However, the amount of money involved and the nature of the crime was deemed too minor to raise as an issue, so the information was held in reserve in case it was needed as leverage during a high-level debate. Up until December 1988, there had been one gas station in Kassel, West Germany, that was suspected of being used by the Soviets to exchange coupons for profit. In January 1989, there was a significant increase in patronage by SMLM-F of that Kassel station, which continued over the following months.

Kassel was not a standard location of SMLM-F touring activity, but Det A analysts established that they visited the location when either traveling from the SMLM-F compound to the Herleshausen border station or when returning to Frankfurt from East Germany. The use of this gas station was anomalous in that this deviation from their standard route added an hour to the travel. USCF analysts determined that two SMLM-F officers had been stockpiling gas coupons for at least the two previous years and were exchanging the coupons in large amounts each time they traveled in and out of the sector. Obviously, the officers had reached a deal with the gas station owner to take the coupons. And under this arrangement, the Soviets and gas station were sharing pure profits, as the coupons were provided by USAREUR to SMLM-F at no cost.

Again, USCF and USAREUR had been aware of SMLM-F personnel taking advantage of gas coupons, tobacco coupons, alcohol coupons, and other perks afforded mission members, but this activity at the Kassel gas station was on a much grander scale. As a counterintelligence organization, Det A had no interest in implicating SMLM-F personnel with a petty crime, but this did provide opportunities for further exploitation: notably, information regarding the illicit and likely unsanctioned activity could be used as "leverage" for recruitment as an intelligence source or to induce a defection. But more so at this point, such abuses of the Huebner–Malinin Agreement could serve to further antagonize USAREUR and prompt authorization for downtown ops.

Det A was authorized to conduct surveillance on SMLM-F tour activity anytime the commander desired. Travel through the sector to or from East Germany could be considered as "tour" activity as SMLM-F might spontaneously collect on targets of opportunity. SMLM-F was required to provide a 24-hour notice prior to departing or returning to the sector. Based on the activity detected at the Kassel gas station, Det A devised a plan to deploy the OST when either of the two officers in question was scheduled to depart the sector. When the first opportunity presented itself, the OST deployed elements to Kassel and conducted a surveillance of the SMLM-F vehicle when it departed the compound, but the vehicle traveled directly to the border station without deviation. However, when the vehicle and officer of interest returned a few days later, the OST was similarly prepared if the vehicle visited the Kassel gas station, which it did. The OST positioned the OP van (Lima), and other callsigns and operators were prepared to photograph the SMLM-F activity. As anticipated, the OST photographed the SMLM-F officer exchanging coupons for cash with the gas station owner. The OST was prepared to record the amount of gas the vehicle did actually take to demonstrate the large discrepancy, but ended up videotaping the fact that the officer did not even attempt to cover his actions by even pumping a nominal amount of gas. That day's take was estimated to have been a $1,200 profit for the SMLM-F officer, assuming a 50 percent split with the gas station.

The activity was recorded and documented, and the case presented to the USAREUR counterintelligence leadership for further exploitation. Had it been 10, five, or even three years earlier, it would have been a discovery of high-level interest. But with the perception that the missions might be coming to an end, the leadership did not want to risk anything going wrong which might taint the legacy of a long-standing postwar agreement that was concluding on very positive terms. However, it did prove that SMLM-F personnel were actively calling in some markers and tying up loose ends, so the stage was set for one final press for downtown surveillance operations of SMLM-F.

In late April 1990, USAREUR again authorized Det A to conduct downtown ops on SMLM-F. However, the 66th MI Brigade argued that ongoing support to counterespionage investigations was a priority. Det A was providing surveillance support to multiple counterespionage investigations, providing countersurveillance support to clandestine HUMINT operations, and conducting periodic SMLM-F tour surveillance. In addition, Det A needed time during May and June to prepare for their annual surveillance training which was a high priority, and also needed to conduct their annual high-speed driving training in June, so the 66th was able to justify a delay in downtown ops.

At this point, it was very questionable whether the MLM era would end without the U.S. ever trying to determine what SMLM-F had been doing all of those years when touring did not appear to be a priority. But there was one more play left.

Although this opportunity did not rate high enough to pursue given the range of considerations, there was still one looming unknown that Det A and the USAREUR counterintelligence leadership knew would forever remain so, unless a final series of operations was executed.

The Lost Reflection

On 18 May 1990, the two German states signed a treaty agreeing on monetary, economic, and social union, which came into force on 1 July with the West German deutsche mark replacing the East German mark as the official currency of East Germany. On 2 July 1990, the two Germanys completed negotiations on the terms for a reunification treaty that would be presented to their parliaments for debate. At this point, the only parties not in favor of reunification were West German hardliners who knew what a financial burden it would be on the West German economy. The U.S. and the Soviets understood and agreed that the MLMs would need to be disestablished prior to German reunification.

The Det A master training plan included an annual three-week training course to qualify special agents nominated throughout Europe to qualify as OST surveillance operators. The training course was a key element of the continuing effort to sustain a robust "bench" of augmentees. The three-week training event required extensive preparation to develop instructional surveillance scenarios to play out in the streets of Frankfurt and surrounding areas. The training was conducted from 9 to 27 July 1990.

In a last-ditch effort to conduct downtown ops, Det A added an addendum to the master training plan. After the conclusion of the training, the OST with trained augmentee support would conduct downtown ops against the SMLM-F target. The rationale was that this provided newly arrived OST members and the newly trained surveillance operators an opportunity to "train" against a sophisticated target. Further rationale was that errors made against the Soviets, who were eventually departing, would be much less costly than an error made during a high-priority counterespionage surveillance operation. The 66th MI Brigade supported the plan as it made operational sense to leverage downtown ops as a "live environment training" opportunity.

With a few reminders to the hawks on the USAREUR staff regarding the brazen countersurveillance on their European turf, and the brash money-making efforts of SMLM-F tour officers, downtown ops was green-lighted. It was also seen as almost fitting that given the Soviet affinity for deception and disinformation, that if surveillance were detected while SMLM-F officers were downtown, it might compel them to question the long-held belief that their activities had never been monitored when conducting non-tour, off-compound activities.

After a one-week delay to meet a priority operational requirement, Det A was prepared to launch downtown ops on 20 August. The downside to the timing of the plan for downtown ops was that many OST members had been operationally deployed since July of the previous year, and had "use or lose" vacation time that they needed to use prior to the 31 September end of the fiscal year, or it would be taken from them. Among the OST members who had returned to the states for a well-deserved and long-overdue vacation was the Sierra Charlie. This meant that the "live environment training" with SMLM-F would also provide deserving operators the opportunity to shine as the Sierra Charlie.

The first three days of the operation were disappointing in that there was very little activity of interest. There were daily visits to the American post exchange and a couple of officers who went for a walk in the neighborhood around the compound, but nothing of operational interest.

The DCSMLM-F was a GRU colonel with a legacy of experience to include multiple tours at SMLM-F and as a military attaché at the Soviet Embassy in

Washington DC. If there were a GRU case officer operating out of SMLM-F, he would be it.

At 1:00 PM on 23 August, the DCSMLM-F departed the compound as a passenger in a USMLM tour vehicle, and the OST began a seamless pickup and follow. The vehicle (now X-Ray 1) began traveling to the center of Frankfurt, crossing the Main river at the Untermainbrücke, a bridge that provided a natural chokepoint and channelized terrain for surveillance detection purposes. After crossing the bridge X-Ray 1 entered the Bornheim area of Frankfurt, which was the most densely trafficked area in Frankfurt, and perhaps all of West Germany. It was apparent that the SMLM-F driver was familiar with the area and comfortable maneuvering through the chaotic downtown Frankfurt traffic. Entering the heart of Bornheim, X-Ray 1 abruptly pulled over on a busy street, dropped the DCSMLM-F off, and drove away. OST callsigns immediately maneuvered to drop off foot operators who seamlessly transitioned to the foot surveillance of DCSMLM-F (Zulu 1). Zulu 1 was not wearing a hat and his uniform without

St. Paul's Church (Paulskirche), Frankfurt, Germany. (Wikimedia Commons)

insignia or other markings did not make him stand out among the crowds of faceless pedestrians. Zulu 1 walked what appeared to be a "three sides of a box" surveillance-detection route and then arrived at the base of the plaza leading to St. Paul's Church (Paulskirche).

St. Paul's Church remains the symbol of German democracy. Construction began in 1789 but it was not completed until 1833. In 1849, it became the seat of the first freely elected German legislative body and is where the first German democratic constitution was signed. The church was destroyed during Allied bombings on 18 March 1944, but due to its symbolic importance as the cradle of German democracy, it was one of the first buildings in Frankfurt to be reconstructed after the war. The site was also a classic location for an agent meet.

The church had a large plaza leading to the front of the structure that was only open to foot traffic. Open terrain such as a pedestrian plaza is a common location to conduct surveillance detection. Since following a target over open spaces exposes surveillance operators, they may choose to walk along the perimeter of the open terrain where more adequate cover and concealment is available. By doing so, however, they may make themselves more noticeable by walking at a faster rate in order to maintain pace and to be positioned to close distance with the target when moving out of the open area and into a more densely trafficked area. As with the drive over the channelized terrain of the long bridge and the likely surveillance detection route walked by Zulu 1, the OST was trained and ready to react securely to this standard surveillance-detection effort.

In addition to the open plaza providing one final surveillance-detection opportunity before entering, the layout of the church was perfect for surveillance detection and security for a clandestine agent meet. There was one main entrance which provided a chokepoint, so once inside, a potential target of surveillance could see everyone entering after them. The interior of the church was large enough to give surveillance operators a sufficient sense of cover and security to enter behind a target, but was small enough to enable the target to scan and see everyone in the church at any given time.

When Zulu 1 entered the church, it would have been preferred to have a touristy looking male and female couple of surveillance operators enter behind him. However, the less-experienced Sierra Charlie was not able to coordinate this, and the team needed to get eyes on Zulu 1, so a lone male surveillance operator was sent into the church. The delay in getting an operator into the church may have worked to the team's advantage, because it was likely that Zulu1 had completed his surveillance-detection regimen before the operator had entered the church. By the time the operator was inside, Zulu 1 was sitting in an isolated pew next to another man. The two were clearly interacting, but in a low-key manner; they were talking but not looking at each other like in a normal conversation. The surveillance operation now had a Zulu 2. This meant that the priority of the operation should shift to the surveillance of Zulu 2 to identify the SMLM-F contact.

The advantage to having a couple enter a location such as this meet site was that they could communicate with the team outside while appearing to be speaking with each other. Conversely, the lone operator could not transmit voice communications effectively because this would have appeared suspicious to any third parties inside the church, any of which could have been countersurveillance. With a lone operator inside the church where voice communication was not feasible, the method used to communicate with the team is through the "interrogation" of the operator.

When the operator needed to transmit information to the team, he sent a series of static transmissions by multiple taps on the push-to-talk transmission button wired inside his pants pocket. Interrogation is a method in which the Sierra Charlie asks the operator a series of "yes" or "no" questions, and the surveillance operator presses one static transmission for "yes" or twice for "no." This is a difficult process requiring much practice, and the less experienced Sierra Charlie was not able to establish that there was a Zulu 2 who should have become the priority of the surveillance operation.

Within three minutes of the operator having identified Zulu 1 sitting with Zulu 2, Zulu 2 stood up and departed. Although it was clear that the two Zulus had been discreetly interacting, Zulu 2 stood up and walked toward the entrance without a word, a nod, or a gesture toward Zulu 1. As he walked away, Zulu 1 turned to observe the church occupants and the entrance; now he was the one conducting countersurveillance observation of Zulu 2. The operator knew that it would be extremely poor tradecraft to follow Zulu 2 out while Zulu 1 was watching, but also knew that the team did not have sufficient details to lock onto Zulu 2. The operator made the sound decision and Zulu 2 walked away. By the time the operator was we able to exit the church and broadcast the information, Zulu 2 was nowhere in sight. All available foot operators began clearing down the most likely routes of foot travel from the church looking for an individual meeting the description of Zulu 2, which in downtown Frankfurt was an improbable effort. With the team's priority singularly focused on finding Zulu 2, Zulu 1 went unobserved after the operator exited the church. The tour officer (Zulu 1) returned to the SMLM-F compound in the same vehicle and with the same driver less than 30 minutes after having been last observed inside the church.

Despite the missed opportunity to identify a suspected clandestine intelligence contact of SMLM-F, the surveillance had netted observations of operational activity and there was now justification for having initiated and continuing downtown ops. From the car drop-off, to the precisely timed walk and contact in the church, to what can only be assumed to have been a clean pickup and return to the compound, the known GRU officer was observed to have conducted a well-orchestrated and apparently often-repeated process. And again, the church was a classic clandestine agent meet location.

When the Det A commander returned to his office, anxious to make a secure call to the USAREUR Chief of Counterintelligence and relay the results of the day's events, he was handed an urgent message to call the 527th MI Battalion director of operations. The call was made, and the message was received, that the authorization to conduct downtown ops had been rescinded.

The date, again, was 23 August 1990. Earlier that day, the East German parliament passed a resolution declaring the accession of the German Democratic Republic to the Federal Republic of Germany, and the extension of the field of application of the Federal Republic's Basic Law to the territory of East Germany as allowed by the West German Basic Law. On 31 August, the two German governments signed the German Reunification Treaty, effective 3 October 1990. The U.S., British, French, and Soviets agreed "to immediately terminate all operational activities" and that the MLMs would officially close on 1 October 1990, two days prior to German reunification.

Epilogue

On 1 October 1990, USMLM was deactivated with much fanfare in a ceremony covered by international media and attended by U.S., British, French, Russian, German, and other national military and diplomatic representatives. As was historically the case, all eyes were on USMLM. On that same morning in Frankfurt, a lone USAREUR representative, the CACS, waived farewell as the 14 SMLM-F members departed from "sleepy hollow" on their final trek to exit West Germany, ending that legacy of the Cold War. The OST was busy at work on a counterespionage surveillance operation, but the USCF side of Det A was busy receiving sighting reports as the SMLM-F convoy traveled east. However, by noon that day, the mission of the fictitious USCF would also unceremoniously come to an end. At 11:43 AM, the Herleshausen border station called to notify the USCF that all SMLM-F personnel and vehicles had departed the U.S. sector—a sector that would also become history in a mere 36 hours.

Before Det A could pay the final DART rent payment for the month of October, the Germans took custody of the vacated SMLM-F compound and leveled the grounds to make room for upscale row houses. The Germans quickly removed all vestiges of the MLMs that had been imposed upon their sovereignty for over four decades.

U.S. and Soviet leadership declared the Cold War over at the Malta Summit on 3 December 1989, but historians generally recognize the official dissolution of the USSR on 26 December 1991 as the end of the Cold War. The true cold warriors, however, consider the final day of a divided Germany, 2 October 1990, as the final day of the Cold War.

Detachment A was awarded the Army Superior Unit Award—the U.S. Army's highest recognition for organizational excellence—for the period of 1 January 1989 to 2 October 1990. The award citation read:

> During the period of 1 January 1989 to 2 October 1990, Detachment A, 527th Military Intelligence Battalion, accomplished its mission in the difficult operational environment created by the fluid West–East political situation, the unique demands of its mission, and limited and shrinking resources. The unit planned and conducted sensitive intelligence operations in response to theater and national level requirements. Balancing counterintelligence and political concerns, the unit executed operations which resulted in valuable intelligence on the modus operandi of hostile intelligence services operating against United States forces and activities in the Federal

Republic of Germany. Mission accomplishment required personal sacrifice and dedication from each member of the unit. Their exemplary performance has brought great credit to themselves, the United States Army Intelligence and Security Command, and the United States Army.

The Army Superior Unit Award was established to recognize units that accomplished difficult, challenging missions in peacetime. It was the highest peacetime recognition of organizational excellence. At the time of award, Det A was the second counterintelligence unit to receive the award and the first with roots dating back to the CIC in Europe. The Det A award was unique in that USAREUR, and not INSCOM, submitted the recommendation for the award to the Department of the Army.

Although the Det A heritage of counterintelligence coverage of SMLM-F can be traced back to the 1950s, the Army Superior Unit Award citation was purposefully dated from the first month that Det A began the mission to transform and attack the SMLM-F enigma. In spite of all of the political obstacles and competing priorities, Det A never lost focus on that mission and was postured and actively identifying indications of the activities that SMLM-F had long been suspected of conducting. But just as some clarity to the ambiguity that was SMLM-F was in sight, the Soviets capitulated and the Eastern Bloc dissolved. USAREUR leadership recognized and appreciated that this 21-month period represented the first time in the 43-year MLM era that DoD Counterintelligence had addressed the threat with a world-class capability.

With the termination of the SMLM-F counterintelligence mission, Det A was able to focus on fully employing the capability it had developed during the unanticipated last years of the Cold War. On 29 March 1991, after an investigation comprised largely of an extensive Det A surveillance operation, the only DoD member convicted of espionage during Operation DESERT SHIELD/STORM was arrested after being recorded admitting his guilt to an undercover agent posing as a foreign agent. There were other elements of the 527th MI Battalion involved in this investigation, but Det A performed the large majority of the investigative effort. The 527th MI Battalion was awarded the Army Superior Unit Award in recognition of this successful national security investigation, giving Det A its second superior unit award in as many years.

By the end of 1991, the Det A commander had turned over the reins after three intensive years, as had the original Sierra Charlie. The stakes of the spy-versus-spy business in Europe were suddenly low-to-irrelevant, as the U.S. leadership rushed to cash in on the peace dividend. Counterintelligence warriors who had cut their teeth wrestling with the Russian bear were no longer in high demand. And those KGB and GRU adversaries whom they did war with lamented the loss of their U.S. counterparts who had given them a reason to live. Det A, too, had become a capability seen as a Cold War relic, and the world slept as an industry of competition was closing that would never be seen again. But there will be a day when the one who remembers the lessons of those long-lost days will be the one who takes the other's king.

Just as the wilderness of mirrors is a metaphor for the Cold War in general, Det A should be seen as symbolic of the fact that, although U.S. counterintelligence took a beating overall, there were some counterintelligence professionals who fought the Communist menace as hard as possible to the very end.

In the end, the Det A legacy is one of "what was" and "what could have been."

As for what it could have been, Det A very nearly chased down the final reflection in the Cold War wilderness of mirrors, as surveillance operators feverishly chased the ghost who was a SMLM-F contact leaving St. Paul's Church in downtown Frankfurt.

As for what it was, Det A did see the final reflection, in the face of a young KGB decoy on a crisp winter night in Munich.

Post-Cold War Revelations

By 1988, the Defense Intelligent Agency had joined USAREUR in recognizing that there was compelling information to conclude that the true potential SMLM threat had been ignored for four decades. Although this conclusion was reached based on the information at the time, information developed after the end of the Cold War further justified these concerns. The following are some examples.

Yes, They Did Know All

Clyde Conrad

Clyde Conrad never admitted to spying or disclosed the identities of any of his recruits, so the full details of his treachery were not known until members of his network were arrested after the Cold War ended. In the end, the ring worked so well that it is still unknown how many people were involved, but 11 persons in addition to Conrad are known to have been complicit. After Conrad's arrest, Szabo agreed to cooperate with the German government in exchange for leniency, and provided information which led to the 1990 arrest of Roderick Ramsay. The investigation of Ramsay led to the 1992 arrest of Jeffrey Rondeau and the 1993 arrest of Jeffrey Gregory. During the surveillance of Conrad, he was observed meeting with the husband of Kelly Warren, who was of interest due to her G3 plans access. The couple was interviewed in 1988, and although investigators did not believe their denials, they did not have any other evidence and had higher priorities at the time. The joint army/FBI investigative team began again with Warren in 1994 with nothing more to go on than her ex-husband's meeting with Conrad and their suspicions. After over 20 interviews, Warren was arrested in 1997 after she confessed to allowing Conrad to read and copy war plans documents in her office, knowing that he was providing them to a foreign government. On 8 January 1998, the 50-year-old Clyde Conrad died of heart failure in his West German prison cell. Since he was convicted in West German courts, and not by the U.S., Conrad continued to receive his U.S. Army retirement pension until he died.

The U.S. did not bring the West Germans into the CANASTA PLAYER investigation until there was no other choice, due to security concerns. After the U.S. Department of Justice refused to convict Conrad, and the realization set in that he would only go to jail if the Germans would take the case, U.S. officials anticipated some uncomfortable conversations when it was disclosed that they had been conducting a three-year investigation in West Germany with significant national security implications without their knowledge. However, when BfV leadership was briefed on the investigation, they wanted to put the arrest of Conrad on a very accelerated timeline, noting that "they had their own problems with security." By this time, there were many knowns, but probably more unknowns. FCA opened the CANASTA PLAYER investigation in January 1985. In August 1985, perhaps prompted by Yurchenko's defection to the U.S. three weeks prior, Hans-Joachim Tiedge, one of the most senior chiefs of counterintelligence in the BfV, defected to East Germany. Unknown to Tiedge at the time of his defection, his deputy in the BfV, Klaus Kuron, had been spying for the East Germans since 1982. Kuron confessed to spying for East Germany in October 1990 in an effort to gain leniency knowing that he was about to be exposed after German reunification. Tiedge and Kuron were two among the many examples of why sharing information with West German intelligence and counterintelligence agencies was usually an unacceptable risk. If Eastern intelligence had learned of an investigation to roll up its most productive spy network in Europe, Conrad could have quietly moved to the East after his August 1985 retirement, which would have remained unnoticed until he was identified as a prime suspect in early 1986. As senior officers in the BfV, Tiedge and Kuron would have had visibility over all BfV support to U.S. counterintelligence investigations in West Germany, to include LANCE BLADE; which would explain how the Soviets were able to set such a precise and elaborate countersurveillance trap on that crisp winter night in Munich.

James Hall

In 1989, Hall was given a relatively low sentence of 40 years due to his cooperation in detailing all of the information he had compromised. Although Army Counterintelligence had no way of knowing at the time, they would shortly be receiving virtually all of the information Hall traded for a lighter sentence from an unlikely source. Based on a request from NSA in 1992, the newly established German Federal Commissioner for Stasi Records provided all but 200 of the nearly 13,300 documents Hall provided to the Stasi. Hall was released from prison in 2011 after serving 22 years.

Hall's late 1988 admission to compromising embarrassing USMLM photographs which he surmised led to Nicholson's death was fodder for counterintelligence conspiracy theorists, with speculations ranging from embarrassed commanders admonishing sentries to be more diligent to it being a targeted act of retaliation.

However, none of the conjectures along this range could pass the "sniff test." The USMLM legacy of allowing shooting incidents to recur rather than risking the viability of the Huebner–Malinin Agreement, and other basic facts, easily dispelled any such notion. The fact was that USMLM had literally been "dodging the bullet" for decades. Nicholson's fate was determined by a lone Soviet sentry.

The Nicholson shooting occurred over a year after the Hall compromise. Had the shooting been the result of increased diligence due to the embarrassing failure, there would have logically been other indications of a more confrontational approach. In contrast, the only discernable change during this period was actually a decrease in dangerous incidents following the March 1984 killing of a French MLM officer which appeared to be the last in a campaign of premeditated vehicle ramming efforts that had been ongoing since 1979. The last shooting incident prior to the Nicholson shooting occurred in February 1983, meaning that the Nicholson shooting was the first one in over two years and the only one since the Hall compromise. Had the shooting been intended as retaliation for the brazen USMLM collection effort, it would have logically occurred much sooner after the triggering event.

In addition to the facts surrounding the incident, a pure counterintelligence perspective would strongly argue against any association among Hall's espionage relationship with the KGB and the Stasi and the Nicholson shooting. The Soviets would not have risked compromising such a valuable source by acting on the information by admonishing commanders or sending emphasis notices that would reach the sentry level in a manner that might alert the U.S. to their knowledge that these very specific USMLM collection activities had been compromised. This was reinforced by the fact that leading to the Nicholson shooting, there was no discernable change to the already intensive East German and Soviet defensive measures. The Soviets managed their intelligence and counterintelligence activities in a very centralized and coordinated manner, and would never have risked disclosing the existence of a source of Hall's value to prevent USMLM photography of military equipment or retaliate for brazen USMLM collection successes.

Finally, this seemingly isolated incident of a compromise of USMLM intelligence-collection activity conveniently fed the urban legend of the Nicholson event, but the fact that it was not an isolated compromise adds context beyond Hall's confession. Although this may have been the singularly most embarrassing compromise for the Soviets, having known all since at least 1969, if the Soviets had a propensity to retaliate for embarrassing USMLM collection successes, this tendency would have likely manifested itself long before 1985.

George Trofimoff

In 1992, a defector named Vasili Mitrokhin provided British intelligence 25,000 pages of secrets he transcribed between 1972 and 1984 while working as the chief of the KGB archives. The information did not name Trofimoff, but details provided by the British to the German government enabled investigators to pinpoint his legacy of espionage.

Trofimoff and Igor Susemihl were arrested by German authorities for suspected espionage just prior to Trofimoff's planned departure to the U.S. in 1994. German authorities were aware that they had no evidence of Trofimoff committing espionage since 1987, which exceeded the five-year German statute of limitations, but needed to make their move before Trofimoff left the country, hoping that they could get him or Susemihl to confess. However, neither broke under interrogation and the case was dropped because of the statute of limitations law. Following his acquittal, Trofimoff made the mistake of continuing with his plan of retiring to the U.S., where there is no statute of limitations for espionage, and where the investigation was being continued by U.S. officials. In late 2000, Trofimoff was approached by an FBI agent posing as a Russian officer who offered a "special payment" for additional information. Trofimoff met with undercover FBI agents several times and was videotaped fully admitting his past involvement in espionage. Trofimoff was arrested on 14 June 2000 at the age of 73 in Tampa, Florida, and charged with spying for Russia for 25 years. Trofimoff, the highest-ranking U.S. officer ever convicted of spying, was sentenced to life imprisonment on 27 September 2001. He died in prison in 2014.

When Trofimoff was unsuccessfully placed on trial in 1994, the Cold War had been won by the West years prior and the case did not get much attention in the U.S., because it did not seem relevant to most. Although George Trofimoff compromised everything he had access to for nearly 20 years, including all USMLM reporting, the U.S. did not become aware of these compromises until long after USMLM was disestablished and the Cold War won. George Trofimoff was one of the less-renowned Cold War spies because the information he compromised, although of severe damage to the U.S. and NATO at the time, was not completely known until over a decade after the end of that war. Had Trofimoff been discovered during the peak of his espionage career, he would have been seen in the same light as those spies who were discovered during the Cold War, when their treachery was recognized as giving the Soviets a decisive advantage in the event of a hot war. By the time he was finally convicted in 2001, the damage which became public record was known to be substantial, but again, the crime was a relic of an era that had ended over a decade prior. The nuance of a Russian spy having lived among the Tampa retirement community was of much more interest than the reality of the damage he would have inflicted on the U.S. had the Cold War gone hot.

Spetsnaz Caches and Suitcase Nukes

At the close of the Cold War, the weapons caches and suitcase-nuke legacy remained one of the most nagging unsolved mysteries of the era. Despite two credible and independent sources who would have no rationale for fabricating the information, the notion of caches sprinkled throughout Western Europe was still viewed by many as a perpetuation of the myth, due to the fact that a cache was never reported to have been uncovered during the entirety of the Cold War or beyond. Like so many of the Soviet secrets of the Cold War era, the existence of the GRU and KGB cache programs were only alleged in the closing years of the Cold War, and were not confirmed until many years after the end.

In 1992, GRU officer Stanislav Lunev defected to the U.S., and in addition to confirming the previous accounts of the Soviet cache programs, he provided additional information that many of the caches were booby-trapped with explosive devices that were designed to destroy all materials in the cache and be lethal to anyone in its immediate proximity. Lunev also confirmed information provided by Gordievsky in 1985 by asserting that some of the hidden caches could contain portable tactical nuclear weapons known as RA-115 "suitcase bombs," and that these devices were not only emplaced in Western European countries, but also in the U.S.

Also, in 1992, Vasili Mitrokhin, the defector who provided the information leading to Trofimoff's arrest, provided information that transformed this myth to legend. Since the Russians were not aware that Mitrokhin had meticulously hand-transcribed KGB archive pages over the years, the British diligently chose the priority for the information they exploited to keep the source of the information protected, which they successfully did until 1999. The information Mitrokhin provided had specific locations for several of the Cold War cache sites, but this information was not initially exploited while other more immediate leads were. It was not until December 1998 that a cache identified by Mitrokhin as being located in a wooded area near Bern, Switzerland, was detonated when Swiss authorities fired upon it using a high-pressure water cannon. There were no casualties from the explosion, but the Swiss federal prosecutor reviewing the evidence noted that anyone who tried to move the KGB container would have been killed. Several other caches that were not booby-trapped with explosives were also removed successfully, including at a KGB radio equipment cache found in a wooded area outside of Brussels, Belgium in 1999. Also in 1999, Austrian authorities tried but failed to locate a similar cache documented to have been planted in 1963 outside Vienna, where road construction had altered the terrain and removed the landmarks needed to locate it. As a testament to the stealth and secrecy under which Soviet Spetsnaz and other agents operated in West Germany during the duration of the Cold War (and perhaps beyond), the existence of the cache program was not confirmed until 43 years after the first caches were reported to have been established, and nearly 10 years after the end of the Cold War.

Mitrokhin was able to provide pinpoint data on some of the Soviet weapons and spy equipment caches based on the information he stole from the KGB archives, but the nuclear suitcases were planted by the GRU, which was information that Mitrokhin did not have access to, as his access was only to KGB information. Lunev also reported on the suitcase nuclear device caches after his 1992 defection. Although this level of information regarding GRU caches was never attained, the fact that information regarding KGB and GRU cache sites was only first reported more than 30 years into the Cold War, and then only confirmed nearly 10 years after the end of the Cold War based on information provided by another fortuitous defection, demonstrates how the Soviets effectively protected the existence of these programs.

In 1997, former Russian National Security Adviser Aleksandr Lebed claimed in a televised interview on the news magazine program *Sixty Minutes* that the Russian military had produced 250 "suitcase-sized nuclear bombs" and had lost track of over a hundred of these devices. Lebed stated that these devices were made to look like suitcases, and that he had learned of their existence only a few years earlier. Although not specified, "lost track" could include devices that were cached and never recovered, as the number Lebed cited corresponded with number Gordievsky reported in 1985. Lebed repeated these claims in his 1998 testimony to the U.S. Congress. From 1998 to 2000, the U.S. Congress held inconclusive hearings on the claims that the Soviets emplaced suitcase nukes in the U.S., which included testimony from Lunev.

Libyan Bombing Suspicions Confirmed

Immediately following the 1986 bombing of the West Berlin disco, SIGINT confirmed Libyan complicity. However, the investigation to bring the culprits responsible to justice went cold until the 1990 reunification of Germany and the subsequent disclosure of the Stasi archives.

Stasi files disclosed that the Libyan mastermind of the La Belle bombing (and the Lockerbie, Scotland aircraft attack) had been the senior intelligence service representative in the Libyan East Berlin embassy, and was also listed as a Stasi agent. His 1996 arrest led to the arrest of four additional suspects and the actual chain of events of that fateful night. More than 15 years after the bombing, a German court convicted a Libyan "diplomat" and three accomplices on murder charges. During the four-year trial, prosecutors proved that the Libyan intelligence agent recruited a Palestinian employee of the Libyan Embassy in East Berlin to help carry out the attack. The men recruited a German of Lebanese descent to carry out the bombing, who was listed as a Stasi agent and potentially referred to Libyan intelligence by the Stasi.

Ultimately, the intended bomber convinced his German wife to carry out the bombing. The female accomplice, accompanied by her sister, carried the explosives into the nightclub in a travel bag, and departed five minutes before the blast. In 2001, the knowingly witting female bomber was imprisoned for 14 years on the charge of murder, while the other planners were sentenced to between 12 and 14 years for attempted murder or aiding and abetting attempted murder. The witting bomber's sister was acquitted for lack of proof that she knew a bomb was in the travel bag.

By the time of the Berlin disco bombing, Libya's status as a rogue nation and state sponsor of terrorism was well established. And while the Stasi leadership had always harbored great disdain for the U.S., support to such an operation at the time highlighted the dichotomy of the final five years of the Cold War. It is very unlikely that the Stasi could have or would have supported such an operation without at least the tacit approval of the KGB. During this fledgling period of *glasnost* for which the Soviet leadership was endeavoring to demonstrate openness to gain economic relief for its failing economy, complicity in the Berlin bombing was counter to these efforts, and served no apparent pragmatic purpose for the Soviets.

The USMLM Legacy

The USAREUR lack of oversight and management of USMLM resulted in safety and security risks to USMLM personnel as cited. In fact, it was largely recognized that USMLM was extended a high degree of autonomy to provide USAREUR plausible deniability when incidents occurred. These decades later, it might appear to have been reckless for USAREUR to permit USMLM to operate so aggressively in such a high-risk environment, but that was simply the Cold War mentality. Regardless, USMLM was a highly professional organization that was, and remains, recognized as among the most prolific intelligence-collection and -analysis organizations the DoD ever fielded.

As a testament to the USMLM legacy—and like so many of the successes or near successes that occurred just as the Cold War was coming to an end—USMLM chased down one of the longest-running and most deceptive reflections in the Cold War wilderness of mirrors. By the late 1970s, USMLM began to collect indications that the Soviets' most elite and combat-ready forces (GSFG) might have been critically undermanned. For nearly the entire Cold War, the U.S. intelligence community maintained an assessment of Soviet military strength that drove NATO to plan for, and wargame against, a Red Army that was sustained at nearly 100-percent strength. As USMLM developed mounting information to support a dissenting assessment, the intelligence agencies that were vested in their perspectives demonstrated the bureaucratic tendency to dismiss information that did not agree with "conventional wisdom." Once again, when the deception theory is effectively employed, intelligence analysts adopt the narrative that the perpetrating intelligence service intended as the deception, and the "deceived" intelligence staff becomes its own deceiver. After a decade-long debate, and 42 years into the Cold War, the 1989 U.S. National Intelligence Estimates concluded that Soviet forces were manned at no higher than 55 percent of their professed wartime strength, and in many cases, less than 50 percent strength. On 9 November of that same year, a few sections of the Berlin Wall were opened, and the weaknesses of the Soviet military that USMLM had first observed were soon to be in full view.

Directly after disestablishment in 1990, the USMLM core members and infrastructure transitioned to a joint U.S. and German organization named the Combined Analysis Detachment-Berlin (CAD-B). The GSFG was renamed as the Group of Western Forces and continued the process of removing Russian forces from Germany, which was completed in 1994. CAD-B exploited the intelligence-collection opportunities that existed while Russian forces remained in Germany.

Arthur Nicholson, who was posthumously promoted to lieutenant colonel, remains the most publicized facet of USMLM history. Although Nicholson's tragic killing tends to overshadow the USMLM legacy of operational excellence, this event remains a source of unity for former USMLM members. USMLM alumni have regularly congregated over the years to reminisce with each other, and honor the memory of their fallen comrade, Lieutenant Colonel "Nick" Nicholson.

The Huebner–Malinin Agreement

AGREEMENT BETWEEN THE MILITARY LIAISON MISSIONS ACCREDITED TO THE SOVIET AND UNITED STATES COMMANDERS-IN-CHIEF OF THE ZONES OF OCCUPATION IN GERMANY, APRIL 5, 1947

In conformity with the provisions of Article 2 of the Agreement on "Control Mechanism in Germany," November 14, 1944, the US and the Soviet Commanders-in-Chief of the Zones of Occupation in Germany have agreed to exchange Military Liaison Missions accredited to their staffs in the zones and approve the following regulations concerning these missions:

1. These missions are military missions and have no authority over quadri-partite military government missions or purely military government missions of each respective country, either temporarily or permanently, on duty in either zone. However, they will render whatever aid or assistance to said military government missions as is practicable.
2. Missions will be composed of air, navy, and army representatives. There will be no political representatives.
3. The missions will consist of not to exceed fourteen (14) officers and enlisted personnel. This number will include all necessary technical personnel, office clerks, personnel with special qualifications, and personnel required to operate radio stations.
4. Each mission will be under the orders of senior member of the mission who will be appointed and known as "Chief of the United States (or Soviet) Military Mission."
5. The Chief of the Mission will be accredited to the Commander-in-Chief of the occupation forces.
   In the United States Zone the mission will be accredited to Commander-in-Chief, United States European Command. In the Soviet Zone the mission will be accredited to the Commander-in-Chief of the Group of Soviet Occupational Forces in Germany.
6. In the United States Zone the Soviet Mission will be offered quarters in the region of Frankfurt.

7. In the Soviet Zone the United States Mission will be offered quarters at or near Potsdam.

8. In the United States Zone the Chief of the Soviet Mission will communicate with A/C of Staff, G3, United States European Command.

9. In the Soviet Zone the Chief of the United States Mission will communicate with the Senior Officer of the Staff of Commander-in-Chief.

10. Each member of the missions will be given identical travel facilities to include identical permanent passes in Russian and English languages permitting complete freedom of travel wherever and whenever it will be desired over territory and roads in both zones, except places of disposition of military units, without escort or supervision. Each time any member of the Soviet or United States mission wants to visit United States or Soviet headquarters, military government offices, forces, units, military schools, factories, and enterprises which are under United States or Soviet control, a corresponding request must be made to Director, Operations, Plans, Organization and Training, European Command, or Senior Officer, Headquarters, Group of Soviet Occupational Forces in Germany. Such requests must be acted upon within 24–72 hours. Members of the missions are permitted allied guests at the headquarters of the respective missions.

11.
   a. Each mission will have its own radio station for communication with its own headquarters.
   b. In each case couriers and messengers will be given facilities for free travel between the headquarters of the mission and headquarters of their respective Commander-in- Chief. These couriers will enjoy the same immunity which is extended to diplomatic couriers.
   c. Each mission will be given facilities for telephone communication through the local telephone exchange at the headquarters, and they also will be given facilities such as mail, telephone, telegraph through the existing means of communication when the members of the mission will be traveling within the zone. In case of breakdown in the radio installation, the zone commanders will render all possible aid and will permit temporary use of their own systems of communication.

12. The necessary rations, P.O.L. supplies and household services for the military missions will be provided for by the headquarters to which accredited, by method of mutual compensation in kind, supplemented by such items as desired to be furnished by their own headquarters. In addition, the respective missions or individual members of the missions may purchase items of Soviet or United States origin which must be paid for in currency specified by the headquarters controlling zone where purchase is made.

13. The buildings of each mission will enjoy full right of extra-territoriality.

14.

    a. The task of the mission will be to maintain liaison between both Commanders-in-Chief and their staffs.

    b. In each zone the mission will have the right to engage in matters of protecting the interests of their nationals and to make representations accordingly as well as in matters of protecting their property interests in the zone where they are located. They have the right to render aid to people of their own country who are visiting the zone where they are accredited.

15. This agreement may be changed or amplified by mutual consent to cover new subjects when the need arises.

16. This agreement is written in Russian and English languages and both texts are authentic.

17. This agreement becomes valid when signed by Deputy Commanders of United States and Soviet Zones of Occupation.

C.R. HUEBNER
Lieutenant-General Huebner
Deputy Commander-in-Chief, European Command
Colonel-General Malinin
Deputy Commander-in-Chief
Chief of Staff of the Group of Soviet Occupation Forces in Germany

Glossary of Abbreviations and Terms

Abbreviations

AAFES	Army and Air Force Exchange Service
ACS	Allied Contact Section
BfV	Bundesamt für Verfassungsschutz
BND	Bundesnachrichtendienst
BRIXMIS	British Military Liaison Mission
CACS	Chief Allied Contact Section
CI	counterintelligence
CIA	Central Intelligence Agency
CIC	Counterintelligence Corps
CINC	commander-in-chief
CPSU	Communist Party of the Soviet Union
CSERB	Chief Soviet External Relations Bureau
CUSMLM	Chief U.S. Military Liaison Mission
DCSERB	Deputy Chief Soviet External Relations Bureau
DCSINT	Deputy Chief of Staff for Intelligence
DCUSMLM	Deputy Chief U.S. Military Liaison Mission
DIA	Defense Intelligence Agency
DoD	Department of Defense
DoJ	Department of Justice (Justice Department)
FBI	Federal Bureau of Investigations
FCA	foreign counterintelligence activity
FMLM	French Military Liaison Mission
FRG	Federal Republic of Germany
GDR	German Democratic Republic
GRU	Glavnoye Razvedyvatel'noye Upravlenie
GSFG	Group of Soviet Forces in Germany
HQ	headquarters
HUMINT	human intelligence
IIR	intelligence information report
IMINT	imagery intelligence

INSCOM	(U.S. Army) Intelligence and Security Command
JIC	Joint Interrogation Facility
KGB	Komitet Gosudarstvennoi Bezopasnosti
MfS	Ministerium für Staatssicherheit
MI	military intelligence
MLM	Military Liaison Mission
MMS	Mission Militaire Sovietique
MRS	MLM Restriction Sign
NATO	North Atlantic Treaty Organization
NCO	non-commissioned officer
NSA	National Security Agency
OP	observation post
OPSEC	operations security
POL	Petroleum, Oil, and Lubricants; P.O.L in Huebner–Malinin Agreement
PRA	Permanently Restricted Area
PX	post exchange
QRT	quick reaction team
SERB	Soviet External Relations Bureau
SIGINT	signals intelligence
SIS	Secret Intelligence Service
SMLM	Soviet Military Liaison Mission (commonly pronounced "smell 'em")
SMLM-F	Soviet Military Liaison Mission, Frankfurt
SOP	standard operating procedure
SOXMIS	Soviet Exchange Mission
TASS	Telegrafnoya Agentstvo Sovyetkovo Soyuza
TRA	Temporary Restricted Area
TSCM	technical surveillance counter measures
USAINSCOM	U.S. Army Intelligence and Security Command (same as INSCOM)
USAREUR	U.S. Army Europe (pronounced use-ar-yur)
USCF	USAREUR SMLM Control Facility
USEUCOM	U.S. European Command
USMLM	U.S. Military Liaison Mission (commonly pronounced "you smell 'em")
USSR	Union of Soviet Socialist Republics
VOPO	Volkspolizei

Terms

agent: a person who engages in clandestine intelligence activities under the direction of an intelligence organization, but is not an officer, employee, or coopted worker of that organization.

agent handler: an intelligence officer or principal agent who directly manages an agent or agent network.

agent network: an intelligence-gathering unit of agents supervised by a principal agent who is operating under the direction of an intelligence officer; an agent net can operate in either the legal or illegal field.

agent provocateur: an agent who provides information to an intelligence service that is intended to induce that service to take actions that damage its interests; similar to an agent of influence or confusion agent.

Agreement on Control Machinery in Germany: agreement signed by the U.S., Britain, and Soviet Union before the conclusion of the war in Germany which detailed how the Allies would administer Germany after its unconditional surrender, and specifying the need for military liaison process.

Akt: incident report issued on USMLM by a GSFG Kommandant; term for legal document or indictment.

Allied Contact Section: the element established to perform as the day-to-day interface between USAREUR and SMLM-F; ACS.

antisurveillance: actions taken to evade an identified or suspected surveillance.

asset: any resource—human, technical, or otherwise—available to an intelligence or security service for operational use.

asylum seeker: a person who has left their home country as a political refugee and is seeking asylum in another.

Basic Law: provision in the West German constitution that expressed West German intent to ultimately reunify the separated parts of Germany under "Germany as a whole."

biographical information/intelligence: information collected, often during official government contacts, on individual foreign personalities of actual or potential importance; information may serve to prepare senior leaders for engagements, to build rapport during engagements, or as leverage against the individual to elicit information or to recruit the individual as an agent.

bona fides: the lack of fraud or deceit; a determination that a person is who he/she says he/she is.

box (surveillance box): The logical positioning of surveillance vehicles or operators to cover all routes of travel out of a specified area.

break the box: When the target of a surveillance passes a surveillance vehicle or operator in a box position and the vehicle or operator executes a pick up and follow for a mobile surveillance.

Bundesamt für Verfassungsschutz: West German Federal Office for the Protection of the Constitution; West Germany's primary counterintelligence and protective security agency; BfV.

Bundesnachrichtendienst: the foreign intelligence agency of West Germany; BND.

bug: term for a surreptitious audio device.

burned: when a case officer or agent is compromised, or a surveillant has been identified (made) by a target.

cache: a hiding place, especially one in the ground, for munitions, equipment, documents, or other items to be recovered when needed; derived from the French verb *cacher* meaning "to hide."

case officer: an intelligence officers who runs or directs an agent in the field.

callsign: cover term for a surveillance vehicle.

chief of station: the CIA officer in charge of intelligence operations run out of U.S. embassy or consulate.

clandestine operations/intelligence: any activity or operation sponsored or conducted by governmental departments or agencies with the intent to assure secrecy or concealment.

clandestine collection: the acquisition of protected intelligence information in a way designed to protect the source, and conceal the operation, identity of operators and sources, and actual methodologies employed.

clean off: an antisurveillance routine performed to ensure that any potential surveillance is evaded/eluded prior to conducting operational activities such as an agent meet or servicing a dead drop.

codename: the name given to an agent or operation, usually printed in capital letters, to hide the true name and to enable the reference of a classified issue in unclassified discussions/correspondence.

collection requirement: a valid need to close a specific gap in intelligence holdings in direct response to a request for information.

Communist Bloc: Soviet Bloc.

compartmentation: the principle of controlling access to sensitive information so that it is available only to those individuals or organizational components with an official "need-to-know" and only to the extent required for the performance of assigned responsibilities.

compromise (intelligence): a communication or physical transfer of classified information to an unauthorized recipient.

compromise (operation): discovery by one intelligence service of another competing intelligence service's operations (to include agents) through intelligence compromise, investigation, or other means.

control: in intelligence human source operations, the capacity of a case officer (and his service) to generate, alter, or halt agent behavior by using or indicating his capacity to use physical or psychological means of leverage.

counterespionage (CE): that aspect of counterintelligence designed to detect, destroy, neutralize, exploit, or prevent espionage activities through identification, penetration, manipulation, deception, and repression of individuals, groups, or organizations conducting or suspected of conducting espionage activities.

counterintelligence analysis: the methodical process of examining and evaluating information to determine the nature, function, interrelationships, personalities, and intent regarding the intelligence capabilities of foreign powers; largely focused on the identification of the friendly information that a foreign intelligence agency will attempt to collect and the likely methods the service will employ to collect the information.

Counterintelligence Corps: U.S. Army Counterintelligence organization established in 1942 to provide domestic and international support to army elements until it was disestablished in 1961 during a reorganization of Army Intelligence; CIC.

counterintelligence investigation: formal investigative activities undertaken to determine whether a particular person is acting for or on behalf of, or an event is related to, a foreign power engaged in spying or committing espionage, sabotage, treason, sedition, subversion, assassinations, or international terrorist activities, and to determine actions required to neutralize such acts.

counterintelligence operations: proactive activities designed to identify, exploit, neutralize, or deter foreign intelligence collection and terrorist activities.

countermeasures: the employment of devices and/or techniques to counter the operational effectiveness of enemy activity.

countersurveillance: a sophisticated surveillance-detection practice involving a team of specially trained and equipped operators who observe the activities of a potential surveillance target to detect surveillance of that target.

coup de grâce: a decisive finishing blow, act, or event; French phrase meaning blow of mercy, that is, a final killing blow.

coup de main: a swift attack that relies on speed and surprise to accomplish its objectives in a single blow; French for blow (stoke) with the hand.

cover: a protective guise used by a person, organization, or installation to conceal true affiliation with clandestine or other sensitive activities.

cover for action: actions a case office, agent, or surveillance operator takes to establish a plausible reason for being in a given location or undertaking specific activities.

cover organization: entity established by an intelligence service to provide cover, plausible occupations, and a means of income for their covert agents in foreign countries; front organization.

covert action: an activity or activities that a government takes to influence political, economic, or military conditions abroad, where it is intended that the role of the sponsoring government will not be apparent or acknowledged publicly.

covert operations/intelligence: method of conducting operations that hides the true intent, affiliation, or relationship of its participants; covert activities differ from clandestine in that covert conceals the identity of the sponsor and not necessarily the act, whereas clandestine conceals the identity of the operation.

credible information: information that, considering its source and other corroborating information, is evaluated as being true.

cutout: an intermediary or device used to obviate direct contact between members of a clandestine organization.

damage: a loss of friendly effectiveness due to adversary action; often associated with damage caused by the loss of classified information.

damage assessment: a determination of the effect of a compromise of classified information on national security.

dangle: a person controlled by one intelligence service who is made to appear as a lucrative and exploitable target to an opposing intelligence service.

dangle operation: an operation in which an enticing intelligence target is dangled in front of an opposition service in hopes they will think him or her a bona fide recruit; mostly employed to initiate a double-agent operation.

dead drop: a clandestine location for transferring material to or from an agent or asset where information is left to be picked up, obviating the need for direct contact between an agent and the agent handler; leaving documents or material in a dead drop or retrieving the contents of a dead drop are both referred to as "servicing" the dead drop.

debriefing: systematically covering topics and areas with a voluntary source who consents to a formal interview.

deception: measures designed to mislead the enemy by manipulation, distortion, or falsification of evidence to induce the enemy to react in a manner prejudicial to the enemy's interests.

deception theory: the concept involving the abstract calculus of Cold War double-cross with the placement of false agents within enemy ranks and the planting of false information with enemy analysts.

deception channel: a means by which controlled, deceptive information can be reliably transmitted to the target.

defection: an individual who abandons loyalty, duty, and principle to one's country and offers the same to another country.

defector: a person who consciously abandons loyalty to his/her country and commonly uses personal knowledge or stolen information/materials to demonstrate value to another country or countries.

defector-in-place: a defector who continues to work, apparently as usual, after he has changed from serving his country to serving its enemy.

defense attaché: a U.S. DoD military member or civilian representing the U.S. in defense- and military-related matters with foreign governments around the world.

demarche: an official protest delivered through diplomatic channels from one government to another.

denied area: an area under enemy or unfriendly control in which friendly forces cannot expect to operate successfully within existing operational constraints unless extraordinary security measures are taken.

Department of Defense: executive branch department of the U.S. federal government charged with coordinating and supervising all agencies and functions of the government directly related to national security and the United States Armed Forces; DoD.

Department of Justice: executive branch department of the U.S. federal government responsible for the enforcement of the law and administration of justice in the United States; equivalent to the justice or interior ministries of other countries; DoJ; also called Justice Department.

Department of State: executive branch department of the U.S. federal government responsible for the nation's foreign policy and international relations; DoS; also called State Department.

détente: the period of the easing of Cold War tensions between the U.S. and the Soviet Union from 1967 to 1979; French translation – relaxation.

diplomatic immunity: a status wherein diplomatic officers accredited to a foreign government as ambassadors, or other public ministers, are immune from the jurisdiction of all courts and tribunals of the receiving states whether criminal or civil.

disinformation: carefully contrived information prepared by an intelligence or counterintelligence service for the purpose of misleading, deluding, disrupting, or undermining confidence in individuals, organizations, or governments.

disinformation agent: agent employed to deliver disinformation.

double agent: agent in contact with two opposing intelligence services, only one of which is aware of the double contact or quasi-intelligence services.

Eastern Bloc: Soviet Bloc.

electronic surveillance: the acquisition of a communication by electronic means without the consent of a person who is party to an electronic communication or, in the case of a nonelectronic communication, without the consent of a person who is visibly present at the place of communication.

electronic tracking device: direction finder including electronic tracking devices, such as radio frequency beacons and transmitters, vehicle locator units, and the various devices that use a Global Positioning System (GPS) or other satellite system for monitoring non-communication activity.

elicitation: in intelligence usage, the acquisition of information from a person or group in a manner that does not disclose the intent of the interview or conversation.

espionage: intelligence activity directed towards the acquisition of information through clandestine means.

exfiltration: the removal of personnel or units from areas under enemy control by stealth, deception, surprise, or clandestine means.

exploitation: the process of obtaining information from any source and taking advantage of it.

extraterritoriality: form of diplomatic immunity wherein foreign representations are exempted from the jurisdiction of local law of the hosting country; largely recognized as embassies, homes, offices, and vehicles being considered to be situated on the soil of the home country.

false flag: development or execution of any imitative or operation under false national sponsorship or credentials; typically, a false flag is an agent recruitment method which involves an intelligence officer of a country (e.g., Russia) approaching an individual and acting as a representative of another country (e.g., America) which the individual is more likely to support.

front organization: entity established by an intelligence service to provide cover, plausible occupations, and a means of income for their covert agents in foreign countries; cover organization.

glasnost: the concept of *glasnost* (openness) led to changes in Soviet society when it was introduced into domestic politics in 1985 by Mikhail Gorbachev; it was accompanied by a policy of *perestroika*, which required restructuring Soviet society; the twin policies aimed to reduce corruption and increase efficiency in Soviet government and industry, and encourage liberal views in politics; in time it led to unrest, nationalist demands, and the destruction of the Soviet Union, the displacement of the Communist party, and the formation of the Commonwealth of Independent States.

Glienicke Bridge: bridge, crossing the Havel River which was the official entry and exit point to and from East and West Berlin.

Glavnoye Razvedyvatel'noye Upravlenie: Chief Intelligence Directorate of the General Staff; Russian Military Intelligence; GRU.

handler: an intelligence officer or coopted worker directly responsible for the operational activities of an agent; also agent handler or case officer.

hard target: a person, nation, group, or technical system often hostile to the U.S. or heavily protected, with a well-honed counterintelligence capability that presents a potential threat to the U.S. or its interests, and provides significant difficulty for agent infiltration or penetration; against surveillance a hard target is surveillance conscious and practices surveillance detection and antisurveillance.

honey trap: an operation undertaken to ensnare an unwary target in a compromising sexual encounter that may leave the victim vulnerable to blackmail that might result in espionage.

Huebner–Malinin Agreement: short title for the Agreement on Military Liaison Missions Accredited to the Soviet and United States Commanders in Chief of the Zones of Occupation in Germany; the agreement establishing the U.S. and

Soviet MLMs which was signed on 5 April 1947 by Lieutenant General Clarence Huebner, Deputy CINC, U.S. European Command, and Colonel-General Mikhail Malinin, Deputy CINC, Group of Soviet Forces in Germany (GSFG).

human intelligence (HUMINT): a category of intelligence derived from information collected and provided by human sources.

human source: a person who wittingly or unwittingly conveys by any means information of potential intelligence value; also HUMINT source.

illegal: an officer, employee, or agent of an intelligence organization who is dispatched abroad and who has no overt relationship with the intelligence service with which he/she is connected or with the government operations that intelligence service; term is derived from the fact that the individual is in the host country illegally.

imagery intelligence (IMINT): the technical, geographic, and intelligence information derived through the interpretation or analysis of imagery and collateral materials.

information operations: the integrated employment, during military operations, of information-related capabilities in concert with other lines of operations to influence, disrupt, corrupt, or usurp the decision-making of adversaries and potential adversaries, while protecting friendly information.

intelligence: the product resulting from the collection, processing, integration, evaluation, analysis, and interpretation of available information concerning foreign nations, hostile or potentially hostile forces or elements, or areas of actual or potential operations.

intelligence analysis: the process by which collected information is evaluated and integrated with existing information to facilitate intelligence production.

intelligence collection: the acquisition of information or intelligence information and the provision of it to processing and/or production elements.

intelligence contingency funds (ICF): funds accounted for in classified channels to protect and use for intelligence activities when the use of other funds is not applicable or would either jeopardize or impede the mission.

intelligence information report (IIR): the primary vehicle used to provide HUMINT information to the consumer; utilizes a message format structure that supports automated data entry into the intelligence community databases.

intelligence officer: a professionally trained member of an intelligence service; he or she may be serving in the home country or abroad as a member of a legal or illegal residency.

intelligence requirement: any subject, general or specific, upon which there is a need for the collection of information, or the production of intelligence to fill a gap in knowledge.

intelligence source: the means or system that can be used to observe and record information relating to the condition, situation, or activities of a targeted location, organization, or individual.

intelligence sources and methods: sources are persons, images, signals, documents, data bases, and communications media capable of providing intelligence information through collection and analysis programs, e.g., HUMINT, IMINT, SIGINT, and MASINT; methods are the strategies, tactics, operations and technologies employed to produce intelligence products; the compromise or disclosure of intelligence sources and methods without authorization may substantially negate or impair their effectiveness.

interrogation: systematic effort to procure information by direct questioning of a person under the control of the questioner.

intrigue: the use of underhanded machinations or deceitful stratagems; secret planning of something illicit or detrimental.

investigation: the systematic inquiry into an allegation of unfamiliar or questionable activities, wherein evidence is gathered to substantiate or refute the allegation or questionable activity.

investigative lead: a person who possesses information about or was a witness to an incident under investigation or a record which contains information of value to the investigation.

Iron Curtain: the de facto frontier between Soviet-dominated countries in Eastern Europe and the non-Communist countries of Western Europe.

Kommandant: local GSFG military police commander.

Komitet Gosudarstvennoi Bezopasnosti: the Soviet Union's Committee of State Security, acted both abroad and within the Soviet Union to secure the nation; KGB.

lead: in intelligence usage, a person with potential for exploitation, warranting additional assessment, contact, and/or development.

legal residency: an intelligence apparatus in a foreign country composed of intelligence officers assigned as overt representatives of their government, but not necessarily identified as intelligence officers.

listening post: a secure site at which signals from an audio operation are monitored and/or received.

load: tradecraft term meaning to put something in a dead drop; to service a dead drop.

manipulation: the mixing of factual and fictitious or exaggerated evidence.

Ministerium für Staatssicherheit: the East German Ministry of State Security, known as Stasi, the German Democratic Republic's internal security force; MfS.

migrant: a person who moves from one place to another, especially in order to find work or better living conditions.

military attaché: a military expert who is attached to a diplomatic mission, often an embassy.

misdirection: the tactic of supplying an ostensibly plausible explanation for an event actually caused by something quite different, probably by an individual or an operation, deemed sufficiently valuable to require protection; typically employed to lead an intelligence agency away from a mole in its ranks.

modus operandi (MO): Latin phrase translated as "method of operating;" a distinct pattern or method of procedure thought to be characteristic of or habitually followed by an individual or an organization involved in intelligence activity.

mole: a member of an organization who is spying and reporting on his/her own organization on behalf of a foreign country; also called a penetration.

mole hunt: the search for a mole in one's own secret service.

National Security Agency: a national-level intelligence agency of the U.S. DoD, responsible for global monitoring, collection, and processing of information and data for foreign and domestic intelligence and counterintelligence purposes, specializing in a discipline known as signals intelligence (SIGINT); NSA.

neutralize: to render an enemy agent no longer able to effectively operate through arrest, termination, or other means.

non-official cover (NOC): term used for case officers who operate overseas without cover of diplomatic protection or sponsoring government employment.

North Atlantic Treaty Organization: an intergovernmental military alliance between European and North American countries to constitute a system of collective defense whereby its independent member states agreed to mutual defense in response to an attack by any external party—notably a Soviet Bloc attack; the U.S., UK, France, Belgium, Luxemburg, and the Netherlands were the original members, with Greece, Turkey, and Spain joining the alliance during the Cold War; NATO.

observation post: a fixed site that provides cover and concealment to enable the secure, continuous observation of a specific area; OP.

on bumper: A surveillance vehicle is "on bumper" when it is in its box position and ready to establish a pickup.

operations security: process of identifying critical information/activities, determining vulnerabilities that might enable adversary intelligence to observe or collect the critical information/activities, and implementing countermeasures to reduce or eliminate the risk of observation or collection by adversary intelligence; OPSEC.

order of battle: the formal, hierarchical structure of an organization—usually military— and the names of the people assigned to each position in that structure; sometimes it includes the tasks allocated to the positions.

overt collection: intelligence activities with the ultimate goal of intelligence information collection which are not designed or executed to conceal sponsorship, collection activity, identity of operators, or methodologies employed.

passage material: classified information provided to a double agent by an intelligence agency to pass to an opposing intelligence service to strengthen the bona fides of the double agent; intelligence agencies commonly use passage material that is known to have already been compromised to the opposing intelligence service by another source.

penetration: the recruitment of agents within or the infiltration of agents or technical monitoring devices in an organization or group for the purpose of acquiring information or of influencing its activities.

Permanent Restricted Area (PRA): areas that MLMs were permanently restricted from traveling until/unless the PRA was officially changed or eliminated; normally established to protect fixed military facilities and infrastructure such as major installations, airfields, and missile sites from MLM intelligence collection efforts.

persona non grata: an international diplomatic term for a legal status applied to diplomats who have been caught by the host country in espionage or other unlawful activities and are expelled and thereafter denied access to the host country; Latin for "unwelcome person;" PNG.

pickup (surveillance pickup): when the surveillance team transitions from static (box) positions to initiate the mobile follow of a surveillance target.

production: the preparation of reports based on analysis of information to meet the needs of intelligence users.

provocation: activity designed to induce an individual, organization, intelligence service, or government to take action damaging to itself.

quid pro quo: a favor or advantage granted or expected in return for something; "something for something" in Latin.

recruit: an individual, or "asset," who is persuaded to cooperate with an intelligence service, and then come under the control of the case officer or handler who recruited him or her.

recruitment: the deliberate and calculating effort to gain control of an individual and to induce him or her to furnish information or to carry out intelligence tasks for an intelligence or counterintelligence service.

Red Army: shortened term for the Workers' and Peasants' Red Army established immediately after the 1917 October Revolution; Russian Army.

refugee: a person who owing to a well-founded fear of being persecuted for reasons of race, religion, nationality, membership of a particular social group or political opinion, is outside the country of his or her nationality and is unable or, owing to such fear, is unwilling to avail himself or herself of the protection of that country.

repatriate: to return to one's own country; a person who returns to his or her country of citizenship, having left said native country either against his or her will, or as one of a group who left for reason of politics, religion, or other pertinent reasons.

residency: KGB or GRU intelligence and active measures offices; legal residencies operate out of official establishments such as Soviet embassies and consulates; illegal residencies operate out entities that are not sanctioned for Soviet foreign presence; Rezidentura.

run: to manage, control, supervise, or otherwise direct and handle the activities of a spy or agent in the field.

safe house: an innocent-appearing house or residence established by an organization for the purpose of conducting clandestine or covert activity in relative security.

SANDDUNE: USMLM collection, analysis and production program which exploited trash and other items left behind at vacated Soviet and East German training sites.

screen: the evaluation of an individual, or a group of individuals, to determine their potential to answer collection requirements, or to identify individuals who match a predetermined source profile coupled with the process of identifying and assessing the areas of knowledge, cooperation, and possible approach techniques for an individual who has information of intelligence value.

Secret Intelligence Service: the British foreign intelligence service tasked mainly with covert overseas collection; SIS; commonly referred to as MI6.

security clearance: an administrative determination by competent authority that an individual is eligible, from a security standpoint, for access to classified information.

sentry: a soldier stationed to keep guard or to control access to a facility, compound, or other designated area.

sensitive sources and methods: a collective term for those persons, organizations, things, conditions, or events that provide intelligence information and those means used in the collection, processing, and production of such information which, if compromised, would be vulnerable to counteraction that could reasonably be expected to reduce their ability to support future intelligence activities.

service: load or unload a dead drop.

signals intelligence (SIGINT): a category of intelligence comprising either individually or in combination all communications intelligence, electronic intelligence, and foreign instrumentation signals intelligence, however transmitted; largely associated with communication intercept.

sleeper: an illegal agent in a foreign country who does not engage in intelligence activities until he or she is activated at a future time.

sleepy hollow: term derived from the Washington Irving story *The Legend of Sleepy Hollow* that characterizes a town or locale that is very inactive/tranquil; "listless repose."

socks: cover term for vehicle license plates.

source: a person, thing, or activity from whom information or services are obtained.

Soviet Bloc: the communist nations closely allied with the Soviet Union, including Bulgaria, Cuba, Czechoslovakia, East Germany, Hungary, Poland, and Romania, whose foreign policies depended on those of the former Soviet Union; also referred to as the Communist Bloc and Eastern Bloc.

Soviet External Relations Branch: the element established to perform as the day-to-day interface between GSFG and USMLM; SERB.

Soviet Union: see Union of Soviet Socialist Republics (USSR).

special agent: a qualified U.S. Army counterintelligence agent.

Spetsnaz: Soviet military's elite special forces elements primarily under the control of the GRU.

spy: either a professional intelligence officer who works for an intelligence service, or to a foreign source or asset who steals secrets on behalf of that intelligence service.

station: a CIA operational center overseas; usually, but not always, located under cover in a U.S. official installation such as an embassy or consulate.

Stasi: commonly used name for the German Democratic Republic (GDR) Ministerium für Staatssicherheit (MfS) or Ministry for State Security; the internal security force of East Germany.

SVR: the Russian Federation Foreign Intelligence Service established after the fall of the Soviet Union; successor to the KGB.

surveillance: systematic observation of a target; continuous watching or listening (overtly or covertly) of people, vehicles, places, or objects to obtain information concerning the activities and identities of individuals.

surveillance detection: measures taken to detect and/or verify whether an individual, vehicle, or location is under surveillance.

surveillance detection route (SDR): a carefully crafted route, of varying lengths and complexity depending on the operational environment, used by a potential target of surveillance to detect surveillance; commonly employed by a case officer and/ or agent to get to a personal meeting site, and after leaving the meeting site, to determine that the case officer and agent are not under surveillance before going to and after the meeting.

sweep: to electronically and/or physically examine a room or area in order to detect any concealed/clandestine devices; a search for "bugs."

target: in intelligence usage, a country, area, installation, agency, or person against which intelligence operations are directed, also the subject of a surveillance.

TASS: the official state-controlled news agency of the former Soviet Union.

technical surveillance countermeasures (TSCM): techniques to detect, neutralize, and exploit technical surveillance technologies and hazards that permit the unauthorized access to or removal of information; synonymous with "sweep."

Temporary Restricted Area (TRA): areas that MLMs were restricted from for periods ranging from three to 30 days; normally designated to prevent MLMs from observing exercises or other military movements.

theater: the geographical area for which a commander of a geographic combatant command has been assigned responsibility.

three sides of a box surveillance detection route: method of surveillance wherein the potential target of surveillance travels a "three sides of a box" pattern which takes a more lengthy and illogical path from the beginning point of the route to the end point of the route; the route enables a potential target to identify persons or vehicles also following along this illogical route as potential surveillance operators.

tradecraft: specialized methods and equipment used by intelligence organizations, especially techniques and methods for handling communications with agents.

triple agent: an agent who serves three intelligence services in an agent capacity but who, like a double agent, wittingly or unwittingly withholds significant information from two services at the instigation of the third service.

unwitting: person who is not aware of affiliation with an intelligence service; for example, an unwitting source would be one who provides assistance to an intelligence service but does not realize he or she is assisting the service.

Union of Soviet Socialist Republics (USSR): a federal state, consisting of 15 constituent Soviet Socialist Republics, each with its own government closely resembling the central government of the USSR; it comprised Russia, Belorussia, Ukraine, the three Baltic states—Estonia, Latvia, and Lithuania—Georgia, Armenia, Moldova (Moldavia), Azerbaijan, Kazakhstan, Kirghizia, Turkmenistan, Tajikistan, and Uzbekistan; also referred to as Soviet Union; USSR.

verification channel: one of the two necessary channels of communication employed in the deception theory to confirm and verify to the perpetrating intelligence service that an operation is having the intended result, and ensure that it is not the service being deceived.

volunteer: a person who initiates contact with a government, and who volunteers operational or intelligence information.

Volkspolizei: East German People's Police; local police responsible for districts throughout East Germany; VOPO.

vulnerability: in intelligence, any aspect of a government system that could potentially be exploited by an adversary intelligence service; also in intelligence, individual attributes, usually weaknesses, that render an individual susceptible to blackmail or other forms of recruitment by an intelligence service as a spy.

vyshaya mera: the highest measure of Soviet punishment for a traitor in which the condemned person is taken into a room, made to kneel, and shot in the back of the head.

walk-in: an unexpected agent; one who presents himself at an embassy or other foreign intelligence service entity and states that he has documents or access to documents he is willing pass to the embassy.

Warsaw Pact: pact formed among the Soviet Union, Albania, Bulgaria, Czechoslovakia, the German Democratic Republic, Hungary, Poland, and Romania as a counter to NATO.

wild west: the western U.S. during the 19th-century era of settlement; commonly believed to be lawless and unruly; term commonly applied to a place or situation in which disorderly behavior prevails.

wilderness of mirrors: term coined by James Angleton, the CIA Chief of Counterintelligence from 1954–74 to depict the organizational culture of the secret services; the phrase centers on the problem of the reliability of the secret information about espionage and the identity of spies; the mirrors comprise information from defectors, disinformation from the opposing sides in the Cold War, deviously covered false trails, and facts thought to be valid but incomplete (and later established as totally untrue).

witting: a term of intelligence art that indicates that one is not only aware of a fact or piece of information but also aware of its connection to intelligence activities.

A Note on Sources

This work is based on exhaustive research and extensive interviews with individuals having first-hand knowledge that was critical to the content. The author also has first-hand experiential knowledge which contributed to the content. Many individual sources requested anonymity due to the perceived sensitivity of the information provided, and the fact that there are governments that continue to act against their enemies, new and old. As such, all individuals contributing first-hand information will remain anonymous.

Part I (Chapters 1–2)

This accurate and often first-hand account of the MLM era in Cold War East and West Germany is based on multiple, redundant sources. The MLM history is based on USAREUR Unit History reports, the USAREUR Nicholson incident report, and studies by Seman, Williams, Vodopyanov, and Hoyt as referenced. Declassified USAREUR documents, to include the USAREUR USMLM Unit History reports from 1964 through 1988 provide the DoD's official record on the history of the MLMs. Other declassified reports such as the Major Nicholson incident investigation provide reinforcing historical, on-the-record context. Declassified U.S. Army Intelligence and Security Command Annual History reports from 1977 through 1990 provide historical detail on U.S. efforts to counter SMLM-F, but the preponderance of this information was provided by first-hand accounts including those of the author. Many first-hand sources requested anonymity, but the veracity of the information provided was verified. The "1978 Protocol Guiding Cooperation between the Stasi and the KGB" is initially referenced in Part I and then again throughout.

Part II (Chapters 3–6)

The "Strategic Wilderness of Mirrors" section is based on multiple, redundant books and U.S. government resources to include the CIA library and the U.S. National Counterintelligence Center's *Counterintelligence Reader* book. James Angleton's record of policies, depiction of the "wilderness of mirrors," and the concept of the "deception theory" are well established in multiples references. U.S. government reports in the cause and effects of the Ames and Hanssen espionage cases provide substantive detail as do other cited references. The details of the U.S. Army Counterintelligence Corps were derived largely from *In the Shadow of the Sphinx* as referenced. Details of Project DART are based largely on the declassified U.S. Freedom of Information Act case as referenced, with isolated first-hand details. Details regarding Operation GOLD and the Pyotr Popov case were largely derived from CIA Library reports, but both of the cases are well documented and very well referenced. Details regarding the Pyotr Sokolov network also involving Heinz Kiefer is based on the declassified CIA analysis report "KGB Exploitation of Heinz Felfe" and the U.S. National Counterintelligence Center, *Counterintelligence Reader* book, Volume III. Details on the George Trofimoff case are based on multiple credible references, on-the-record distribution channels for USMLM reporting, and isolated first-hand details. Details regarding the Clyde Conrad and James Hall cases largely reference the first-hand accounts derived from *Traitors Among Us* as referenced, and on-the-record distribution channels for USMLM reporting. The discussion on the deception theory as it applied to the MLMs draws on USMLM Unit History reports from the years specified and the author's informed analysis. Details regarding the 1979 drugging event is based on information derived directly from released Stasi files, the referenced article which first publicized the incident, the USMLM Unit History report from 1979 and 1980, and first-hand accounts from the officers involved and other members of USMLM at the time. The discussion of the 1980/1 Poland crises and the involvement of Ryszard Kukliński is based on redundant credible sources as referenced and the USMLM Unit History reports from 1978 and 1980. The details of the 1981 attempted KGB recruitment of a U.S. defense attaché in the Ukraine are based on first-hand details in *Moscow Memoir* and as acknowledged by a U.S. State Department press release to *The Washington Post*, both as referenced. The chapters on the Nicholson negotiations are based on the U.S. Army Europe Nicholson incident case study as referenced, the 1985 and 1986 USMLM Unit History reports, the U.S. Army Intelligence and Security Command 1985 Annual History Report, and the author's analysis. Details confirming the SMLMs as GRU residencies and the GRU and KGB cache programs is based on the British SIS debriefings of Vladimir Rezun as subsequently detailed in the books authored under the pseudonym of Viktor Suvorov. Additional details of the GRU cache program and the first information regarding the GRU suitcase nuke program were provided by Oleg Gordievsky as detailed in his referenced book on the KGB. Additional details regarding the GRU cache and suitcase nuke programs were provided after the Cold War by Vasili Mitrokhin which led to the discovery of cache sites and by Stanislav Lunev in his testimonies to the U.S. Congressional Select Committee on Intelligence and his book *Through the Eyes of the Enemy*. Details on Operation LANKY MISS are based on the referenced *Secret Warriors*, the 1975, 1981, and 1986 USMLM Unit History reports, interviews of persons with first-hand knowledge, and the author's analysis.

Part III (Chapters 7–9)

Details regarding the Clyde Conrad and James Hall cases largely reference the first-hand accounts derived from *Traitors Among Us* as referenced, and on the record of distribution channels for USMLM reporting. The "Wartime Mentality" is a reshaped retelling of conventional historic understanding which draws on the referenced Executive Order 12333, ABLE ARCHER studies, the 1988 USMLM Unit History report, and the author's first-hand experience. Chapter 8 is based on well-documented Soviet clandestine HUMINT tradecraft, interviews of persons with first-hand knowledge, and the author's first-hand experience. Chapter 9 is based on interviews of persons with first-hand knowledge and the author's first-hand experience.

Select Bibliography

Andrew, Christopher and Oleg Gordievsky. *KGB: The Inside Story of its Foreign Operations from Lenin to Gorbachev*. London: Hodder & Stoughton, 1990.

Andrew, Christopher and Vasili Mitrokhin. *The Sword and the Shield: The Mitrokhin Archive and the History of the KGB*. New York, NY: Basic Books, 1999.

Bagley, Tennent, H. "Ghosts of the Spy Wars: A Personal Reminder to Interested Parties." *International Journal of Intelligence and Counterintelligence* Vol. 23 (pp. 1–37). Taylor & Francis Group, 2015.

Bearden, Milt and James Risen. *The Main Enemy: The Inside Story of the CIA's Final Showdown with the KGB*. New York, NY: Random House, Inc., 2003.

Burke, Matthew M. and Marcus Kloeckner. "Disgraced U.S. Air Force Officers Were Set Up, Stasi Documents Show Decades Later." *Stars and Stripes*, 10 October 2019.

Carter, Donald A. *Forging the Shield: The U.S. Army in Europe, 1951–1962*. Center of Military History United States Army. November 2014.

Central Intelligence Agency. "About the CIA, The Berlin Tunnel." November 2012.

Central Intelligence Agency. Full Text of CIA Files Relating to Heinz Felfe, originally classified "Secret."

Central Intelligence Agency. "James. J. Angleton, Anatoliy Golitsyn, and the 'Monster Plot': Their Impact on CIA Personnel and Operations," *Studies in Intelligence* Vol. 55, No. 4. December 2011, originally classified "Secret."

Central Intelligence Agency. "KGB Exploitation of Heinz Felfe: Successful Penetration of a Western Intelligence Service." March 1969, originally classified "Secret."

Central Intelligence Agency. "Special National Intelligence Estimate, Soviet Support for International Terrorism and Revolutionary Violence." November 1981, originally classified "Top Secret NOFORN/NO CONTRACT/ORCON."

Central Intelligence Agency Library. "Career Trainee Program, GRU Style," approved for release 1994, originally classified "Secret."

Central Intelligence Agency Library. *Of Moles and Molehunters*, 1993.

Central Intelligence Agency Library. *The James Angleton Phenomenon*, 2001.

Central Intelligence Agency Library. *Tolkachev, A Worthy Successor to Penkovsky*, 2007.

Central Intelligence Agency Library. "Unrecognized Potential in the Military Attaches," approved for release 1994, originally classified "Confidential."

Central Intelligence Agency, News and Information. "A look Back … CIA Asset Pyotr Popov Arrested." January 2011.

Central Intelligence Agency, News and Information. "The Capture and Execution of Colonel Penkovsky." 1963.

Congressional Select Committee on Intelligence United States Senate. "An Assessment of The Aldrich H. Ames Espionage Case and Its Implications for U.S. Intelligence." 1 November 1994.

Congressional Select Committee on Intelligence United Stated Senate. "Meeting the Espionage Challenge: A Review of United States Counterintelligence and Security Programs." 3 October 1986.

Dennis, Mike. *The Stasi: Myth and Reality*. London: Pearson Education Limited, 2003.

Der Spiegel, "Active Repentance: This week the trial of a double agent who fled to the GDR and back begins before the Higher Regional Court in Stuttgart." *Der Spiegel*, 1 September 1984.

Emerson, Steven. "Where Have all His Spies Gone?" *The New York Times* magazine, 8 December 1990.

Emerson, Steven. *Secret Warriors: Inside the Covert Military Operations of the Reagan Era*. New York, NY: G. P. Putnam's Sons, 1988.

Ermarth, Fritz W. "Observations on the 'War Scare' of 1983." Parallel History Project on NATO and the Warsaw Pact (Stasi Intelligence on NATO), 6 November 2003.

Fagone, Jason. "The Amazing Story of the Russian Defector Who Changed His Mind." *Washingtonian* magazine, February 2018.

Fahey, John F. *Licensed to Spy: With the Top Secret Military Liaison Mission in East Germany*. Annapolis, MD: Naval Institute Press, 2002.

Fischer, Ben F. "ABLE ARCHER 83." Parallel History Project on NATO and the Warsaw Pact (Stasi Intelligence on NATO), 6 November 2003.

Gilbert, James and Jon Finnigan, Ann Brey. *In the Shadow of the Sphinx: A History of Army Counterintelligence*. History Office, Office of Strategic Management and Information, U.S. Army Intelligence and Security Command, 2005.

Headquarters US Army EUROPE and 7th Army Military History Office. "The Nicholson Incident: A Case Study of US–SOVIET Negotiations." June 1988, declassified 1988.

Herrington, Stuart. *Traitors Among Us: Untold Stories of Cold War Espionage*. Novato, CA: Presidio Press, 1999.

Heuer, Richards J. Jr. "Nosenko: Five Paths to Judgement." *Studies in Intelligence* Vol. 31, No. 3 (Fall 1987)(pp. 71–101), originally classified "Secret."

Holbrook, James. *Moscow Memoir: An American Military Attaché in the USSR 1979–1981*. Bloomington, IN: AuthorHouse, 2018.

Holbrook, James. *Potsdam Mission: Memoir of a U.S. Army Intelligence Officer in Communist East Germany*. Bloomington, IN: AuthorHouse, 2008.

Hoyt, Stephen V. "Cold War Pioneers in Combined Intelligence and Analysis." *Intelligence and National Security Publication* Vol. 23, No. 4 (pp. 63–487). August 2018, Taylor & Francis Group.

Klose, Kevin. "Moscow Said to Solicit U.S. Attaché." *The Washington Post*, 16 February 1981.

Lunev, Stanislav and Ira Winkler. *Through the Eyes of the Enemy: Russia's Highest Ranking Military Defector Reveals Why Russia is More Dangerous Than Ever*. Washington D.C.: Regnery Publishing, 1998

Martin, David C. *The Wilderness of Mirrors: Intrigue, Deception, and the Secrets that Destroyed Two of the Cold War's Most Important Agents*. New York, NY: Harper Collins Publishers, Inc., 1980.

Mastny, Vojtech. "Did East German Spies Prevent a Nuclear War?" Parallel History Project on Cooperative Security (Stasi Intelligence: Nuclear War), 28 October 2016.

McCaslin, Leland. *Secrets of the Cold War: US Army Europe's Intelligence and Counterintelligence Activities Against the Soviets*. West Midlands, England: Helion & Company Limited, 2010.

Murphy, David E. and Sergei A. Kondrashev. *Battleground Berlin: CIA vs. KGB in the Cold War*. New Haven, CT: Yale University Press, 1997.

Myagkov, Aleksei. *Soviet Analyst, Soviet Sabotage Training for World War III*, 20 December 1979.

National Counterintelligence Center, *Counterintelligence Reader: An American Revolution into the New Millennium* Vol. 3: The Angleton Era in CIA (pp. 109–16), Erich Englehardt and Karl-Heinz Kiefer (p. 187), Michal Goleniewski (pp. 192–3), Aleksandr Nikolayevich Cherepanov (pp. 195–6), Yuri Ivanovich Nosenko (pp. 196–7), Oleg Vladimirovich Penkovsky (p. 199), Executive Order 12333 (pp. 219–31), The Walker Spy Ring (pp. 233–6), Clyde Lee Conrad (pp. 257–8); James Hall III (pp. 263–4), Edward Lee Howard (p. 268), Clayton John Lonetree (pp. 271–2), Ronald William Pelton (pp. 276–7), Aldrich Hazen Ames (pp. 306–34), Earl Edwin Pitts (pp. 364–90),

Roderick James Ramsay (pp. 412–13), Jeffrey Stephen Rondeau (p. 413), Albert T. Sombolay (pp. 413–14).

Olson, James M. *To Catch a Spy: The Art of Counterintelligence.* Washington D.C.: Georgetown University Press, 2019.

Omand, David and Mark Phythian. *Principled Spying: The Ethics of Secret Intelligence.* Oxford: Oxford University Press, 2018.

Parallel History Project on NATO and The Warsaw Pact (PHP), translation of the report provided by the East German Intelligence Service to the Group of Soviet Forces Germany following the death of USMLM member Major Nicholson, 26 March 1985.

Pond, Elizabeth. "Complex Spy Swap: East German superspy for West German agents." *The Christian Science Monitor*, 29 September 1981.

Richelson, Jeffrey T. "Truth Conquers All Chains: The U.S. Army Intelligence Support Activity, 1998–1989." *International Journal of Intelligence and Counterintelligence* Vol. 12, No. 2 (pp. 168–200). October 2010.

Robarge, David, "Moles, Defectors, and Deceptions: James Angleton and CIA Counterintelligence." *The Journal of Intelligence History* Vol. 3 (Winter 2003), International Intelligence History Association, 2003.

Schector, Jerrold and Leona Schector. *Sacred Secrets: How Soviet Intelligence Operations Changed American History.* Sterling, VA: Brassy's Inc., 2002.

Seman, Timothy Alan. *Cold War Intelligence: The United States Military Liaison Mission in East Germany 1947–1990.* The American University, 1994.

Shafer, Bernd. "Stasi Files and GDR Espionage Against the West." Norwegian Institute for Defense Studies, 2000.

Shebelskie, Michael C. "The Major Nicholson Incident and the Norms of Peacetime Espionage." *Yale Journal of International Law* Vol. 11, No. 2, 1986.

66th Military Intelligence Brigade, 527th Military Intelligence Battalions (Counterintelligence) Unit History Report, Chapter IX: Detachment A, 1988, originally classified "Secret"/redacted.

66th Military Intelligence Brigade, 527th Military Intelligence Battalions (Counterintelligence) Unit History Report, Chapter VIII: Detachment A, 1989, originally classified "Secret"/redacted.

66th Military Intelligence Brigade, 527th Military Intelligence Battalions (Counterintelligence) Unit History Report, Chapter VIII: Detachment A, 1991, originally classified "Secret"/redacted.

Sulick, Michael J. *American Spies: Espionage Against the United States from the Cold War to the Present.* Washington D.C.: Georgetown University Press, 2013.

Suvorov, Viktor. *Inside Soviet Military Intelligence.* New York, N.Y: Macmillan Publishing Co., Inc., 1984.

Suvorov, Viktor. *Inside the Aquarium: The Making of a Soviet Spy.* London: Hamish Hamilton, 1986.

Suvorov, Viktor. *Inside the Soviet Army.* New York, N.Y: Macmillan Publishing Co., Inc., 1982.

Suvorov, Viktor. *Spetsnaz: The Inside Story of the Soviet Special Forces.* New York, NY: W. W. Norton & Company, 1988.

Suvorov, Viktor. *Spetsnaz: The Story of the Soviet SAS.* New York, NY: Harper Collins Publishing, 1989.

U.S. Army Intelligence and Security Command, Freedom of Information/Privacy Office, Case # 0402F-19 (Project DART), declassified and released 21 June 2019/redacted.

United States Military Liaison Mission Annual History Report (1961, 1964–86, 1988), originally classified "Confidential" or "Secret."

U.S. Department of Justice, Office of the Inspector General, "A Review of the FBI's Performance in Deterring, Detection, and Investigating the Espionage Activities of Robert Philip Hanssen." August 2003.

U.S. Department of State, Foreign Affairs Note, "Expulsions of Soviet Officials Worldwide." 1986/ January 1987.

U.S. Executive Branch. Executive Order 12333: United States Intelligence Activities, 4 December 1981.

Williams, Peter. "BRIXMIS in the 1980s: The Cold War's 'Great Game'—Memories of Liaising with The Soviet Army in East Germany." Parallel History Project on Cooperative Security, 2007.

Wilson Center. East German Ministry of State Security. "US and NATO Military Planning on Mission of V Corps/US Army During Crises and in Wartime" (excerpt). Digital Archive International History Declassified, 16 December 1982.

Wilson Center. East German Ministry of State Security. "Assessment of Adversary's Intelligence on Development of Warsaw Pact Forces, 1983–1985" (excerpt). Digital Archive International History Declassified, 16 December 1985.

Wilson Center. "Protocol Guiding Cooperation Between the Stasi and the KGB, 1978." Digital Archive, International History Declassified, 29 March 1978.

Wilson Center. "Report Warning of Soviet Intervention." History and Public Policy Program Digital Archive, CIA Release, Ryszard Kukliński documents, December 1980.

Winkler, Christopher and Anna Locher, Christian Nuenlist. "Allied Military Liaison Missions, 1946–1990." Parallel History Project on Cooperative Security, July 2005.

Wise, David, "Thirty Years Later, We Still Don't Truly Know Who Betrayed These Spies." *Smithsonian* magazine, November 2015.

Vodopyanov, Anya. "A Watchful Eye Behind the Iron Curtain: The U.S. Military Liaison Mission in East Germany, 1953–61." Honors program in International Security Studies Center for International Security and Cooperation, Stanford University, 21 May 2004.

Index